# A CONCISE LOGIC

# A CONCISE LOGIC

**WILLIAM H. HALVERSON**
OHIO STATE UNIVERSITY

RANDOM HOUSE · NEW YORK

First Edition
987654321

Copyright © 1984 by Random House, Inc.

Library of Congress Cataloging in Publication Data

Halverson, William H.
    A concise logic.

    Includes index.
    1. Logic.  I. Title.
BC71.H175  1984      160      83-21280
ISBN 0-394-32905-8

*Text design by Dana Kasarsky Design*
Manufactured in the United States of America

# TO KAY,
## WHO IS ALWAYS LOGICAL
## AND SOMETIMES CONCISE

# preface

Logic courses have been growing in popularity recently, for a number of reasons. One reason is that many people have become concerned about an apparent decline in the writing skills of today's students, and have encouraged the study of logic in the hope that clearer thinking will lead to clearer writing. Another reason is the current explosion of interest in microcomputers: students know that computers are "logical" devices, and assume that an understanding of the fundamental principles of logic will be of value to them in a world in which computers are destined to play increasingly important roles. The principal reason, however, is that logic is being taught more imaginatively today than it was in the past. The field of logic has in recent years attracted many superb teachers, and they are making the study of logic a far more exciting experience than it used to be.

The study of logic can and should be rigorous without being tedious. The need for rigor is obvious. The point of studying logic is to understand the relationships between premises and conclusions in arguments of various types, and to master certain techniques for determining when arguments succeed or fail in establishing their conclusions. Whether or not a given argument establishes its conclusion is not a matter of opinion: it either does or doesn't. With respect to rigor, logic is like mathematics. But the *mastery* of this rigor, which is what one seeks to acquire through the study of logic, should be an inherently exciting learning experience for the student.

*A Concise Logic* attempts to capture both the rigor and the excitement of logic. It covers all of the topics commonly included in a first course in logic. Part I, "Logic and Language," deals with the relation of logic to ordinary language. Part II, "Informal Logic," builds on the concepts developed in Part I, and includes a typology of fallacies as well as an extended discussion of the fallacies most frequently encountered in ordinary discourse. Part III introduces the logic of the syllogism. Syllogistic logic is of course a part of predicate logic, and for that reason might have been dealt with after sentential logic, which is logically more fundamental. For pedagogical reasons, however, I have chosen to treat syllogistic logic first. Because syllogistic logic stays relatively close to ordinary language, it is more accessible to most students than symbolic logic. A study of the logic of the syllogism gives students an opportunity to master such concepts as validity, logical equivalence, and formal proof in a context in which these concepts make immediate and intuitive sense. Moreover, I can think of no more effective way to demonstrate the superior power and elegance of symbolic logic than by contrast with the much more cumbersome techniques of traditional logic. Symbolic logic is discussed in Part IV, up to and including the logic of monadic predicate arguments. The relationship of modern predicate logic to the logic of the syllogism is carefully explained, and the power of modern techniques to prove the validity of extended predicate arguments is demonstrated. Much of this section is devoted to the presentation of a powerful system for the construction of formal proofs of validity. The mastery of this system, however, requires time and a good deal of practice. As an aid to students while they are attempting to acquire such mastery, I have included a one-page summary of the Formal Proof System, which appears on the back endpaper of the book. With sufficient practice, students should be able to construct correct formal proofs without such aid. During the learning process, however, the summary should be helpful.

Part V, "Induction and Scientific Method," consists primarily of an examination of several types of inductive arguments. Mill's Methods are discussed in a modified form suggested by the work of Georg Henrik von Wright. The book concludes with an extended discussion of the reasoning involved in the creation and confirmation of scientific hypotheses.

A substantial amount of space is devoted to student exercises. These have been carefully designed to serve two purposes: to reinforce the logical concepts discussed in the text, and to provide practice in the use of each new logical technique that is introduced. Solutions are provided in Appendix B for approximately half of these exercises, thus giving students an opportunity to receive immediate feedback on their efforts.

This book could not have been written without the help and cooperation of many people. I express my special thanks to Jane Cullen, who first encouraged me to write it; to Robert Burch of Texas A & M University, Diane Barense of Southeastern Massachusetts Technological Institute, Jeffrey Olen of the University of Wisconsin at Stevens Point, and Peter Asquith of Michigan State University, who gave me the benefit of their valuable comments on the manuscript; to Marolyn Halverson for help in polishing the prose; to C. Steven Pensinger and the Random House staff members who shepherded the book through its various stages; and to my colleagues at Ohio State University, who allowed me the luxury of a four-month leave of absence during which I finished the writing.

*William H. Halverson*

# contents

# P A R T  I V
## SYMBOLIC LOGIC    149

### eight / Symbolic Notation    151

### nine / Sentential Arguments    181

## ten / Predicate Arguments    221

# PART V
# INDUCTION AND SCIENTIFIC METHOD    249

## eleven / An Introduction to Induction    251

# A CONCISE LOGIC

# PART ONE

# LOGIC AND LANGUAGE

# one
# Logic

We are going to study logic. The subject matter of logic is arguments, that is, bits of reasoning concerning which it is claimed that some statement or statements (the premise or premises) provide evidence for the truth of some other statement (the conclusion). To define the field or domain of logic, then, we need to understand precisely the ways in which logic is concerned with reasoning, statements, and arguments. We shall begin by attempting to clarify the basic concepts involved in that definition.

## 1.1 REASONING

First, reasoning. It is evident that reasoning is a particular kind of thinking. What kind? The kind in which one derives a conclusion from certain alleged facts and/or hypothetical assumptions. If I say, "There was no snow on the ground last evening, but there is snow on the ground this morning, so obviously it snowed during the night," I am reasoning—in this case, from certain alleged facts to the **3** conclusion that it snowed during the night. And if I say, "We're going to have higher prices on the stock market now because the Republicans won the election and stocks always do better when the Republicans are in power," I am also reasoning—this time from a fact (a recent Republican victory) and an alleged general truth (stocks always do better when the Republicans are in power) to the conclusion that there will be higher prices on the stock market.

Now it is evident that when somebody is reasoning, something is going on in the mind or brain of the person doing the reasoning. It is not the process in the mind or brain that is of interest to the logician, however—though that process might well be of interest to a psychologist or a neurophysiologist. Logic is concerned with the *product*, not the *process*, of reasoning. The product of reasoning can always be stated as an argument. "Reasoning," therefore, in the sense that is of interest to logic, is a synonym for "argument." In this book, as in many logical writings, the two terms will be used interchangeably.

## 1.2 STATEMENTS

Reasoning always concerns relations between and among statements. A statement is a verbal formulation affirming or denying that something is the case.[1]

Statements have the important property of being either true or false. To say that a statement is true is to say that what it asserts to be the case is in fact the case. Otherwise it is false. In the case of a general statement, to say that it is true is to say that what it asserts to be the case is the case *without exception*. If all the houses in the world but one were white, the statement "All houses are white" would be false, not true. And if there were but one white house in the world, the statement "No houses are white" would be false, not true. A statement may be close to the truth, in the sense that a slight modification of the statement would make it true, but a statement cannot be partly true and partly false, nor can it contain some truth and some falsehood. A statement that in popular parlance is said to be partly true and partly false, or to contain some falsehood, is simply false.

Moreover, it is not the case that the same statement is sometimes true and sometimes false. It might be thought that such a statement

---

[1] This is intended to be a neutral definition of the word "statement." This word will be used consistently throughout this book to refer to the basic components of arguments, in preference to the words "proposition" and "sentence," as there is much controversy concerning the exact meanings of those words.

as "The current president of the United States is a Republican" is an exception to this claim, but it is not. What we have here is an ambiguous statement, a statement whose exact meaning depends on when it is uttered. The word "current" obviously refers to a date. If we specify a date—January 1, 1983, let us say—one statement is being affirmed, and that statement is true because Ronald Reagan, a Republican, was president of the United States on that date. If we specify a different date—January 1, 1980, for example—what is being affirmed is the different (and false) statement that the *then* president of the United States—Jimmy Carter—was a Republican. To repeat: every statement is either true or false, since what it states to be the case either is or is not the case. Examples that may appear to contradict this claim will be found, upon closer examination, to contain some ambiguity by virtue of which the sentences involved actually express multiple statements, some of which may be true and some false.

Although every statement is true or false, it of course does not follow that we or anyone else can in all cases know whether a given statement is true or false. The statement "There is at least one place in the universe other than the earth where intelligent life exists," for example, is either true or false, but we do not know which. Indeed, the whole of humanity's quest for knowledge might be described as an effort to determine which statements are true and which are false.

# 1.3 ARGUMENTS

There is no need to belabor the point that logic is concerned with arguments only in the sense in which arguments are understood to be instances of reasoning. Logic has no special interest in arguments in the sense of disagreements ("The argument concerned who was best qualified to serve as mayor") or quarrels ("The Bickersons had their usual end-of-the-month argument over family finances"). But everything—absolutely everything—that is of interest to logic has to do with arguments as instances of reasoning. Let us look at some important features of such arguments.

Arguments have already been defined as instances of reasoning concerning which it is claimed that some statement or statements (the premise or premises) provide evidence for the truth of some other statement (the conclusion). An argument, then, always contains a minimum of two statements, that is, at least one premise and a conclusion. And some arguments, as we shall see later, contain many premises.

Logicians commonly distinguish two fundamental types of

arguments: deductive and inductive. A **deductive argument** is one for which it is claimed that the premises constitute conclusive evidence for the truth of the conclusion. In a correct deductive argument, if the premises are true, the conclusion must be true. Here is an example of such an argument:

> All college students are literate.
> Joe Smith is a college student.
> ———————————————
> ∴ Joe Smith is literate.[2]

Note that this argument does not establish absolutely that Joe Smith is literate. It establishes that Joe Smith is literate (that the statement "Joe Smith is literate" is true) *if the premises of the argument are true.* The strength of correct deductive arguments is that their conclusions follow necessarily from their premises. The weakness of such arguments is that their premises are frequently doubtful, if not obviously false.

An **inductive argument** is one for which it is claimed that the premises merely offer some evidence in support of the conclusion. It is logically possible for the premises of a correct inductive argument to be true and the conclusion false; the truth of those premises establishes only that there is some probability that the conclusion is true. Here is an example of an inductive argument:

> College student 1 is literate.
> College student 2 is literate.
> College student 3 is literate.
> .
> .
> .
> College student $n$ is literate.
> ———————————————
> ∴ All college students are literate.

The advantage that inductive arguments have over many deductive arguments is that their premises, as in the above example, are typically assertions of observable fact that can be easily verified. One can often be reasonably sure that the premises of such an argument are true. The weakness of inductive arguments is that their conclusions do not follow necessarily from their premises: the conclusion may be false even if the premises are true.

Inductive and deductive reasoning are often combined in what looks like a single argument. Consider the following example:

A recent poll of a group of voters believed to be representative of the entire electorate yielded the following findings:

---

[2] The symbol ∴ will be used regularly throughout this book to identify a statement as the conclusion of an argument. Read "Therefore."

58 percent of those polled favored Candidate Smith.
37 percent of those polled favored Candidate Jones.
5 percent of those polled were undecided.

We can reasonably conclude, then, that Smith will receive approximately 58 percent of the votes cast on election day. Any candidate who receives 58 percent of the votes cast on election day will be elected. Therefore, Smith will be elected.

This is essentially an inductive argument, as is evident from the fact that the conclusion follows from the premises not with certainty but only with some degree of probability. The premises, if true, make it likely that approximately 58 percent of those who vote on election day will vote for Smith. Since 58 percent constitutes a majority of the votes cast, and since a majority of the votes cast guarantees election, it is concluded that Smith will be elected.

If you study the argument carefully, however, you will see that some deductive reasoning is also involved. Look carefully at the following statements:

1.  A recent poll shows 58 percent of those polled favoring Candidate Smith, 37 percent Candidate Jones, and 5 percent undecided.
2.  Approximately 58 percent of those who vote on election day will vote for Candidate Smith.
3.  Any candidate who receives approximately 58 percent of the votes cast on election day will be elected.
4.  Candidate Smith will be elected.

When we review these four statements, it is clear that statement 2 is an inductive inference from the evidence summarized in statement 1, and statement 4 is a deductive inference from statements 2 and 3. Statement 2 in this example is therefore the conclusion of an inductive argument and the premise of a deductive argument. What appears initially to be a single argument is in reality two arguments, one inductive and one deductive. Only by careful analysis can we sort out the various strands of reasoning that are often intertwined in a given piece of discourse.

# EXERCISE 1.1–1.3[3]

Each of the following passages contains at least one argument. For each passage (a) identify the premise(s) and the conclusion of the argument and (b) state whether the argument is deductive or inductive.

---

[3] Answers to selected exercise problems will be found in Appendix B.

1. Our bank is committed to serving you. We have made a multimillion-dollar investment in data processing equipment. We are open more hours each week than any of our competitors. Our automatic teller is open twenty-four hours a day, seven days a week. And our staff consists only of trained professionals.

2. Inflation is caused by an excess of money in circulation. Deficit spending by government results in too much money being in circulation. Thus federal deficit spending is the root cause of inflation. If the federal government would balance its budget, inflation would cease.

3. Jones deserves this award for outstanding public service. He is a leader in this community, a deacon in his church, a member of the school board, and chairman of the United Fund.

4. I expect my new Rabbit to give me much better mileage than my old car, because according to recent tests the Rabbit gives the best mileage of any car sold in this country.

5. It is necessary that the land and the surrounding waters have the figure which is cast by the shadow of the earth, for during an eclipse it projects on the moon the circumference of a perfect circle. Therefore the earth is not a plane . . . or a cylinder . . . but it is perfectly round.
   —Copernicus, *On the Revolution of the Heavenly Bodies*

6. The student body always elects as homecoming queen the most beautiful girl on campus. Some years ago the students at a certain midwestern university elected a heifer as homecoming queen. It is clear, therefore, that the heifer was the most beautiful girl on campus that year.

7. No month can possibly have more than 23 weekdays, since the longest months contain only 31 days, and in any 31-day period there must be at least four Saturdays and four Sundays.

8. Evidently working with computers is good for one's health, for according to a recent study, nearly all of the people who have ever worked with computers are still living.

9. Franklin Delano Roosevelt became president in 1932. During his campaign for the presidency, he wore leg braces as a result of his bout with polio, so it is clear that he had polio at some time before 1932.

10. As more and more nuclear power plants have started up, more and more nuclear accidents have occurred. Ten years from now, according to present plans, there will be twice as many nuclear power plants as there are today. Thus it is inevitable that the frequency of such accidents will increase.

# 1.4 LOGICAL IMPLICATION

If we assume that (*a*) all crows are black, (*b*) there are some birds in Beltrami County, and (*c*) at least 50 percent of the birds in Beltrami County are crows, what are we entitled to conclude about the truth or falsity of the following statements?

1.   Some birds in Beltrami County are black.
2.   Some birds in Beltrami County are not black.
3.   Some crows in Beltrami County are not black.
4.   Some birds in Beltrami County are not crows.
5.   Some noncrows are not black.
6.   No crows in Beltrami County are nonblack.

Can we, given our assumptions, conclude that one or more of these statements is true? Yes. It follows from our assumptions that statements 1 and 6 are true. Do our assumptions allow us to conclude that one or more of these statements is false? Yes. Given our assumptions, we may infer that statement 3 is false. Is the truth or falsehood of any of these statements still undetermined, given only the above assumptions? Yes. Statements 2, 4, and 5 cannot be shown to be either true or false on the basis of these assumptions.

Statements, then, are sometimes related in such a way that if one knows or assumes the truth or falsity of some statements, one can infer the truth or falsity of certain other statements. This relationship is called **logical implication.** Deductive logic is concerned exclusively with this relationship, and it is important that we understand it.

Note, first, that logical implication does not presuppose that the statements that are so related are actually true. No assumption whatsoever is made about their actual truth or falsity. The statement "All crows are black," in conjunction with the other statements that constitute our assumptions, has certain logical implications even if it should be the case that there are albino crows—that is, even if the statement "All crows are black" is false. Indeed, there may not in fact be such a place as Beltrami County. That possibility in no way affects the logical implications of the statements that constitute our assumptions.

Logical implication has to do with the truth or falsity of certain statements on the provisional assumption that certain other statements are true or false. If I assume that the statement "All crows are black" is true, then it follows that the statement "Some crows are not black" is false. These two statements are related in such a way that the truth of one implies the falsity of the other. This relationship, as well as the relationship in which the truth of one or more statements implies the truth of another statement, constitutes logical implication.

This relationship does not hold between all statements, nor even between all true statements. Given our general knowledge of the various colors of birds, and given the assumptions stated above, we may be inclined to *believe* that statements 2, 4, and 5 are true, but their truth or falsity cannot be inferred from our assumptions. And that is equivalent to saying that there is no relationship of logical implication between the stated assumptions and those statements.

Logical implication, then, is a relationship between and among statements such that we can infer the truth or falsity of certain statements on the assumption that a given statement or set of statements is true (or false). All deductive reasoning is an attempt to discern this relationship between and among statements.

# 1.5 PROBABLE INFERENCE

Suppose that you are driving down the freeway in your car, and two things happen: (*a*) the engine sputters and stops, and (*b*) you observe with dismay that the fuel gauge is on EMPTY. Can you, on the basis of these facts, infer that the fuel tank is empty?

It seems clear, on the one hand, that you cannot infer *with absolute certainty* that the fuel tank is empty. There is no relationship of logical implication between the statements "The engine stopped" and "The fuel gauge shows EMPTY" and the statement "The fuel tank is empty." It is possible, for example, that something has gone wrong with the electrical system, causing the engine to stop and the fuel gauge to malfunction, and that there is in fact a plentiful supply of fuel in the tank. It seems equally clear, however, that under the above circumstances it is not unreasonable to conclude that the fuel tank *probably* is empty. The sputtering and stopping of the engine and the fact that the fuel gauge shows EMPTY are not irrelevant to the conclusion that the fuel tank is empty, even though those facts do not conclusively establish the conclusion. You are likely to be right more often than you are wrong if, under these circumstances, you conclude that the fuel tank really is empty and act accordingly.

The reasoning involved in any case in which the premises are clearly relevant to the conclusion of the argument but the conclusion cannot be rigorously deduced from those premises is called **probable inference.** All inductive arguments involve such inferences.

We will be analyzing such arguments in detail in Part Five of this book, but let us note in passing several types of arguments of great practical importance that involve this kind of reasoning.

One type is illustrated by the above example of the car that appeared to have an empty fuel tank, and may be called an argument leading to a *presumption of determinate fact:* from certain observed determinate facts we infer an unobserved determinate fact. We often make inferences of this kind in our everyday lives. From the fact that the thermometer registers 100° F. we infer that we have a fever. From the fact that the barometer is falling we infer that there will be rain tomorrow. From the fact that it is September we infer that the leaves will soon be turning. And so on.

A second type of reasoning involving probable inference is that in which we infer an empirical generalization. An **empirical generalization** is a general statement about a class of objects made on the basis of observation of some members of the class. If a biologist states, for example, that "all female salmon, when they are about to lay their eggs, return to the fresh-water streams where they were hatched," the biologist is stating an empirical generalization. The generalization is obviously based on the observation of the actual behavior of some representatives of the class of salmon, most of which clearly have not been observed by anyone. All scientific generalizations are statements of this type, and the arguments establishing such generalizations always involve probable inference.

A third type of argument involving probable inference is one in which the conclusion of the argument is a **theoretical hypothesis.** Consider, for example, the wave theory of light. This theory is not an empirical generalization, for it is not a statement about all instances of light based on an examination of some lesser number of instances. One cannot observe the wavelike character of some representative rays of light, whereas one can observe the spawning of salmon. What is observed is a range of phenomena (the behavior of light as it passes through a prism, refraction phenomena, alterations in the velocity of light as it passes through media of varying density, and so on) that are said to be satisfactorily explained by the hypothesis that light is wavelike rather than corpuscular in nature.

Although all of these types of reasoning involve probable inference, the precise nature of the reasoning varies in several important and interesting ways from one type to another. Since the detailed analysis of probable inference belongs to inductive logic, however, we will reserve that analysis for Part Five of this book.

# 1.6 LOGIC

Against the background of the foregoing discussion and definitions, we can now define **logic** as *the science of distinguishing between correct and incorrect reasoning or arguments.* The subject matter of logic is reasoning, arguments, the drawing of inferences. The specific task of logic is to provide methods for distinguishing between good and bad reasoning, correct and incorrect arguments, allowable and unallowable inferences.

In pursuing this task, logicians typically engage in three distinct activities: analysis, classification, and assessment. Let us note briefly how each of these activities is involved in the logician's task.

Logic begins with analysis, because before one can get on with the task of distinguishing between correct and incorrect arguments, one must determine what is and what is not an argument. In ordinary language, arguments rarely are stated with their premises and conclusions neatly labeled as such. The logician's first task, therefore, is to disentangle the argument (if there is one) from the logically irrelevant language in which it may be embedded—the rhetoric, the flowery language, the vague terminology—in order that the argument may be assessed on its own merits. And this, it is clear, is an analytical task.

As logicians study the enormous variety of arguments that they encounter in both spoken and written discourse, they observe certain similarities and certain differences between and among arguments. These similarities and differences are the basis for the *classification* of arguments into types and subtypes. We have already noted the grand distinction between deductive and inductive arguments (Section 1.3) and have looked briefly at some subtypes of the latter (Section 1.5), but there is more to come. These classifications are of immense importance in the study of logic, for they enable us to focus our attention at any given time on a manageable range of arguments, and to be reasonably confident that we have mastered the logic involved in such arguments. We may then go on to study the logic of other types of arguments, and then others, until finally we have familiarized ourselves with all of the types in which we are interested.

Analysis and classification are, however, only preludes to the chief business of logic, which is the *assessment* of arguments, the determination of their correctness or incorrectness. Some arguments establish their conclusions and some do not—though they may appear to do so. Our reasoning may be correct or it may be faulty, and it is not always easy to tell intuitively which is the case. By far the greatest part of logic consists, therefore, in developing methods for determining whether arguments of a particular form[4] are correct or incorrect. A number of methods appropriate to the several types of arguments will be presented in subsequent chapters of this book.

## 1.7 THE USES OF LOGIC

If one accepts the dictum that knowledge is better than ignorance, one really does not need a practical justification for studying anything: one studies it simply in order to know. A knowledge of the principles

---

[4] The concept of an *argument form* is very important in logic. See Section 4.1.

of logic, like all knowledge, has such intrinsic value, and for many students of logic that is all the justification that is required. But it happens to be the case that this particular knowledge—an understanding of the principles of logic—is likely to have significant practical value for anyone who possesses it, and we may as well take note of it as we begin our study.

First, an understanding of these principles is likely *to reduce the likelihood of being deceived by the faulty arguments of others.* All of us are subject to a constant barrage of words—in the newspapers, on television, in public speeches, in private conversation—words that sometimes take the form of arguments intended to persuade us to draw certain conclusions about this candidate, this policy, this product, this proposal, this theory, this belief. Logic has no magic formula to enable us to distinguish unerringly between true and false statements—that would be expecting too much—but it can help us to avoid being taken in by phony arguments. In a world of advertising and elections, that is a prize worth seeking.

Second, an understanding of these principles should *enhance one's ability to clarify one's beliefs.* All of us arrive at adulthood with a large fund of beliefs—beliefs about the world, about society, about the meaning and value of human life, and so on—which we have acquired in a variety of ways. Some of these beliefs are in all likelihood only half-formed and somewhat hazy. Logic gives us tools to restate them in such a way that we may more readily decide whether they are worthy of assent. Some of our beliefs are in all probability in conflict with each other. Logic teaches us to discern the relationships of logical implication between and among our various beliefs, and in so doing helps us to rid our belief system of internal contradictions. For a belief, be it noted, is simply a statement to which one assents, and every statement is related by logical implication to many other statements.

Third, an understanding of the principles of logic may be expected to *aid us in the quest for knowledge.* Surely it is obvious on the face of it that all rational inquiry involves reasoning, and logic is the science of distinguishing between correct and incorrect reasoning. Both inductive and deductive reasoning are involved in scientific research, in historical inquiry, in research in the social sciences and humanities—indeed, in any endeavor whose goal is to determine the truth about some phenomenon or range of phenomena. Applied logic, which goes beyond the scope of this book, is a study of the application of the principles of logic to specific kinds of inquiries.

The study of logic, then, should be both intrinsically interesting and of practical value. The remaining chapters of this book will attempt to demonstrate that this is indeed the case.

## EXERCISES 1.4–1.7

**A.** Each of the following numbered statements is followed by a series of other statements, some of which are logically implied by the numbered statement and some of which are not. Using intuitive judgment, identify the statements that *are* logically implied by the immediately preceding numbered statement.

1. Susan is taller than Carol and Beth is taller than Susan. Therefore:
   a. Beth is taller than Carol.
   b. It is not the case that Beth is taller than Carol.
   c. It is not the case that Carol is taller than Beth.
   d. It is not the case that Carol is taller than Susan.
   e. Carol is shorter than Susan.
   f. Carol is shorter than Beth.
   g. It is not the case that Carol is shorter than Beth.
   h. Carol is shorter than Beth and Susan.
   i. Carol and Susan are shorter than Beth.
   j. Either Carol is shorter than Susan or Beth is shorter than Susan.

2. All Minneapolitans are trustworthy, and all Minneapolitans are Minnesotans. Therefore:
   a. All Minnesotans are trustworthy.
   b. All Minnesotans are Minneapolitans.
   c. No Minneapolitans are untrustworthy.
   d. It is not the case that some Minneapolitans are untrustworthy.
   e. It is not the case that all Minnesotans are untrustworthy.
   f. It is not the case that all Minnesotans are trustworthy.
   g. It is not the case that some Minnesotans are non-Minneapolitans.
   h. It is not the case that some Minneapolitans are non-Minnesotans.
   i. It is not the case that some Minneapolitans are not trustworthy.
   j. It is not the case that some Minneapolitans are not Minnesotans.

3. Either John will pass the final in this course or he will flunk out of school. Therefore:
   a. If John does not pass the final in this course he will flunk out of school.
   b. If John passes the final in this course he will not flunk out of school.
   c. It is not the case both that John will not pass the final in this course and that he will not flunk out of school.
   d. It is not the case both that John will pass the final in this course and that he will flunk out of school.
   e. If John does not flunk out of school, then it must be the case that he will pass the final in this course.
   f. John will pass the final in this course.
   g. John will not pass the final in this course.
   h. John will flunk out of school.
   i. John will not flunk out of school.
   j. John will flunk out of school or he will pass the final in this course.

4. Some Ohioans are politicians and some politicians are honest. Therefore:
   a. Some Ohioans are honest.
   b. Some Ohioans are not honest.
   c. Some politicians are Ohioans.
   d. Some honest people are Ohioans.
   e. Some honest people are politicians.
   f. It is not the case that all honest people are nonpoliticians.
   g. It is not the case that all honest people are non-Ohioans.
   h. It is not the case that all Ohioans are nonpoliticians.
   i. It is not the case that all politicians are non-Ohioans.
   j. It is not the case that no politicians are honest.

5. If Lynn buys a stereo she will not be able to go home for Christmas, but if she does not buy a stereo she will not be able to listen to her favorite records. She is determined to go home for Christmas, so it is obvious that:
   a. There must be some attraction back home in addition to her family.
   b. Lynn either will or will not buy a stereo.
   c. Lynn will not buy a stereo.
   d. Lynn will not listen to her favorite records.
   e. Lynn will not go home and she will listen to her favorite records.
   f. Lynn will not both forgo buying a stereo and listen to her favorite records.
   g. It is not the case both that Lynn will go home and that she will buy a stereo.
   h. It is not the case both that Lynn will buy a stereo and that she will listen to her favorite records.
   i. It is not the case that either Lynn will go home for Christmas or she will buy a stereo.
   j. It is not the case that either Lynn will buy a stereo or she will listen to her favorite records.

B. Indicate what probable inference, if any, you would be inclined to draw from each of the following sets of premises. In any case in which you do draw a probable inference, state whether the inference is a presumption of determinate fact, an empirical generalization, a theoretical hypothesis, or a probable inference of some other kind.

   1. In a recent road test, five Toyotas achieved mileage readings of 34, 31, 32, 34, and 33 miles per gallon respectively, whereas five comparably equipped Hondas in the same weight class achieved mileage readings of 37, 35, 39, 36, and 35 miles per gallon. Therefore . . .

   2. Returning home from a recent vacation, the Smiths discovered that their back door was smashed, clothes and other items were strewn about in several rooms, and a number of valuables—including jewelry, silverware, and photographic equipment—were missing. It seems evident that . . .

   3. On the way home from work the next day, Mr. Smith stopped at a pawnshop to find out whether anyone had tried to pawn the

items that were missing. As he walked into the pawnshop, a teenaged boy whom he recognized as his son's best friend was attempting to pawn a camera of the same make as one that was missing from Mr. Smith's house. Upon seeing Mr. Smith, the boy dropped the camera and ran out of the pawnshop. Mr. Smith would appear to be justified in concluding . . .

4. Mr. Smith inspected the camera that the boy had left behind, and determined that although it was similar to one of the items missing from his house, it was not in fact his camera. He then concluded that . . .

5. It has often been observed that a flash of lightning is usually followed by the sound of thunder apparently emanating from the same location. When we bear in mind that lightning is a light phenomenon and thunder a sound phenomenon, it seems clear that . . .

6. Tonight's baseball game will determine the winner of the National League pennant. Pitching for team A will be Lefty Robinson, whose record going into this game is 24 wins and 5 losses. On the mound for team B is Speedball Marsh, who has 7 wins and 13 losses for the year, but who claims that he now feels the best he has felt all season. All of the starters on both teams are healthy, and the two teams have identical team batting averages. Which team would you bet on to win the pennant?

7. People who live by the sea have long been aware that as a ship recedes from land, it disappears from view a bit at a time: first the lower portion of the ship cannot be seen, then the middle portion, and finally the uppermost portion passes from view. The opposite is true of a ship sailing toward an observer on land: the uppermost part can be seen first, then the middle part, and finally the part nearest to the water. As everyone knows, the explanation of these facts is to be found in . . .

8. According to a recent study, the average weight of American adult males is approximately 170 pounds. A random sample study of defensive tackles playing in the National Football League, however, gave these results: none weighed under 200 pounds, three weighed between 200 and 220 pounds, seven weighed between 220 and 240 pounds, and five weighed over 240 pounds. It seems clear, therefore, that . . .

9. Of 212 students who ate dinner at the commons on a certain Tuesday evening, 37 became ill and were diagnosed as having food poisoning. These 37 students reported having eaten the following:

6 had beef, potatoes, gravy, peas, and ice cream.
8 had beef, rice, gravy, peas, and cake.
9 had chicken, rice, gravy, peas, and ice cream.
5 had chicken, sweet potatoes, peas, and no dessert.
9 had beef, rice, gravy, peas, and ice cream.

The above facts would seem to indicate that the probable cause of the food poisoning was . . .

10. A zoology student was assigned to do a research project on a certain species of frog. She collected 20 living specimens, of which 11 were male and 9 female. Upon weighing them, she discovered that the weight of the females ranged from 97 grams to 134 grams, whereas that of the males ranged from 119 grams to 164 grams. She also observed that all of the males emitted a certain croaking sound that was emitted by none of the females in her sample group. On the basis of her observations she concluded that . . .

# BRAIN-STRETCHERS

Brain-stretchers are logical puzzles that can be solved by careful reasoning from the information given in each case. Their solution requires the drawing of inferences, and each time one draws an inference, one is of course formulating an argument. Clues to the solutions (if you need them) will be found in Appendix A. Do your best to solve them on your own. If you get stuck, check Appendix A.

## 1.  Twin Souls

Once upon a time there lived six pairs of twins, and their names (in descending order of age) were Alex and Alice, Brian and Barbara, Charles and Constance, David and Diana, Edgar and Eileen, Frank and Florence.

In the course of time they all grew up and married—amongst themselves. Most of the men and maids had known each other for a long time. The only exception was in the case of Brian's wife and Alex. At no time had these two met; at least not until after their respective marriages.

There is not much else I can tell you about them apart from the fact that David's wife was younger than Brian's, and that Charles's wife was younger than Alice's husband.

Oh yes, there is just one more point I have remembered; one of the weddings was a double-wedding. On that occasion a brother and sister married a sister and brother.

What were the names of the husbands and wives in the case of each of the six happy couples?[5]

## 2.  The Wise Fool

Long ago in a forgotten country of the east there existed a remarkable oracle. Unlike most oracles it was not the mouthpiece of a single deity but of three, the God of Truth, the God of Falsehood, and the God of Diplomacy. These

[5] Douglas St. P. Barnard, *One Hundred Braintwisters* (Princeton, N.J.: D. Van Nostrand, 1966), pp. 51–52.

gods were represented by three identical figures seated in a row behind the altar at which their petitioners knelt. The gods were always ready to answer their mortal supplicants, but since their identities were impossible to determine because their images were exactly alike, no one ever knew whether the reply to his question came from the God of Truth and hence could be relied on, or whether it came from the God of Falsehood and so was certainly untrue, or whether it came from the God of Diplomacy and hence might be either true or false. This confusion of course did not deter the multitude from seeking advice, though it did create a very profitable sideline for the priests of the temple who, for a price, were always ready to interpret the utterances of the oracle.

One day a sacrilegious fool came to the altar vowing to do what the wisest men of the past had failed to accomplish, namely to expose the identity of each god.

Said he to the figure on the left, "Who sittest next to thee?"

"The God of Truth," was the answer.

Then said the fool to the image in the center, "Who art thou?"

"The God of Diplomacy," was the answer.

Lastly to the image on the right the fool said, "Who sittest next to thee?"

"The God of Falsehood," came the reply.

"Oho," said the fool to himself, "so that's the way of it."

And straightaway he established an interpreting concession just outside the temple and soon had driven the priests out of business through the uncanny accuracy of his interpretation.

Can you, like the fool in the legend, determine the identity of each god from the answers they made to the three simple questions they were asked?[6]

## 3.  You Can't Tell the Teachers Without a Program

In the Stillwater High School the economics, English, French, history, Latin, and mathematics classes are taught, though not necessarily respectively, by Mrs. Arthur, Miss Bascomb, Mrs. Conroy, Mr. Duval, Mr. Eggleston, and Mr. Furness. The mathematics teacher and the Latin teacher were roommates in college. Eggleston is older than Furness but has not taught as long as the economics teacher. As students, Mrs. Arthur and Miss Bascomb attended one high school while the others attended a different high school. Furness is the French teacher's father. The English teacher is the oldest of the six both in age and in years of service. In fact he had the mathematics teacher and the history teacher in class when they were students in the Stillwater High School. Mrs. Arthur is older than the Latin teacher.

What subject does each person teach?[7]

---

[6] C. R. Wylie, Jr., *101 Puzzles in Thought and Logic* (New York: Dover Publications, 1957), no. 47. Reprinted by permission of Dover Publications, Inc.

[7] Ibid., no. 12. Reprinted by permission of Dover Publications, Inc.

### 4.  If It's Tuesday

In one of the most famous resort towns of Europe, where tourists from a dozen countries may always be encountered, four travelers once struck up an acquaintance. They were of different nationalities and although each man could speak two of the four languages, English, French, German, and Italian, there was still no common tongue in which they could all converse. In fact, only one of the languages was spoken by more than two of the men. Nobody spoke both French and German. Although John couldn't speak English he could still act as interpreter when Peter and Jacob wanted to speak to each other. Jacob spoke German and could also talk to William although the latter knew not a word of German. John, Peter, and William could not all converse in the same language.

What two languages did each man speak?[8]


### 5.  The Lineup

Four men were eating dinner together in a restaurant when one of them suddenly struggled to his feet, cried out "I've been poisoned," and fell dead. His companions were arrested on the spot and under questioning made the following statements, exactly one of which is false in each case:

> *WATTS:*   I didn't do it.
> I was sitting next to O'Neil.
> We had our usual waiter today.
>
> *ROGERS:*  I was sitting across the table from Smith.
> We had a new waiter today.
> The waiter didn't do it.
>
> *O'NEIL:*  Rogers didn't do it.
> It was the waiter who poisoned Smith.
> Watts lied when he said we had our usual waiter today.

Assuming that only Smith's companions and the waiter are implicated, who was the murderer?[9]

---

[8] Ibid., no. 35. Reprinted by permission of Dover Publications, Inc.
[9] Ibid., no. 52. Reprinted by permission of Dover Publications, Inc.

# two
# Language

Arguments are linguistic entities; they occur only in the form of oral or written language. Language is an extremely complex phenomenon, one that serves many purposes in addition to that of expressing arguments. Some facts about language, however, are especially important for the study of logic. The features of language that are of special importance for logic are the subject of the present chapter.

## 2.1 FUNCTIONS OF LANGUAGE

Language is used for many purposes, of which four may be said to be basic: to make assertions, to ask questions, to direct behavior, and to express feeling. We may call these, respectively, the assertoric, the interrogative, the directive, and the expressive functions of language.

Language is being used **assertorically** when it is used to state that something is or is not the case. Such discourse is also said to express a *truth claim*, since to assert that something is or is not the case is to claim that what is asserted (the statement) is true. "All birds are bipeds," "No human beings are nine feet tall," and "Some houses are blue" are examples of such discourse, but not all examples are so easily recognized as these. One reason we may fail to recognize an assertion when we hear one is that language may be *obliquely* informative, and when it is, we may have to do a bit of detective work to isolate the assertion(s) involved. When a traffic cop says, for example, "Why were you driving 45 miles per hour in that 30-mile zone?" the question clearly assumes the following assertions: (*a*) the zone in question is a 30-mile zone, (*b*) you drove through that zone, and (*c*) your speed while driving through that zone was 45 miles per hour. That these assertions are obliquely contained in the officer's question is evident from the fact that it would not be beside the point (though perhaps untrue) to reply (*a*) "But officer, that's not a 30-mile zone," (*b*) "You've got the wrong person; I never drove on that street in my life," or (*c*) "You are mistaken: I was only going 30." In general, any time discourse contains something that is capable of being contradicted, we may safely conclude that an assertion is being made.

A second basic function of language is the **interrogative** function, the asking of questions. While this function is normally served by sentences ending in a question mark ("Is it raining?"), this is not always the case. "I wonder if it is raining" is an oblique way of asking whether it is raining, as is evident from the fact that it would make sense to say, "Yes, it is," whereas it would not make sense to say, "No, you don't." So we must conclude that language may serve an interrogative *function* even in the absence of an interrogative *sentence*, just as in an earlier example we found it serving an informative function under the guise of a sentence that is unmistakably interrogative in form.

The **directive** function of language may be seen in the issuing of commands, requests, instructions, or recommendations. This function is often served by sentences in the imperative mood ("Forward march," "Please hand me my glasses," "Cut on dotted line"), but again there are numerous exceptions. When a mother says, "Young man, you will be in bed in ten minutes," she is not making a prediction: she is issuing a command, using language directively. The same is true of announcements (signs) such as "Overnight parking is forbidden," "No hunting," and "Violators will be prosecuted."

The expressive function of language is exemplified by such ejaculations as "Whoopee!" "Great!" "Rats!" "Darn!" and the like. Since discourse serving this function is generally recognizable as such, we will not dwell on it here.

As is evident from several of the preceding examples, a single piece of discourse—even a single sentence—may serve more than one function. Moreover, as the examples also make clear, one cannot determine the function of a piece of discourse simply on the basis of its grammatical form. Rather, one must pay attention to the apparent *meaning* of what is being said, and make a reasoned judgment about its function.

Now since arguments consist of statements, and statements are without exception instances of language used assertorically, it is obvious that it is language in its assertoric function that is of primary interest to logic. So far as logic is concerned, the other functions of language are mere distractions that may prevent us from getting at the underlying argument. For logic, the principal value in identifying these nonassertoric functions is to enable us to recognize them and get them out of the way so that we can focus our attention on the argument, if any, that may lie concealed beneath them.

## EXERCISE 2.1

Identify the function or functions served by each of the following examples of discourse. Remember that a given piece of discourse may serve more than one function.

1. Exeter lies in a surpassingly beautiful slice of southern New Hampshire, where the Atlantic, tall pine forests, and pre-Revolutionary homes have joined to create a background for a mystery—a mystery as fantastic and sweeping as the legend of Sleepy Hollow, mixed with the most vivid trappings of science fiction.
   —John G. Fuller, *Incident at Exeter*

2. Future shock is a time phenomenon, a product of the greatly accelerated rate of change in society. It arises from the superimposition of a new culture on an old one. It is culture shock in one's own culture.
   —Alvin Toffler, *Future Shock*

3. The only possible way out of chaos is for us to come once more under the control of the ideals of true civilization through the adoption of an attitude toward life that contains those ideals. But what is the nature of the attitude toward life in which the will to general progress and to ethical progress are alike founded and in which they are bound together? It consists in an ethical affirmation of the world and of life.
   —Albert Schweitzer, *Out of My Life and Thought*

4. Johnny's first explorations of the external world were in the form of pictures—graphic art. Some of his paintings still hang on the walls in the house in Madison, Connecticut. The violence with which a child sees nature! The brilliant savagery of the struggles already precipitated in an infant's mind!
   —John Gunther, *Death Be Not Proud*

5. Arrest! Need it be said that it is a breaking point in your life, a bolt of lightning which has scored a direct hit on you? That it is an unassimilable spiritual earthquake not every person can cope with, as a result of which people often slip into insanity?
   —Aleksandr I. Solzhenitsyn, *The Gulag Archipelago*

6. Through the windshield, Warren swept the harbor with the binoculars. "Good God, Jan, Ford Island's a junkyard! I don't see one undamaged plane. But there must be many left in the hangars. Lord, and there's a battlewagon *capsized*. I'll bet a thousand guys are caught inside that."
   —Herman Wouk, *The Winds of War*

7. My mind turned to another decision facing me: what would I do when called upon to testify? I couldn't predict where or when, but I was sure it would happen. The president had tucked me under the wing of his office and said his counsel could never be called upon to testify in a Senate Committee investigation. It would be different, however, should a grand jury call me.
   —John Dean, *Blind Ambition*

8. Ask any philosopher who claims to have constructed a sound argument supporting his belief that solipsism is false, what he would do if it were conclusively demonstrated to him that his argument was unsound. Now while philosophers may very rarely admit in any particular case that their arguments are actually fallacious, they all eagerly profess to be fallible and openminded and agree that any of their arguments could in principle be proven wrong and in that case they would withdraw them. Thus, to the question what a philosopher would do if his argument in support of the existence of other minds was proven mistaken the answer will be: he would retract it.
   —George N. Schlesinger, "Do We Have to Know Why We Are Justified in Our Beliefs?"

9. It's a little late to be proving that a behavioral technology is well advanced. How can you deny it? Many of its methods and techniques are really as old as the hills. Look at their frightful misuse in the hands of the Nazis! And what about the technique of the psychological clinic? What about education? Or religion? Or practical politics? Or advertising and salesmanship? Bring them all together and you have a sort of rule-of-thumb technology of vast power.
   —B. F. Skinner, *Walden Two*

10. One need not be a partisan of the provincial governments to argue that Mr. Trudeau is making a grave mistake in trying to railroad through London a bill of rights the Canadian provinces cannot agree on. . . . Imposing constitutional provisions from outside . . . can only aggravate the already bitter conflicts in Canada about language, energy and the balance of federal and provincial powers.
    —Editorial, *The Wall Street Journal*

## 2.2 LANGUAGE AND METALANGUAGE

Ordinarily, language is used to talk about the world—about football and politics and automobiles and thunderstorms and all of the other objects and events that make up what we call "the world." So long as we are using language in this way, we are usually quite clear about the fact that the world is one thing and the language we use to talk about that world is another. We drive cars—machines made of steel and aluminum and rubber and so on—and in talking *about* cars we use such terms as "speed" and "gas mileage" and "automatic transmission." We observe thunderstorms—real thunderstorms—and in *describing* them we use such words as "frightening" and "awesome" and "destructive." The world is a physical entity, a complex system of objects and events occurring in space and time. Language is a linguistic entity, and its most obvious components are not objects and events but *words.* So long as we are using language to talk about the world, we are rarely if ever tempted to confuse the two.

But language can also be used to talk about language, and when it is used in that way we may easily confuse the language being spoken about with the language that is being used to speak about it. Consider, for example, the following statements:

**1.** Lightning is a discharge of electrical energy in the atmosphere.
**2.** Lightning is a noun.

Are both of these statements true? If so, it would seem to follow that there is something in the world that is both a discharge of electricity and a noun, and on the face of it that seems rather strange. The problem, of course, is that statement 2 is a statement about language—about the *word* "lightning"—not about an event in the heavens. As it stands, it confuses two languages—the language spoken about and the language being used to speak about it.

Let us call a language being spoken about an **object language** and a language being used to speak about it a **metalanguage.** A metalanguage must have some way of indicating that the objects to which it is referring are words in the object language, not entities in the physical world. The most common way of doing so is to enclose a word in quotation marks when it is being used in this way. Thus, to avoid confusion statement 2 should be written like this:

**2'.** "Lightning" is a noun.

Now everything in this example is clear: statement 1 is a statement in the object language about an event in the heavens, and statement 2' is a statement in the metalanguage about a word in the object language. The puzzle about whether there is something in the world that is both a discharge of electricity and a noun does not arise.

Another common way of avoiding confusion between an object language and a metalanguage is to make some kind of typographical or format distinction between statements in the two languages. A grammarian, for example, might offer a list of nouns, and the fact that the words appear in the form of a list would be sufficient to mark the distinction between the two languages. Indentation, underlining, and parentheses are other devices that are sometimes used.

## EXERCISE 2.2

Identify the statements in the following list that can most reasonably be interpreted as being statements in a metalanguage. Insert quotation marks as necessary to make the statements thus identified correct and meaningful.

1.   Wisdom, courage, temperance, and justice were considered by the Greeks to be the principal virtues.
2.   Justice is sometimes represented pictorially as a blindfolded woman holding a scale.
3.   Justice comes from the Latin *justitia*.
4.   Nouns have cases, verbs have tenses.
5.   Go, went, and will go are, respectively, the present, past, and future tenses of the verb to go.
6.   I am firm, you are stubborn.
7.   Firmness and stubbornness are the same thing; it's just a question of who you're talking about.
8.   Firm means stubborn.
9.   I wouldn't go so far as to say that my roommate is hard to get along with, but I will say that a certain kind of grass was named after him.
10.  The definition of crab as an ill-tempered person is thought to derive from the behavior of the marine animal of that name.

## 2.3  EXTENSION AND INTENSION OF WORDS

The principal components of a language are, of course, words. From one point of view, a word is merely a noise made by a human being (a spoken word) or a mark on a piece of paper (a written or printed word). What distinguishes words from other noises (such as the babbling of an infant or a random series of letters of the alphabet) is the fact that they have *meaning*. Words always point beyond themselves, and they may do so in at least two ways.

Many words point beyond themselves in the sense of denoting— referring to—certain objects or events. A word is said to **denote** if there are objects or events to which it can be correctly applied— objects or events to which one can point, or that one can name or describe. The word "automobile," for example, denotes a large number of individual machines that have existed, now exist, or will exist in the future. The word "running" denotes a large number of events involving people, dogs, antelopes, and other creatures capable of such activity. The word "red" denotes the color of blood, of many apples, of certain flowers, and so on.

The totality of objects or events denoted by a word constitutes the **extension** of that word. The word "automobile," for example, cannot be indiscriminately applied to just anything: it denotes some objects and not others. Those objects to which the word "automobile" *can* be correctly applied constitute the extension of the word "automobile." An object or event to which a word can be correctly applied is said to be "included in the extension" of that word.

But words may also point beyond themselves in another way: they may signify certain characteristics or properties that an object or event must have in order to be included in the extension of that word. Something is called an "automobile" by virtue of having certain characteristics—wheels, a motor, a steering mechanism, and so on. These properties—the list of characteristics that an object or event must have in order to be included in the extension of a word— constitute the **intension** of that word. In order for something to be a triangle, for example, it must be a closed plane figure having three straight sides. These characteristics, then—being a closed plane figure and having three straight sides—constitute the intension of the word "triangle." The properties of being an adult male and being unmarried constitute the intension of the word "bachelor." Other examples could easily be given.

The correct identification of the properties that constitute the intension of a word is not always an easy task, however. The philosopher Plato devoted many pages to an attempt to pin down the intensions of such words as "religion," "virtue," and "justice." The current controversy concerning abortion turns in part on the question: What, exactly, is the intensional meaning of the word "human"? You should not be discouraged, then, if you sometimes have difficulty determining the intension of a word, perhaps even a word with which you are quite familiar. You are in good company.

## 2.4 EXTENSIONAL AND INTENSIONAL DEFINITIONS

That certain words (sounds, marks) have certain meanings is, of course, a matter of convention. There is no objectively *correct* sound or mark to denote the writing instruments that English-speaking people denote by the word "pen"; "zarf" or "mert" or something else would have served equally well had it been chosen instead. It just happens to be the case that English-speaking people use the word "pen" to denote these particular kinds of objects. It is equally a matter of convention that German-speaking people use instead the word "Feder," French-speaking people the word "plume," and so on.

Within the context of a particular language, however, certain words have, by common agreement, certain meanings. To indicate the meaning of a word is to give a **definition** of that word. Corresponding to the two ways in which words may point beyond themselves, there are two basic kinds of definitions: extensional definitions and intensional definitions.

One gives an **extensional definition** of a word by pointing to or naming some examples of the objects or events that are included in the extension of that word. One might, for example, define the word "vegetable" as meaning "peas, beans, carrots, spinach, and things like that." To be sure, that is not a very satisfactory definition, for someone who does not already know the meaning of the word "vegetable" might well remain puzzled about what is supposed to be covered by the catchall phrase "and things like that." But it is better than no definition at all. It gives one *some* idea of what the word means. A person just learning the language would at least know that "vegetable" means certain kinds of food, and could then pay attention to other uses of the word to determine more precisely its extension.

Pointing to examples of objects or events included in the extension of a word, rather than naming some examples, is an even more primitive type of extensional definition. Such a definition is termed **ostensive** (from a Latin word meaning "displayed"). It is obvious, when you think about it, that the process of attaching meanings to words must begin with ostensive definitions. Imagine yourself charged with the task of teaching English to someone who does not know a single word of English, and whose native tongue is totally foreign to you. How would you go about it? Clearly, you would have to begin by pointing to objects while pronouncing the English words by which those objects are called: "tree," "boy," "car," "house," "bus," and so on. No doubt there would be some confusion, for a boy can also be called a child, a car can also be called a vehicle, and so on. Our bewildered pupil might understandably be puzzled at first about the relative extension of such words as "boy," "child," "car," "vehicle," and many others as well. But there is no other way. The fundamental bond between words and the world is by means of extension, and in its most primitive form this bond is indicated by means of pointing to some representative objects and events that are included in the extension of the word in question.

Extensional definitions are the only definitions most of us ever have (or need) for color words. If we were asked to define "red," for example, we would either point to something having the appropriate color (that is, define it ostensively) or say something like "The color of blood." For other purposes, of course, a color might also be defined in terms of a precise range in the color spectrum.

**Intensional definitions** state the properties that an object or event must have in order to be included in the extension of the word being defined. Intensional definitions, therefore, are always verbal; they give a rule for the use of the word being defined. The word being defined is sometimes called the **definiendum,** the rule stated for its use the **definiens.**

For most words, an adequate intensional definition will be such that anything that satisfies the definiens (i.e., anything that fits the definition) will be included in the extension of the definiendum, and anything that fails to do so will be excluded from the extension of that word. *The Random House Dictionary of the English Language* defines "colony," for example, as "any people or territory separated from but subject to a ruling power." The adequacy of this definition depends on the answers to the following questions: Does this definition include everything to which English-speaking people would normally apply the word "colony"? Does it exclude everything that English-speaking people normally would *not* call a "colony"? The definition is adequate if both questions can be correctly answered in the affirmative.

The same word (definiendum) may, however, require a different definition (definiens) when it is used in a different context. The definition of "colony" in the preceding paragraph, for example, is adequate only when the word is used in a *political* context. In biology the word has another meaning, in ecology yet another, and so on. Usually the intended meaning is clear from the subject matter under discussion. In dictionaries, the various possible meanings are typically listed in a numbered series, often with some indication of the context in which a given definiens is applicable. (*The Random House Dictionary*, for example, lists nine definitions for the word "colony.")

Words whose meaning varies from one context to another are said to be **ambiguous.** Much logical confusion is due to the ambiguity of language. We will return to this topic in our discussion of informal fallacies (Chapter 4).

Some words are inherently imprecise in such a way that one cannot *in a way consistent with actual usage* define them so precisely as to be able to determine absolutely what is and what is not included in their extension. Such words are said to be **vague.** Consider, for example, the word "warm" as used in the expression "a warm bath." Clearly, 32° F. is too cold to qualify as "warm," and 212° F. is too hot to qualify. What, then, is the precise temperature range that constitutes a warm bath? How cold may the water be before we would call it cool rather than warm? How hot may it be before we would call it hot rather than warm? We cannot say. Any answer that we might give would define the term more precisely than is allowed by actual usage. In this case, therefore, an adequate intensional definition does not enable us to determine precisely what is and what is not included in the extension of the term, since actual usage is itself vague on this point.

There is, of course, nothing to prevent us from formulating combined definitions—definitions that are both intensional and extensional—when we are faced with the task of defining a word. If we were asked to define the word "food," for example, we might reasonably reply, "'Food' means anything that living organisms eat to nourish their bodies—in the case of human beings, bread, meat, vegetables, and things like that." Typically, we feel more confident about the extensional part of such an off-the-cuff definition than we do about the intensional part. The intensional part of such a definition is typically subject to revision as we search for a rule—a summary of required characteristics—that is consistent with actual usage.

## EXERCISES 2.3–2.4

A. Distinguish the following: ostensive definition, verbal extensional definition, intensional definition.
B. Explain how one might define the following words ostensively for someone who does not know the English language: "boy," "girl," "child," "man," "woman," "human being."
C. Write extensional definitions for the following words: "tree," "car," "animal," "blue," "straight," "heavy."
D. Write intensional definitions for the following words: "house," "clothing," "machine," "toy," "bowl," "school."

# 2.5 CONTEXTUAL DEFINITIONS

Some words cannot be defined either extensionally or intensionally. Consider: in order for a word to be definable extensionally, there must be some objects or events to which that word refers, some objects or events that one can point to or name that are included in the extension of that word. Any word that cannot be related to some object or event in this way cannot be defined extensionally. Moreover, if a word does not refer to (denote) any real or possible or imaginable objects, then it cannot be defined intensionally either, for an intensional definition states the properties that an object or event must have in order to be included in the extension of the word to be defined (the definiendum).

Among the words that cannot be defined either extensionally or intensionally are some that are very important to logic: such words as "all," "some," "either," "or," "and," "if," and "not." Such words are usually defined *contextually*, or *in use*. Note that their function is to connect other words—words that can be defined extensionally and/or intensionally—in meaningful sentences. The words "brothers males" do not, by themselves, make a meaningful statement. If we add the words "all" and "are," combining them with these two words according to the relevant rules of English sentence structure, we get the meaningful statement "All brothers are males." The meanings of "all" and "are" are exhibited when their respective functions are shown or described in meaningful linguistic expressions. Their meaning consists not in their reference but in their use.

Contextual definitions will be given for a number of logically important words in later chapters of this book, and it would be premature to give examples at this time. The only point you need take note of at this stage of our study is that there are words that cannot be defined either extensionally or intensionally, and the reason is that they do not denote anything. Their meaning consists in their use in statements of the forms "All ___ are ___," "If ___, then ___," and the like.

## 2.6 SYNONYMOUS DEFINITIONS

One further kind of definition—albeit a kind that is scarcely worthy of the name "definition"— is what is called a **synonymous definition**. As the name implies, it consists of a synonym of the word to be defined. In this sense, "car" may be defined as "automobile," "toy" as "plaything," and so on. Any word for which there is an equivalent word or phrase in the same language can be "defined" in this way.

Dictionaries frequently offer synonymous definitions of words that cannot easily be defined in other ways. The word "if," for example, can—strictly speaking—be defined only contextually. To define a word contextually, however, requires a number of examples, and they may take more space than is available. So the dictionary may instead offer some synonyms: "in case," "provided that," "on the condition that," and so on.

Synonymous definitions are not without value. Their principal value, however, consists in clarifying the meanings of obscure words or phrases by providing verbal equivalents that are presumed to be already understood. Someone who does not know the meaning of the word "equitation," for example, might find it helpful to learn that "equitation" means "horsemanship." It is less likely that someone who does not understand the word "horsemanship" would find it helpful to be told that it means "equitation." A good synonymous definition should offer a verbal equivalent that is more likely to be understood than the word being thus defined.

## 2.7 DEFINITIONS AND LOGIC

People formulate definitions for a variety of purposes, and the purposes may vary depending on whether those formulating the definitions are lexicographers, propagandists, scientists, philosophers, logicians, or whatever. What is the specific interest of *logic* in the formulation of definitions? For what purposes do logicians seek or create definitions?

One important purpose is to create a terminology appropriate for the discussion of the subject matter of logic. In the preceding paragraphs, for example, I have occasionally used the words "definiendum" and "definiens." I could have gotten along without those words. Each time I wanted to use the word "definiendum" I could have used instead the phrase "word to be defined," and each time I wanted to use the word "definiens" I could have used instead the phrase "phrase used to define." It is convenient, however, to have single words to take the place of phrases that one has occasion to use over and over again. It is convenient not only in the sense that it is easier to *write* a single word rather than a phrase; it is in the long run easier to *think* in such terms as well. To define a word is, in a sense, to capture a concept, to *organize* some facet of our experience. Concepts enable us to move about more efficiently in the booming, buzzing confusion of experience, and words embody concepts. I shall define many words in this book for the specific purpose of developing a terminology that will enable you to discuss more efficiently and precisely the subject matter of logic.

A second purpose is to make precise the terms and phrases that determine the logical structure of language. I will, in due course, formulate precise contextual definitions of such logically important words and phrases as "some," "all," "if . . . then," "if and only if," and so on. The precision that has been achieved in modern logic would not have been possible without such definitions.

Third, logic is interested in definitions because of the desire to identify and eliminate errors in reasoning resulting from the vagueness or ambiguity of language. Reasoning can go astray in a wide variety of ways, and we can eliminate some of those ways by defining precisely the key words involved in our reasoning. As the science of distinguishing between correct and incorrect reasoning, logic has a permanent interest in definitions as tools for the elimination of specious arguments.

# three
# Arguments

Since logic is concerned solely with arguments and arguments consist solely of statements, one might think that it would be a simple matter to determine when a piece of discourse is of interest to logic and when it is not. In concept, at least, the formula seems clear enough: discourse containing one or more arguments is of interest to logic, discourse containing no argument is not of interest to logic. In practice, however, this distinction is not always easy to apply. In ordinary discourse, arguments frequently appear intertwined with, submerged under, and obscured by elements of discourse that make it exceedingly difficult to determine whether an argument is indeed present beneath all those words, and if so, exactly what the argument is. In this chapter we will look at some of the ways in which arguments may be embedded in ordinary discourse, and will consider some techniques for isolating such arguments from the surrounding verbiage.

## 3.1 IDENTIFYING STATEMENT CONTENT

Arguments consist of statements. The first step in locating a hidden argument, then, consists in trying to isolate the statements that may be contained, however obscurely, in the discourse under considera- **33** tion. There are no hard and fast rules for doing so, but two methods have been found useful. One is to apply the true–false test: identify anything of importance stated, assumed, or implied in the sample discourse that is *capable of being true or false*. State these items separately. They and they alone constitute the informative content of the discourse. A second technique is to apply the contradiction test: identify anything of importance stated, assumed, or implied in the sample discourse that is *capable of being contradicted*. State these items separately. They and they alone constitute the informative content of the discourse. Obviously, with respect to any given sample of discourse, the two methods should yield the same results.

Let us apply these methods to a piece of actual discourse. Andrei Sakharov has written as follows:

> Freedom of thought is the only guarantee of the feasibility of a scientific democratic approach to politics, economy, and culture. But freedom of thought is under a triple threat in modern society—from the opium of mass culture, from cowardly, egotistic and narrow-minded ideologies, and from the ossified dogmatism of a bureaucratic oligarchy and its favorite weapon, ideological censorship. Therefore, freedom of thought requires the defense of all thinking and honest people.[1]

Applying the methods described above, we find the following statements assumed, stated, or implied in this short passage:

1. All thinking and honest people desire that there be a scientific democratic approach to politics, economy, and culture.
2. Freedom of thought would guarantee the feasibility of a scientific democratic approach to politics, economy, and culture.
3. Nothing other than freedom of thought would guarantee the feasibility of a scientific democratic approach to politics, economy, and culture.
4. Freedom of thought is threatened by mass culture.
5. Freedom of thought is threatened by certain ideologies.
6. Freedom of thought is threatened by governmental dogmatism.
7. Freedom of thought is threatened by ideological censorship.
8. Freedom of thought requires the defense of all thinking and honest people.
9. All thinking and honest people should oppose mass culture, certain ideologies, governmental dogmatism, and ideological censorship.

---

[1] Andrei Sakharov, *Progress, Coexistence, and Intellectual Freedom* (New York: W. W. Norton, 1968), pp. 29–30.

Let us pause to note two things about this restatement of the informative content of Sakharov's argument. First, note that in the restatement the terms "opium," "cowardly," "egotistic," "narrow-minded," and "ossified" have been omitted. The reason for omitting them is that they are highly emotive terms that contribute little or nothing to the informative content of the passage under consideration. "The opium of mass culture" is simply mass culture, "cowardly, egotistic and narrow-minded ideologies" are simply certain ideologies of which the author strongly disapproves, and so on. The informative content of his discourse—the statements he is making—can be more clearly seen if one simply eliminates these terms.

Second, note that statement 1 is not explicitly stated by Sakharov. We state it, however, because it is clearly assumed by his argument. The stated reason that all thinking and honest people should defend freedom of thought (which is the conclusion of the argument) is that something that they prize (a scientific democratic approach to politics, economy, and culture) is threatened by mass culture, certain ideologies, governmental dogmatism, and ideological censorship, and freedom of thought is the only defense against those enemies. Thus the argument makes sense only on the supposition that statement 1 is being taken for granted, and when we attempt to do justice to Sakharov's argument—identifying anything stated, assumed, or implied that is capable of being true or false or of being contradicted—it is appropriate that we make explicit this implicit assumption.

It is evident that the analysis of discourse for the purpose of identifying the statement content should not be done in a purely mechanical fashion. One has to use common sense, applying either or both methods (the true–false test and/or the contradiction test) in such a way as to produce results consistent with the apparent intentions of the speaker or writer who produced the discourse. If one's analysis is correct, the author of the discourse would recognize in the results an accurate statement of the informative content of the discourse. Since one rarely has the opportunity to check one's results with the author, however, it follows that one can rarely be absolutely sure that one's analysis is correct.

## EXERCISE 3.1

Using the true–false test or the contradiction test, identify and restate the informative content of the following passages:

1. Nature hath made men so equal, in the faculties of the body and the mind, as that, though there be found one man sometimes manifestly stronger in body or of quicker mind than another, yet when all is reckoned together, the difference between man and man is not so

considerable, as that one man can thereupon claim to himself any benefit, to which another may not pretend as well as he. For as to the strength of the body, the weakest has strength enough to kill the strongest, either by secret machination, or by confederacy with others that are in the same danger with himself.

—Thomas Hobbes, *The Leviathan*

2. The voice of conscience may sound loud and clear. But it may conflict not only with the law but with another man's conscience. Every conscientious objector to a law knows that at least one man's conscience is wrong, viz., the conscience of the man that asserts that *his* conscience tells him that he must not tolerate conscientious objectors. From this, if he is reasonable, the conscientious objector should conclude that when he hears the voice of conscience, he is hearing not the voice of God but the voice of a finite, limited man in this time and in this place, that conscience is neither a special nor an infallible organ of apprehending moral truth, that conscience without conscientiousness, conscience which does not cap the process of critical reflective morality, is likely to be a prejudice masquerading as a First Principle or a Mandate from Heaven.

—Sidney Hook, "Neither Blind Obedience nor Uncivil Disobedience"

3. Religion is an attempt to master the sensory world in which we are situated by means of the wishful world which we have developed within us as a result of biological and psychological necessities. But religion cannot achieve this. Its doctrines bear the imprint of the times in which they arose, the ignorant times of the childhood of humanity. Its consolations deserve no trust. Experience teaches us that the world is no nursery. The ethical demands on which religion seeks to lay stress need, rather, to be given another basis; for they are indispensable to human society and it is dangerous to link obedience to them with religious faith.

—Sigmund Freud, *New Introductory Lectures on Psychoanalysis*

4. Black Power, whatever the form of its implementation, has to solve the question of massive unemployment and underemployment, massive bad housing, massive inferior education. It must also deal with the massive problems of institutionalized white racism manifested in subtle forms of discrimination that result in blacks being denied equal access to and use of existing public accommodations and services. From access to medical facilities through the injustices suffered by blacks in the courts, to the pervasive problem of racist, repressive police practices, Black Power has to come up with the solutions.

—Eldridge Cleaver, "The Fire Now"

5. It is apparent from this brief description of the *kibbutz* that most of the functions characteristic of the typical nuclear family have become the functions of the entire *kibbutz* society. This is so much the case that

the *kibbutz* as a whole can almost satisfy the criteria by which Murdock defines the "family." This observation is not meant to imply that the *kibbutz* is a nuclear family. Its structure and that of the nuclear family are dissimilar. This observation does suggest, however, that the *kibbutz* can function without the family because it functions as if it, itself, were a family; and it can so function because its members perceive each other as kin, in the psychological implications of that term.

—Melford E. Spiro, "Is the Family Universal?"

6. The possibilities which confront us are few and ascertainable. One possibility is that we continue in the direction we have taken. This would lead to such disturbances of the total system that either thermonuclear war or severe human pathology would be the outcome. The second possibility is the attempt to change that direction by force or violent revolution. This would lead to the breakdown of the whole system and violence and brutal dictatorship as a result. The third possibility is the humanization of the system, in such a way that it serves the purpose of man's well-being and growth, or in other words, his life process. In this case, the central elements of the second Industrial Revolution will be kept intact. The question is, Can this be done and what steps need to be taken to achieve it?

—Erich Fromm, *The Revolution of Hope*

7. All that we lack at birth and need in maturity is given us by education. This education we receive from three sources—Nature, men, and things. The spontaneous development of our organs and faculties constitutes the education of Nature, the use to which we are taught to put this development constitutes that given us by men, and the acquirement of personal experience from surrounding objects constitutes that of things.

—Jean-Jacques Rousseau, *Emile*

8. From a scientific point of view, we can make no distinction between the man who eats little and sees heaven and the man who drinks much and sees snakes. Each is in an abnormal physical condition, and therefore has abnormal perceptions. Normal perceptions, since they have to be useful in the struggle for life, must have some correspondence with fact; but in abnormal perceptions there is no reason to expect such correspondence, and their testimony, therefore, cannot outweigh that of normal perception.

—Bertrand Russell, *Religion and Science*

9. Given our new, fast-accumulating knowledge of genetics, we shall be able to breed whole new races of blue people—or, for that matter, green, purple or orange. In a world still suffering from the moral lesion of racism, this is a thought to be conjured with. Should we strive for a world in which all people share the same skin color? If we want that,

we shall no doubt have the technical means for bringing it about. Or should we, instead, work toward even greater diversity than now exists?

—Alvin Toffler, *Future Shock*

10.    In order to prove that a thing *can* be done, all that is necessary is to do it—once. This may not always be easy, but once it has been done it has been proved possible and there is no need to pursue that question further. But to prove that a thing *cannot* be done is an assignment of a completely different order. It is equivalent to claiming that every single possible way has been tried and failed—and this is a bold claim for anyone to make.

—Douglas St. Paul Barnard, *Adventures in Mathematics*

# 3.2   ARGUMENT INDICATORS

Let us suppose that we have analyzed a piece of discourse for its statement content and have determined that it contains two or more statements. Does the presence of two or more statements establish the presence of an argument? Clearly not, for an argument involves the claim that one or more statements (the premise or premises) provide evidence for the truth of some other statement (the conclusion). How can one determine that such a claim is being made?

Once again, we must admit that there are no hard-and-fast rules for making such a determination. One has to pay close attention to the sense of the discourse and make a judgment about whether some statement (or statements) is (are) being offered in support of some other statement. In attempting to get at the sense of the discourse, one asks questions such as these: What is the author trying to establish? How is he or she trying to establish it? A correct answer to the first question should give us the conclusion of the argument (if there is one), and a correct answer to the second should give us the premise or premises.

It would greatly simplify matters if the conclusion always appeared at the end of an argument, as the last statement, but unfortunately this is not the case. Ordinary language is so flexible that the conclusion of an argument may appear anywhere—at the beginning, in the middle, or at the end of the argument. Thus position within the argument is not a useful criterion for identifying the conclusion. It is necessary to pay attention to the sense of the discourse.

Certain words and phrases are often indicators, however, that a given statement is being offered as a premise or as the conclusion of an argument. In the Sakharov excerpt in Section 3.1, for example, the conclusion of the argument is signaled by the word "therefore." Let us call any word or phrase that signals the presence of the conclusion of an argument a **conclusion indicator,** and any word or phrase that signals the presence of a premise a **premise indicator.** Among the words and phrases that often function in these ways are the following:

| **CONCLUSION INDICATORS** | **PREMISE INDICATORS** |
|---|---|
| consequently | as |
| ergo | because |
| hence | for |
| it follows that | if it be allowed that |
| so | if it be granted that |
| then it must be the case that | if we assume |
| therefore | inasmuch as |
| thus | since |
| we may conclude that | |

It goes without saying that the presence of one or more of these words or phrases in a piece of discourse is no guarantee that an argument is present, just as their absence is no guarantee that an argument is not present. Premise indicators and conclusion indicators are just what their names imply: indicators that the statements following them *may* be the premises or the conclusion of an argument. They call our attention to the possible presence of an argument within a piece of discourse, and may provide a clue to the structure of that argument. They cannot take the place, however, of a reasoned judgment about the sense of the discourse under consideration. Indeed, they are of value only insofar as they aid us in discerning that sense.

# EXERCISE 3.2

Each of the following passages contains at least one argument. Identify the premise(s) and conclusion of each argument.

1. The denial of theism is logically compatible with a religious outlook upon life, and is in fact characteristic of some of the great historical religions. For . . . early Buddhism is a religion which does not subscribe to any doctrine about a god; and there are pantheistic religions and philosophies which . . . are not theistic.
   —Ernest Nagel, "Philosophical Concepts of Atheism"

2. If, then, all experience is absolutely individual in its existence, all intrinsic good must be individual, for intrinsic good is experience.
   —Gardner Williams, "Individual, Social, and Universal Ethics"

3. The very essence of the moral decision as it is experienced is that it is a decision whether or not to *combat* our strongest desire, and our strongest desire *is* the expression in the situation of our character as so far formed. Now clearly our character cannot be a factor in determining the decision whether or not to *oppose* our character. I think we are entitled to say, therefore, that the act of moral decision is one in which the self is for itself not merely 'author' but 'sole author'.

   —C. A. Campbell, *On Selfhood and Godhood*

4. All states of consciousness in us, as in [brutes], are immediately caused by molecular changes of the brain-substance. It seems to me that in men, as in brutes, there is no proof that any state of consciousness is the cause of change in the motion of the matter of the organism. If these positions are well based, it follows that our mental conditions are simply the symbols in consciousness of the changes which take place automatically in the organism.

   —T. H. Huxley, "On the Hypothesis That Animals Are Automata and Its History"

5. We say of an old regiment, that it did such a thing a century ago, though there now is not a man alive who then belonged to it. We say a tree is the same in the seed-bed and in the forest. A ship of war, which has successively changed her anchors, her tackle, her sails, her masts, her planks, and her timbers, while she keeps the same name, is the same. The identity, therefore, which we ascribe to bodies, whether natural or artificial, is not perfect identity.

   —Thomas Reid, *Essays on the Intellectual Powers of Man*

6. Personality is essentially a matter of organization. Certain events, grouped together by means of certain relations, form a person. The grouping is effected by means of causal laws—those connected with habit-formation, which includes memory—and the causal laws concerned depend upon the body. If this is true—and there are strong scientific grounds for thinking that it is—to expect a personality to survive the disintegration of the brain is like expecting a cricket club to survive when all its members are dead.

   —Bertrand Russell, *Religion and Science*

7. Every being, which during its natural lifetime produces several eggs or seeds, must suffer destruction during some period of its life, . . . otherwise, on the principle of geometrical increase, its numbers would quickly become so inordinately great that no country could support the product. Hence, as more individuals are produced than can possibly survive, there must in every case be a struggle for existence.

   —Charles Darwin, *Origin of Species*

8. The Iranians, to be sure, often had reason to be suspicious of foreigners. The British, who seemed to think of Iran as their own naval petroleum reserve, bullied the Iranians for decades. And when the American CIA

joined British intelligence in organizing the 1953 coup, it gave a generation of Iranians a new focal point for their rage—and for their sense of insecurity.
>                          —David Ignatius, "How U.S. Relations with Iran Fell Apart"

9.  Because economic and social phenomena are so forbidding, or at least so seem, and because they yield few hard tests of what exists and what does not, they afford to the individual a luxury not given by physical phenomena. Within a considerable range he is permitted to believe what he pleases.
>                          —John Kenneth Galbraith, *The Affluent Society*

10. Science predicts, and it is because it predicts that it is useful and can serve as a rule of action.
>                          —Henri Poincaré, *The Value of Science*

# 3.3 COMBINED ARGUMENTS

If one could be sure that a given piece of discourse contained just one single argument, the analysis of the logic of that discourse would be much simpler than in fact it usually is. One could then, using the techniques already discussed, simply isolate the statements contained in that discourse, identify the conclusion, and then proceed on the assumption that the remaining statements (if they are relevant to the argument) must function as premises. The reason that one cannot do this is that in ordinary discourse chains of reasoning sometimes occur in which two or more arguments are combined in any of a variety of ways. Thus one must be prepared to find arguments within arguments (for example, when a subargument is introduced to support a premise of the principal argument), successive arguments related in such a way that the conclusion of one argument serves as the premise of another, and so on.

Consider, for example, the following passage from Robert Paul Wolff's *The Ideal of the University:*

> A large university in contemporary America simply cannot adopt a value-neutral stance, either externally or internally, no matter how hard it tries. . . . For example, let us suppose that a university cooperates with the Selective Service System, motivated in part by a simple desire to be helpful to legitimate government agencies and interested students, and in part by the conviction that deliberate refusal to cooperate would constitute an institutional opposition to the draft which would violate the principle of political neutrality. Obviously, the university strengthens the draft system, positively by its cooperation and negatively by its failure to take the deliberate step of opposition which was open to

it. To be sure, public refusal would have a greater political effect against, than quiet cooperation would have for, the government. Hence there must be better reasons for opposition than there are for cooperation. But the reasons need not be overwhelming or apocalyptic, and in any event, the action, positive or negative, is a political act based on *political* considerations. No major institution can remain politically innocent in an open society.[2]

We shall not take time to analyze this passage in detail, but it is evident from even a cursory reading that it contains more than one argument. The main thesis of the passage—the principal conclusion that the author is attempting to establish—is stated in the first sentence. The main premise offered in support of this conclusion is that, faced with the choice of cooperating or not cooperating with Selective Service, the university has no value-neutral alternative available to it. This premise, however, is the conclusion of another argument in which it is pointed out that if the unversity cooperates, it strengthens the draft system, and if it refuses to cooperate, it weakens it. There is another argument, whose conclusion (signaled by the word "hence") is that "there must be better reasons for opposition than there are for cooperation," and the concluding sentence of the passage functions as a premise in a deductive argument whose conclusion is the main thesis with which the passage begins.

Need I say it again? There are no hard-and-fast rules by which one can confidently identify and set forth the underlying logic of ordinary discourse. One must first do one's best to determine the exact meaning of the discourse under consideration. One must then isolate the informative content and, with the help of premise indicators, conclusion indicators, and any other clues that may be present, try to determine the structure of the argument or arguments. Only when one has determined that structure can the central business of logic—the *assessment* of arguments—get under way.

# EXERCISES 3.3

**A.** Locate an editorial in a recent edition of your local newspaper. Identify any arguments contained in it, and analyze those arguments into their premises and conclusions.

**B.** Review the quotation from Robert Paul Wolff on p. 41–42. Isolate the arguments contained in this passage, and identify the premises and conclusions of each.

---

[2] Robert Paul Wolff, *The Ideal of the University* (Boston: Beacon Press, 1969), pp. 71–72.

# 3.4 RESTATING THE ARGUMENT

In order to facilitate the assessment of arguments that occur in ordinary discourse, it is often desirable to restate those arguments in such a way as to expose clearly their logical structure. The following **Rules for the Restatement of Arguments** are offered as guides for this process.

*Rule 1: So far as possible, formulate all statements that are constitutive of the argument in emotively neutral language.* The purpose of this rule is to eliminate from the argument those noninformative elements that may tend to impair one's objectivity in assessing the argument. We have already considered (Section 3.1) a piece of discourse in which it was necessary to observe this rule.

*Rule 2: Eliminate synonymous terms and phrases through consistent use of one of the synonyms.* In the Robert Paul Wolff selection quoted in Section 3.3, for example, the phrase "adopt a value-neutral stance" in the first sentence is evidently synonymous with the phrase "remain politically innocent" in the last sentence. According to Rule 2, a careful restatement of the argument should adopt one phrase or the other and use it consistently.

*Rule 3: In discourse containing more than one argument, state each argument separately.* Each argument should be able to stand on its own premises. It is much easier to judge whether or not a given argument does so if you disentangle it from everything that is not part of that argument, including any other arguments that may be present in the discourse under consideration.

*Rule 4: In restating an argument, always state the conclusion last.* This is purely a matter of convention, but it is a convention so universally observed that it would be silly to ignore it. Moreover, many of the formal tests of validity (to be discussed later) presuppose the statement of the argument in standard form, one requirement of which is that the conclusion be stated last.

*Rule 5: Make explicit any statement that is or appears to be tacitly assumed in the discourse under consideration.* This rule is sometimes called the "principle of charity," since it charitably assumes that the author of the discourse is offering a cogent argument, and makes explicit the unstated premise or premises that exhibit that cogency. To take a simple example, the statement "It couldn't have been raining an hour ago because the pavement is perfectly dry" contains an argument that is cogent only if we assume that the speaker is tacitly asserting that "If it was raining an hour ago, the pavement would not be dry." Rule 5—the principle of charity—states that we should make such an assumption whenever it seems reasonable to do so.

Let us now carry out a careful analysis of a piece of discourse, restating its arguments in accordance with the above rules. The subject of our analysis will be the following passage from Martin Luther King's famous "Letter from Birmingham Jail":

> You[3] express a great deal of anxiety over our[4] willingness to break laws. This is certainly a legitimate concern. Since we so diligently urge people to obey the Supreme Court's decision of 1954 outlawing segregation in the public schools, at first glance it may seem rather paradoxical for us consciously to break laws. One may well ask: "How can you advocate breaking some laws and obeying others?" The answer lies in the fact that there are two types of laws: just and unjust. I would be the first to advocate obeying just laws. Conversely, one has a moral responsibility to disobey unjust laws.

Our first step is to formulate (in random order) all of the important statements that appear to be assumed, stated, or implied in the discourse under consideration. In carrying out this step we must be careful to observe Rules 1 and 2. Our first attempt to accomplish this step—subject to possible modification in accordance with Rule 5 at a later stage of our analysis—yields the following list of statements:

1. The civil rights activists consciously break laws.
2. The civil rights activists are not morally justified in consciously breaking laws.
3. The ministers of Birmingham are concerned about the fact that the civil rights activists sometimes consciously break laws.
4. This concern on the part of the ministers of Birmingham is legitimate.
5. A 1954 Supreme Court decision outlaws segregation in the public schools.
6. The civil rights activists advocate obedience to the 1954 Supreme Court decision outlawing segregation in the public schools.
7. Anyone who advocates obedience to the 1954 Supreme Court decision outlawing segregation in the public schools is not morally justified in consciously breaking laws.
8. Some laws are just.
9. Some laws are unjust.
10. The conscious breaking of just laws is not morally defensible.
11. The conscious breaking of unjust laws is morally defensible.
12. The laws that are consciously broken by the civil rights activists are unjust laws.

---

[3] The ministers of Birmingham—W.H.H.
[4] The civil rights activists—W.H.H.

13.  The conscious breaking of laws by the civil rights activists is morally defensible.

Let us next try to identify the *arguments* of which some of these statements (and perhaps others yet to be identified) are a part. Which of these statements are premises, which are conclusions, and which are neither?

It is clear that the main thesis of Dr. King's argument—the principal conclusion that he is trying to establish—is statement 13, "The conscious breaking of laws by the civil rights activists is morally defensible." The argument by which this conclusion is established appears to be this:

> The conscious breaking of unjust laws is morally defensible (statement 11).
>
> The laws that are consciously broken by the civil rights activists are unjust laws (statement 12).

∴  The conscious breaking of laws by the civil rights activists is morally defensible (statement 13).

It is equally clear that this argument is offered in opposition to the following argument of the ministers of Birmingham, an argument by which they have reached an opposite conclusion:

> Anyone who advocates obedience to the 1954 Supreme Court decision outlawing segregation in the public schools is not morally justified in consciously breaking laws (statement 7).
>
> The civil rights activists advocate obedience to the 1954 Supreme Court decision outlawing segregation in the public schools (statement 6).

∴  The civil rights activists are not morally justified in consciously breaking laws (statement 2).

When we reread the original passage, it is clear that the two arguments stated above faithfully set forth the principal reasoning contained in the passage. Are there additional arguments, either implicit or explicit, in this passage? Yes. Implicit in the position of the ministers of Birmingham is the following argument:

> Anyone who advocates obedience to law is not morally justified in consciously breaking laws.
>
> The 1954 Supreme Court decision outlawing segregation in the public schools is law.

∴  Anyone who advocates obedience to the 1954 Supreme Court decision outlawing segregation in the public schools is not morally justified in consciously breaking laws (statement 7).

Dr. King also suggests (but does not explicitly state) the following argument:

> Any concern about the conscious breaking of laws based on respect for law is legitimate.
>
> The concern of the ministers of Birmingham about the fact that the civil rights activists consciously break laws is based on respect for law.

∴  The concern of the ministers of Birmingham . . . is legitimate.

What is the function of the remaining statements in our list? Let us review them. Statements 1, 3, and 5 are simple statements of fact that play no direct role in the argument. Statements 8 and 9 make a conceptual distinction that is presupposed by statements 10 and 11. Statement 10 is the correlate of statement 11, and should perhaps be regarded as a premise in the following implicit argument:

> The conscious breaking of just laws is not morally defensible.
>
> The Supreme Court decision of 1954 outlawing segregation in the public schools is a just law.

∴  The conscious breaking of the law as represented by the Supreme Court decision of 1954 is not morally defensible.

It is evident from the above discussion that the identification and explicit statement of the arguments embedded in ordinary discourse is no easy task. Most of the time—fortunately!—there is no need to spell arguments out in this detailed and laborious way, since it is rarely necessary to wring the last hint of possible reasoning from a piece of discourse. As students of logic, however, we need to be able to recognize an argument when we encounter one, and to restate it in such a way as to be able to judge its cogency. The value of exhaustively analyzing the reasoning in sample pieces of argumentative discourse is that it heightens our ability to analyze the logic of discourse in which the structure of the argument is difficult to discern.

## EXERCISES 3.4

A.  Review what you have written in response to Exercises 3.2 and 3.3, and make any revisions that are necessary in order to satisfy the Rules for the Restatement of Arguments.

B.  Analyze the argument in the Sakharov passage on p. 34, restating that argument in accordance with the Rules for the Restatement of Arguments.

# PART TWO

# INFORMAL LOGIC

# four
# Informal Fallacies

In a correct argument, the premises are related to the conclusion in such a way that the assumed truth of the premises provides good grounds for assenting to the conclusion. In a correct inductive argument, the truth of the premises makes it more or less likely that the conclusion is true. In a correct deductive argument, the truth of the premises implies that the conclusion *must* be true.

Arguments can fail to support their conclusions in a variety of ways. The premises may be true, and yet those premises may fail to support the conclusion by virtue of some flaw, some logical error, in the argument. Such errors are called **fallacies,** and they are of several kinds. In this chapter we shall consider a number of what are called *informal* fallacies. *Formal* fallacies will be discussed in connection with our study of categorical syllogisms (Chapter 6).

## 4.1 FORMAL AND INFORMAL FALLACIES

In order to understand the concept of an informal fallacy, we must first distinguish between the *form* and the *content* of an argument. Consider the following arguments:

| | |
|---|---|
| All humans are mortal. | All sorority women are brilliant. |
| All Ohioans are human. | All Thetas are sorority women. |
| All Ohioans are mortal. | ∴ All Thetas are brilliant. |

With respect to content, these arguments are obviously very different: one is about Ohioans, humans, and mortality, the other about Thetas, sorority women, and brilliance. But there is something that is identical in these two arguments, namely, their form. That form might be represented as follows:

All A's are B's.
All C's are A's.

∴ All C's are B's.

Substitute any groups of things you please for *A*, *B*, and *C* and the result will be an argument identical in form to the two arguments stated above. Arguments are said to "instantiate" (that is, be an instance of) a certain argument form. A deductive argument that instantiates a correct argument form is said to be "valid." A valid argument is one in which the conclusion must be true if the premises are true (see Section 6.2). The form of the above arguments is correct, so any argument of this form having true premises will also have a true conclusion.

A deductive argument that does not instantiate a correct argument form is said to contain a **formal fallacy**. An example of an argument containing a formal fallacy is the following:

All communists are socialists.
Some members of the British Parliament are socialists.

∴ Some members of the British Parliament are communists.

An argument that is incorrect in any way other than with respect to its form is said to contain an **informal fallacy**. Informal fallacies occur in both deductive and inductive arguments. Numerous examples of such fallacies will be given later in this chapter.

Some fallacies are so obvious that nobody in his or her right mind is likely to be fooled by them. One need not be a logician to recognize that there is something wrong with the argument "All cats are animals and all dogs are animals, therefore all cats are dogs." Other arguments, however, mimic correct arguments in such a way that they tempt us to assent to the conclusion even though, upon analysis, it can be shown that the premises do not support that conclusion. Such arguments substitute psychological persuasion for rational argument, but in such a way that the careless reader or hearer is unaware of being taken in. They are the stock in trade of those who deliberately engage in nonrational persuasion. (Interestingly enough, the Latin word *fallacia*, from which the word "fallacy" is derived, means "a trick" or "a deliberate deceit.")

# 4.2   TYPES OF INFORMAL FALLACIES

There is no limit to the number of ways in which errors in reasoning can occur, and it is therefore impossible in principle to offer an exhaustive list of types of informal fallacies. Aristotle, in a treatise titled *De Sophistici Elenchi*, identified thirteen types of fallacies, and later writers have identified another hundred or so that apparently escaped Aristotle's attention. It would be a tedious task just to list them, let alone describe and illustrate them, and fortunately there is no need to do so. We shall, however, discuss a few of the informal fallacies that occur most frequently in the kinds of persuasive discourse that we are most likely to encounter.

Following Aristotle, logicians commonly distinguish between material fallacies and fallacies of ambiguity. A **material fallacy** is a mistake in the content of an argument such that the premises do not in fact support the conclusion even though they may appear to do so. Material fallacies are often further subdivided into two subclasses: fallacies of insufficient evidence and fallacies of relevance. A **fallacy of ambiguity** occurs when the meaning of a crucial word or phrase changes during the course of the argument in such a way as to render the argument incorrect. Such fallacies are possible because of the vagueness and ambiguity of language (see Section 2.4).

The broad classes of fallacies that we have discussed thus far are summarized in Figure 4-1. I must quickly add, however, that the classification and identification of types of informal fallacies is by no means an exact science. Competent logicians may disagree about the exact nature of the logical error that is occurring in a given case, and different names are sometimes given to the same fallacy. The principal value in acquainting oneself with some of the most common types of informal fallacies is not that one learns thereby to *name* them, but rather that one learns to avoid being taken in by them. One studies fallacies in order to develop what might be called a "sense for logical nonsense."

# 4.3   FALLACIES OF INSUFFICIENT EVIDENCE

Inductive arguments always offer conclusions that in some sense go beyond the evidence. It is not a fault in an inductive argument, then, if it asserts something in the conclusion that is not contained in the

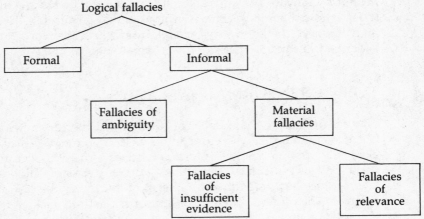

**Figure**
**4-1** Types of logical fallacies

premises, since all inductive arguments do so. Indeed, the unique value of inductive arguments consists precisely in the fact that they provide a way for us to extend our knowledge beyond that which has been directly observed. Only so can we draw conclusions about the TV viewing preferences of all Americans on the basis of actual evidence concerning some smaller number of Americans, about the chemical properties of hydrogen on the basis of observations concerning a small sample of hydrogen, and so on.

In a correct inductive argument, however, the evidence offered in the premises should make it reasonably probable that the conclusion is true. What constitutes a "reasonable probability" varies with the circumstances. If the conclusion of the argument is that Smith is guilty of murder, it is reasonable to demand that the evidence be extremely convincing (Smith must be proved guilty "beyond a reasonable doubt"). If, however, the conclusion concerns merely the cause of a certain small dent on the side of one's automobile, it is reasonable to conclude on perhaps quite meager evidence that it was probably caused by a carelessly opened car door in a parking lot.

The evidence stated in the premises, then, should provide adequate support for the conclusion that is being offered. An argument in which this is not the case is said to commit the fallacy of insufficient evidence. There are two principal kinds of such fallacies, corresponding to two ways in which the evidence may be inadequate to support the conclusion.

First, the evidence may be inadequate in the sense that there just is not enough of it to support the conclusion. "All bankers are conservative. I ought to know: my uncle is a banker, and he's as conservative as they come!" is an example of such an argument. That one banker is conservative is, of course, relevant to the conclusion that all bankers are conservative, but it is clearly insufficient to support such a sweeping conclusion. Evidence that a hundred out of a hundred bankers are conservative would be more convincing, similar evidence concerning a thousand bankers would be yet more convincing, and so on. At some point we would perhaps be ready to accept the conclusion, particularly if it were softened by the substitution of "most" or "nearly all" for "all."

Arguments that offer too little evidence to support a general conclusion (like the one about the bankers) are sometimes said to commit the fallacy of **hasty generalization.** The essence of this fallacy is that the quantity of evidence is not commensurate with the scope and the importance of the conclusion being drawn. Whether a given argument commits this fallacy is in some cases a matter of judgment.

The evidence offered in the premises may be inadequate in another way: it may be drawn from an unrepresentative sample. We may call this the **biased sample** fallacy. During the presidential election campaign of 1980, for example, a major TV network attempted to sample voters' reactions to the Reagan-Carter debate by inviting viewers to phone in their vote for the "winner" of the debate. The results of this telephone poll indicated that Reagan was favored by a much wider margin than had been anticipated. Subsequent analysis indicated that the wide margin was due in part to a biased sample: those who participated in the telephone poll incurred a small long-distance charge, and people at the higher income levels—those most inclined to support Reagan on other grounds—were found to be more likely to make such calls than those at lower income levels. Thus the results of the poll led to a false conclusion.

The principal defense against the biased sample fallacy is what statisticians call a "random sample." A random sample of a given population is a sample in which each member of the population has the same likelihood of being selected as every other member. Drawing names out of a hat is a primitive method of securing a random sample, but more sophisticated methods—such as those involving the use of a table of random numbers—have precisely the same purpose: securing a sample that is genuinely random.

One is most likely to be deceived by an argument containing a fallacy of insufficient evidence when that argument is offered in support of a conclusion that one is inclined to assent to on other grounds. From a single publicized case of welfare fraud we too easily conclude that "all welfare recipients are defrauding the public," from a single report of embezzlement by a public official we too easily conclude that "corruption by public officials is the main reason for high taxes," and so on. Perhaps it would be wise to adopt the policy of regarding as suspect any argument that reinforces one's prejudices, for it is such arguments that are likely to be the most seductive.

# 4.4 FALLACIES OF RELEVANCE

A fallacy of relevance occurs when the premises of an argument are irrelevant to the conclusion of that argument. Fallacies of relevance are material fallacies; in this respect they are like fallacies of insufficient evidence. But they differ from the latter in a very important way: the evidence that they offer in the premises is of *the wrong kind* to establish the stated conclusion. The premises of such an argument support a different conclusion, and the conclusion of such an argument requires different premises if it is to be established.

How, then, do such arguments even superficially *appear* to support their conclusions? Often they do so by establishing an emotional link between the premises and the conclusion so that an unwary reader or hearer is made to *want* to assent to the conclusion even though the stated premises do not support that conclusion. Where one should find an evidential link one finds instead pity, or fear, or awe, or the force of public opinion, or something else that tempts one to assent *notwithstanding the absence of relevant evidence.* Such arguments can be extremely deceptive.

There are many types of fallacies of relevance, depending on what it is that is offered in the place of relevant evidence. We shall consider a few of the most common types. Some of these fallacies are often referred to by their Latin names. In these cases the Latin name is given in parentheses after the English equivalent.

### a. *Appeal to Authority (argumentum ad verecundiam)*

There are, of course, numerous occasions when it is appropriate to appeal to an authority to substantiate a given assertion. Although experts can err, it is not unreasonable to consult the opinions of astronomers with respect to questions of astronomy, physicists with respect to questions in physics, historians with respect to historical questions, and so on. And since articles in encyclopedias and other reference books are normally written by people who are presumed to be experts on the subjects about which they are writing, it is not unreasonable to consult such books when one wishes to know the facts about some matter with which those books deal.

Expertise, however, is *field-specific*. To be an expert is to be an expert about something, not about everything. The appeal to authority is fallacious, therefore, whenever the appeal is to someone who is not an authority *on the subject in question*. Robert Redford may be an expert on movie making, but there is no reason to suppose that he is especially knowledgeable about the relative merits of various brands of shampoo, shaving cream, or men's suits. The president of the United States has access to a great deal of information that is not available to the average citizen, but this information does not make him an expert on constitutional law. The opinions of Robert Redford and of the president on these matters, then, should carry no more weight than those of anyone else—but of course they tend to do so. To give special credence to nonexpert opinions as if they were expert opinions is to fall prey to this fallacy.

A fallacious appeal to authority substitutes general eminence for genuine expertise. Thus we could also call this fallacy "the appeal to general eminence" or "the appeal to a famous person." We are tempted to assent to the conclusion not because the opinion of the famous person in question is genuinely relevant, but because we are unduly impressed with that person's eminence.

### b. *Appeal to Force (argumentum ad baculum)*

Not every appeal to force constitutes a fallacy, since to say that a fallacy is present is to say that a faulty *argument* is being presented. Thus a naked show of force, whether by a gunman who intends to steal your wallet or a nation threatening atomic war, involves no fallacy, as in neither case are we being asked to *believe* anything. Looking into the barrel of a revolver may be unnerving, but it is unlikely to lead us into errors of reasoning. If one's only options are to give up one's wallet or to receive a bullet in one's heart, it is clearly more reasonable to give than to receive.

The fallacy of an appeal to force is a much more subtle matter. It occurs whenever one is constrained to *believe* something because one perceives that it would be dangerous to believe otherwise. A plausible appeal to force presupposes an environment of intellectual coercion. Apart from such an environment, an appeal to force would deceive nobody.

Consider, for example, a Russian scholar who wishes to write, say, a biography of Karl Marx. Could this scholar write an objective biography? Could he acknowledge weaknesses in Marx's character, inconsistencies in his theories, or errors in his reports of alleged facts? Probably not. The threat of repression, the danger of losing professional standing, would be so great that such a scholar would be under constant (albeit unspoken) pressure to make the facts fit the accepted picture of Marx as an unassailable source of Communist wisdom. The ever-present threat would tend to make our harried scholar *believe* that the facts were as the reigning orthodoxy decreed that they must be, and thus would function as a constant implicit appeal to force in the course of his work.

The essential clue to the probable presence of a fallacious appeal to force, which is to say an appeal that attempts to force belief rather than merely behavior, is the existence of a reigning orthodoxy that is able to convey the impression that dissent is dangerous. If one is constrained to believe something because one is made to feel that to believe otherwise would jeopardize one's job, or one's social standing, or one's freedom, or one's eternal salvation, or anything else, such constraint constitutes an implicit appeal to force. The appeal to force is totalitarianism in the realm of intellect, and when stated as an argument it is always fallacious.

### c. *Appeal to Pity (argumentum ad misericordiam)*

The fallacy of an appeal to pity occurs when pity is evoked to support a statement despite the fact that pity is logically irrelevant to the truth of the statement in question. The paradigm example of this fallacy is the courtroom scene in which a defense attorney gives a heartrending account of the unhappy childhood that the accused was forced to endure, the series of misfortunes that later befell him, the suffering that he has experienced through many years as a result of a war injury, and so on. When this tale of woe has brought the members of the jury to the verge of tears, they are urged to find the accused innocent. How could they think of adding to his miseries? Yet the poor man's previous suffering (assuming that it really occurred) is logically irrelevant to the question of fact that the jury is supposed to decide: Did he or did he not do what he is accused of having done?

The appeal to pity is sometimes used also to solicit support for phony charities that in fact do little or nothing to help those for whom the pity is evoked. For example, an organization that claimed to be providing services to people who are physically disabled recently solicited funds in Ohio and several other midwestern states. The brochure accompanying the request for funds was filled with pictures of children and young people wearing leg braces, sitting in wheelchairs, using physical therapy equipment, and so on. The caption read, "They need your help!" And how could one help them? By giving—generously—to the organization in question. How would one's donation help them? The brochure did not say. Subsequent investigation revealed that the organization was a fraud, that funds given to this organization accomplished nothing for the handicapped. The appeal to pity was obviously intended to precipitate the false belief that a gift to the "charity" in question would result in some benefit for the people for whom pity was being evoked. It was therefore a clear example of a fallacious appeal to pity.

**d.** *Appeal to Popular Sentiment (argumentum ad populum)*

The appeal to popular sentiment occurs when one attempts to influence the judgment of one's hearers or readers by appealing to prejudices and attitudes that have nothing to do with the matter on which one is attempting to secure agreement. A political speaker, for example, may wish to persuade an audience that Candidate A should be elected. One way to do this, of course, would be to present the relevant facts about Candidate A—his experience, his views on certain issues, evidence concerning his commitment to public service, and so on. But what if evidence of this kind favors Candidate B? Well, as many political speakers have demonstrated, all is not lost. The speaker can still attempt to arouse the emotions of the audience in favor of his or her candidate, and thus divert attention from the objective facts. One can imagine something like the following occurring at a political rally:

SPEAKER: Have you had enough inflation?
CROWD: Yes!
SPEAKER: Have you had enough unemployment?
CROWD: Yes!
SPEAKER: Have you had enough international bungling?
CROWD: Yes!
SPEAKER: Do you want a congressman who will truly represent our interests?
CROWD: Yes!
SPEAKER: Do you want a congressman who is really *one of us*?
CROWD: Yes!
SPEAKER: Do you want a congressman who will *listen* to you?
CROWD: Yes!
SPEAKER: Well, I'm here to tell you that you can have that congressman. He is a man who served our nation in World War II and in Korea, a man whose sons fought in Vietnam, a man who is an elder in his church and a leader in his community. Ladies and gentlemen, I give you the congressman you've been seeking, your own Jerry Mander!

An appeal to popular sentiment can attempt to arouse the negative emotions of one's hearers as well as the positive ones. The late senator Hubert Humphrey's famous "but not Senator Goldwater" speech at the 1964 Democratic National Convention is an example of such an argument. Humphrey, a skilled political orator, recited a long list of legislative accomplishments that he said had won the support of all clear-thinking and forward-looking Americans—"but not Senator Goldwater." As the list grew longer and longer, the chanting of the crowd—repeating the catchphrase—grew louder and louder, and the millions of television viewers watching the performance had to be very astute indeed not to draw the conclusion that a vote for Barry Goldwater would be a vote against progress.

Not all arguments containing an ad populum fallacy are of the "bandwagon" variety. Advertisements, for example, often urge us to buy a certain product because it is allegedly the "in" thing to do. "Beer belongs," "Join the Pepsi generation," and "Go with number one" are examples of ads that appeal to the desire of many people to do what lots of other people are doing. Now the fact that many people are purchasing a given product does not in any way support the conclusion that the product is superior to its competitors. That is quite obvious if you eliminate the emotional element and simply state the argument: "More people are smoking Stogies than any other brand of cigarette. Therefore Stogies are superior to the other brands." That people are sometimes influenced by such appeals is due not to the cogency of the argument but simply to the desire to be "one of the crowd."

### e. *Argument Against the Person (argumentum ad hominem)*

Rational discussion requires that views be considered on their own merits, no matter who may happen to hold or express those views. It is reasonable to assent to well-supported views, it is reasonable to withhold assent from views that are not well supported, and it is not reasonable to assent or to withhold assent on any other basis. The fallacy of argument against the person occurs when someone who wishes to oppose a certain view attempts to discredit the person who holds the view rather than assessing the merits of the view itself. This may be done in a number of ways; thus this fallacy has several different forms.

One way of directing one's argument against the person is to attack his or her character, or to point to some fact or alleged fact about that person that is likely to arouse negative feelings toward him or her on the part of one's hearers. The hearers are then supposed to transfer that negative feeling toward the person to the views held by that person. This is called the **abusive** form of this fallacy. An example of such an argument would be "Edward Kennedy's proposals for a national health insurance program aren't worth listening to.

Remember Chappaquiddick!" Another is "Don't waste your time studying the philosophy of Nietzsche. Not only was he an atheist, but he ended his days in an insane asylum." And perhaps the most famous example of all is "Pay no attention to that rabble-rouser. Can any good come out of Nazareth?"

A second form of this fallacy is called the **circumstantial** argument against the person. Here the object is to discredit a person's views by suggesting that the circumstances of that person's life are such that he or she could be expected to hold exactly those views. Suppose, for example, that a researcher, Dr. X, claims to have found evidence that, contrary to the findings of other researchers, there is no causal link between cigarette smoking and lung cancer. To argue against this finding on the grounds that "Dr. X's family has been in the tobacco-growing business for many years; moreover, his research was financed by the tobacco industry" would be to present an argument containing this kind of fallacy. Other examples are "Of course John Paul II holds that birth control and abortion are morally wrong. He's the pope!" and "Your opinion of rock music is perfectly understandable; I'd probably feel the same way if *my* husband had run off with a rock singer."

It should be noted, however, that it is not fallacious to present evidence that calls a person's veracity into question when the veracity of that person is relevant to the truth of the statement in question. If the main reason for believing a certain statement is the testimony of someone who claims to have been an eyewitness to some event, and if there is reason to believe that the alleged eyewitness is lying, then it is perfectly reasonable to present evidence challenging that testimony—for example, evidence that the witness has been bribed, or was seen elsewhere at the time of the event that he or she claims to have witnessed, or has admitted lying under oath in the past, and so on. The fallacy of arguing against the person occurs when the view in question is capable of being assessed on its own merits, and when the character or circumstance of someone who advocates that view is logically irrelevant to its truth or falsity.

A third kind of argument against the person might be called the **you-too** argument (in Latin, *tu quoque*). It consists in an attempt to defend oneself against some accusation by making a countercharge against one's accuser, the purpose being to shift the discussion from one's own alleged misdeeds to those of one's accuser. Example:

MARY:  Oh, John, have you started smoking again? You know that before your surgery the doctor said that your system just couldn't stand any more nicotine.

JOHN:  *You're* a fine one to talk! Why, I'll bet you're forty pounds overweight. What does the doctor think about that?

Obviously, Mary's weight problem has nothing to do with whether or not it is inadvisable for John to resume smoking. The two issues are unrelated. To bring up the second issue as if it were somehow relevant to the first is therefore to introduce a you-too fallacy. Such fallacies occur rather frequently in the course of heated arguments.

### f. *Genetic Fallacy*

The genetic fallacy is similar to the argument against the person in that it attempts to discredit a statement or belief by discrediting the *source* of that statement or belief. If that source is an identifiable person, the argument commits the fallacy of argument against the person. If that source is not an identifiable person, it commits the genetic fallacy.

An example of an argument containing this fallacy is Sigmund Freud's famous claim that religious doctrines are unworthy of belief because they have arisen out of people's desire for knowledge about the origin of the universe, their need for protection against the dangers and vicissitudes of life, and their quest for authoritative direction as to how life is to be lived. So far as the logic of the matter is concerned, the suggestion that belief in God arose out of and is sustained by certain psychological needs of humankind is irrelevant to the truth of the statement affirming that belief. Thus any inference based on Freud's view would constitute a clear example of the genetic fallacy.

## EXERCISES 4.1–4.4

**A.** Write a brief response to each of the following:
  1. What is a fallacy?
  2. Explain the difference between a formal and an informal fallacy and give one example of each.
  3. Explain the difference between a material fallacy and a fallacy of ambiguity and give one example of each.

**B.** Each of the following arguments contains one of the fallacies discussed above. For each argument, do the following: (*a*) identify the fallacy and (*b*) state why the conclusion does not follow from the premises.
  0. *Example:* "Mr. Smith, you say that this town needs a new high school because the old one isn't big enough to handle our growing population. Answer me this: Isn't it true that you yourself have only a grade school education?"
    (*a*) Fallacy: Argument against the person (abusive).
    (*b*) The fact (if it is a fact) that Mr. Smith had only a grade school

education is irrelevant to the question of whether or not the town needs a new high school.

1. Samuel Dickerman Burchard to Republican presidential candidate James G. Blaine: "We are Republicans, and don't propose to leave our party and identify ourselves with the party whose antecedents have been rum, Romanism, and rebellion."

2. Student: "Professor, I want to ask you to please reconsider my grade in your course last semester. If you don't change my grade I'm going to be dismissed from school, and I'm sure you don't want to be responsible for that—especially when I tell you that my mother is a widow who has enough to worry about without this added burden."

3. "Are you doing anything in the stock market these days?" I asked. "Not on your life!" my friend replied. "I lost a bundle in the slump of '73–'74, and believe me, I learned my lesson. Putting money in the stock market is like throwing it away."

4. Senator Smith's arguments against gun-control legislation do not deserve the dignity of a reply. It is a matter of public record that the senator recently accepted a large campaign contribution from the American Rifle Association.

5. There's no doubt about it: women just aren't as good at mathematics as men. There are over fifty students in my math class, and on a recent test the top four students in the class were men and the three lowest were women. My roommate says that most of the good students in his class are men, too.

6. There certainly are cases in which capital punishment is morally justified. Even Abraham Lincoln declined to pardon a young soldier who had been condemned to death for desertion.

7. Russian spokesman: "Don't presume to lecture *us* about human rights. How do you treat black people in your own country? What are you doing for American Indians, or for Hispanics? Put your own house in order!"

8. Attorney: "Ladies and gentlemen of the jury, I think you would want to know that during the time the defendant has been awaiting trial on this charge he has lost both of his parents in a tragic auto accident, and his wife has recently filed for divorce. His young son, who sits there beside him, has a serious birth defect that will require him to spend the rest of his life in a wheelchair. Surely it is evident to all of you that this man has already had more than his share of suffering. Do not, by your decision in this case, add to his suffering."

9. My uncle is the president of a large university, and he says the best place to put your savings in these days of high inflation is in gold. He says that if one had invested just one thousand dollars in gold ten years ago, that same gold today would be worth about fifteen thousand dollars. I don't know any other place where you can get a return like that.

10. Politician: "Mr. Governor, you say that the taxes of this state

need to be raised if we are going to maintain governmental services at their present level. Is it not true that, through clever use of tax loopholes that an honorable man would never deign

11. Foreign students are rabble-rousers and should not be allowed to attend American universities. An Iranian student in my dorm actually had the audacity to burn an American flag, and then he and some of his friends boasted that their country had made the United States cry "uncle" when they took the hostages. Two other foreign students that I know are communists, and are here only to cause trouble. We should send all foreign students back where they came from.

12. Union spokesman (to fellow union members): "Some people say that it's the declining productivity of the American worker that is causing inflation, but you and I know better. It's the excessive profit of the owners and the high salaries of management that cause it, that's what it is. Right?" (Loud cheers.)

13. Prosecuting attorney: "Jones, why don't you think over what you observed on the day of the robbery, and see if you can't remember more clearly exactly who it was that pulled the trigger. I'm sure you know without my telling you that an improved memory could substantially reduce your own sentence."

14. I don't understand how anyone can be a skeptic or, worse yet, a downright unbeliever when you consider that every American president in this century has been a devout believer, and has endorsed religious faith as a bulwark of democracy.

15. Sales manager: "Bascomb, we've just got to get more sales in your territory or else we're going to have to replace you. I want you to stop worrying about those reports you've been hearing about our product being dangerous for small children. Those reports are all exaggerated—and besides, if we don't start making a few sales to families with small children, both you and I are going to be out of a job."

16. Political spokesman: "I'm sick and tired of answering questions about our candidate's conviction for income tax evasion. Besides, your candidate has recently been charged with drunk driving. What do you say about that?"

17. Political candidate: "People ask me how Republicans will explain the eighteen-and-a-half-minute gap in the Nixon tapes. I tell them it will take the Democrats a lot longer to explain the twelve-and-a-half-hour gap at Chappaquiddick."

18. Federal Communications Commission official to owner of TV station: "I would like to ask you to be more careful about the impression of the administration that you are conveying in your newscasts. The president is personally displeased with what he has been seeing on your station, and so are a lot of other powerful people around him. I note, incidentally, that your license comes up for renewal next year. It would be too bad if poor handling of the news were to result in your losing your license, wouldn't it?"

19. Political candidate: "It's time to put an end to these giveaway

programs. You've worked hard for your money and so have I. We have scrimped and saved and gone without in order to get where we are today. Why should we pay taxes in order to feed and clothe people who are too lazy to go out and earn a living?"

20. Beer is by far the favorite beverage among college students today. We verified that fact recently by taking a poll among the students on our campus, and it showed that beer was more than twice as popular as its nearest competitor.

# 4.5 MORE FALLACIES OF RELEVANCE

We shall now consider briefly six additional fallacies of relevance.

### g. *Argument from Ignorance (argumentum ad ignorantiam)*

The fallacy of argument from ignorance occurs when it is asserted that a given statement must be true (or false) because there is no evidence to the contrary. "Why do I believe that UFO's are piloted by beings from other planets? Because there's no evidence that they're piloted by earthlings, that's why. Until you can produce some evidence to the contrary, I shall continue to hold my belief." Obviously, if one could reasonably argue in this way one could "prove" the truth of any statement that is not clearly contrary to fact. Arguments of this kind are always fallacious.

Two practical principles, however, to some extent modify the general rule against arguing from ignorance. The first may be called the **presumption of falsity with respect to unsupported statements of fact.** According to this principle, in the absence of any evidence one way or the other, a statement affirming some alleged matter of fact is presumed to be false. For example: I am aware of no evidence that would indicate either that there is or that there is not at this moment a group of evil men plotting to kill me within the next thirty days. According to the principle just stated, under these circumstances I am justified in assuming that the assertion that there is such a group is false. The second principle has to do with one's guilt or innocence in a court of law, and is called the **presumption of innocence:** in the absence of evidence indicating guilt, one is presumed to be innocent. It is these principles that determine who has the burden of proof in a debate as well as in a court of law—and, for that matter, in ordinary rational conversation.

Note, however, that these principles do not make the absurd claim that in the absence of evidence the falsity of the statement of alleged fact or the innocence of the accused are *proved*. They merely establish the convention that under these circumstances proof will not be required.

### h. *Begging the Question (petitio principii)*

The fallacy of begging the question is the mistake that is committed when a given statement is offered as evidence that that very statement is true. The reason that such arguments are likely to deceive us is that the statement in question may be stated in different terms in the premises and in the conclusion of the argument, and thus may not be immediately recognizable as the same statement. Examples of such arguments are the following: "Women should not be drafted, because no woman should be required to render military service"; "Philosophy is the noblest of callings, for nothing is nobler than the love of wisdom"; and "Freedom of speech is advantageous to the state, for it is conducive to the interests of the community that citizens should have an opportunity to say what they please."

A more complex version of an argument that begs the question is what is called a **circular** argument. A circular argument involves two or more statements that are presented in such a way that each of them is offered in support of the other, but none of them breaks out of the circle so as to establish a connection with any supporting facts. A charming example of such reasoning occurs in one of the Dr. Seuss poems, in which we are told that the way to distinguish between ziffs and zuffs is that ziffs live on cliffs whereas zuffs live on bluffs. How, then, are we to distinguish between cliffs and bluffs? Simple: the cliffs are inhabited by ziffs, and the bluffs by zuffs! A more astonishing example of arguing in a circle—astonishing because it is offered seriously rather than in jest—appears in the following passage from a once widely used theological textbook:

> That the Word of God . . . really possesses causative authority, or the power of attesting itself as the divine truth, independently of any external proof, is clearly taught in Holy Scripture. [Here follows a series of biblical quotations and paraphrases.] In this way, then, and only in this way, do we receive divine assurance of the truth of God's Word: Scripture attests itself as the true Word of God through the power of the Holy Ghost, who operates through the divine Word.[1]

The circularity of this reasoning is evident: one should believe the Scriptures because they are authoritative, and the evidence that they are authoritative is that certain passages in those very Scriptures

---

[1] John Theodore Mueller, *Christian Dogmatics* (St. Louis: Concordia, 1951), p. 122.

declare them to be so. The authority of the Scriptures is offered as
the reason for believing these passages, and the testimony of these
passages is offered as the reason for believing in the authority of the
Scriptures. The author adds: "Against the charge . . . that theology
here argues in a circle we reply that, if Scripture cannot be relied
upon in its testimony concerning itself, it cannot be relied upon in
any other of its teachings." Such reasoning has the curious result of
resting confidence in the credibility of the Scriptures on the very
shaky foundation of a logical fallacy.

### i. *Complex Question*

In essence, the complex question fallacy is nothing more than a trick
to induce someone to assent to (or dissent from) a statement that he
or she would not assent to (or dissent from) apart from the trick.
The trick, in this case, consists in asking a question in such a way
that *if one answers the question as stated* one is assenting to (or dissenting
from) at least one statement that is assumed by the question. A
complex question, no matter how sophisticated it may be, is merely
a variant of the age-old question "Have you stopped beating your
wife?"

The error in reasoning in the case of a complex question is the
error of extracting a false conclusion by concealing that conclusion
in a premise that the victim of the fallacy is given no opportunity to
deny. A witness in a courtroom proceeding may, for example, be
induced to make statements that he or she had no intention of
making, but from which implications can be drawn that are damaging
to the position that the witness represents. "Mrs. Jones, did anyone
help you kill your husband?" appears to require a yes or no answer—
but if Mrs. Jones had nothing to do with the death of her husband,
either response would lead to a false conclusion. If she answers
either yes or no, she has implicitly admitted killing her husband—
either alone (if she answers no) or with the help of an accomplice (if
she answers yes).

The proper response to a complex question is to *divide the
question*, and in so doing to identify the assumption or assumptions
that lie hidden within it. One can then state one's agreement or
disagreement with each such assumption. In the case of the courtroom
interrogation, for example, Mrs. Jones might reasonably say, "Counsel, your question assumes that I killed my husband, either alone or
with somebody else's help. I deny this. There is therefore no way
for me to answer your question, for it makes no sense to talk about
whether or not anyone helped me do something that I had no part
in."

### j. *False Cause*

What does it mean to say that a particular event A is the "cause" of a particular event B? This is a much more difficult question to answer than it may seem, but for our present purposes we shall say that A is the cause of B if (1) A occurred before B, (2) B would not have occurred if A had not occurred, and (3) a recurrence of an event similar in all important respects to event A would be followed by a recurrence of an event similar in all important respects to event B. (The concept of causality is discussed more fully in Section 13.2.)

The fallacy of false cause occurs when an event, A, is identified as the cause of another event, B, on grounds that are not by themselves sufficient to establish a causal relationship. There are two forms of the false cause fallacy.

One form of this fallacy consists in arguing that A is the cause of B solely *because A occurred before B*. This is called the **post hoc** fallacy, from the Latin phrase *post hoc ergo propter hoc* (after this, therefore because of this). Such reasoning, although fallacious, is extremely common. Examples: "Each year for the past four years we have had a deficit in the federal budget, and each such deficit has been followed by more inflation. Thus it is clear that federal deficits are the main cause of inflation." "Prayer works. Every time there is a storm I pray that our house will be spared, and not once have we been hit by lightning."

In the second form of the false cause fallacy, simple correlation is mistaken for a causal relationship. Events of type A may be regularly followed by events of type B not because A is the cause of B, but because A and B are the joint effects of some other cause, X. It would be fallacious to argue, for example, that the fact that lightning regularly precedes thunder proves that lightning causes thunder, since it may equally well be the case (and, as we know, is the case) that both phenomena are caused by something else (an electrical discharge) that has both visible and audible consequences. It would be fallacious to argue from the fact that there is an unusually high divorce rate among counseling psychologists to the conclusion that the practice of counseling psychology leads to (causes) divorce, since it may equally well be the case that the field of counseling psychology tends to attract people who for other reasons are divorce-prone. And so on.

The correct identification of the cause of a given phenomenon is often a matter of considerable importance, as is demonstrated by the long and thus far largely unsuccessful search for "the" cause of cancer. Only if one knows what causes events of a certain kind to occur can one make them occur at will (in the case of desirable events) or prevent them from occurring (in the case of undesirable events).

Thus it is sometimes a matter of great practical importance to avoid the kind of simplistic thinking represented by the false cause fallacy.

### k. *Irrelevant Conclusion (ignoratio elenchi)*

The fallacy of irrelevant conclusion occurs when an argument is presented that supports a conclusion different from the conclusion that is actually stated. The arguer presents an argument that in fact supports statement A, but offers it instead in support of statement B, which does not follow from those premises. The conclusion that would actually follow from the stated premises and the one actually given are related in such a way, however, that an unwary reader or hearer may be deceived by the argument. Here is an example. The legislature in a certain state recently considered a proposal to require national testing agencies to make public each year the tests used in that state during the preceding year. The testing agencies vigorously opposed this measure on the grounds that its enactment would result in significantly higher costs to students, as totally new tests would then have to be developed annually. A proponent of the measure argued, however, that the proposal should be adopted *since these tests serve no worthwhile purpose anyway*. Now if that premise could be established, the proper conclusion is not that the testing agencies should be required to publish their tests annually; rather, they should be enjoined from giving those tests at all. Thus the argument commits the fallacy of irrelevant conclusion.

How do such arguments achieve even the appearance of plausibility, since the briefest analysis shows them to be fallacious? The answer appears to be that they first engender a positive or negative *attitude* toward the person or entity about whom the desired conclusion is to be drawn, and then suggest a conclusion consistent with that attitude. In the above case, for example, the proponent of the testing legislation may simply have been trying to arouse sentiment against the testing agency in the hope that his colleagues would support any measure hostile to those agencies, even though his argument did not support the particular measure under consideration. Such arguments are sometimes very effective, but their strength is the strength of emotion, not of logic.

### l. *Straw Man Fallacy*

The straw man fallacy consists of two steps: first, one misrepresents the position that one wishes to oppose, and then one attacks the position thus misrepresented as if it were the actual position of one's opponent. In short, one creates a straw man and then proceeds to demolish it. A good example of such an argument is the oft-repeated attack on the theory of evolution as "the ridiculous theory that human beings are descended from baboons, and are first cousins of orang-utans and chimpanzees." A critic of the theory of evolution who is able to convince his hearers that that is what the theory affirms does not need to concern himself with the tedious task of assessing the enormous body of evidence on which the theory is based. Indeed, he does not even have to attack his own straw man; it is so patently absurd that it will simply collapse under the weight of its own absurdity.

Straw man arguments are often used in political debate. A proposal to increase welfare payments to compensate for the effects of inflation becomes, in the mouth of a critic, "a plan to steal more of your hard-earned money and give it to people who are too lazy to work." A proposal to enter into a strategic arms limitation agreement with the Soviet Union may be caricatured as "a sell-out to the commies," a bill to deregulate the trucking industry as "giving the big trucking companies a license to destroy the smaller companies," and so on. Such arguments, though fallacious, can be very effective.

As can be seen from these examples, straw man arguments frequently substitute ridicule for rational argument. The person who puts forth a straw man argument is saying, in effect, "A really means B, but B is patently absurd; therefore, you should reject A." The fallacy in the argument consists in the identification of A with B, the authentic position with the straw man. Once the inaccuracy of the identification is perceived, the argument ceases to be convincing.

## EXERCISES 4.5

**A.**  Find or invent one argument to illustrate each of the following fallacies: argument from ignorance, begging the question, complex question, false cause, irrelevant conclusion, straw man fallacy.

**B.**  Each of the following arguments contains one of the fallacies listed above. For each argument, identify the fallacy and state why the conclusion does not follow from the stated premises.

  **1.**  Every major change in the intellectual, cultural, religious, and political forms of any society have been preceded by a substantial change in the economic system in that society. The conclusion is clear: intellectual, cultural, religious, and political ideas and institutions result from economic realities.

  **2.**  The Supreme Court has ruled that persons accused of crimes cannot be interrogated unless their lawyer is present. I think this shows more concern for criminals than for the victims of crime.

Laws exist to protect law-abiding citizens, not criminals. The police have a duty to get the facts, and one way to do that is to question the criminal. I think the Supreme Court is way off base on this point.

3.  I recommend that a Community Service Award be given to one of our most distinguished alumni, Dr. X. Q. Jones. As a young man, he brought worldwide recognition to this university as an Olympic athlete. He is a successful veterinarian with one of the largest practices in the state. His family life is exemplary, and he is also a generous contributor to this school. We couldn't make a better choice.

4.  The idea of treating frostbite by putting snow on it is absurd. It is one of many folk remedies that originated among poor and ignorant people who had no access to competent medical help.

5.  Corporate spokesman: "It is true that we have been burying our chemical wastes in this area for several years, and it is also possible that some of those waste materials have made their way into the water supply of the surrounding area. But there is no evidence whatsoever to link these admitted facts with the higher incidence of fetal death and birth defects that have been noted in this area in recent years. Thus it is clear that our company is not to blame."

6.  Each autumn, as soon as the frost comes, the leaves begin to turn. Some years, when the first frost is very severe, the leaves seem to turn almost overnight, and the entire countryside explodes in the most glorious hues of crimson and gold.

7.  The conservatives, on balance, oppose efforts at purposeful change because they believe that things are about as good as they are ever likely to get, and that any change is likely to be for the worse rather than for the better. If our ancestors had been conservatives, the human race would never have gotten beyond the Stone Age. Every single advance that has ever been achieved in human affairs has been achieved in opposition to the stay-put, no-progress stance of conservatives.

8.  He: "All competent music critics agree that the music of Mozart is the most exquisite—the *best*—music ever composed." She: "But how can you tell a competent music critic from an incompetent one?" He: "That's easy. If they're competent, they know that the music of Mozart is superior to all other music."

9.  Accuser: "The Actors Guild is loaded with communists and fellow travelers." Defender: "That's a pretty serious charge. Can you prove it?" Accuser: "Where's the evidence that what I say is not true? Can you prove that the members of the Guild are loyal Americans?"

10. Member of Parliament: "My dear colleagues, it is time to put an end to the importation of bananas. I have recently studied statistics covering the past forty years—forty years, I say—and I note with horror that the increase in the incidence of tuberculosis in our land runs almost exactly parallel to the increase in the volume of bananas imported here from Central America. We owe it to our

constituents to ban once and for all the root cause of this terrible malady that afflicts so many of our countrymen."

11. Salesman: "Well, folks, I can see that you really like that model. Would you like to order it with or without power steering?" (Sales manuals call this the "implied consent" approach to closing a sale, but the logical fallacy on which it is based has another name.)

12. Sect spokesman: "True believers will never die, but will be taken straight to heaven." Skeptic: "But many members of your group have died." Spokesman: "They were not true believers." Skeptic: "How do you know that?" Spokesman: "Because they died."

13. Professor Jones, I understand that you have made a special study of extinct species of animal life. On the basis of your study, would you say that dinosaurs became extinct before, during, or after the great flood from which Noah and his family were spared?

14. I wish to speak in favor of the proposal to establish at this university a department of library science with an initial operating budget of $500,000. There are thousands of libraries in this country, and they all need librarians. Many other universities have such programs, and we should too. Good libraries make for a better-informed public, and that is important in a democracy. If we want good libraries, we must support them in every way we can.

15. The decision to turn over the Panama Canal to Panama was a great mistake that is sure to have disastrous consequences. The whole idea originated in an administration that had little experience and no sense of direction in foreign affairs. This sad episode shows how important it is to have experienced people heading up the government.

16. Professor: "Your assignment for next week is as follows: first, read the three short articles that were handed out at the beginning of the period; second, write a brief summary of each; third, identify the one you liked *least* well; and fourth, tell me to what defect in your character you attribute this dislike."

17. The liberal, old style or new style, swears by the evangels of Progress. He thinks of society as a machine for attaining material aggrandizement, and of happiness as the gratification of mundane desires. Now surely we all know that not all change is progress, that society is not merely a goods-producing machine, and that the satisfaction of trivial desires does not lead to happiness. How anyone with a modicum of intelligence can accept these silly ideas is beyond comprehension.

18. Man to bank teller: "I'd like to cash a check." Teller: "Do you have any identification?" Man: "Yes, my friend here can identify me." Teller: "But I don't know your friend." Man: "No problem. I'll introduce you."

19. Senator Joe McCarthy (concerning a State Department employee whom he had accused of being a communist sympathizer): "I do not have much information on this except the general statement of the agency that there is nothing in the files to disprove his communist connections."

20. For the past twenty-five years, the standardized test scores of high school seniors have been slowly declining. During that same period of time, the television viewing time of the average American school-age child has been steadily increasing. The conclusion to be drawn from these facts is obvious: increased television viewing time results in lower test scores.

# 4.6 FALLACIES OF AMBIGUITY

Some words and phrases, as we have seen (Section 2.4), have more than one meaning. They are, as we say, ambiguous. So long as the intended meaning is specified, or is clear from the context, such ambiguity creates no logical problems. When the intended meaning is not clear, however, ambiguity can lead to errors in reasoning. Such errors are called **fallacies of ambiguity.** We shall consider six of the most common types of these fallacies.

### a. Accent

Language is so pliable that a given sentence may have several different meanings, depending on which word or phrase in the sentence is stressed. Consider, for example, the sentence "The senseless murder of John Lennon was a tragedy." The meaning of that sentence seems clear enough, and is presumably noncontroversial. But note what happens if, in reading the sentence, you emphasize the word "senseless." In this reading there is a suggestion that if the murder had not been *senseless*—if, for example, it had been motivated by robbery or jealousy or a desire to settle an old grudge, or something else that in some way made sense—it would not have been a tragedy. Or note what happens if you emphasize the name "John Lennon." Suddenly the meaning seems to be that, while the senseless murder of *John Lennon* was a tragedy, it would not have been a tragedy if someone other than John Lennon had been senselessly murdered. Almost any declarative sentence can be construed to mean a variety of things depending on where one places the accent.

The fallacy of accent occurs when a false conclusion is drawn from premises at least one of which has been rendered misleading or false by a misplaced accent. Suppose, for example, that a male chauvinist argues as follows: "According to the Declaration of Independence, all *men* are created equal. Now it is obvious that women are women, not men; therefore it is obvious that the Declaration of Independence does not support the thesis that women are or should be equal to men." The accent, in this case, leads us to construe "men" as "adult males" rather than as "human beings," which was the evident intent of the framers of the Declaration of Independence. Thus that hallowed document is misquoted to support an erroneous conclusion, but the misquotation involves only a change of accent, not a change in wording.

When the incorrectly accented statement is from a well-known source, as in the above example, the argument is unlikely to deceive anyone, since it can be assumed that most people would recognize the misquotation for what it is. Arguments containing fallacies of accent can be highly deceptive, however, when the misquoted source is unknown to the persons to whom the argument is directed. If a politician says, for example, "In a speech on November 12, 1982, my opponent said, and I quote," the quotation may be word for word and yet be a misquotation by virtue of a deliberate change of accent. Moreover, there is no magic formula by which one can detect this fallacy. One needs to be sensitive to situations in which the speaker might have a motive to deceive, and take with a grain of salt anything that sounds suspicious if not downright preposterous. The best defense against deliberate deceit, of which an argument containing the fallacy of accent is but one example, is a habit of intellectual caution.

### b. *Amphiboly (syntactic ambiguity)*

Just as the meaning of a sentence is determined in part by where one places the accent, so also is it determined in part by the grammatical structure of the sentence. When the grammatical structure of a sentence is ambiguous, the sentence is said to be *amphibolous*. When an inference is drawn from premises at least one of which is amphibolous, the argument is also amphibolous and is said to commit the fallacy of **amphiboly**. Another name for this fallacy is the fallacy of **syntactic ambiguity**.

Let us look first at an example of an amphibolous sentence. Consider the sentence "The candidate warned against a lot of errors in his speech." This sentence is amphibolous in two ways. First, it is not clear whether "his speech" means the candidate's own speech or that of someone else, since "his" could refer either to himself or to another male speaker. Second, if we assume that "his speech" refers to the candidate's own speech, it is not clear whether the sentence states that the speech contains the warning or the errors. If the former, the sentence would be more clear (that is, the amphiboly would be removed) if it read "In his speech, the candidate warned against a lot of errors." If the latter meaning is intended (although this seems unlikely), a clearer reading would be "The candidate warned that his own speech contained a lot of errors."

Suppose, now, that someone uses this amphibolous sentence in the following way: "According to the morning paper, the candidate warned against a lot of errors in his speech. Since he himself acknowledges that his speech contains errors, I think we can safely ignore everything he has to say." This is an amphibolous argument: it draws an unwarranted conclusion from a premise that is misinterpreted as a result of an ambiguity in its grammatical structure.

Amphibolies are usually the result of carelessness rather than deliberate deceit, and it is in reading printed materials containing amphibolies that we are most likely to draw such unwarranted inferences. Amphibolous arguments are typically arguments that we frame for ourselves in the process of reading materials containing this particular kind of ambiguity.

### c. *Composition*

In order to understand the fallacy of composition we must first understand the difference between collective and distributive predication. Consider the statement "The Bach children were both numerous and musical." In this example, the quality of being numerous is predicated of the Bach children as a group, whereas the quality of being musical is predicated of each of them individually. If we assent to this statement, we are then agreeing that Elisabeth Juliana was musical, and Johann Christian was musical, and Carl Philipp Emanuel was musical (and so on), but we are not thereby agreeing that Elisabeth Juliana was numerous, and Johann Christian was numerous, and Carl Philipp Emanuel was numerous (and so on). The quality of being musical is predicated of the Bach children *distributively*, whereas the quality of being numerous is predicated of them *collectively*.

The fallacy of composition consists in treating a distributed characteristic as if it were collective. It occurs when one makes the mistake of attributing to a group (or a whole) some characteristic that is true only of its individual members (or its parts), and then makes inferences based on that mistake. The following argument, for example, contains a fallacy of composition: "All of the starters on this year's football team are highly talented individuals; highly talented teams generally win all or most of their games; so this year's football team should have a winning season." It is obvious, when you think about it, that a talented *team* is more than a group of talented *individuals*. In order for those talented individuals to constitute a talented team, they must be well coached in the fundamentals of the game, must know their plays well, must have their timing down to a fine point, and so on. That the members of the team are talented individuals is evidence in support of the statement that the team is talented, but it is not by itself sufficient to establish the statement that the team is talented, and it certainly is not equivalent to the statement that the team is talented. The argument cited above treats the statement about the team's talent as if it were equivalent to the statement about the talent of the individual members, and in so doing it commits the fallacy of composition.

### d. *Division*

The fallacy of division is just the opposite of the fallacy of composition: it consists in treating a collective attribute distributively, and then drawing inferences from the statement thus obtained. In the case of a statement such as "The Bach children were numerous," common sense is enough to prevent us from committing this fallacy, since it would be obviously silly to conclude that each and every one of the Bach children was numerous. In other cases, however, the mistake is more subtle and may easily escape our notice. For example, the person who says to a college student, "Well, I suppose you are pretty concerned about what career you're going to follow; I understand that's a growing concern among college students these days," is committing the fallacy of division. A growing concern about careers is a characteristic of college students as a *group*, not of each and every college student as an individual. Any inference about any individual college student based on the supposition that college students as a group are characterized by a growing concern about careers is therefore unwarranted.

The fallacies of composition and division are called fallacies of ambiguity because they result from the fact that ordinary language makes no distinction between attributes that are to be construed collectively and those that are to be construed distributively. Ordinary language is genuinely ambiguous on this point. There is no grammatical clue that tells us that "numerous" is a collective predicate, "tall" a distributive predicate, and "talented" one or the other depending on the context. The distinction between collective predication and distributive predication is a purely logical distinction, indeed a logical distinction that is easily made and understood in clear-cut cases. In cases that are not so clear-cut, however, we need to keep our wits about us lest we inadvertently draw conclusions about some group on the basis of premises that are true only of the individual members (the fallacy of composition) or, alternatively, draw conclusions about the individual members on the basis of premises that are true only of the group (the fallacy of division).

### e. *Equivocation*

The fallacy of equivocation occurs because of the fact that a given word or phrase may have more than one meaning. In ordinary discourse, we usually know from the context which meaning is intended, and in such cases no problem results. When we assess arguments, however, we may sometimes discover that the same word or phrase is used with two different meanings, whereas the plausibility of the argument depends on the consistency of the meaning throughout the course of the argument. Such arguments are said to commit the fallacy of equivocation.

Consider, for example, the following argument, which is attributed to St. Augustine: "Deep within the heart of every man is a desire for freedom; but bondage to God is the highest form of freedom; therefore, all men secretly long for this bondage, in order that they may be truly free." This argument, which has been stated in one form or another in many a sermon, commits the fallacy of equivocation. The term on which it equivocates is "freedom." The statement "Deep within the heart of every man is a desire for freedom" is plausible (if it is) only on the supposition that "freedom" means something like "the opportunity to do as one pleases." But it is very unlikely that this is the meaning in the second premise, for then St. Augustine would be saying, "Bondage to God gives one the maximum opportunity to do as one pleases"—and that is clearly not a very saintly thing to say. For this premise to be plausible (if it is), "freedom" must mean something else—"the fullest realization of true humanity," for example. Now "the opportunity to do as one pleases" and "the fullest realization of true humanity" are very different concepts, but the difference is hidden by the fact that both are acceptable meanings of the single term "freedom."

The fallacy of equivocation is most likely to occur when the meanings involved in the equivocation are somewhat related. Nobody would be fooled by arguments that tried to take advantage of the several meanings of such words as "lock," "sock," "suit," "crank," and so on, because the meanings are so different. Such words lend themselves to humor, not to seriously misleading arguments. The words to watch out for are the fuzzy abstractions—such words as "law," "freedom," "happiness," "justice." Their very fuzziness is due in part to the fact that they can mean any one of several things, and it frequently is not clear from the context *which* of these several things is meant in a given instance. Even the speaker or writer who is using the term may not be absolutely clear about its exact meaning in a given context. Thus it can very well happen that a speaker or writer, with no intent to deceive, puts forward an argument that on close inspection proves to be equivocal.

If one suspects that a given argument may be equivocal, there is a way to test one's suspicion. That is to do as we did above in the case of the "freedom" argument: (*a*) define the term that you suspect of being equivocal in such a way as to make the statement in which it first occurs plausible, and (*b*) use that definition in place of the term at each subsequent appearance of the term. If one's suspicion is correct, the result will be an argument that either is logically incorrect or contains premises that no longer appear plausible. This method is not foolproof, however, for there may be some other definition of the suspect term that would result in plausible statements in all cases, in which case the charge of equivocation would not be correct.

### f. *Quotation out of Context*

Most of us have had the experience on more than one occasion of joining a group that is engaged in conversation and being initially bewildered about what on earth the conversation is about. Somebody makes a statement, and we *think* we understand what that person says, but what is said next doesn't make sense, or doesn't seem appropriate, if the first speaker meant what we thought he or she meant. So we continue to listen, searching all the while for—what? For the *context* of the discussion. We cannot really understand the various contributions to the conversation—and certainly cannot intelligently participate in it—until we are clear about what is being discussed.

The lesson to be learned from this experience is that the meaning of individual bits of discourse is often determined in part by the context in which they occur. Considered in its original context, a passage may have one meaning; considered apart from that context, it may appear to have quite a different meaning. The fallacy of quotation out of context occurs when the meaning of the quoted excerpt is so intimately related to its context that the elimination of the context has the effect of changing the meaning of the quoted passage. Any inferences drawn from the misinterpreted excerpt will then be unwarranted, since they will be starting from a false premise.

Suppose, for example, that candidate Jones writes an article in which he states, "Some people say we ought not to worry about those who are unemployed. They say we shouldn't use public funds to support these people, because if they weren't so lazy they would go out and find a job. Well, I don't agree with that view. I think most of the people who are out of work today really want to work, and we have a public obligation to keep food on their tables until they get back on their feet." Suppose now that Jones's opponent, candidate Smith, makes a speech in which he states, "My opponent claims that he is concerned about the poor and the unemployed, but the truth is that he is not. I have before me an article written by Mr. Jones in which he states—and I quote his very words: '. . . we shouldn't use public funds to support these people, because if they weren't so lazy they would go out and find a job.' I submit to you that those are not the words of a man who cares about the poor and the unemployed. They are the words of a cynical, uncaring man who is not qualified to hold public office." Clearly, although Smith's quotation of Jones is perfectly accurate as far as it goes, the omission of the context leads to the erroneous conclusion that Jones is unconcerned about the unemployed. Smith is using the fallacy of quotation out of context to discredit his opponent.

The fallacy of quotation out of context may be either innocent or malicious. It is innocent when, perhaps as a result of carelessness, someone inadvertently creates a misunderstanding by failing to note or make explicit the context. It is malicious when, as in the above example, the context is deliberately suppressed in order to deceive. Whether innocent or malicious, however, quotation out of context is a logical fallacy whenever the quotation is used as a basis for further inferences.

## 4.7 DETECTING INFORMAL FALLACIES

The perceptive reader will have noted during this long discussion of informal fallacies that no formula has been provided for detecting such fallacies. If reasoning could go astray only in a small number of ways, perhaps a formula for detecting those ways might be devised. But reasoning can err in any number of ways, only some of which have been discussed here. How, then, can one be even moderately certain in the case of any particular argument that one is not being misled? How can one at least *attempt* to detect any fallacies that may be present, and so guard against error? I shall conclude this discussion of informal fallacies by setting forth what may be called *informal rules for detecting informal fallacies*. Following these rules will not guarantee that we will not be misled by fallacious arguments, but it will greatly reduce the likelihood of being so misled.

The first rule is this: *Be clear about the exact meaning of the statement to which you are being asked to assent* (the conclusion of the argument) *and the exact meaning of each statement offered in support of that statement* (the premise or premises). If you are tenacious about this, you should be able to detect most if not all of the fallacies of ambiguity that may be foisted upon you. Fallacies of ambiguity deceive us (when they do) because we do not insist on the clarity that should be demanded before we yield our assent.

The second rule is this: *Be clear about the kind of evidence that would be relevant to establishing the conclusion in question, and regard with suspicion any argument that does not offer such evidence.* If we really are clear about the exact meaning of the statement to which we are being asked to assent (Rule 1), we should be able to state what would have to be the case in order for this statement to be true. But if we know this, we must also have some idea of the kind of evidence that would show that this is indeed the case. If, then, an argument is presented in support of this statement that does not appeal to the appropriate evidence, we are surely justified in suspecting that it is a fallacious argument. Only detailed analysis of the argument, of course, can determine whether it is indeed fallacious and, if so, in exactly what way it is fallacious.

Third, *be suspicious of arguments that tend to evoke emotion of any kind.* As we have seen, many informal fallacies accomplish their deception under the protective cover of some emotion. They appeal to us in such a way that we are made to *want* to assent to a given conclusion, no matter what the evidence may indicate. Such wanting, however, is irrelevant to the truth or falsehood of the statement in question, and irrelevant also to the reasoning that might establish or fail to establish that statement. Whenever we are presented with an argument that appears to appeal to our emotions, therefore, we would be well advised to restate the argument in as unemotive a way as we can find. If the argument is cogent, its cogency will then be apparent. If the argument is not cogent, that will also be apparent. In either case, we will have eliminated the possibility of being misled by a fallacious appeal to emotion.

Fourth, *be suspicious of arguments presented by anyone who might have a motive to deceive.* It is to be hoped that in most of our dealings with our fellows we can count on their veracity as well as their intent not to deceive us, at least not willfully. There are situations, however, in which it is only prudent to be on one's guard. People who want to sell us something, people who want our vote, people who are committed to a party line or ideology, people who have a personal stake in persuading us that so-and-so is the case—these are the people who might be expected deliberately to deceive us. It is only prudent, therefore, to receive their arguments with caution and to examine them with due care.

Finally, *trust your instincts whenever you encounter an argument that just doesn't sound right to you, and try to figure out why it doesn't sound right*. Most people of adult age and normal intelligence have encountered enough good and bad reasoning in the course of their lives to have developed a kind of sense of cogency, and can sometimes intuit that something is wrong with an argument without being able immediately to say *what* is wrong with it. Do not be embarrassed about this. Do not hesitate to place a question mark over an argument when it sounds questionable to you, even if you cannot determine immediately *why* it sounds questionable. You may eventually conclude that the argument is all right, and if so, fine—no harm has been done. But often, very often, when an argument sounds fishy to you, careful analysis will reveal that your initial hunch was right: the argument contains a fallacy. Your own sense of cogency is one of the most effective weapons available to defend you against fallacious arguments. Don't be afraid to use it!

## EXERCISES 4.6–4.7

A.  Find or invent one argument that illustrates each of the following fallacies of ambiguity: accent, amphiboly, composition, division, equivocation, quotation out of context.

B.  Each of the following bits of discourse contains or suggests an argument that contains one of the above fallacies. Identify the fallacy in each, and state why the conclusion does not follow from the premise or premises. (See pp. 60–61 for an example.)

1.  It is silly to pass laws against discrimination, since it is obvious that we can't live without it. We discriminate between pleasant and unpleasant tastes in selecting our food, between pleasant and unpleasant sounds in selecting our music, between harmonious and unharmonious colors in decorating our homes, between interesting and uninteresting people in choosing our friends, and so on. We can't live without discriminating.

2.  We have it on good authority that it is our duty to render unto Caesar that which is Caesar's. Now one of Caesar's—which is to say the government's—prerogatives is to keep the armed forces at whatever level may be judged necessary to maintain national security. It follows, therefore, that the government has the right to institute a military draft whenever it perceives a need to do so, and those who are in the prescribed age range have a corresponding duty to register and, if called upon, to serve.

3.  Mother recently asked me to watch my little brother while she went to the store, and I did. I watched him go out in the street and stop the traffic. I watched him climb a ladder and come down again. I watched him sit down in a mud puddle and put mud in his hair. I did exactly what mother asked me to do, and still she was angry when she got home. I wonder why.

4.  Thomas Jefferson, in a letter to Dr. Benjamin Rush, wrote as follows: "They [the clergy] believe that any portion of power confided to me, will be exerted in opposition to their schemes.

And they believe rightly: for *I have sworn upon the altar of God, eternal hostility against every form of tyranny over the mind of man."* (Italics added.) The italicized words are engraved on the Jefferson Memorial in Washington, D.C. Seeing the engraved words, a visitor commented, "Why, I never realized that Jefferson was such a religious man."

5. All human beings, regardless of their political persuasion, desire peace. The memory of war and its attendant miseries is sufficiently fresh in the minds of many living today, and the fear of the terrible holocaust that would be likely to occur in any future war is sufficiently strong in the hearts of many more, that no one but a madman would consider war a viable solution to any problem. Since, therefore, all nations desire peace, we may be confident that, notwithstanding occasional *talk* of war, we will in fact have peace.

6. Reporter: "Senator, you have been quoted as saying that you have never made a public statement that was not, to the best of your knowledge, fully and absolutely true. The issue that we are discussing, however, concerns private statements made by you to members of your staff and to certain of your colleagues in the Senate. Since your disclaimer concerns only your public statements, may we not reasonably conclude that the veracity of those statements is open to question?"

7. The impending bankruptcy of the Chrysler Corporation, if it really occurs, will certainly be a terrible blow to the president and officers of the corporation. Imagine what it must be like to spend half a lifetime acquiring a modest estate, and then to see it completely wiped out in a single day in bankruptcy court.

8. The duke said to his servant, "Saddle the ass." So he saddled him, and the duke was sorely angered.

9. I know that the Bible says, "Thou shalt not bear false witness against thy neighbor." But the fellow I was testifying against lives clear cross town, so surely that commandment doesn't apply to me.

10. John Stuart Mill: "Each person's happiness is a good to that person, and the general happiness, therefore, a good to the aggregate of all persons."

11. Father to son: "I heard today that yours is one of the unruliest classes ever to attend Walhalla High School. In my book, unruliness deserves to be punished. Therefore, I am removing your driving privileges until there is evidence that your unruly behavior has been terminated."

12. Jesus of Nazareth once said, "The poor ye always have with you." Thus it is obviously futile to attempt to eradicate poverty, since the enterprise is clearly doomed to failure.

13. The Bible says that the meek shall inherit the earth. Let us, therefore, be bold in the hope that we may instead inherit heaven.

14. "How do you like your tea?" he asked. "I like it fine," I replied. He looked at me to see if I was trying to be funny, but quickly

realized that I was just a country boy who was not accustomed to afternoon tea. "No," he said, "I mean, with milk or lemon?" Puzzled, I said, "Yes, I like it that way too."

15. Some people will tell you that there are no such things as angels. Poppycock! Every compassionate man or woman who visits the sick and the aged and the dying is an angel. Every traveler who stops to assist a stranded motorist is an angel. Fortunately for all of us when we are in need, the world is full of angels. Anybody who denies it is either ignoring the facts or an outright liar.

16. Traveler: "My wife and I recently returned from [name of country deleted], and we were amused to observe how people there decorate their houses. Almost never does one see evidence of any effort at color coordination. I don't know if they really proceed in this way or not, but their houses *look* as if they were decorated on the theory that any number of beautiful colors thrown together in any combination will yield a beautiful result. In short, their decorating practice is a continuous demonstration of the fallacy of _____."

17. At the end of the course, Professor Jones told us that we were the best class he had ever had. That's why I am sure that the *F* that appeared on my grade report is a mistake. Surely, if we were as good a class as Professor Jones said we were, none of us deserved to fail.

18. A book reviewer wrote of a certain book, "If you like silly plots, shallow characters, and sloppy writing, you will find this book interesting. If not, don't bother with it. It's almost unbelievable that a book as poor as this one ever got into print." The advertisement said, "Reviewer calls this book 'interesting' and 'almost unbelievable.' Read it! Find out for yourself!"

19. It is a fundamental principle of this society that all men are created equal. It follows, therefore, that the inequalities that we observe—in wealth, intelligence, strength, stature, health, athletic ability, and so on—are the result of societal conditions that can and should be altered. The dream of our founding fathers will not be realized until we achieve a society in which the equality in which all men are created is realized in maturity as well.

20. According to some people in the oil ministry in Riyadh, Saudi Arabia, you can almost set your watch by the daily schedule of Sheikh Ahmed. Each morning at precisely 9:00 A.M., it is said, he leaves his chauffeur-driven Mercedes wrapped in a flowing white robe, and each afternoon at precisely 4:00 P.M. he reenters it to begin the journey to his private palace. Hoping to catch a glimpse of him, I once stationed myself near the entrance to the oil ministry as one Mercedes after another drove up to discharge its passengers. Among all those beautiful cars, however, I did not see a single car wrapped in a flowing white robe, and to this day I do not know which of the many chauffeured passengers whom I saw that morning was the legendary Sheikh Ahmed. Moreover, I am highly inclined to doubt the story about a white-robed Mercedes.

# PART THREE

# SYLLOGISTIC LOGIC

# five
# Categorical Statements

We now turn our attention to one of the main subdivisions of logic, the study of deductive arguments. Deductive arguments, it will be recalled (Section 1.3), are arguments in which it is claimed that the premises constitute conclusive evidence for the truth of the conclusion. In a correct deductive argument, if the premises are true, the conclusion must also be true. Deductive logic consists in the identification of the several types of deductive arguments, the analysis of the structure of such arguments, and the development of methods for testing the correctness of arguments of each type.

The first type of deductive argument that we shall consider is the categorical syllogism. A categorical syllogism is a deductive argument that contains two premises and a conclusion, all of which are categorical statements. We begin, therefore, with a discussion of categorical statements.

## 5.1 CATEGORICAL STATEMENTS AS STATEMENTS ABOUT CLASSES

Categorical statements, in the sense that is important to us at this stage of our study, can be construed as statements about classes of things. A **class** is the total group of objects that possess the feature **85** or features that constitute the defining characteristic(s) of that group. The class of "green things," for example, consists of everything in the world that is green—blades of grass, the leaves of many trees, the skins of avocados and unripe bananas, and so on. The class of "books" includes all of the objects normally called by that name that are in libraries, homes, bookstores, schoolrooms, and so on. The class of "one-eyed Russians" includes all Russians who, for whatever reason, have but one eye. *Any* characteristic or set of characteristics can be used to define a class.

A class may have many members (as in the case of green things, books, things made of wood, and so on), few members (as in the case of one-eyed Russians, living ex-presidents of the United States, and people who regularly commute between New York and Chicago), or no members (people over nine feet tall, automobiles that have been driven on Mars, stones that are lighter than air). A class that has no members is called an **empty** or **null class.**

Every class divides the whole world into two groups of entities: entities that are members of that class and entities that are not members of that class. The class of green things *includes* everything in the world that has the characteristic of being green and *excludes* everything in the world that does not have that characteristic (including plans and theories and speed limits and other things that have no color at all). The class of one-eyed Russians excludes not only two-eyed Russians and no-eyed Russians, but absolutely everything in the world that is not a one-eyed Russian—including the Declaration of Independence and the Empire State Building and so on.

Since every class divides the world into things that are and things that are not members of that class, we can equally well say that for every class X there is another class whose defining characteristic is *not* being a member of class X. No matter what you take to be the defining characteristic(s) of X, everything in the world is either an X or a non-X. Thus we arrive at the concept of **complementary classes.** Every class has a complement, and every class together with its complement includes everything in the world. We shall return to the concept of complementary classes later.

A **categorical statement** is defined for our purposes as a statement of the subject-predicate type in which both the subject term and the predicate term designate classes, and in which the subject and the predicate terms are joined by a copula, that is, by some form of the verb "to be." The general form of categorical statements, then, is:

S copula P

where S stands for the subject term, P for the predicate term, and "copula" for some form of the verb "to be" (is/is not, are/are not, and so on).

As statements about classes, categorical statements can be construed as statements about the inclusion of some or all of the members of one class (designated by the subject term) in another class (designated by the predicate term) or their exclusion from that class. The categorical statement "No living ex-presidents of the United States are women," for example, can be construed to mean "None of the members of the class consisting of ex-presidents of the United States is a member of the class consisting of women." The categorical statement "No woman has ever served as Chief Justice of the Supreme Court" can similarly be construed to mean "No member of the class consisting of women is a member of the class consisting of past or current Chief Justices of the Supreme Court."

Note the terminology: characteristics *define* a class, a subject or predicate term *designates* a class, and a class *includes* its members.

## EXERCISE 5.1

Listed below are several categorical statements. For each statement, do the following:
a. Identify the class designated by the subject term.
b. Identify the class designated by the predicate term.
c. Identify the complement of each class listed in answer to a and b above.
d. Identify the copula.
e. Identify any classes included in your answers to a, b, and c that you know or believe to be empty (null) classes.
   1. All buyers of Japanese cars are satisfied customers.
   2. No college presidents are illiterate people.
   3. All people who cannot write legibly are people who ought to type.
   4. Some college graduates are underemployed workers.
   5. Some fictional characters are characters who are represented as being faster than a speeding bullet.
   6. All people who can leap tall buildings in a single bound are superpeople.
   7. No congressmen are people who can walk on water.
   8. All congressmen are vote getters.
   9. All fair-minded people are supporters of the Equal Rights Amendment.
   10. No nonsupporters of the Equal Rights Amendment are fair-minded people.
   11. Some college teachers are not American citizens.
   12. Some noncitizens are people whose primary loyalty is to the country from which they came.

13. All nongraduates are nonholders of an advanced degree.
14. All ping-pong players are people who love pizza and beer.
15. No lazy people are people who are unwillingly unemployed.
16. All people who are frightened by absurdities are nonphilosophers.
17. Some space travelers will be women.
18. Some people who drive westward at sundown are people who cannot see without sunglasses.
19. No UFO's have been craft piloted by extraterrestrial beings.
20. All Martians are two-headed creatures.

# 5.2 QUANTITY AND QUALITY OF CATEGORICAL STATEMENTS

A categorical statement may assert something about all members of a class, about some members of a class, or about a single individual (who—or which—we might say constitutes "a class of one"). With respect to *quantity*, therefore, categorical statements may be *universal* (about all members of a class), *particular* (about some members of a class), or *singular* (about a single individual). Here are some examples of each kind:

**UNIVERSAL STATEMENTS:**
U1. All cowboys are horse lovers.
U2. Every motor is a consumer of energy.
U3. Anything that has feathers and flies is fair game for hunters.
U4. No pygmies are over five feet tall.
U5. Only veterans are eligible to join the American Legion.

**PARTICULAR STATEMENTS:**
P1. Some apples are not sweet.
P2. Some New Yorkers are subscribers to *The New York Times*.
P3. Not all politicians are corrupt.
P4. Buffalo once roamed this plain.
P5. Some detergents are nontoxic.

**SINGULAR STATEMENTS:**
S1. Jimmy Carter is a southerner.
S2. The fortieth president of the United States was a resident of California.
S3. The oldest building on campus is University Hall.
S4. The best advice my father ever gave me was: "Whatever you are, be it completely."
S5. My favorite chair is a rickety old rocker.

Note that it is the status of the *subject* term that determines whether a statement is universal, particular, or singular. If the statement asserts something about all of the members of $S$, it is universal; if about some but not all, it is particular; if about some one identifiable individual, it is singular. The status of the predicate term is irrelevant to this determination.

How many is "some"? One? Two? Five? Ten? Any answer that one might give seems a bit arbitrary, as indeed it is. Yet it is clear that some definition must be adopted; otherwise it would not be possible to determine when a particular statement is true and when false. The convention that has been adopted by logicians, therefore, is this: *"some" means "at least one."* Thus the precise meanings of the particular statements listed above are as follows:

**P1.** At least one apple is not sweet.
**P2.** At least one New Yorker is a subscriber to *The New York Times*.
**P3.** At least one politician is not corrupt.
**P4.** At least one buffalo once roamed this plain.
**P5.** At least one detergent is nontoxic.

Because particular statements are understood to assert the existence of at least one member of the class designated by $S$, such statements are said to have **existential import.** "Some $S$ is $P$" means "At least one $S$ is $P$," or "There exists at least one $S$ that is $P$." "Some $S$ is not $P$" means "At least one $S$ is not $P$," or "There exists at least one $S$ that is not $P$." Universal statements, however, are construed by modern logicians as *not* having existential import. The statement "Anyone [ = all persons] who descends into the crater of an active volcano will be asphyxiated," in accordance with this convention, is not construed to assert that some people actually exist who will descend into the crater of an active volcano and, in so doing, be asphyxiated. The construed meaning is, rather, that *if* anybody descends into the crater of an active volcano, *then* that person will be asphyxiated. Universal statements are construed as asserting merely that *if* something is a member of the class designated by the subject term, then it is either included in or excluded from the class designated by the predicate term. Whether what is being asserted is inclusion in or exclusion from the class designated by the predicate term depends on the *quality* of that statement.

With respect to quality, a categorical statement may be either *affirmative* or *negative*. It is affirmative if it states that some or all of the members of the class designated by $S$ are *included in* the class designated by $P$. It is negative if it states that some or all of the members of the class designated by $S$ are *excluded from* the class designated by $P$. Thus, for example, of the five universal statements listed on page 88, U1, U2, U3, and U5 are affirmative and U4 is negative. You might find it instructive to determine for yourself the quality of each of the particular and singular statements listed on that page.

## EXERCISE 5.2

Refer once again to the statements in Exercise 5.1. Name the quantity and quality of each.

# 5.3 STANDARD-FORM CATEGORICAL STATEMENTS

In order to simplify the study of categorical arguments, it is desirable to reduce the variety of categorical statements that we must deal with to the minimum number of logically important types. The preceding discussion suggests that we may reasonably hope to reduce all categorical statements to just six types: universal affirmative and negative, particular affirmative and negative, and singular affirmative and negative. This is indeed the case. It happens, however, that in categorical syllogisms the logical behavior of singular statements is identical to that of universal statements. The statement "Socrates is bald," for example, can be restated as follows: "All of the members of the class of which Socrates is the only member are bald"; and this, of course, is a universal affirmative statement. In order to study the logic of categorical arguments, therefore, we can for most purposes ignore the existence of singular statements (affirmative and negative) and concentrate on the other four types.

A further simplification is achieved by the creation of a *standard form* for each of the remaining four types of statement. This simplification, which goes all the way back to Aristotle (384–322 B.C.), may be summarized as follows:

**A** Universal affirmative: All $S$ is $P$.
(Example: "All Californians are sun lovers.")
**E** Universal negative: No $S$ is $P$.
(Example: "No automobiles are horse-drawn vehicles.")
**I** Particular affirmative: Some $S$ is $P$.
(Example: "Some vacationers are spendthrifts.")
**O** Particular negative: Some $S$ is not $P$.
(Example: "Some athletes are not football players.")

The letters **A, E, I,** and **O** that appear in this summary are traditional symbols that uniquely identify the four types of standard-form categorical statement. That is to say, "an **A** statement" is another name for "a universal affirmative standard-form categorical statement," "an **E** statement" is another name for "a universal negative standard-form categorical statement," and so on. We will be using these letters regularly from now on to denote these four types of statement.

In order to be a standard-form categorical statement, then, a statement must exemplify one of the above four patterns. The first word of a standard-form categorical statement must be "all," "no," or "some." The copula may be any form of the verb "to be," except that in the case of **A, E,** and **I** statements the copula must be affirmative, and in the case of **O** statements it must be negative. Although it is sometimes permissible to use tensed copulas (were/ were not, will be/will not be, and so on), certain logical errors can be avoided by restricting one's use to present-tense copulas. Tensed copulas are easily eliminated by making them a part of the predicate: "All kings were tyrants," for example, can be restated in the form "All kings are people who were tyrants."

## 5.4 RESTATING NONSTANDARD CATEGORICAL STATEMENTS IN STANDARD FORM

Most of the categorical statements that one encounters in ordinary discourse are not in standard form. Of the categorical statements listed on page 88, for example, only five—U1, U4, P1, P2, and P5— are in standard form. Many of the methods that have been developed for assessing categorical arguments require, however, that the statements that constitute those arguments be in standard form. In order to use those methods, therefore, it is necessary to restate nonstandard statements in standard form—and one must, of course, do so in such a way as to retain the meaning of the original statement. The nonstandard statements on page 88, for example, can be restated as follows:

U2. All motors are consumers of energy.
U3. All things that have feathers and fly are fair game for hunters.
U5. All persons who are eligible to join the American Legion are veterans.
P3. Some politicians are not corrupt.
P4. Some buffalo are animals that once roamed this plain.

In translating categorical statements from nonstandard into standard form, one must be careful not to change the meaning of the original statement. Someone, for example, might carelessly restate U5 as follows:

All veterans are eligible to join the American Legion.

Now this may or may not be a true statement—that is not the issue here—but it is not what the original statement asserts. What U5 asserts is that nobody who is not a veteran is eligible to join the American Legion, that all of those who are eligible to join the

American Legion are veterans. P3, too, lends itself to incorrect restatement. One might, if one were careless, attempt to restate P3 like this:

>    Some politicians are corrupt.

or like this:

>    No politicians are corrupt.

Neither of these statements asserts what the original statement asserts, however—though it happens that one or the other of them must be true. What the original statement asserts is that it is not the case that all politicians are corrupt, which is equivalent to saying that some politicians are not corrupt—which is, therefore, a correct standard-form restatement of the original statement.

Unfortunately, there are no general rules governing the reformulation of statements from nonstandard to standard form. One must simply attend carefully to the *meaning* of the original statement, and then be careful to preserve that meaning in one's restatement. Some particularly tricky types of nonstandard statements, and a correct restatement of each, are the following:

| NONSTANDARD STATEMENT | CORRECT RESTATEMENT |
| --- | --- |
| Not all (or every) $S$ is $P$. | Some $S$ is not $P$. |
|   Not all men are tall. |   Some men are not tall. |
| None but $P$ is $S$. | All $S$ is $P$. |
|   None but the brave |   All of those who deserve |
|   deserve the fair. |   the fair are brave. |
| Only $P$ is $S$. | All $S$ is $P$. |
|   Only those who have been in- |   All of those who may come are |
|   vited may come. |   those who have been invited. |
| $S$ is not $P$. | No $S$ is $P$. |
|   Logicians are not saints. |   No logicians are saints. |
| All that is $S$ is not $P$. | Some $S$ is not $P$. |
|   All that glitters is not gold. |   Some things that glitter are not gold. |
| $S$ is always $P$. | All $S$ is $P$. |
|   Oranges are always sweet. |   All oranges are sweet. |
| $S$ is not always $P$. | Some $S$ is not $P$. |
|   Oranges are not always sweet. |   Some oranges are not sweet. |
| $S$ is all $P$. | All $S$ is $P$. |
|   Swedes are all good-looking. |   All Swedes are good-looking. |
| All $S$ (action verb). | All $S$ is $P$. |
|   All engineering students study math. |   All engineering students are people who study math. |

There are, of course, many types of nonstandard categorical

statement in addition to those listed above, but most of them can be restated in standard form without difficulty. They include such types as the following:

1. Statements beginning with "each," "every," or "any," restatable as "All *S* is *P*."
2. Statements that contain no quantifier, but that clearly imply "all" or "no." (Examples: "Tigers are ferocious"; "Dogs are not cats.")
3. Statements beginning with "no one," "none of," or "nothing," restatable as "No *S* is *P*."
4. Statements beginning with "many," "a few," "quite a few," "a number of," "several," or some other word or phrase correctly translatable as "some."
5. Statements that contain no quantifier, but that clearly imply "some." (Example: "Indians once hunted in these hills.")

But I repeat: the essential thing in restating nonstandard categorical statements in standard form is to pay careful attention to the exact meaning of the original statement, and then to capture that exact meaning in one's restatement. There is some value in becoming especially familiar with the tricky types of nonstandard statements listed above, as it is these types that most frequently give rise to errors in restatement. Do not, however, succumb to the temptation merely to memorize some mechanical formula for restating, say, "none but" and "not all" statements into standard-form **A** and **O** statements, respectively. Such formulas do not work, if only because one is likely to get confused about which term to treat as *S* and which as *P*. The only safe route from a nonstandard-form categorical statement to a standard-form categorical statement is through the brain of an alert restater.

It should perhaps be noted that in order to be absolutely rigorous in adhering to the canons of standard form, we would have to insist that the predicate term in the restatement always be a substantive, not an adjective. Thus, for example, in the "correct restatements" listed on page 92 we would have to write "Some men are not tall *people*" instead of "Some men are not tall," "All of those who deserve the fair are brave *people*" instead of "All of those who deserve the fair are brave," "All oranges are sweet *things*" instead of "All oranges are sweet," and so on. For most purposes, however, no problems result if we allow the predicate term to be an adjective, provided that we bear in mind that what is really designated by *P* is the class of things to which that adjective applies. We should, however, be prepared to supply a substantival term whenever it becomes necessary to do so—for example, in stating some of the logical equivalents of standard-form categoricals that we shall be discussing shortly (Section 5.6).

Finally, you may have noted that in identifying the categorical statements on page 88 that require restatement in order to be in standard form, I made no mention of the singular statements listed there. It is, of course, possible to reformulate singular statements as standard-form **A** or **E** statements; we saw an example of such a reformulation on page 90. Such reformulations are typically rather clumsy, however, and since in syllogistic logic singular statements behave logically like the corresponding universal statements, it is customary not to restate them. It is imperative, however, that any singular statement used in a syllogistic argument have a copula. If a copula is lacking, the statement should be reformulated in such a way as to introduce one. (The nonstandard statement "Ronald Reagan came from California," for example, could be restated as "Ronald Reagan is a person who came from California.")

## EXERCISES 5.3–5.4

**A.** Refer again to the categorical statements on pages 87–88, all of which are in standard form. Identify each as an **A, E, I,** or **O** statement.

**B.** Listed below are categorical statements that are not in standard form. Restate them in standard form, and identify each of your reformulations as an **A, E, I,** or **O** statement.

1. It is not only the poor that suffer when inflation runs rampant.
2. Not all Democrats support massive welfare spending.
3. Only those who work hard deserve to succeed.
4. Everyone who arrives by six o'clock in the morning will receive free admission.
5. None but the sturdiest survived the Bataan death march.
6. It is not the case that the only things in life that are certain are death and taxes.
7. Elderly professors are not always distinguished-looking people.
8. Distinguished-looking people are often tall.
9. Not everyone who can write can write a book.
10. People are not machines.
11. All musicians can count to four.
12. All ducks swim.
13. Logicians are not always logical.
14. Everybody is entitled to his or her day in court.
15. Nobody who is employed by the state is eligible to participate in the state lottery.
16. Many regular readers of our local newspaper are badly misinformed about current events.
17. The hostages in Iran all returned home safely.
18. People who live in glass houses should not throw stones.

19.   Only the gullible would believe the defendant's story about how the stolen property came into his possession.
20.   All of those who earn good grades are not naturally brilliant.

# 5.5 DISTRIBUTION

We have already encountered the concept of distribution in connection with the informal fallacies of composition and division (Section 4.6). This concept is also of exceptional importance in syllogistic logic. Each subject and predicate term that occurs in a categorical statement is either distributed or undistributed. A term is said to be **distributed** if the statement in which it occurs asserts something about every member of the class designated by that term. When the statement in which a given term occurs does not assert something about all members of the class designated by that term, the term is said to be **undistributed.** As a matter of semantics it should be noted that in logic, as in ordinary usage, "to distribute" is a transitive verb: statements are said to "distribute" certain terms and "not to distribute" certain other terms.

A simple rule governs the distribution of terms in all standard-form categorical statements. The **Rule of Distribution** is this: Universal statements distribute their subject terms, negative statements distribute their predicate terms, and all other terms are undistributed. When this rule is applied to the four standard forms of categorical statement, it follows that:

A    statements distribute the subject term but not the predicate term.
E    statements distribute both subject and predicate terms.
I    statements distribute neither the subject nor the predicate term.
O    statements distribute the predicate term but not the subject term.

Statements that distribute both or neither of their terms are said to be **symmetrical** with respect to distribution. Statements that distribute either the subject or the predicate term (but not both) are said to be **asymmetrical** with respect to distribution. Thus E and I statements are symmetrical with respect to distribution, whereas A and O statements are asymmetrical.

Although the Rule of Distribution can be easily memorized, and can then be applied to individual statements of each type to determine infallibly which terms are distributed and which are not, the serious student of logic will want to understand *why* certain terms are distributed whereas certain others are not. I assume that all readers of this book are serious students of logic. I shall therefore discuss briefly the grounds for the rule.

I have said that to assert that a term is distributed means that the statement in which that term occurs asserts something about every member of the class designated by that term. It is evident, then, that the subject term of an **A** statement (all *S* is *P*) will always be distributed, for no matter what classes are designated by *S* and *P*, every member of the class designated by *S* will be in the class designated by *P* as well. Thus it is clear that **A** statements do assert something about every member of the class designated by the subject term, and that is equivalent to saying that **A** statements distribute the subject term. It is equally clear, however, that **A** statements do not distribute the predicate term, for when we assert that all *S* is *P* we are asserting nothing about all *P*'s. The statement "All wives are women" does not assert that every woman is a wife, nor does it assert anything else about every woman; and the same thing will be true no matter what classes are assumed to be designated by *S* and *P*. Thus it is clear that **A** statements do not distribute the predicate term.

Turning now to **E** statements (no *S* is *P*), one can easily see that they do assert something about every member of the class designated by *S*, namely, that it is not a member of the class designated by *P*. If it is asserted that no crows are able to whistle "Yankee Doodle," then it is asserted that every crow is excluded from the class of beings that can whistle "Yankee Doodle." Thus it is clear that **E** statements distribute the subject term. In this case, however, unlike the case of **A** statements, it turns out that the predicate term is also distributed, for if no *S* is *P*, it must also be the case that no *P* is *S*. If no crows are beings that are able to whistle "Yankee Doodle," then it is also the case that no beings that are able to whistle "Yankee Doodle" are crows, that every member of the class of beings that are able to whistle "Yankee Doodle" is excluded from the class of crows. Thus it is evident that **E** statements distribute the predicate term as well as the subject term.

In the case of **I** statements (some *S* is *P*), it is clear on the face of it that they do not distribute the subject term. Whatever an **I** statement may assert about *some S*, it clearly asserts nothing about *all S*. But by the same token, such a statement says nothing about all the members of *P* either, for if you know that some *S* is *P*, the only thing you know about *P* is that *some P* is *S*. If it is asserted that some weight lifters are Englishmen, it obviously is not being asserted that all Englishmen are weight lifters, nor is anything else being asserted about all Englishmen. Hence we may conclude that **I** statements do not distribute the predicate term.

Finally, **O** statements (some *S* is not *P*). As with **I** statements, the phrase "some *S*" makes it evident that the subject term is not distributed. In this case, however, something *is* being asserted about every member of the class designated by the predicate term, namely, that none of them is the particular *S* denoted by the subject term in this statement. If some vegetables are not cabbages, then it is true of every member of the class of cabbages that it is not one of the vegetables denoted in the statement "Some vegetables are not cabbages." Hence it is clear that **O** Statements do distribute the predicate term.

Thus we arrive at the result summarized in the Rule of Distribution. **A** and **E** statements are universal in quantity, and both distribute their subject terms; hence the generalization, stated in the rule, that universal statements distribute the subject term. **E** and **O** statements are negative in quality, and both distribute their predicate terms; hence the generalization, stated in the rule, that negative statements distribute the predicate term. Since these two generalizations account for all the terms that we have found to be distributed, we are justified in making the further generalization that all other terms are undistributed. Thus the Rule of Distribution merely summarizes the results obtained from a careful analysis of the subject and predicate terms of each of the four standard-form categorical statements.

## EXERCISES 5.5

**A.** Refer to the standard-form categorical statements on pages 87–88. State whether each subject and predicate term is distributed or undistributed.
**B.** Write four standard-form categorical statements of your own invention, including one of each type (**A, E, I,** and **O**). Identify the terms in your four examples that are distributed, and explain in each case what is being asserted about all members of the class designated by each such term.

## 5.6 IMMEDIATE INFERENCES: LOGICAL EQUIVALENTS OF STANDARD-FORM CATEGORICAL STATEMENTS

If you know that a given statement is true (or false), you can draw certain conclusions about the truth or falsity of certain other statements. If you know, for example, that the statement "All infants are adorable" is true, then you can infer that the following statements are also true:

No infants are nonadorable.
No nonadorable things are infants.
All nonadorable things are noninfants.

If you assume instead that the statement "All infants are adorable" is false, then it follows that the above statements are false, not true. Indeed, if any one of the above statements is true, then it follows that all of them are true; and if any one of them is false, then they must all be false.

A deductive inference drawn from a single premise is called an **immediate inference.** Some inferences of this kind are possible by virtue of the fact that certain statements are logically equivalent to certain other statements (as in the above example). Some of these equivalences are of considerable importance in deductive logic and have been given special names. We will consider three such types of immediate inference: conversion, obversion, and contraposition.

**Conversion** is merely the process of exchanging the subject and predicate terms. The statement that results from this process is termed the **converse** of the original statement, and the original statement is also the converse of its converse. Thus the converse of the statement "No sophomores are pirates" is the statement "No pirates are sophomores," and vice versa. Conversion yields logical equivalents only for **E** and **I** statements.

**Obversion** involves two steps: (1) changing the quality of the statement (from affirmative to negative or from negative to affirmative) and (2) replacing the predicate term with its complement (see above, page 97). Thus the obverse of the statement "All Scots are penny pinchers" is the statement "No Scots are non–penny pinchers"; the obverse of the statement "No Swedes are photographers" is the statement "All Swedes are nonphotographers"; and so on. Just as any statement is the converse of its converse, so also is any statement the obverse of its obverse. Obversion yields logical equivalents for all four types of standard-form categorical statement.

**Contraposition** also involves two steps: (1) replacing the subject term with the complement of the predicate term and (2) replacing the predicate term with the complement of the subject term. The statement thus derived is called the **contrapositive** of the original statement. Thus the contrapositive of the statement "All senators are Presbyterians" is the statement "All non-Presbyterians are nonsenators"; the contrapositive of the statement "Some senators are not Presbyterians" is the statement "Some non-Presbyterians are not nonsenators"; and so on. The symmetry that we have noted in the case of conversion and obversion also holds in the present case: a standard-form categorical statement is the contrapositive of its contrapositive. Contraposition yields logical equivalents only for **A** and **O** statements.

The **Rule of Conversion, Obversion, and Contraposition** may be stated as follows: Conversion may be applied only to statements that are symmetrical with respect to distribution, contraposition only to statements that are asymmetrical with respect to distribution, and obversion to all. Thus there are logically equivalent converses only of **E** and **I** statements, logically equivalent contrapositives only of **A** and **O** statements, and logically equivalent obverses of all four types.

The following table summarizes the above information with respect to conversion, obversion, and contraposition and the applicability or nonapplicability of each to the four standard forms of categorical statement:

| TYPE | FORM | CONVERSE | OBVERSE | CONTRA-POSITIVE |
|---|---|---|---|---|
| A | All S is P. | — | No S is non-P. | All non-P is non-S. |
| E | No S is P. | No P is S. | All S is non-P. | — |
| I | Some S is P. | Some P is S. | Some S is not non-P. | — |
| O | Some S is not P. | — | Some S is non-P. | Some non-P is not non-S. |

We may note, finally, that by the successive application of conversion and obversion to a given standard-form categorical statement, it is possible to derive logically equivalent statements in addition to those summarized above. Consider, for example, the **A** statement "All spiders are pests." According to the above table, this statement has two logical equivalents: "No spiders are nonpests" (the obverse) and "All nonpests are nonspiders" (the contrapositive). But the statement "No spiders are nonpests" has an allowable converse, "No nonpests are spiders," which is also the obverse of the contrapositive. Similarly, if one starts with the **E** statement "No schoolboys are policemen," one can derive not only the converse ("No policemen are schoolboys") and the obverse ("All schoolboys are nonpolicemen") but also the obverse of the converse ("All policemen are nonschoolboys"), which is also the contrapositive of the original statement. As a matter of fact, all of the logical equivalents of standard-form categorical statements (including the contrapositive) can be derived by conversion and obversion alone. The contrapositive is merely the obverse of the converse of the obverse of an **A** or **O** statement. Going directly from an **A** or **O** statement to its contrapositive is merely taking a shortcut to a destination that could be reached in another way.

# 5.7 IMMEDIATE INFERENCES: THE BOOLEAN SQUARE OF OPPOSITION

It will be recalled that statements are sometimes related in such a way that if one knows or assumes the truth or falsity of some statements, one can infer the truth or falsity of certain other statements, and that this relationship is called *logical implication* (Section 1.4). In order to have an instance of logical implication, then, one must have a minimum of two statements that are related in such a way that from the truth or falsity of one you can correctly infer the truth or falsity of the other. The question that we shall now consider is this: Assuming constant values for S and P, what inferences can be drawn about the truth or falsity of the remaining standard-form categorical statements, given the truth or falsity of any one of them? If one assumes, for example, that a statement of the form "All S is P" is true, what inferences can one make about the truth or falsity of the corresponding E, I, and O statements?

The answer to our question is displayed in what is called the Boolean Square of Opposition (see Figure 5-1), named after the English mathematician and logician George Boole (1815–1864). What the **Boolean Square of Opposition** shows is that **A** and **O** statements that have the same subject and predicate terms are contradictories, as are also standard-form **E** and **I** statements that have the same subject and predicate terms. Two statements are said to be **contradictories** if they are related in such a way that both cannot be true and both cannot be false. It follows, therefore, that if any statement is true its contradictory must be false, and if any statement is false its contradictory must be true. Moreover, since every standard-form categorical statement has a standard-form contradictory, it follows that if we make any assumption concerning the truth or falsity of any standard-form categorical statement, we can immediately infer the falsity or truth of at least one other standard-form categorical statement.

Are there other immediate inferences that can be drawn between or among corresponding **A**, **E**, **I**, and **O** statements? The answer is no, not if we adhere consistently to the convention of treating particular statements as having existential import and universal statements as not having existential import (see p. 89). If one does not adopt this convention (as Aristotle, for example, did not), certain other immediate inferences are possible. In accordance with most modern logicians, however, we shall continue to treat particular statements as having existential import and universal statements as not having existential import. Thus, the only immediate inferences

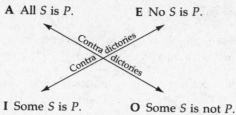

**A** All *S* is *P*.          **E** No *S* is *P*.

Contradictories

Contradictories

**I** Some *S* is *P*.          **O** Some *S* is not *P*.

**Figure**
**5-1**    Boolean Square of Opposition

that we can make are those allowed by the relation of contradictoriness as displayed in the Boolean Square of Opposition.

It may seem strange that according to the Boolean Square of Opposition it is not permissible to infer an **I** statement from the corresponding **A** statement. "Surely," it may be objected, "if we know that all apples are ripe, we know also that some apples are ripe, do we not?" That we cannot make this inference follows, however, from the decision to treat only **I** and **O** statements as having existential import (see Section 5.2). Given this decision, an **A** statement has the meaning "If anything is *S*, then it is *P*." "All violators will be prosecuted," for example, means "If any individual is a violator, that individual will be prosecuted." Now it clearly does not follow from this assertion by itself that there is in fact at least one individual who is a violator and who will therefore be prosecuted. The inference from an **A** statement to the corresponding **I** statement could be made only if the **A** statement were supplemented with another statement to the effect that the class designated by the subject term has at least one member. That such a statement is required in order to make the inference, however, means that the inference cannot be made from the **A** statement alone. It *appears* that we can infer "Some apples are ripe" from "All apples are ripe" because we are tacitly assuming that there are indeed some apples—that the class designated by the term "apples" is not empty. Now that happens to be a perfectly reasonable assumption when we are talking about apples, and logic has no interest in preventing us from making this assumption. All that logic requires is that we state that assumption explicitly, that we not treat **A** and **E** statements as if they were always about real existing things. That we must state that assumption means, however, that the inference to the corresponding **I** statement does not follow from the **A** statement alone, which is the point we are discussing. Similar reasoning applies to the relationship between corresponding **E** and **O** statements.

## EXERCISES 5.6–5.7

A. Refer to the standard-form categorical statements on pages 87–88.
  1. Identify the statements that have logically equivalent converses. State the converse of each.
  2. Identify the statements that have logically equivalent contrapositives. State the contrapositive of each.
  3. State the obverse of each.
  4. By the use of some allowable combination of conversion and obversion, derive from each statement one logically equivalent statement that is not the converse, the obverse, or the contrapositive of the original statement.

B. Assume that each of the statements on pages 87–88 is true. Using the Boolean Square of Opposition, formulate a standard-form categorical statement that must then be false.

## 5.8 VENN DIAGRAMS OF CATEGORICAL STATEMENTS

Since standard-form categorical statements are construed as statements about classes, they lend themselves to visual representation by means of circles representing the classes designated by the subject and predicate terms. A simple system for this process was developed by the English mathematician and logician John Venn (1834–1923). We shall consider the Venn system at this point as a method for diagramming standard-form categorical *statements*, and shall return to it later as a method for also diagramming standard-form categorical *arguments* (Section 6.6).

In the Venn system, a single circle diagrams both a class and its complement. (Remember that a class divides the whole world into two groups of entities, those that are members of that class and those that are not.) Everything that is *within* the circle is a member of the class represented by that circle; everything that is *outside* the circle is a member of its complement. Suppose, for example, that S is the class of senators. Then the circle representing S, as in Figure 5-2, includes within it everything that is a senator, and excludes from it everything that is a nonsenator. Thus a single circle diagrams both the class of senators and the class of nonsenators.

Suppose now that we wish to state that class S has some members (at least one). We indicate this situation by placing an X inside the circle (see Figure 5-3). Thus, on the supposition that S designates the class of senators, Figure 5-3 diagrams the assertion "There are senators" or "Some senators exist."

If we wish to state instead that the class designated by S is

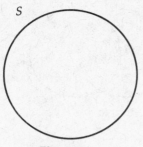

Figure 5-2

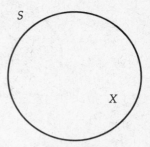

Figure 5-3

empty—that it has no members—we shade the entire circle. Thus, again assuming *S* to designate the class of all senators, to represent the assertion "There are no senators," we shade the circle, as in Figure 5-4.

A standard-form categorical statement, as we have seen, involves two classes, one designated by the subject term and one by the predicate term. Let us, then, use two *overlapping* circles to represent the classes designated by the subject (*S*) and the predicate (*P*) terms of a standard-form categorical statement, as in Figure 5-5.

Note that with the introduction of overlapping circles we have now represented four classes:

1. Everything that is *S* but not *P*.
2. Everything that is both *S* and *P*.
3. Everything that is *P* but not *S*.
4. Everything that is neither *S* nor *P*.

With these simple elements, we can now diagram any standard-form categorical statement. The diagrams for standard-form **A**, **E**, **I**, and **O** statements are shown in Figure 5-6.

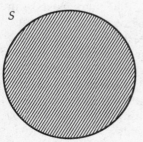

Figure 5-4

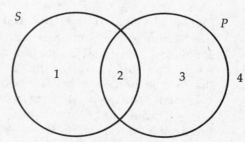

Figure 5-5

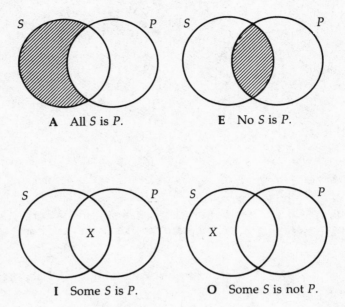

**A** All S is P.        **E** No S is P.

**I** Some S is P.        **O** Some S is not P.

**Figure 5-6**

Note that we diagram universal statements by *shading* the appropriate space, whereas we diagram particular statements by placing an X in the appropriate space. You will find this convention easy to remember if you bear in mind that an X means "Some S's [or P's] exist," and that only particular statements are to be construed as affirming that something exists (that is, as having existential import). Universal statements, therefore, must always be understood to express the assertion that some class is *empty* (= shaded), whereas particular statements must be understood to express the assertion that some class has at least one member (represented by an X).

Of the four diagrams shown in Figure 5-6, most readers will probably find those representing the **I** and **O** statements intuitively obvious. "Some S is P" obviously means that there exists something that is both an S and a P, and so it is obvious where one must place the X. Similarly, "Some S is not P" clearly means that there exists something that is an S but not a P, and once again it is obvious where one ought to place the X. Things are a little less obvious in the case of the two universal statements, however. In diagramming such statements, you must remember always to ask: What class is being affirmed to be *empty*? In the case of **A** statements, you may find it helpful to think of the obverse: if all S is P, then no S is non-P (the obverse), which is to say that the class consisting of things that are *S* but not *P* is empty. In the case of **E** statements, it is perhaps less difficult to see intuitively that "No *S* is *P*" means that nothing is both *S* and *P*, that the class of things that are both *S* and *P* is empty.

The importance of Venn diagrams consists primarily in their value in testing the correctness of a certain type of deductive argument, namely, standard-form categorical syllogisms. The method works, however, only if one has correctly diagrammed the premises of the argument being tested. You should therefore master thoroughly the technique of diagramming statements before proceeding to the analysis of arguments whose correctness is to be tested by the use of such diagrams.

## EXERCISES 5.8

A.   Refer once again (this is the last time, I promise) to the standard-form categorical statements on pages 87–88. Then do the following:
  1. Draw a Venn diagram that correctly diagrams each statement.
  2. State the obverse of each statement, and draw a Venn diagram for each.

B.   Think about the following questions. If anything occurs to you that seems worth writing down, write it down.
  1. What relationship, if any, do you see between (*a*) the symmetry or asymmetry with respect to distribution of **A, E, I,** and **O** sentences, and (*b*) their respective Venn diagrams? If you do see a relationship, can you think of any explanation for it?
  2. Why do Venn diagrams work? Why does it make intuitive sense to visualize standard-form categorical statements in terms of over-lapping circles?

# six
# Categorical Syllogisms

Some of the reasoning that we encounter in everyday discourse occurs in the form of syllogisms, and much of the reasoning that does not occur in this form can be restated syllogistically. A syllogism is a certain kind of deductive argument, and a categorical syllogism is a certain kind of syllogism. In this chapter we shall examine the logic of categorical syllogisms. We begin by defining some of the key terms that we shall be using in the course of our discussion.

## 6.1 TERMINOLOGY

A **syllogism** is a deductive argument consisting of two premises and a conclusion. A **categorical syllogism** is a syllogism in which all three of the statements that make up the syllogism—the two premises and the conclusion—are categorical statements. A **standard-form categorical syllogism** is a syllogism in which the premises and the conclusion are standard-form categorical statements that are arranged in a certain prescribed order, which I shall specify shortly. Categorical statements and standard-form categorical statements were defined in **106** Chapter 5 (Sections 5.1 and 5.3).

A standard-form categorical syllogism contains just three terms (class names), each of which is used in two of the three statements that constitute the argument. These three terms are called the major term, the minor term, and the middle term. To determine which is which, one must attend to the conclusion of the argument. The predicate term of the conclusion is the **major term,** the subject term of the conclusion is the **minor term,** and the remaining term (which appears once in each premise but never in the conclusion) is the **middle term.** Sometimes, for brevity, these three terms are referred to simply as "the major," "the minor," and "the middle."

Since it is obvious that no term can serve as both the subject term and the predicate term of the same statement, it follows that the major term will appear in one premise and the minor term in the other. The premise in which the major term appears is called the **major premise,** and that in which the minor term appears is called the **minor premise.** In order for a categorical syllogism to be in standard form, the major premise must be stated first. Thus the pattern for a standard-form categorical syllogism is:

Major premise
Minor premise

∴ Conclusion

Hereafter we shall, for the sake of brevity, use the abbreviation "SFC syllogism" to mean "standard-form categorical syllogism." An SFC syllogism is a syllogism consisting of standard-form categorical statements arranged in the pattern just described.

## EXERCISE 6.1

Listed below are several categorical syllogisms, some in standard form and some not. For each syllogism, do the following:
a. Identify the major, minor, and middle terms.
b. Identify the major premise and the minor premise.
c. State whether or not the syllogism is in standard form.
d. If the syllogism is not in standard form, state why. (For example: "The major premise is not a standard-form categorical statement.")

1. All fathers are obligated to provide for the welfare of their children. Some sixteen-year-olds are fathers.

∴ Some sixteen-year-olds are obligated to provide for the welfare of their children.

2.  No pilots are people who are legally blind.
    Some people who have taken flying lessons are legally blind.

    ∴ Some people who have taken flying lessons are not pilots.

3.  Some intoxicated people drive when they ought not to do so.
    All people who drive when they ought not to do so are people who
    endanger the lives of others.

    ∴ Some intoxicated people are people who endanger the lives of others.

4.  High-calorie foods are bad for one's waistline.
    Desserts are high-calorie foods.

    ∴ Desserts are bad for one's waistline.

5.  All flutists are musicians.
    No tone-deaf people are musicians.

    ∴ No tone-deaf people are flutists.

6.  No fish are animals that bark.
    Dogs are animals that bark.

    ∴ No dogs are fish.

7.  All students in good academic standing are eligible for financial aid.
    Some residents of this dormitory are students in good academic
    standing.

    ∴ Some residents of this dormitory are eligible for financial aid.

8.  All members of the legislature are people who have been duly elected.
    Some people who have been duly elected are not people who are
    qualified to hold office.

    ∴ Some people who are qualified to hold office are not members of the
    legislature.

9.  All sailors are lovers of the sea.
    Some sailors are not people who like to travel.

    ∴ Some people who like to travel are not lovers of the sea.

10. All students who successfully complete this course will receive a grade
    of S in the course. .
    Some students who will receive a grade of S in the course will not live
    to be a hundred.

    ∴ Some students who successfully complete this course will not live to
    be a hundred.

11. All cases of involuntary servitude are morally reprehensible.
    All cases of military conscription are cases of involuntary servitude.

    ∴ All cases of military conscription are morally reprehensible.

12.   All great music is uplifting.
      Some rock and roll music is uplifting.

∴   Some rock and roll music is great music.

13.   No music that is painful to listen to is great music.
      Some so-called classical music is painful to listen to.

∴   Some so-called classical music is not great music.

14.   All pilots of UFO's are extraterrestrial beings.
      All extraterrestrial beings should be regarded as dangerous.

∴   All pilots of UFO's should be regarded as dangerous.

15.   Many of the greatest composers of all time were Germans.
      All Germans are beer drinkers.

∴   Many of the greatest composers of all time were beer drinkers.

16.   Some people are people who are frightened by absurdities.
      No philosophers are people who are frightened by absurdities.

∴   Some people are not philosophers.

17.   Some alumni are generous contributors to their alma mater.
      No pinchpennies are generous contributors to their alma mater.

∴   Some pinchpennies are not alumni.

18.   Some college graduates are semiliterate.
      Some semiliterate people are congressmen.

∴   Some congressmen are college graduates.

19.   All forms of cheating are to be condemned.
      Some methods of getting good grades are forms of cheating.

∴   Some methods of getting good grades are to be condemned.

20.   Any future war will have the potential of annihilating the human race.
      Anything that has the potential of annihilating the human race should
          be avoided at all costs.

∴   Henceforth, war should be avoided at all costs.

# 6.2  VALIDITY AND SOUNDNESS

To understand the concept of validity in the sense in which logicians use the term, we must bear in mind the distinction between the form and the content of an argument (Section 4.1). The content of an argument is what we might call its "subject matter"; it is what the argument is about. The form is the structure, or pattern, of the argument. It is what two arguments have in common when they are constructed according to the same pattern.

Two SFC syllogisms have the same form when (1) statements of a certain type (**A, E, I,** or **O**) occur in the same relative positions in the two arguments, and (2) the major, minor, and middle terms occur in the same relative positions in the two arguments. Using the letters, *P, S,* and *M* for, respectively, the major, minor, and middle terms, one can then represent the form of SFC syllogisms as follows (these are examples, not an exhaustive list):

All *M* is *P.*
All *S* is *M.*
_____
∴ All *S* is *P.*

All *P* is *M.*
All *M* is *S.*
_____
∴ All *S* is *P.*

Some *M* is *P.*
All *S* is *M.*
_____
∴ Some *S* is *P.*

Some *P* is *M.*
All *M* is *S.*
_____
∴ Some *S* is *P.*

Validity concerns only the form of an argument, not its content. A **valid argument** is one whose form is such that the conclusion follows from (is logically implied by) the premises. To say that an argument is valid is to say that if the premises are true, then the conclusion must also be true. Such an argument is said to **instantiate** (that is, be an instance of) a valid argument form. An **invalid argument,** then, is one that does not instantiate a valid argument form. Only deductive arguments may be valid or invalid, and every deductive argument is either valid or invalid. Most of this chapter will be devoted to a discussion of techniques for testing SFC syllogisms for validity.

Soundness, too, is a characteristic that can be attributed only to deductive arguments. Unlike validity, however, soundness concerns both the form and the content of the argument. A **sound argument** is a valid argument that contains only true premises. To claim that an argument is sound, therefore, is to claim that the conclusion is true absolutely, since it follows from true premises. To claim that an argument is valid is to make the weaker claim that the conclusion is true *if* the premises are true.

How can one determine whether the premises of a given argument are true? There is, of course, no general answer to this question, except perhaps the common-sense one: look at the evidence. Logic cannot tell you whether a given statement is true or false; it can only tell you (sometimes) how the truth or falsity of one statement is related to the truth or falsity of some other statement or statements. Determining the truth or falsity of statements is a matter for common sense and, at a higher level, for science. The business of logic is to assess the correctness of our reasoning once we have—from whatever source—gotten some statements to reason about.

### EXERCISES 6.2

A.   Review the syllogisms listed on pages 107–109. Using your intuitive judgment, try to determine which syllogisms are valid and which are invalid.

B.   Which of these syllogisms, if any, do you think are sound? In each case, on what basis do you affirm that the syllogism is sound or unsound?

## 6.3 MOODS AND FIGURES

It was stated earlier (Section 6.2) that two SFC syllogisms have the same form when (1) statements of a certain type (**A, E, I,** or **O**) occur in the same relative positions in the two arguments and (2) the major, minor, and middle terms occur in the same relative positions in the two arguments. These two characteristics of SFC syllogisms are called, respectively, the mood and the figure of such syllogisms.

The **mood** of an SFC syllogism is identified by a three-letter symbol naming in order the types of statements (**A, E, I,** or **O**) that constitute, respectively, the major premise, the minor premise, and the conclusion of the argument. The moods of the four argument forms in Section 6.2, for example, are respectively **AAA, AAA, IAI,** and **IAI.** Here are some additional examples:

1.   **AII**   All *M* is *P*.
              Some *S* is *M*.
              _____
              ∴ Some *S* is *P*.

2.   **AEE**   All *P* is *M*.
              No *S* is *M*.
              _____
              ∴ No *S* is *P*.

3.　**AOO**　All *M* is *P*.
　　　　　Some *M* is not *S*.
　　　　　―――――――――
　　　　　∴ Some *S* is not *P*.

4.　**EAE**　No *P* is *M*.
　　　　　All *M* is *S*.
　　　　　―――――――――
　　　　　∴ No *S* is *P*.

Since there are four types of statements (**A, E, I, O**) and three statements in each syllogism, it follows that there are 4 × 4 × 4 or 64 different moods in which SFC syllogisms may occur.

If you will examine the arguments stated above, however, you will discover another difference in addition to the differing mood of each, namely, the relative positions of the major, minor, and middle terms in each of the premises. The relative positions of the three terms in the premises of an SFC syllogism constitute the **figure** of the syllogism. Since there are two premises in an SFC syllogism and two terms in each premise, there are four possible patterns in which these terms may occur. Moreover, since the predicate term always occurs in the major premise and the subject term in the minor premise, one really need pay attention only to the position of the middle term. The four patterns, or figures, in which the terms may occur in the premises are as follows·

| **FIRST FIGURE** | **SECOND FIGURE** | **THIRD FIGURE** | **FOURTH FIGURE** |
|---|---|---|---|
| *M–P* | *P–M* | *M–P* | *P–M* |
| *S–M* | *S–M* | *M–S* | *M–S* |
| *S–P* | *S–P* | *S–P* | *S–P* |

In order to describe the form of an SFC syllogism, then, one must state both its mood and its figure. The four argument forms stated schematically on pages 111–112, for example, are exhaustively described as **AII-1, AEE-2, AOO-3,** and **EAE-4** syllogisms, respectively. Since there are 64 moods, each of which may occur in 4 figures, it follows that there are 64 × 4 or a total of 256 unique forms of SFC syllogisms. Only a few of them are valid argument forms, however. The important question, then, is: How can one determine which forms are valid and which are not? The rest of this chapter will provide several methods of testing for validity.

# EXERCISES 6.3

**A.**　Identify the syllogisms on pages 107–109 that are in standard form. Name the mood and figure of each.

**B.**   Identify the syllogisms on pages 107–109 that are not in standard form. Restate them in standard form, and name the mood and figure of each.

**C.**   Using the letters *P*, *S*, and *M* for the major, minor, and middle terms, show the respective forms of SFC syllogisms of the moods and figures listed below:

*Example:*  **AOO-2**   All *P* is *M*.
Some *S* is not *M*.
_____

∴ Some *S* is not *P*.

| | | | |
|---|---|---|---|
| AEE-1 | AOO-4 | AAA-4 | IAO-4 |
| AII-3 | EIO-1 | AEO-2 | EIO-3 |
| EIO-2 | IAI-1 | EII-1 | IEO-2 |

# 6.4   TESTING FOR VALIDITY: CONSTRUCTING A PARALLEL ARGUMENT

We begin with an informal, imperfect, but intuitively convincing method of testing the validity of SFC syllogisms. It consists quite simply in attempting to construct another argument of the same form, but one in which the premises are obviously true and the conclusion obviously false. Suppose, for example, that someone presents an argument that, reduced to syllogistic form, asserts the following:

All communists are people who favor socialized medicine.
Some residents of this city are people who favor socialized medicine.
_____

∴ Some residents of this city are communists.

Now since an argument is valid or invalid solely by virtue of its form, any argument instantiating that same form (in this case, **AII-2**) will be valid if that form is valid, and invalid if it is not.[1] If,

_____

[1] Establishing invalidity is slightly more complicated than this statement would seem to indicate, but for now you can safely ignore this complication. The problem is that a deductive argument may be said to instantiate more than one argument form, and one or more of the argument forms instantiated by a given argument may be valid while one or more of the other argument forms instantiated by that same argument are invalid. To be absolutely correct, therefore, one would have to say that a valid argument is one that instantiates at least one valid argument form (though it may also instantiate one or more invalid argument forms), and an invalid argument is one that instantiates no valid argument form. An SFC syllogism, however, instantiates only one *syllogistic* argument form. Thus, it is true without exception that any SFC syllogism that instantiates a valid syllogistic argument form is valid, and one that instantiates an invalid syllogistic argument form is invalid.

therefore, one constructs a *parallel argument*—that is, another argument instantiating exactly the same form—in which the premises are true and the conclusion false, one will have proved the argument (and, indeed, any argument of that form) to be invalid. In the case of the above argument, for example, one might reply, "That's a silly argument. It is as if I said:

> "All college graduates are people who can read.
> Some people who never went to school are people who can read.

∴ Some people who never went to school are college graduates."

Let us note very carefully what is going on when we prove invalidity in this way. A valid argument, we have said, is one that instantiates a valid argument form. If an argument instantiates a valid argument form, it is valid; otherwise it is invalid. Validity, then, has to do only with the form of the argument. If a given argument form is valid, then any argument of that form will be valid. By the same token, if a given syllogistic argument form is invalid, any syllogism of that form will be invalid. To say that an argument form is valid, however, is to say that if the premises of an argument instantiating that form are true, the conclusion must also be true. If, therefore, one can produce a syllogism instantiating a given argument form in which the premises are true and the conclusion false, one has thereby shown that *any syllogism instantiating that argument form is invalid*.

This method, which is often used in informal conversation and debate, has some obvious limitations. For one thing, one has to suspect in advance that a given argument is fallacious before one is likely to exert the effort to try to establish its invalidity in this way. For another, even when one is quite sure that a given argument is invalid, one may have difficulty inventing a parallel argument with indisputably true premises and an obviously false conclusion. It is desirable, therefore, to find other methods for testing for validity, methods that escape the limitations of the parallel-argument technique.

## EXERCISE 6.4

The arguments listed below are invalid. Read each one carefully, then construct a parallel argument to demonstrate its invalidity. Remember that to show invalidity your parallel argument must be of the same form (mood and figure) as the syllogism you are attacking, and must have indisputably true premises and an obviously false conclusion.

1.  No communists are loyal Americans.
    No admirers of Adam Smith are communist.

    ∴ No admirers of Adam Smith are loyal Americans.

2.  Some students are avid readers of history.
    Some avid readers of history are people who are more at home in the past than in the present.

    ∴ Some people who are more at home in the past than in the present are students.

3.  All loyal Americans are supporters of the president in his desire to trim the federal budget.
    All loyal Americans are people who willingly pay their taxes.

    ∴ All people who willingly pay their taxes are supporters of the president in his desire to trim the federal budget.

4.  All Japanese-made automobiles are vehicles that get better mileage than their American counterparts.
    Some vehicles that get better mileage than their American counterparts are unsafe vehicles.

    ∴ Some unsafe vehicles are Japanese-made automobiles.

5.  All supporters of the Iranian revolution are Muslims.
    Some residents of Cleveland are Muslims.

    ∴ Some residents of Cleveland are supporters of the Iranian revolution.

6.  All mermaids are legless.
    All legless beings are aquatic.

    ∴ Some aquatic beings are mermaids.

7.  No dinosaurs are extant creatures.
    Some extant creatures are members of endangered species.

    ∴ No members of endangered species are dinosaurs.

8.  Some students of logic are not geniuses.
    All geniuses are people who can see logical connections at a glance.

    ∴ Some people who can see logical connections at a glance are not students of logic.

9.  All geniuses are people who can see logical connections at a glance.
    Some students of logic are not geniuses.

    ∴ Some students of logic are not people who can see logical connections at a glance.

10.  All valid arguments are arguments whose conclusions follow from their premises.
     No arguments on this page are arguments whose conclusions follow from their premises.

∴  Some arguments on this page are valid arguments.

11.  All opponents of the Equal Rights Amendment are male chauvinists.
     Some male chauvinists are insecure people.

∴  Some insecure people are opponents of the Equal Rights Amendment.

12.  Some great composers were people who died young.
     Haydn was not a person who died young.

∴  Haydn was not a great composer.

13.  Some great composers were people who died young.
     Mozart was a person who died young.

∴  Mozart was a great composer.

14.  All active players in the National Football League are men who weigh over 175 pounds.
     Some men who weigh over 175 pounds are overweight men.

∴  Some overweight men are active players in the National Football League.

15.  No soccer players are people who do not enjoy outdoor sports.
     Some people who have quit smoking are people who do not enjoy outdoor sports.

∴  Some people who have quit smoking are soccer players.

16.  All centaurs are four-footed creatures.
     All four-footed creatures are animals.

∴  Some animals are centaurs.

17.  No centaurs are unicorns.
     All unicorns are beings with one horn.

∴  No beings with one horn are centaurs.

18.  Some illnesses are maladies that do not respond to medication.
     Some maladies that do not respond to medication are incurable.

∴  Some illnesses are incurable.

19.  Some people who are over fifty years of age are young at heart.

No people who are young at heart are people who have a fear of flying.

∴  Some people who have a fear of flying are not people who are over fifty years of age.

20.   Some syllogisms are arguments whose validity or invalidity is not readily apparent.
      All syllogisms are arguments whose validity or invalidity needs to be established.

∴  Some arguments whose validity or invalidity needs to be established are not arguments whose validity or invalidity is not readily apparent.

# 6.5 TESTING FOR VALIDITY: AXIOMS OF VALIDITY

We may test the validity of any SFC syllogism by determining whether or not it observes each and every one of five **axioms of validity,** which we shall state in a moment. For now, you will have to accept the claim that these axioms provide a reliable method of testing the validity of such syllogisms. Later, when another method of testing for validity has been introduced (Section 6.6), you may determine for yourself whether or not they do so.

Let us assume, then, that we have determined that the argument we are going to assess is an SFC syllogism as defined in Section 6.1. The syllogism will be valid if and only if it satisfies all of the following axioms:

*Axiom 1. The middle term must be distributed at least once.* The reason for this axiom, to state the matter simply, is that the intent of every SFC syllogism is to connect the subject term with the predicate term through the middle term. Now if the middle term is undistributed in both premises, then neither premise asserts anything about *all* members of $M$ (the middle term), and so the desired connection between $S$ and $P$ is lost. SFC syllogisms that fail to observe this axiom are said to commit the **fallacy of an undistributed middle.**

An example of a syllogism containing this fallacy is the following:

All students are readers of books.
Some readers of books are colorblind.

∴  Some students are colorblind.

*Axiom 2. If a term is distributed in the conclusion, it must also be distributed in the premises.* The reason for this axiom is simply that you cannot assert anything in the conclusion of a valid argument that is not contained in the premises. If a term is undistributed in the premises but distributed in the conclusion, then the conclusion will be affirming something about all members of the class designated by that term, whereas the premise in which that term occurs does not do so. Therefore, a syllogism in which this fallacy occurs will be invalid. A syllogism that violates this axiom is said to commit the **fallacy of illicit process of the (major or minor) term.** More briefly, such an argument is said to contain an "illicit major" or an "illicit minor," depending, of course, on which term is distributed in the conclusion but not in the premises.

Here are examples of SFC syllogisms containing this fallacy:

1. *Illicit major:*
   Some students are Republicans.
   No Republicans are socialists.
   ───────────────────────────
   ∴ Some socialists are not students.

2. *Illicit minor:*
   No students who are members of the ski club are pot smokers.
   Some pot smokers are students who like to ski.
   ───────────────────────────
   ∴ No students who like to ski are members of the ski club.

*Axiom 3. At least one premise must be affirmative.* Recall, once again, that the intent of every SFC syllogism is to connect the major and the minor terms through the middle term. But negative statements, you will recall, merely *exclude* some or all members of one class from another class. Now if the premises only tell you that some or all of the members of $S$ (the minor) are excluded from $M$, and some or all of the members of $P$ (the major) are excluded from $M$, you have learned nothing at all about the relationship between $S$ and $P$. Any conclusion that asserts some relationship between $S$ and $P$ on the basis of two negative premises will therefore be unwarranted. An SFC syllogism that violates this axiom is said to commit the **fallacy of exclusive premises.** Here is an example of such a syllogism:

No senators are members of the Communist party.
Some members of the Communist party are not people who are trustworthy.
───────────────────────────
∴ Some people who are trustworthy are not senators.

*Axiom 4. If either premise is negative, the conclusion must also be negative.* Affirmative statements, as we have seen, assert the inclusion of some or all members of one class in another, whereas negative statements assert the exclusion of some or all members of one class from another. If, then, one of the premises is negative, it follows that the subject and predicate terms of the conclusion can be connected only by exclusion, which, in turn, can be expressed only in a negative statement. Syllogisms that violate this axiom are so obviously invalid that the fallacy they contain has no generally accepted name. We could perhaps call it the **fallacy of an unallowable affirmative conclusion.** The following example illustrates this fallacy:

> All Christians are believers in God.
> No Muslims are Christians.
>
> ∴ All Muslims are believers in God.

*Axiom 5. If the conclusion is particular, at least one premise must be particular.* The reason for this axiom is that, as we have seen, particular statements are construed as having existential import, whereas universal ones are not. To draw a particular conclusion from universal premises would therefore be to assert the real existence of some entity or entities on the basis of premises that do not warrant that assertion.

An SFC syllogism that violates this axiom is said to commit the **existential fallacy.** An example of an otherwise valid syllogism that commits this fallacy is the following:

> All two-headed creatures are wild beasts.
> All Martians are two-headed creatures.
>
> ∴ Some Martians are wild beasts.[2]

The five fallacies prohibited by these axioms constitute a complete list of the **formal fallacies** that may invalidate an SFC syllogism. A formal fallacy, as distinguished from an informal fallacy (see Chapter 4), is a flaw in the form of a deductive argument such that the conclusion does not follow from the premises. Reviewing the five fallacies prohibited by the axioms, we may note that the first two are related to the distribution of terms, the next two are related to the quality of statements, and the remaining fallacy is related to

---

[2] In Aristotelian logic this would have been considered a valid argument, since Aristotle treated universal statements as having existential import. Aristotle also made it an axiom of validity that a syllogism must have just three terms, each of which must occur just twice in the argument. A syllogism that failed in this regard was said to commit the "fallacy of four terms." In making the occurrence of three terms a defining characteristic of SFC syllogisms (Section 6.1), we avoid the necessity of making this a separate axiom of validity. An argument that has more or fewer than three terms simply does not fit the definition of an SFC syllogism, and thus cannot be tested for validity by any of the methods appropriate for testing the validity of such syllogisms.

existential import. Any SFC syllogism that avoids these fallacies is valid; that is, it instantiates a valid argument form.

## EXERCISES 6.5

**A.** Write out the five axioms of validity. Under each construct a syllogism that fails to satisfy that axiom.

**B.** Review the invalid syllogisms on pages 115–117. Identify the axiom of validity that each fails to satisfy, and name the fallacy that results in each case.

**C.** Test the validity of the following syllogisms by the axioms of validity. If you determine that a syllogism is invalid, state the fallacy that is committed.

1.  No communists are loyal Americans.
    All admirers of Adam Smith are loyal Americans.

    ∴ No admirers of Adam Smith are communists.

2.  Some Russians are Christians.
    No Christians are atheists.

    ∴ Some atheists are not Russians.

3.  No martyrs are people to be envied.
    Some Polish peasants are martyrs.

    ∴ Some Polish peasants are not people to be envied.

4.  Some fiscal conservatives are strong supporters of foreign aid.
    All Republicans are fiscal conservatives.

    ∴ Some Republicans are strong supporters of foreign aid.

5.  All Volkswagens are cars that get good gas mileage.
    Some Volkswagens are American-made vehicles.

    ∴ Some American-made vehicles are cars that get good gas mileage.

6.  All fanatics are sincere people.
    No sincere people are people who should be despised.

    ∴ No people who should be despised are fanatics.

7.  All diagrams are visual aids.
    Some diagrams are things that assist us in understanding abstract concepts.

    ∴ Some things that assist us in understanding abstract concepts are visual aids.

8.  All college students are people who can read.
    Some residents of Jones Hall are not people who can read.

∴   Some residents of Jones Hall are not college students.

9.  All children are people who need adequate nourishment for normal growth.
    Some adolescents are people who need adequate nourishment for normal growth.

∴   Some adolescents are children.

10. All desserts are high-calorie foods.
    No high-calorie foods are sugar-free foods.

∴   No sugar-free foods are desserts.

# 6.6 TESTING FOR VALIDITY: VENN DIAGRAMS

Venn diagrams can also be used to test the validity of SFC syllogisms.[3] For this purpose, *three* overlapping circles must be used representing, respectively, the major term (*P*), the minor term (*S*), and the middle term (*M*). (Remember: the major term is defined as the predicate term of the conclusion, the minor term as the subject term of the conclusion, and the middle term as the remaining term of the syllogism.) Figure 6-1 shows the recommended way to position and label the three circles.

**Figure 6-1**

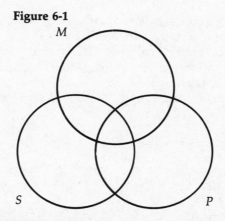

---

[3] It might be advisable to review Section 5.8 before proceeding with this method of testing for validity.

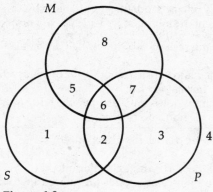

**Figure 6-2**

If we now examine our three overlapping circles, we will find that they mark out eight distinct regions, as identified in Figure 6-2. They are, respectively:

1.   The class of those things that are *S* but not *P* and not *M*.
2.   The class of those things that are *S* and *P* but not *M*.
3.   The class of those things that are *P* but not *S* and not *M*.
4.   The class of those things that are not *S*, not *P*, and not *M*.
5.   The class of those things that are *S* and *M* but not *P*.
6.   The class of those things that are *S* and *P* and *M*.
7.   The class of those things that are *M* and *P* but not *S*.
8.   The class of those things that are *M* but not *S* and not *P*.

To diagram a syllogism, we diagram only the two premises, *being careful to identify correctly the major (P), minor (S), and middle (M) terms.* Since each premise is diagrammed separately, we need to attend to only two circles at a time, diagramming each one as explained in Section 5.8.

Suppose, for example, that we wish to test the validity of the following SFC syllogism:

All artists are individualists.
Some artists are Bohemians.
_____
∴   Some Bohemians are individualists.

We first determine the identity of *S*, *P*, and *M* by examining the conclusion of the argument. In this argument, *S* = Bohemians, *P* = individualists, and *M* = artists.

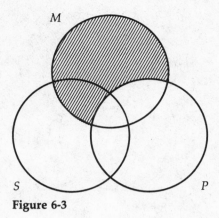

**Figure 6-3**

Next, we exhibit the form of the argument as follows:

All *M* is *P*.
Some *M* is *S*.
∴ Some *S* is *P*.

Now we are ready to diagram our two premises. We shall, for a reason to be explained presently, diagram the universal premise (all *M* is *P*) first. This step gives us a partial diagram as in Figure 6-3.

Next we diagram the remaining premise. This step gives us a completed diagram as in Figure 6-4.

Recall now that in a valid argument the conclusion follows necessarily from the premises: if the premises are true, the conclusion must also be true. The conclusion of a valid argument is, so to speak, already contained in the premises; the argument is merely a way of extracting the conclusion from the premises, showing that it is in fact contained in those premises. What this means with respect to Venn diagrams is this: *If an argument is valid, diagramming the premises will produce a diagram that contains what is asserted in the conclusion; if the argument is invalid, this will not be the case.* Once we have diagrammed the premises, therefore, our diagram is complete. All that remains is to inspect it to see whether or not what is asserted in the conclusion also appears in the diagram.

The conclusion of the syllogism whose validity we are now testing is "Some *S* is *P*" (Some Bohemians are individualists). If our argument is valid, then, we should expect to find an *X* in a space that is within both *S* and *P*. Looking at our completed diagram (Figure 6-4), we see

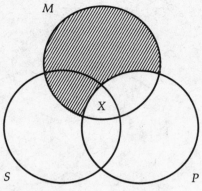

**Figure 6-4**

that "Some S is P" is indeed diagrammed. We conclude, therefore, that the argument is valid.

Let us now use the same technique to test the validity of an SFC syllogism that we have already shown to be invalid by use of the parallel-argument technique (see p. 113):

> All communists are people who favor socialized medicine.
> Some residents of this city are people who favor socialized medicine.
>
> ∴ Some residents of this city are communists.

Following the steps described in the preceding example, we do the following:

1.  Identify terms:
    S = residents of this city.
    P = communists.
    M = people who favor socialized medicine.

2.  Restate schematically:

    All P is M.
    Some S is M.

    ∴ Some S is P.

3.  Diagram the universal premise (Figure 6-5).
4.  Diagram the remaining premise (Figure 6-6).

We now inspect the completed diagram (Figure 6-6) to determine whether the conclusion, "Some S is P," is diagrammed, and we

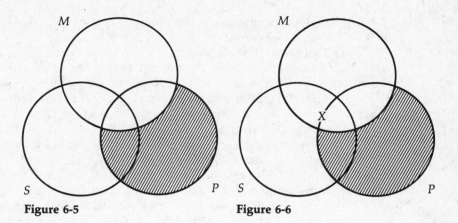

**Figure 6-5**                    **Figure 6-6**

discover that it is not. There is an $X$ on the line that separates that which is $S$ and $M$ but not $P$ from that which is $S$ and $M$ and $P$, but we cannot positively conclude that the class "$S$ and $P$" has any members. The syllogism, therefore, is invalid.

The two examples that we have just considered illustrate the importance of two simple rules that should be followed in the construction of Venn diagrams to test SFC syllogisms. **Rule 1** is this: When you diagram one universal and one particular premise, diagram the universal premise first. The reason for this rule is that once you have done the shading required by the universal premise, you may then see where (and where not) to place the $X$ required by the particular premise. In the case of the premises diagrammed in Figures 6-3 and 6-4, for example, had we attempted to diagram our particular premise first, we would have had to place the $X$ on the line in the region depicting "Some $M$ is $S$." Once we diagram our universal premise, however, we can see that the $X$ cannot be in the region depicting that which is $S$ and $M$ but not $P$, for we know from our universal premise that that region is empty. Thus the $X$ must go in the only remaining part of $M$ that is $S$, and that happens to be the part that is also $P$.

**Rule 2** is: When you diagram a particular premise, if you are in doubt about which part of a divided region should receive the $X$, place it on the line dividing that region. An $X$ on the line means that one part or the other of the class denoted by that region has at least one member, but the premises do not tell you which part. In Figure 6-6, for example, we want to show that "some $S$ is $M$," but the premises do not tell us whether the $S$ that is $M$ is $P$ or not-$P$. It might also be $P$, or it might not. Therefore, we place the $X$ on the line to indicate our ignorance of which part of that divided region it belongs to. Had we, in violation of Rule 2, placed the $X$ in the part of $S$ and

*M* that is also *P*, our diagram would have led us to the erroneous conclusion that the argument in question is valid.

Venn diagrams provide a simple and intuitively convincing method of testing the validity of any SFC syllogism. The method works because, as we noted earlier, validity concerns only the *form* of an argument. No matter what the argument is about, its form can always be represented as some set of relations (of inclusion and exclusion) among the terms *S*, *P*, and *M*, and those relations can be pictorially represented by means of overlapping circles. The diagrams provide, therefore, a means whereby we can literally see the relations (of inclusion and exclusion) among *S*, *P*, and *M* required by the syllogism in question (as well as any other syllogism of the same form). If the conclusion follows when we are reasoning about circles, then an argument of that form will yield a valid conclusion no matter what we are reasoning about. The diagrams allow us to ignore the specific content of an argument and concentrate exclusively on its form, which, so far as validity is concerned, is the only thing of importance.

## EXERCISES 6.6

**A.** Construct a Venn diagram to test the validity of each of the syllogisms on pages 120–121.

**B.** Construct Venn diagrams to test the validity of SFC syllogisms of the following moods and figures:

| | | | |
|---|---|---|---|
| AAA-1 | AII-2 | AII-3 | AEO-4 |
| AEO-1 | AEE-2 | AEO-3 | IAI-4 |
| EAO-1 | AEO-2 | OAO-3 | EAE-4 |
| EIO-1 | EIO-2 | EIO-3 | EIO-4 |

# 6.7 TESTING FOR VALIDITY: TABLE OF VALID ARGUMENT FORMS

We noted earlier (Section 6.3) that of the 256 forms of syllogism that are theoretically possible, only a few are valid. You could at this point determine for yourself which forms are valid and which are invalid by constructing a schematic argument instantiating each of the 256 forms, and then testing your arguments one by one by means of one or more of the methods already discussed. Happily, this task has already been done, and it turns out that there are just fifteen valid argument forms for SFC syllogisms.[4] They are listed below.

---

[4] In Aristotelian logic, which allowed particular conclusions to be drawn from universal premises, nine additional argument forms were considered valid: **AAI-1, EAO-1, AEO-2, EAO-2, EAO-3, AAI-3, AEO-4, EAO-4,** and **AAI-4.**

## VALID ARGUMENT FORMS[5]

1. **Valid syllogisms of the first figure**

| **AAA-1** | **AII-1** | **EAE-1** | **EIO-1** |
|---|---|---|---|
| All *M* is *P*. | All *M* is *P*. | No *M* is *P*. | No *M* is *P*. |
| All *S* is *M*. | Some *S* is *M*. | All *S* is *M*. | Some *S* is *M*. |
| ∴ All *S* is *P*. | ∴ Some *S* is *P*. | ∴ No *S* is *P*. | ∴ Some *S* is not *P*. |
| (Barbara) | (Darii) | (Celarent) | (Ferio) |

2. **Valid syllogisms of the second figure**

| **AEE-2** | **AOO-2** | **EAE-2** | **EIO-2** |
|---|---|---|---|
| All *P* is *M*. | All *P* is *M*. | No *P* is *M*. | No *P* is *M*. |
| No *S* is *M*. | Some *S* is not *M*. | All *S* is *M*. | Some *S* is *M*. |
| ∴ No *S* is *P*. | ∴ Some *S* is not *P*. | ∴ No *S* is *P*. | ∴ Some *S* is not *P*. |
| (Camestres) | (Baroco) | (Cesare) | (Festino) |

3. **Valid syllogisms of the third figure**

| **AII-3** | **EIO-3** | **IAI-3** | **OAO-3** |
|---|---|---|---|
| All *M* is *P*. | No *M* is *P*. | Some *M* is *P*. | Some *M* is not *P*. |
| Some *M* is *S*. | Some *M* is *S*. | All *M* is *S*. | All *M* is *S*. |
| ∴ Some *S* is *P*. | ∴ Some *S* is not *P*. | ∴ Some *S* is *P*. | ∴ Some *S* is not *P*. |
| (Datisi) | (Feriso) | (Disami) | (Bocardo) |

4. **Valid syllogisms of the fourth figure**

| **AEE-4** | **EIO-4** | **IAI-4** |
|---|---|---|
| All *P* is *M*. | No *P* is *M*. | Some *P* is *M*. |
| No *M* is *S*. | Some *M* is *S*. | All *M* is *S*. |
| ∴ No *S* is *P*. | ∴ Some *S* is not *P*. | ∴ Some *S* is *P*. |
| (Camenes) | (Fresison) | (Dimaris) |

Since any valid SFC syllogism must instantiate a valid argument form, the table of valid argument forms provides yet another method to test the validity of such syllogisms. That method is as follows:

---

[5] The names in parentheses in this table of valid argument forms are mnemonic devices invented by medieval logicians to help them remember the valid argument forms. Note that the vowels in each name correspond to the letters that designate the mood of the corresponding argument form.

1. Restate the argument in schematic form.
2. Identify the mood and figure of the argument.
3. Determine whether or not an argument of that mood and figure is listed in the table of valid argument forms. If it is, the argument is valid; if not, the argument is invalid.

Suppose, for example, that we wish to test the validity of the following argument:

Some Minnesotans are avid skiers.
All Minnesotans are lovers of cold weather.

∴ Some lovers of cold weather are avid skiers.

Following the steps outlined above, we first restate the argument in schematic form:

Some $M$ is $P$.
All $M$ is $S$.

∴ Some $S$ is $P$.

We then identify the mood and figure of this argument form as **IAI-3,** and checking the table of valid argument forms, we find that it is listed. We conclude, therefore, that the argument is valid. Had an argument of this form not been listed in the table, we would have concluded that the argument is not valid.

This method of testing the validity of SFC syllogisms is obviously dependent on some other method or methods, since the table is merely a listing of argument forms whose validity has been established in some other way. Once we have satisfied ourselves that the table is both accurate and complete, however, we may use it to test the validity of any SFC syllogism. This method simply saves us the labor of applying over and over again the more fundamental tests of validity, whose results are summarized in the table.

## EXERCISES 6.7

A. Restate the syllogisms on pages 120–121 in schematic form, identify the mood and figure of each, and determine validity by reference to the table of valid argument forms.

B. Test the validity of the argument forms listed in Exercises 6.6 (p. 126) by reference to the table of valid argument forms.

C. Verify the validity of the fifteen argument forms listed in the table of valid argument forms by means of Venn diagrams.

# seven

# Categorical Arguments Not in Standard Form

The tests of validity developed in Chapter 6 are applicable only to SFC syllogisms. Many of the arguments that we encounter in ordinary discourse, however, do not occur as SFC syllogisms. In order to test such arguments, therefore, we must either (a) devise new methods for testing them or (b) convert them into SFC syllogisms and then test those syllogisms by one of the methods already described. In this chapter we discuss some of the ways of doing the latter. In later chapters we will examine some methods of testing arguments that are not restatable as SFC syllogisms.

In general, any *categorical* argument (see Section 6.1) can be restated as an SFC syllogism or a series of SFC syllogisms. Categorical arguments may be nonstandard in a finite number of ways, the most important of which are the following:

1.  The statements of which the argument is composed may be stated in the wrong order.
2.  One or more statements may not be in standard form.
3.  The argument may have more than three terms.
4.  A component statement (usually a premise) may be unexpressed.
5.  The argument may have more than two premises.

# 7.1 ARGUMENTS WHOSE STATEMENTS OCCUR IN NONSTANDARD ORDER

Here a single example will surely suffice. A speaker says, "Some Floridians are not swimmers, for some Floridians are centenarians, and no centenarians are swimmers." This argument is nonstandard only in that the three statements occur in the wrong order. The solution is obvious: identify the conclusion of the argument, identify the major and minor premises, and restate the argument in standard form:

> No centenarians are swimmers.
> Some Floridians are centenarians.
> ───────────────────────────────
> ∴ Some Floridians are not swimmers.

The validity of the argument can then be tested by any of the methods described in Chapter 6.

Logically, it makes no difference whether the statements occur in standard order or not. Indeed, if you are clear about which term is which (*S*, *P*, and *M*) and which premise is which (major and minor), you can even test the argument for validity by some methods without restating it. Restatement is advisable, however, in order to minimize the likelihood of error in identifying the components.

## EXERCISE 7.1

Determine which of the following arguments are and which are not in standard form. Restate the latter in standard form.

1. All native-born Ohioans who are at least eighteen years of age are eligible to vote, for all native-born Ohioans who are at least eighteen years of age are American citizens who have attained their eighteenth birthday, and all American citizens who have attained their eighteenth birthday are eligible to vote.

2. Some Californians are swimmers, and all swimmers are sun lovers, so some Californians are sun lovers.

3. No operations are pleasant, for no things that require incisions are pleasant, and all operations require incisions.

4. Some apples are not tasty, since some apples are rotten, and no rotten things are tasty.

5. All college students are readers, and no two-year-olds are readers, so no two-year-olds are college students.

6. Some pets are not four-legged animals, for some pets are birds, and no birds are four-legged animals.

7. No atheists are Christians, and all saints are Christians, so no saints are atheists.

8.  Some saints are martyrs, and no astronauts are martyrs, so some saints are not astronauts.
9.  Some arguments are silly, for some arguments have absurd premises, and all arguments that have absurd premises are silly.
10. All knowledge is worthy of being desired, but some knowledge is productive of sorrow; so some things that are productive of sorrow are worthy of being desired.

# 7.2 ARGUMENTS IN WHICH ONE OR MORE STATEMENTS ARE NOT IN STANDARD FORM

We have already made a substantial beginning toward dealing with this problem by identifying some of the most common ways in which categorical statements may be nonstandard in form and showing how they may be restated as standard-form categorical statements (Section 5.4). You are encouraged to review that discussion now, as it is directly and importantly relevant to the task of restating categorical arguments in standard form.

In translating premises and conclusions into standard-form categorical statements, however, one must pay attention to the formal requirements of SFC syllogisms as well as to the sense of each individual statement. Otherwise, one might produce a correct translation of each individual statement and still end up with a nonstandard argument that would not be testable by conventional methods.

Consider, for example, the following argument: "People sometimes contract serious diseases while they are patients in a hospital. It doesn't make sense to expose oneself unnecessarily to the risk of disease, so it follows that one ought not to go to the hospital unless it is absolutely necessary." The three statements in this argument could be correctly translated into standard-form categorical statements as follows:

1.  Some people are people who contract serious diseases while they are patients in a hospital.
2.  No people are people who should expose themselves unnecessarily to the risk of disease.
3.  No people are people who ought to go to the hospital unless it is absolutely necessary.

Although all three statements are now in standard form, however, the *argument* is still not in standard form. In formulating our statements we have focused our attention on one statement at a time, carelessly ignoring the structure of the argument. Thus we have ended up with an argument that has four terms, an argument whose validity cannot be tested by any of the standard methods.

Had we paid attention to the formal requirements of an SFC syllogism as well as to the sense of each statement, we could have restated the argument as follows:

> No places where people sometimes contract serious diseases are places that should be entered unless absolutely necessary.
> All hospitals are places where people sometimes contract serious diseases.

∴ No hospitals are places that should be entered unless absolutely necessary.

This is a standard-form **EAE-1** syllogism, and its validity can be easily demonstrated.

Consider a second example: "Whenever the NFC team wins the Super Bowl, the stock market has a bad year. The NFC team just won the Super Bowl, so the coming year is likely to be a bad one for Wall Street." This argument can be restated as follows:

> All seasons in which the NFC team wins the Super Bowl are seasons that will be followed by a bad year in the stock market.
> This season is a season when the NFC team has won the Super Bowl.

∴ This season is a season that will be followed by a bad year in the stock market.

This is a standard-form **AAA-1** syllogism that can easily be shown to be valid.

In both of the above examples, the standard-form translation is achieved by the use of what is called a "parameter," that is, a word whose sole function in the argument is to assist in getting the argument into standard form. The word "places" serves as a parameter in the first argument and the word "seasons" in the second. Other words that are sometimes useful as parameters are "times," "cases," "occasions," "instances," "locations," and "examples."

## EXERCISE 7.2

Restate the following arguments as SFC syllogisms, using parameters if necessary.

1.   People who walk to work are always in good physical shape.
     My father always walks to work.

∴   My father should be in good shape.

2.   Seven-hundred-pound gorillas sleep where they please.
     Priscilla the gorilla weighs 712 pounds.

∴   Priscilla sleeps where she pleases.

3.   Whenever Richard Cory went to town, the people on the pavement
     stared at him.
     Richard Cory went to town yesterday.

∴   The people on the pavement stared at Richard Cory yesterday.

4.   Whoever tells a lie will get his due.
     Molly is a notorious liar.

∴   Molly will get her due.

5.   Whosoever hears my words and obeys them will be twice blessed.
     You, my child, are one who hears my words and obeys them.

∴   You will be twice blessed.

6.   Whenever I have more than one drink within an hour, I get a headache.
     I have had three drinks during the past hour.

∴   I am going to get a headache.

7.   Where there's smoke there's fire.
     I see some smoke coming from behind the barn.

∴   There must be a fire there.

8.   What goes up must come down.
     Prices have been going up for as long as I can remember.

∴   Prices will eventually have to come down.

9.   Whenever I get a few dollars in my savings account, something always
     happens to my car.
     I have just deposited a hundred dollars in my savings account.

∴   I suppose I'd better get ready for a car problem.

10.  Whoever says that I am not an honest man is a liar.
     The witnesses for the prosecution have called me dishonest.

∴   Those witnesses are all liars.

11.  Everybody who voted for Reagan in 1980 was happy with the outcome
     of the election.
     Some of those who voted for Reagan were disgruntled Democrats.

∴   Some Democrats were pleased that Reagan was elected.

12.  Anybody with any sense knows that you can't spend your way to
     prosperity.
     Most Americans have good sense.

∴   Most Americans know that annual budget deficits will not bring
     prosperity.

13. Jim always brags when he gets a good grade on an exam.
Jim is very quiet, though he just got back his exam paper.

∴ Jim did not get a good grade on this exam.

14. Whenever jurors have reached a verdict of innocent, they look the accused in the eye when they enter the courtroom.
The jurors have just filed in, and they are looking the other way.

∴ The jurors have reached a verdict of guilty.

15. Novelists always dream of writing the Great American Novel.
My brother is a novelist.

∴ My brother hopes to write the Great American Novel.

16. There is no excuse for allowing people to die of preventable disease.
Polio is now preventable.

∴ To allow people to die of polio is inexcusable.

17. Any computer built before 1978 is now obsolete.
This one was built in 1972.

∴ This one is clearly obsolete.

18. Whatever is adorable is lovable.
Small children are generally adorable.

∴ Most small children are lovable.

19. I like all Italian foods except pizza.
This is lasagna.

∴ I like it.

20. Network television shows have frequent interruptions for commercials.
I don't enjoy shows with frequent interruptions for commercials.

∴ I don't enjoy network television shows.

# 7.3 ARGUMENTS CONTAINING MORE THAN THREE TERMS

A categorical argument may be nonstandard in that it has, or appears to have, more than three terms. Such an argument *may* be an argument of a kind that cannot be reduced to syllogistic form and tested in the ways discussed in Chapter 6, but before you quickly conclude that that is the case, it is advisable to test whether the number of terms cannot be reduced to three. In certain cases, as we shall see, such a test can be carried out without violence to the argument or to any of its components.

Sometimes, for example, an argument appears to contain too many terms merely because one or more terms appear both complemented and uncomplemented. This is the case, for example, with the following argument:

> All Christians are theists.
> All Catholics are Christians.
> ───────────────────────
> ∴   No Catholics are nontheists.

As it stands, the argument contains four terms: "Christians," "theists," "Catholics," and "nontheists." "Theists" and "nontheists," however, are complementary terms, and we can get rid of one of them by obverting either the major premise ("No Christians are nontheists") or the conclusion ("All Catholics are theists"). If we do the former, the result is a standard-form **EAE-1** syllogism; if the latter, a standard-form **AAA-1** syllogism. Both can be easily shown to be valid.

So: if a categorical argument appears to have more than three terms, check first to see whether one or more terms may not appear in the argument both complemented and uncomplemented. If this is the case, use conversion, obversion, or contraposition as necessary to reduce both occurrences of the term to one form or the other (it does not matter which). Remember, however, that conversion may be applied only to **E** and **I** statements, and contraposition only to **A** and **O** statements (see Section 5.6).

The next thing to look for in an argument that appears to have too many terms is synonymous words and phrases. Consider, for example, the following argument: "All people who refuse to do their duty to their country are unpatriotic. Moreover, anyone who avoids serving in the military is spurning his patriotic duty. It follows, therefore, that all draft dodgers are unpatriotic." With a bit of massaging, this argument can be restated as follows:

> All people who refuse to do their duty to their country are unpatriotic.
> All people who avoid military service are people who refuse to do their
>    duty to their country.
> ──────────────────────────────────────────
> ∴   All people who avoid military service are unpatriotic.

This is a standard-form **AAA-1** syllogism and is, of course, valid.

Since every standard-form categorical statement contains two terms, it is evident that a categorical argument could contain as many as six terms and still be statable as an SFC syllogism by the elimination of synonyms and complementary terms. And a single argument may, of course, contain both complements and synonyms.

## EXERCISE 7.3

The following syllogisms all contain more than three terms. Reduce each of them to three terms by eliminating synonyms and complements. In each case, explain what you are doing to reduce the number of terms. (The first one is done for you as an example.)

### Set A

1. All members of the American Legion are noncommunists.
   No uncles of mine are nonmembers of the American Legion.

   ∴ None of my parents' brothers are communists.

   *Restatement:*
   a. Obvert major: No members of the American Legion are communists.
   b. Obvert minor: All uncles of mine are members of the American Legion.
   c. Eliminate synonym in conclusion: No uncles of mine are communists.

2. Some tunes are unsingable.
   All songs are melodies.

   ∴ Some songs are not singable.

3. Some things that are sublime are inexpressible.
   All nonsublime things are things other than eternal truths.

   ∴ Some eternal truths cannot be expressed.

4. No truths are inherently incomprehensible.
   Some things not easily grasped by the slow-witted are not nontruths.

   ∴ Some things not easily grasped by the slow-witted are comprehensible.

5. All rotten things are nontasty.
   Some rotten things are nonapples.

   ∴ Some apples are not tasty.

6. No nonreaders are non–college students.
   No two-year-olds are able to read.

   ∴ No two-year-olds are college students.

7. All birds are two-legged animals.
   Some birds are not nonpets.

   ∴ Some pets are not four-legged animals.

8. All astronauts are nonmartyrs.
   Some saints are martyrs.

   ∴ Some saints are nonastronauts.

9.  Some people who visit Denver in the winter are people who like Mozart.
    All people who avoid Denver in the winter are people who do not like winter sports.

∴  Some winter-sports lovers are not people who do not like Mozart.

10. All out-of-date checks are worthless.
    Some things of value are not nonnegotiable.

∴  Some negotiable things are not out-of-date checks.

**Set B**

11. No *M* is non-*P*.
    All non-*M* is non-*S*.

    ∴  All *S* is *P*.

12. All *P* is *M*.
    All *S* is non-*M*.

    ∴  All *S* is non-*P*.

13. All non-*P* is non-*M*.
    Some *M* is *S*.

    ∴  Some *S* is *P*.

14. No *P* is non-*M*.
    All *M* is non-*S*.

    ∴  All *S* is non-*P*.

15. All *M* is *P*.
    Some *S* is not non-*M*.

    ∴  Some *S* is not non-*P*.

16. No *M* is *P*.
    All non-*M* is non-*S*.

    ∴  All *S* is non-*P*.

17. All *P* is non-*M*.
    All *S* is *M*.

    ∴  All *S* is non-*P*.

18. Some *M* is *P*.
    No *M* is non-*S*.

    ∴  Some *S* is not non-*P*.

19. Some non-*M* is non-*P*.
    All *M* is *S*.

    ∴  Some *S* is *P*.

20. Some *M* is non-*P*.
    All non-*S* is non-*M*.

    ∴  Some *S* is not *P*.

# 7.4 ARGUMENTS CONTAINING ONE OR MORE UNEXPRESSED STATEMENTS (ENTHYMEMES)

In ordinary discourse, one frequently encounters arguments that resemble categorical syllogisms except for one thing: they appear to have only one premise. Someone says, "The pavement is wet this morning. It must have rained last night," or "The barometer is falling today. There will be rain tomorrow." What is often happening in such cases is that another premise is being taken for granted, a premise that the speaker considers so obvious that it seems superfluous to express it. The first speaker above, at the risk of sounding silly, *could* have said, "All mornings when the pavement is wet are mornings that have been preceded by a night of rain. This morning is a morning when the pavement is wet. Therefore, this morning is a morning that was preceded by a night of rain." The second speaker, at the risk of sounding equally silly, could also have made explicit the missing premise: "All days on which the barometer is falling are days that will be followed by a day of rain." Moreover, anyone hearing either of the above statements would readily understand that the unexpressed premise was implicit in the speaker's statement.

An argument in which a statement (usually a premise) is taken for granted, and therefore left unexpressed, is called an **enthymeme** (from a Greek word meaning "in the mind" or "in thought"). Such an argument is also said to be **enthymematic.**

In restating an enthymematic argument as an SFC syllogism, one should be guided by the principle of charity (see Section 2.6). According to this principle, one should supply a premise that will make the argument valid if it is possible to do so. If the statement that one produces in accordance with this principle is obviously false, one should attempt to determine from the context what statement the speaker probably intended his or her hearers to have in mind when they heard the argument. If one can find no true statement that would yield a valid argument, one is justified in concluding that the argument is at least unsound. Whether the argument is also invalid depends on the intentions of the speaker, which of course cannot be determined by logical analysis.

# EXERCISE 7.4

State the following arguments as SFC syllogisms, supplying the missing premise and restating as necessary.

1. I think Dad must be working too hard. His hair is beginning to turn gray.
2. The Jones family must have a lot of money. They buy a new Cadillac every year or so.
3. There must be a surplus of oranges this year. They are on sale at all the supermarkets.
4. Professor Jones evidently is an easy grader. Even Dumb Dora got an A in his course.
5. Today must be a holiday. The campus is practically deserted.
6. Sam's Steak House must have pretty low prices. Uncle George took Aunt Tillie there for dinner last night.
7. Grandma's age is beginning to show. Yesterday she forgot her own birthday.
8. Jimmy will get well soon. A lot of people are praying for him.
9. Otis must have turned over a new leaf. He's been sober for nearly a week.

10.   Gretchen must be a very strong student. She has been admitted to medical school.

# 7.5 ARGUMENTS WITH MORE THAN TWO PREMISES (SORITESES)

A **sorites** (so-*rite*-eez) is a categorical argument containing three or more premises. A sorites is said to be in standard form if (1) all of the statements that make up the argument are in standard form, (2) each term occurs just twice, (3) each statement has one term in common with each contiguous statement, and (4) the conclusion is stated last. A sorites is valid if the truth of the premises implies the truth of the conclusion.

The following argument is an example of a standard-form sorites:

All scavengers are flesh eaters.
No vegetarians are flesh eaters.
All hoofed mammals are vegetarians.

∴  No hoofed mammals are scavengers.

A sorites may be thought of as a chain of syllogisms in which the unstated conclusion of one syllogism serves as a premise of the next. A sorites must have at least three premises, but there is no upper limit to the number of premises that it may have. The number of syllogisms derivable from a standard-form sorites will always be one less than the number of premises in that sorites (including any premises that may be unexpressed).

In order to test the validity of a sorites by the methods developed in Chapter 6, it is necessary to isolate the constituent syllogisms and test each one separately. A sorites is valid if and only if all of its constituent syllogisms are valid.

The above sorites, for example, may be broken down into two SFC syllogisms:

1.   All scavengers are flesh eaters.
     No vegetarians are flesh eaters.

∴  No vegetarians are scavengers.

and

2.   No vegetarians are scavengers.
     All hoofed mammals are vegetarians.

∴  No hoofed mammals are scavengers.

The syllogisms can now be tested by any of the methods appropriate for the testing of SFC syllogisms, and can easily be shown to be valid. Thus the sorites is valid.

If the premises of a sorites do not occur in standard order, they may easily be put into standard order in the following way:

1. Identify the conclusion of the argument.
2. Identify the predicate term of the conclusion.
3. Identify the premise that contains the term identified in step 2. Let this be the first premise.
4. Identify the premise that has a term in common with the premise previously identified. Let this be the next premise. Continue this process until all premises have been stated. The premises will then be in the proper order.

Here is an example of a sorites whose premises are not in standard-form order:

(1) All foods that are low in calories are foods that I do not especially enjoy eating.
(2) No foods that are served to me on my birthday are foods that I do not especially enjoy eating.
(3) All foods that my diet allows are foods that are low in calories.

∴ (4) No foods that are served to me on my birthday are foods that my diet allows.

Statement 4 is, of course, the conclusion, and its predicate term is "foods that my diet allows." Statement 3 also contains this term, and is therefore the first premise. Statement 1 has a term in common with statement 3, so it is the second premise. That leaves statement 2 to serve as the third premise. Thus we get the following standard-form sorites:

(3) All foods that my diet allows are foods that are low in calories.
(1) All foods that are low in calories are foods that I do not especially enjoy eating.
(2) No foods that are served to me on my birthday are foods that I do not especially enjoy eating.

∴ (4) No foods that are served to me on my birthday are foods that my diet allows.

We can now test the sorites by identifying the constituent syllogisms and testing them separately. Note that in order for statements 3 and 1 to serve as the premises of a valid SFC syllogism, their order has to be reversed:

**(1)** All foods that are low in calories are foods that I do not especially enjoy eating.

**(3)** All foods that my diet allows are foods that are low in calories.

∴ **(5)** All foods that my diet allows are foods that I do not especially enjoy eating.

Statements 1, 3, and 5 instantiate argument form **AAA-1,** which is valid. We can then complete the testing of the sorites by stating the syllogism consisting of statements 5, 2, and 4. This syllogism instantiates argument form **AEE-2,** which is also valid. Thus the sorites is valid.

Note that in stating each syllogism other than the last one in the series, we actually *make* the syllogism valid by formulating the statement (if there is one) that can be validly deduced from the premises. In practice, therefore, a standard-form sorites is proved invalid only if (*a*) the premises of a constituent syllogism will yield no valid conclusion or (*b*) the final syllogism of the series is invalid.

## EXERCISES 7.5

**A.** Restate the following soriteses in standard form.

   **1.** All residents of Arizona are sun lovers.
      All Pueblo Indians are residents of Arizona.
      No sun lovers are cliff dwellers.
      All members of the tribal council are Pueblo Indians.

    ∴ No members of the tribal council are cliff dwellers.

   **2.** Some sausages are spicy.
      No things that burn one's tongue are delectable.
      All delectable things are things that one would serve to one's guests.
      All spicy things are things that burn one's tongue.

    ∴ Some sausages are not things that one would serve to one's guests.

   **3.** All agates are things of value.
      Some items in this bag are marbles of exceptional beauty.
      All marbles of exceptional beauty are agates.
      No things of value are things that should be destroyed.

    ∴ Some items in this bag are not things that should be destroyed.

   **4.** All Arthurian legends are fictitious.
      Some true-life adventures are incredible tales.

No stories in this book are fictitious.
Some incredible tales are stories in this book.

∴ Some true-life adventures are not Arthurian legends.

5. No birds that are messy are things that are desirable to have in one's attic.
Some things bequeathed to me by my father are pigeons.
All things that one treasures are things that are desirable to have in one's attic.
All pigeons are birds that are messy.

∴ Some things bequeathed to me by my father are not things that one treasures.

6. Some occupants of this room are bookworms.
All conceited people are obnoxious.
All occupants of this room are mathematicians.
All mathematicians are conceited.

∴ Some bookworms are obnoxious.

7. All statues sculpted by Michelangelo are things of great worth.
All statues in our local sculpture garden are made of marble.
No things of great worth are things that deserve to be ignored.
Some statues in our local sculpture garden are things that deserve to be ignored.

∴ Some things that are made of marble are not statues sculpted by Michelangelo.

8. All cows are bovine animals.
All animals in this corral are cows.
Some animals in this corral are bad-tempered.
No contented cows are bad-tempered.

∴ Some bovine animals are contented cows.

9. Some gamblers are foolhardy.
All foolhardy people are people who take unnecessary chances.
No people who think before they act are people who take unnecessary chances.
All gamblers are people who always expect good luck.

∴ Some people who always expect good luck are not people who think before they act.

10. Some Egyptians are inhabitants of this apartment building.
All cab drivers are loquacious.

All inhabitants of this apartment building are cab drivers.
No loquacious people are unwelcome guests at a cocktail party.

∴ Some Egyptians are not unwelcome guests at a cocktail party.

**B.**     Test the validity of soriteses 1–5 by means of Venn diagrams.

# 7.6 ARGUMENTS THAT ARE NONSTANDARD IN A VARIETY OF WAYS

Most of the categorical arguments we have been looking at have been nonstandard in just one way. We have looked at arguments whose component statements occur in nonstandard order (7.1), arguments containing statements not in standard form (7.2), arguments containing more than three terms (7.3), arguments containing an unexpressed statement (7.4), and arguments containing more than two premises (7.5). In ordinary discourse, however, arguments are often nonstandard in several ways at the same time. We therefore need a strategy for restating such arguments in standard form, one that will give us a standard-form argument that is logically identical to the nonstandard one whose validity we wish to test.

Let us suppose that we have before us a piece of discourse containing what looks like a categorical argument whose validity we wish to test, but which appears to be nonstandard in a variety of ways. Here is a recommended strategy for getting such an argument into testable form:

1.    Identify and state each of the statements that make up the argument, retaining at this stage the language of the original argument.
2.    Identify any statements not in standard form and restate them in standard form.
3.    Eliminate synonyms and complementary terms, if any, using conversion, obversion, and contraposition as necessary.
4.    Identify the conclusion.
5.    Order the premises.
6.    State unexpressed statements, if any.

The result will be either a standard-form syllogism or a sorites stated as a series of syllogisms. In either case, the argument will be testable by conventional methods.

Let us apply this strategy to the following argument, which is adapted from one invented by Lewis Carroll (the same Lewis Carroll who wrote *Alice in Wonderland*):

My dear sir, you must believe me when I tell you that the romances in this library are, without exception, well written. Surely this is clear when you consider that the only books in this library that I do not recommend for reading are those that are unhealthy in tone, and that the bound books are all well written. Now, as you know, the romances are healthy in tone, and I never recommend for reading any of the unbound books. Do you see?

First, we identify the component statements:

(1) The romances in this library are, without exception, well written.
(2) The only books in this library that I do not recommend for reading are those that are unhealthy in tone.
(3) The bound books are all well written.
(4) The romances are all healthy in tone.
(5) I never recommend for reading any of the unbound books.

Next we restate the component statements in standard form. It is clear from the context that the various subclasses of books mentioned in the argument are books "in this library," so to avoid stating that phrase over and over again we simply stipulate that the entire argument concerns only books "in this library." We may then derive the following standard-form statements:

(1) All romances are well-written books.
(2) All books that I do not recommend for reading are books that are unhealthy in tone.
(3) All bound books are well-written books.
(4) All romances are healthy in tone.
(5) No unbound books are books that I recommend for reading.

Our next task is to eliminate synonyms and complementary terms. We first eliminate a minor difference in terminology between statements 2 and 5 by restating the latter as follows:

(5) All unbound books are books that I do not recommend for reading.

We still have two pairs of terms, however, that in the context of this argument are obviously intended to be construed as complementary (though in a strict logical sense they are not). These two pairs of terms are "books that are healthy/unhealthy in tone" and "bound/unbound books." The simplest (but not the only) way to reduce each pair of complements to a single term appears to be to substitute the contrapositive of statements 2 and 5. This strategy gives us the following:

(2)   All books that are healthy in tone are books that I recommend for reading.
(5)   All books that I recommend for reading are bound books.

It is clear from the original argument that statement 1 is the conclusion, and the predicate term of statement 1 is "well-written books." Statement 3 contains this term, and is therefore the first premise. Using common terms as our clue, we establish the following order of premises: 3, 5, 2, 4. Thus we arrive at the following standard-form sorites:

(3)   All bound books are well-written books.
(5)   All books that I recommend for reading are bound books.
(2)   All books that are healthy in tone are books that I recommend for reading.
(4)   All romances are healthy in tone.

∴ (1) All romances (in this library) are well-written books.

The only unexpressed statements in this argument appear to be the conclusions of the component syllogisms, and they will be made explicit in the process of testing the sorites for validity in accordance with the method described in Section 7.5. Statements 3 and 5 are the premises of an **AAA-1** syllogism whose conclusion is:

(6)   All books that I recommend for reading are well-written books.

Statements 6 and 2 are the premises of an **AAA-1** syllogism having the following conclusion:

(7)   All books that are healthy in tone are well-written books.

We can now see that statements 7, 4, and 1 constitute a valid syllogism of mood and figure **AAA-1**. Thus the argument (a sorites) is valid.

It cannot be emphasized too strongly that when a nonstandard argument is restated in standard form, the most meticulous care must be exercised to make sure that the argument as restated is the *same argument* as the original one. Each step in the process affords an opportunity for error, and a single error is all it takes to invalidate one's results. The value of following a systematic restatement strategy is that it enables one to take a series of allowable steps one at a time, and to recheck those steps for any errors that may have crept in.

Only to the extent that one is confident of the correctness of one's restatement can one be confident that, in testing its validity, one is testing also the validity of the original argument.

## EXERCISE 7.6

Each of the arguments stated below is nonstandard in one or more ways. Restate each argument in standard form, and test its validity by any method you choose. In the case of any argument that you find to be invalid, state the axiom(s) of validity that it fails to satisfy.

### Set A

1. All mothers are parents of at least one child.
   Grandmothers are never nonmothers.

   ∴ Every grandmother has had at least one baby.

2. Sailors have a girl in every port.
   My brothers are all in the Navy.

   ∴ No brothers of mine lack companionship when their ship is in port.

3. Quitters never win.
   Winners sometimes get discouraged.

   ∴ People who sometimes get discouraged are not always quitters.

4. Some medicines are foul-tasting.
   Some good-tasting things are not conducive to health.

   ∴ Some medicines are not conducive to health.

5. Alcoholic beverages are not permitted in the dormitory.
   The beverages in this box are nonalcoholic but good-tasting nonetheless.

   ∴ Good-tasting beverages are permitted in the dormitory.

6. Forenoon is the time when I do my best work.
   All of my classes meet in the afternoon.

   ∴ None of my classes meet at a time when I am able to do my best work.

7. He who attempts to be his own lawyer has a fool for a client.
   My brother-in-law is currently pleading his own case.

   ∴ My brother-in-law is a fool.

8. People of wealth are not always stingy.
   All likable people are generous.

   ∴ Some rich people are unlikable.

9. Uncle Charlie always wins when he plays poker.
   When Uncle Charlie wins, he smiles.

   ∴ Uncle Charlie never frowns when he is playing poker.

10. Every item in our experience, including the smallest and most insignificant detail, is stored in our memory bank.
    Anything that is in our memory is theoretically accessible to consciousness.

    ∴ Nothing that we have ever experienced is inaccessible to our consciousness.

### Set B[1]

1. Babies are illogical.
   Nobody is despised who can manage a crocodile.
   Illogical people are despised.

   ∴ Babies cannot manage crocodiles.

2. All hummingbirds are richly colored.
   No large birds live on honey.
   Birds that do not live on honey are dull in color.

   ∴ No hummingbirds are large.

3. All the old articles in this cupboard are cracked.
   No jug in this cupboard is new.
   Nothing in this cupboard that is cracked will hold water.

   ∴ No jug in this cupboard will hold water.

4. No experienced person is incompetent.
   Jenkins is always blundering.
   No competent person is always blundering.

   ∴ Jenkins is inexperienced.

5. No one takes the *Times* unless he is well educated.
   No hedgehogs can read.
   Anyone who cannot read is not well educated.

   ∴ No one who takes the *Times* is a hedgehog.

6. Colored flowers are always scented.
   I dislike flowers that are not grown in the open air.
   No flowers grown in the open air are colorless.

   ∴ All of the flowers that I like are unscented.

---

[1] Adapted from Charles Lutwidge Dodgson (Lewis Carroll), *Symbolic Logic*, 5th ed. (London, 1896).

7. The only things my doctor allows me to eat are things that are not very rich.
   Nothing that agrees with me is unsuitable for supper.
   Wedding cake is always very rich.
   My doctor allows me to eat anything that is suitable for supper.

   ∴ Wedding cakes do not agree with me.

8. All the policemen on this beat eat supper with our cook.
   No man with long hair can fail to be a poet.
   Amos Judd has never been in prison.
   Our cook's "cousins" all love cold mutton.
   None but policemen on this beat are poets.
   None but her "cousins" ever eat supper with our cook.
   Men with short hair have all been in prison.

   ∴ Amos Judd loves cold mutton.

9. I greatly value everything that John gives me.
   Nothing but this bone will satisfy my dog.
   I take particular care of everything that I greatly value.
   This bone was a present from John.
   The things of which I take particular care are things I do not give to my dog.

   ∴ Nothing that I give to my dog satisfies him.

10. When I work a logic example without grumbling, you may be sure it is one I can understand.
    This sorites, unlike the examples I am used to, is not arranged in regular order.
    No easy example ever makes my head ache.
    I can't understand examples that are not arranged in regular order, like those I am used to.
    I never grumble at an example unless it gives me a headache.

    ∴ This sorites is not an easy example.

# PART FOUR

# SYMBOLIC LOGIC

# eight
# Symbolic Notation

There was a time when the study of deductive logic ended at approximately the point that we have now reached. The syllogism, it was thought, is the basic unit of all deductive reasoning, and all deductive arguments—it was further thought—are reducible to syllogisms. Thus, it was concluded, once you have identified the various types of syllogisms and devised methods for determining which types are valid, you have said all there is to say about deductive logic. Even so astute a philosopher as Immanuel Kant (1724–1804), the dominant figure in eighteenth-century philosophy, expressed the view that the logic of the syllogism constitutes a "closed and completed body of doctrine."[1]

In point of fact, however, the logic of the syllogism constitutes little more than an introduction to the field of logic as that field is defined by logicians today. Some of the most interesting and powerful techniques available for the evaluation of arguments have been developed only recently, and it is to these techniques that we now turn our attention.

---

[1] Immanuel Kant, *Critique of Pure Reason*, trans. Norman Kemp Smith (New York: St. Martin's Press, 1956), p. 17.

# 8.1 NONSYLLOGISTIC ARGUMENTS

Syllogistic logic is of genuine value for the assessment of many arguments that one encounters in ordinary discourse. Any argument that can be stated as a standard-form categorical syllogism, or as a series of such syllogisms, can be tested for validity by the techniques developed in the preceding chapters. Since many of the arguments that come to our attention can in fact be so stated, syllogistic logic can be quite adequate for our needs much of the time.

Syllogistic logic is not adequate, however, for the evaluation of arguments that cannot be stated as categorical syllogisms—and there are many such arguments. Consider the following simple example, which is of a familiar type (called a "constructive dilemma") that we might expect to encounter in a political speech or newspaper editorial:

If the federal government cuts spending, unemployment will increase, and if it doesn't cut spending, inflation will continue. The government either will or will not cut spending. Therefore, either unemployment will increase or inflation will continue.

It is intuitively obvious that this is a valid argument, but it would be quite impossible to restate it in the form of a categorical syllogism, or even a series of categorical syllogisms, without changing its meaning. For one thing, neither the first premise nor the conclusion is a categorical statement, and any attempt to turn them into categorical statements would change their respective meanings. Moreover, the validity of this argument does not depend on relations between and among "classes" designated by various subject and predicate terms. The evaluation of such arguments requires techniques different from those that we have considered thus far. We shall consider first the elements of a system of logic that is competent to handle arguments other than categorical syllogisms (Chapters 8 and 9). We will then consider how this system can be extended to handle categorical arguments as well (Chapter 10).

You will recall that in syllogistic logic the link between the premises and the conclusion of an argument is by means of terms (major, minor, and middle) construed as the names of *classes*. Each premise asserts that some or all of the members of the class designated by the subject term are included in or excluded from the class designated by the predicate term, and on the basis of these assertions of inclusion and exclusion it is stated in the conclusion that some other class relation must also be the case. The various tests for validity that we have discussed are simply so many ways of determining whether the class relation asserted in the conclusion in fact follows from premises of a certain kind.

In many arguments, however, the reasoning involved has nothing to do with relations of inclusion and exclusion between and among classes. Look once again, for example, at the argument on page 152. The reasoning in that argument has to do not with class relations but with something else that we have not yet encountered, namely, *relations of truth and falsity between and among the statements making up the argument.* If the statement that the government is cutting spending is true, then—according to this argument—the statement that unemployment will increase will also be true; and if the statement that the government is not cutting spending is true, then—according to this argument—the statement that inflation will continue will also be true. But, it is asserted, one of those two statements must be true: either the government will cut spending or it will not cut spending. Therefore, one or the other of two other statements will be true— either the statement that unemployment will increase or the statement that inflation will continue.

Arguments whose validity depends on relations of truth and falsity between and among the component statements rather than on relations of inclusion and exclusion between classes are called **sentential arguments.** The logical techniques that we shall shortly be discussing are adequate for the analysis and assessment of such arguments.

The statements that we have been dealing with up to this point have been primarily simple statements. SFC syllogisms, for example, contain only such statements. Sentential arguments, however, always involve one or more compound statements. Let us, before proceeding further, briefly examine the difference between these two kinds of statement.

A **simple statement** is a statement containing no other statement as a component. "All birds have feathers," "My brother is an Eagle Scout," and "The painter of *Guernica* is Spanish" are examples of simple statements. Note that although the phrase "*Guernica* is Spanish" might, under some circumstances, be construed as an independent statement, that statement is not a *component* of the statement "The painter of *Guernica* is Spanish." The statement "*Guernica* is Spanish" is no part of what is being asserted in the statement "The painter of *Guernica* is Spanish."

The statement "*Guernica* is Spanish" is a component, however, of the statement "The *Mona Lisa* is Italian, but *Guernica* is Spanish." "*Guernica* is Spanish" is a part of what is being asserted when one asserts, "The *Mona Lisa* is Italian, but *Guernica* is Spanish." Such a statement—that is, one containing at least one other statement as a component—is termed a **compound statement.**

Although the difference between these two kinds of statement is perhaps intuitively obvious, that difference can be determined objectively by the following test: a phrase that is construable as a statement is a component of another statement if and only if replacing it with any other statement results in a meaningful statement. In the case of the statement "The painter of *Guernica* is Spanish," replacing the phrase "*Guernica* is Spanish" with another statement would frequently result in nonsense. If, for example, one replaced the phrase "*Guernica* is Spanish" with the statement "It rained this morning," the result would be the nonsensical expression "The painter of it rained this morning." In the case of the statement "The *Mona Lisa* is Italian, but *Guernica* is Spanish," however, the result of replacing "*Guernica* is Spanish" with any other statement would always result in a meaningful (though often inelegant) statement. The expression "The *Mona Lisa* is Italian, but it rained this morning," is not nonsense; it is a correct and intelligible compound statement, albeit one that is not likely to occur in ordinary discourse.

Compound statements may be thought of as wholes consisting of two or more smaller parts. The compound statement "The *Mona Lisa* is Italian, but *Guernica* is Spanish," for example, consists of the following elements: (1) the simple statement "The *Mona Lisa* is Italian," (2) the simple statement "*Guernica* is Spanish," and (3) the conjunction "but." One can easily invent examples of more complex statements, statements that contain a large number of component statements and other elements.

Our goal in symbolic logic is to reduce statements and arguments to symbols so as to be able to concentrate on their logical form. To achieve this goal, we need a symbol of some kind to represent each element of a compound statement—component statements, conjunctions, and whatever other logically important elements such a statement may contain. This chapter will introduce all of the symbols needed for the symbolization of sentential arguments. Chapter 9 will show how these symbols can be used for the analysis of such arguments.

## EXERCISES 8.1

**A.** Review the definitions of categorical arguments (Section 7.1) and sentential arguments (Section 8.1). Write your own definition for each in such a way as to distinguish clearly between the two types of arguments.

**B.** Identify each of the following arguments as either categorical or sentential:

1. If John and Mary are married, then they are not siblings. John and Mary are married. Therefore, they are not siblings.

2. If all human beings are fallible and you are a human being, then

you are fallible. You are, therefore, fallible, since you are a human being, and all human beings are fallible.

3. All human beings are fallible, and you are a human being; therefore, you are fallible.

4. Either I neglected to mail it or it got lost in the mail. I did not neglect to mail it. Thus it must have gotten lost in the mail.

5. All sentential arguments are arguments whose validity depends on the logical relations between and among their component statements. This is such an argument. Therefore, this is a sentential argument.

6. If something is a sentential argument, then its validity depends on the logical relations between and among its component statements. The validity of this argument does not depend on such logical relations. Therefore, it is not a sentential argument.

7. If this fish was caught during the time limit prescribed in the contest rules, then you are the winner. It was caught during the specified time limit. Therefore, you are the winner.

8. Only those in formal dress can be admitted. They are not in formal dress. Therefore, they cannot be admitted.

9. None but the brave deserve the fair. Cowards, by definition, are not brave. They therefore do not deserve the fair.

10. If they refueled and received clearance to take off as scheduled, they would be here by now. They are not here. Thus it is clear that either they did not refuel or they did not receive clearance to take off as scheduled.

## 8.2 STATEMENT CONSTANTS AND STATEMENT VARIABLES

A **statement constant** is a symbol that represents a specific simple statement. Upper-case letters—A, B, C, D, and so on—are used for this purpose. Any letter may be used as a symbol for any simple statement. As a matter of convenience, however, it is customary to use letters that will serve to remind one of the statement being symbolized. Thus, for example, one might use the letter G to represent the statement "*Guernica* is Spanish," the letter M to represent the statement "The *Mona Lisa* is Italian," the letter A to represent the statement "Apples are sweet," the letter Z to represent the statement "Zebras are striped," and so on.

Since a statement constant represents a specific statement, statement constants in use should be thought of as being true or false. A statement constant that represents a true statement is true, a statement constant that represents a false statement is false.

The point of using statement constants to represent statements is to expose more clearly the structure of statements and of the arguments in which they occur. Consider once again the argument in the preceding section—the one about government spending, unemployment, and inflation. Using the statement constant $C$ for the statement "The federal government cuts spending," $U$ for "Unemployment will increase," and $I$ for "Inflation will continue," we could state this argument as follows:

> If $C$ then $U$, and if not-$C$ then $I$
> $C$ or not-$C$
> ∴ $U$ or $I$

The structure of such an argument can be exhibited still more clearly when we have mastered the symbols for the remaining elements of the argument.

Notice that the meaning of each statement constant in the above argument is very specific: $C$ means "The federal government cuts spending," $U$ means "Unemployment will increase," and $I$ means "Inflation will continue." Statement constants are simply abbreviations for statements. Once you have chosen a constant to represent a given statement, you can use that constant in place of the statement throughout the argument of which the statement is a part.

A **statement variable** is a symbol used to indicate the occurrence of a statement (any statement) without regard to either its form or its content. Lower-case letters in the middle of the alphabet—$p$, $q$, $r$, and so on—are used for this purpose. "If $p$, then $q$," for example, means "If some statement $p$ is true, then some other statement $q$ is also true." You might find it helpful to think of $p$ as meaning "some statement," $q$ as meaning "some other statement," $r$ as meaning "yet another statement," and so on. The occurrence of a statement variable, in any case, means only that *some statement or other* is to be thought of as occurring at that place.

The function of statement variables is to provide a convenient way to exhibit the *form* of compound statements and arguments. Statements, like arguments, instantiate a certain form. Consider, for example, the following statements:

> **E1.** If $C$, then $U$, and if not-$C$, then $I$.
> **E2.** If $K$, then $L$, and if not-$K$, then $M$.

E1, you may recall, states, "If the federal government cuts spending, unemployment will increase, and if it doesn't cut spending, inflation will continue." We don't know what E2 states, since we haven't been told what statements are symbolized by the constants $K$, $L$, and $M$, but for our present purpose it doesn't matter. What we are interested in is what E1 and E2 have in common, and that is their *form*. With the help of statement variables, that form can be represented as follows:

> **E3.** If $p$, then $q$, and if not-$p$, then $r$.

E1 and E2 are statements. They assert something, though one can know what they assert only if one knows what statements are represented in these particular cases by the constants *C, U, I,* and so on. E3, however, is not a statement. It is, rather, a statement form. A **statement form** is a symbolic formulation that contains statement variables but no statements and is constructed in such a way that when statements or statement constants are substituted for those variables—the same statement or statement constant being substituted for the same statement variable throughout that formulation—the result is a statement.

The statement that results from the substitution of statements or statement constants for statement variables in a statement form is called a **substitution instance** of that statement form. E1 and E2, for example, are substitution instances of E3. The substitution of other statements or statement constants for the statement variables in E3 would result in other substitution instances of that statement form.

A given statement may instantiate more than one statement form. E1 and E2, for example, also instantiate the following statement form:

**E4.** *p* and *q.*

That is to say, E1 and E2 are conjunctive statements, compound statements in which two component statements are joined by a conjunction. In that respect they are identical in form to the statement "Mary is short and Barbara is tall," which might be stated as follows:

**E5.** *M* and *B.*

The component statements that enter into the conjunctive statements E1 and E2, however, are themselves compound statements, whereas in E5 the component statements are simple. E4, one might say, represents *a* form of E1 and E2, whereas it represents *the* form of E5. The form of E1 and E2 can be analyzed further, and the form that emerges as a result of such further analysis is the one exposed in E3.

The statement form that results from the assignment of a statement variable to every *simple* component of a statement constitutes what is called the **specific form** of that statement. E4 exhibits the specific form of E5, whereas E3 exhibits the specific form of E1 and E2.

# 8.3 TRUTH-FUNCTIONAL CONNECTIVES

A **statement connective** is a word, phrase, or symbol that, when attached to one or more statements, creates a new statement. A **truth-functional connective** is a statement connective whose meaning is such that the truth or falsity of the statement created by its use depends solely on the truth or falsity of the statement(s) to which it is attached. The exact meaning of these definitions can perhaps be explained by means of a few examples.

Let us consider first an example of a statement connective that is *not* truth-functional: the phrase "Everybody knows that." This phrase qualifies as a statement connective, since it is a phrase that can be attached to a statement to form a new statement. It can, for example, be attached to the statement "The sun rises in the east" to form the new statement "Everybody knows that the sun rises in the east." But it is not a truth-functional connective, because the truth or falsity of the new statement does not depend solely on the truth or falsity of the statement to which it is attached. From the fact that the statement "The sun rises in the east" is true, we cannot make any inference about the truth or falsity of the statement "Everybody knows that the sun rises in the east."

Now consider an example of a statement connective that *is* truth-functional: the phrase "It is not the case that." This phrase, too, qualifies as a statement connective, since—like the phrase "Everybody knows that"—it can be attached to a statement to form a new statement. But there is an important difference: in the present case, the truth or falsity of the statement created by its use does depend solely on the truth or falsity of the statement to which it is attached. If it is attached to a true statement, the resulting statement is false; and if it is attached to a false statement, the resulting statement is true. If the statement "The sun rises in the east" is true, then the statement "It is not the case that the sun rises in the east" is false. If the statement "All Ohioans are brilliant" is false, then the statement "It is not the case that all Ohioans are brilliant" is true. More generally, if $p$ is true, "It is not the case that $p$" is false, and if $p$ is false, "It is not the case that $p$" is true. (Note that we are here using $p$ as a statement variable.)

All of the statement connectives that we shall be considering are truth-functional. There are just five such connectives, representing the operations of negation, conjunction, disjunction, material implication, and material equivalence.

# 8.4 NEGATION ($\sim$)

The symbol $\sim$ (called **tilde** or **negation sign**) means "It is not the case that." If $p$ is true, then $\sim p$ (read "not-$p$") is false, and if $p$ is false, then $\sim p$ is true. If the statement "Abraham Lincoln was president of the United States in 1864" is true, then the statement

"~(Abraham Lincoln was president of the United States in 1864)" is false. If the statement "This house is red" is false, then the statement "~(This house is red)" is true. The negation sign changes the *truth value* of any statement to which it is attached—from true to false or from false to true.

The symbol ~ may be attached to a statement that already starts with a negation sign. Thus the negation of ~$p$ is ~~$p$, the negation of ~~$p$ is ~~~$p$, and so on.

One simple way of setting forth the meaning of the symbol ~ (and of the other symbols that we shall be discussing shortly) is by means of a **truth table.** A truth table is a matrix that allows one to examine in a systematic way all of the possible relations of truth and falsity among a set of statements. The truth table defining the meaning of the symbol ~ looks like this (T means true and F means false):

| $p$ | ~$p$ |
|---|---|
| T | F |
| F | T |

We will be using truth tables extensively later in our study, and will discuss their construction in greater detail at that time (see Section 9.2). For the present, however, note that to the left of the vertical line are all of the possible truth values of some statement $p$, and to the right of that line are the corresponding values of ~$p$ given those values of $p$. Reading from left to right, we see that if $p$ is true, then ~$p$ is false, and if $p$ is false, then ~$p$ is true.

## 8.5 CONJUNCTION (·)

The symbol · (read "and") denotes the simple conjunction of two statements. It has the same meaning as the English word "and" when "and" signifies merely the joint assertion of two statements. A conjunction is true only on the condition that both of the statements of which it is composed (its **conjuncts**) are true. The precise meaning of the symbol · is defined by the following truth table:

| $p$ | $q$ | $p \cdot q$ |
|---|---|---|
| T | T | T |
| T | F | F |
| F | T | F |
| F | F | F |

The symbol · is called a **binary connective** because it operates on (connects) two statements. All of the connectives that we will be discussing with the exception of the negation sign (for which the name "connective" is a bit of a misnomer) are binary connectives.

It is important to note that the symbol · cannot *always* be used to translate the English word "and." The reason is that the word "and" sometimes means something other than simple conjunction. Consider, for example, the statement "The plane crashed and everyone aboard was killed." In this example, "and" does not mean simply that both conjuncts are true; it means, rather, temporal sequence and causality: first this happened, and then, as a direct result, that happened. The proof that this statement is not a case of simple conjunction is that you cannot reverse the two parts without changing the meaning of the statement. If you said, "Everyone aboard was killed and the plane crashed," you would be making a different statement. The symbol · can be used to translate the English word "and" only when "and" is being used to signify simple conjunction, that is, only when the two statements being so joined can be reversed without changing the meaning of the statement.

In ordinary English, words other than "and" are sometimes used to signify the simple conjunction of two statements. "But," "whereas," and "however" are examples of words that are sometimes used in this way. Commas and semicolons also sometimes take the place of a conjunctive word in ordinary English. The symbol · may be used in all of these cases—provided, of course, that the statement in question can reasonably be interpreted as a simple conjunction. Any of the following expressions, for example, could be expressed symbolically in a statement of the form $p · q$:

> Roses are red but violets are blue.
> Roses are red whereas violets are blue.
> Roses are red, violets are blue.
> Roses are red; violets, however, are blue.

## EXERCISE 8.4–8.5

Write the statements below in symbolic notation, using upper-case letters as indicated for the statements to which appropriate logical connectives are to be attached. For purposes of this exercise, symbolize all negative statements as negations of affirmative statements.

*Example:*
0.   I will go to the party, but I will not wear that silly costume. (G, W)
     Symbolic formulation: $G · {\sim}W$
1.   Roses are red, violets are blue. (R, V)

2. Beth is a doctor and her brother is a pilot. (D, P)
3. I did not see the accident, nor did my brother. (S, B)
4. Cookin' lasts, kissin' don't. (C, K)
5. Love is eternal, infatuation isn't. (L, I)
6. John is in love, and so is Mary. (J, M)
7. Mary loves John, but she doesn't love George. (J, G)
8. Jim was raised by his grandparents, but he remembers his parents from early childhood. (G, P)
9. All the world's a stage, and all of us are actors. (S, A)
10. You can fool some of the people some of the time, but you can't fool all of the people all of the time. (S, A)

# 8.6 DISJUNCTION (∨)

The symbol ∨—called the **wedge** or **vee**—is the symbol for what is called **inclusive disjunction.** Its meaning is the same as that of the English word "or" when that word is used to join two statements in such a way as to assert that *at least one* (and possibly both) of the statements so joined is true. Examples of such disjunctions are the following:

E6. Either John will be at the airport to meet you or else Mary will.
E7. Wages are too low or prices are too high.

The two statements that are joined in a disjunction are called its **disjuncts.** An inclusive disjunction is true if *either or both* of its disjuncts are true; thus it is false only if both disjuncts are false. The truth table that defines the meaning of the symbol ∨ is as follows:

| $p$ | $q$ | $p \lor q$ |
|-----|-----|------------|
| T | T | T |
| T | F | T |
| F | T | T |
| F | F | F |

It is important to be aware that in ordinary English the word "or" is sometimes used to create what is called an **exclusive disjunction**—a disjunction that joins two statements in such a way as to assert that *one and only one* of them is true. The symbol ∨ does *not* correctly translate the word "or" when it is used in this sense.[2] Examples of exclusive disjunctions are the following:

---

[2] Exclusive disjunctions can also be stated symbolically, but it is customary to state them as complex expressions rather than by means of a single connective. See Section 8.9.

E8. For that price you get tinted glass or you get white sidewalls.
E9. Either my father was born in Italy or he was born in Switzerland.

How does one decide whether a disjunction in ordinary language is inclusive or exclusive? The answer is that there is no foolproof way to decide; one simply has to make a reasoned judgment on the basis of the apparent meaning of what is being asserted. In the case of E6 and E7 above, the apparent sense of the statements seems to allow the addition of the words "and maybe both," so we take them to be inclusive disjunctions. In E8 it is quite clear, and in E9 absolutely clear, that the intended meaning is "but not both."

# 8.7 MATERIAL IMPLICATION (⊃)

The truth-functional connectives that we have considered up to this point have stayed fairly close to the meanings of corresponding words in ordinary English. Although we have had to observe a few cautions along the way, we have nonetheless been able to grasp the meanings of the various symbols in terms of the following approximate equivalencies:

~ is approximately equivalent to "not."
· is approximately equivalent to "and."
∨ is approximately equivalent to "or."

The *exact* meanings of these symbols, to be sure, are given in their respective truth tables, but what we find in the truth tables is fairly consistent with what we would expect on the basis of the common-sense meanings of their approximate equivalents in ordinary language.

In the case of material implication, however, the meaning of the symbol is somewhat further removed from the common-sense meanings of the closest approximate equivalents in ordinary language. The symbol for material implication is the **horseshoe:** ⊃. To say that a certain statement $p$ *materially implies* another statement $q$ is to say that it is not the case that $q$ is false and $p$ is true. A statement of the form "$p ⊃ q$" (read "$p$ horseshoe $q$" for now) is false only if $p$ is true and $q$ is false; otherwise it is true. The truth table defining the meaning of the symbol ⊃ is as follows:

| $p$ | $q$ | $p ⊃ q$ |
|-----|-----|---------|
| T | T | T |
| T | F | F |
| F | T | T |
| F | F | T |

A statement affirming a material implication is called a **conditional** (or a **hypothetical**). The first part of a conditional—the part preceding the horseshoe—is called the **antecedent;** the part following the horseshoe is called the **consequent.**

**Material implication,** then, is a relation between two statements $p$ and $q$ such that if $p$ is true, $q$ must also be true. This relation obtains between $p$ and $q$ if both $p$ and $q$ are false, if both $p$ and $q$ are true, and if $p$ is false and $q$ true. It does not obtain in the one case in which $p$ is true and $q$ false. That is the whole meaning of the term "material implication," and we must keep that meaning clearly in mind as we turn now to a discussion of how this relation is linked to expressions in ordinary language.

The closest thing to an equivalent expression in ordinary language is a statement of the form "If . . . then . . ." Here are a few such statements in ordinary language:

**E10.** If it doesn't rain tomorrow, then we'll play tennis.
**E11.** If war breaks out, then there will be many casualties.
**E12.** If this is a circle, then all points on its circumference are equidistant from its center.

Such statements express material implication, as is evident from the fact that they would be false if the antecedent were true and the conclusion false. But they also express more than that. The antecedent and the consequent in each of these examples is, so to speak, about the same subject: there is a "subject matter" connection between the weather and tennis playing, between war and casualties, between being a circle and having all points on the circumference equidistant from the center. In E10 the link is what we might call "common-sense causal": it just doesn't make very good sense to play tennis in the rain. In E11 it is straightforwardly causal: if war occurs it will *cause* casualties. In E12 the link is definitional: having all points on the circumference equidistant from the center is part of the definition of a circle.

Material implication has nothing to do with this subject-matter link between the antecedent and the consequent of ordinary-language conditionals. To affirm a relation of material implication between $p$ and $q$ is not to affirm that $p$ causes $q$, or that the definition of $p$ includes $q$, or anything else relating to the content of the statement. It is to affirm simply that it is not the case that $p$ is true and $q$ false. That is the *truth-functional* connection between antecedent and consequent that is common to all of the above examples (and, indeed, to most statements of the form "If . . . then . . ."). In translating ordinary-language conditionals into symbolic statements of the form $p \supset q$, therefore, one is leaving behind everything except this truth-functional relation. So far as the logic of the matter is concerned—

that is, with respect to the role that such a statement may play in a sentential argument—this relation is the only thing that counts.

Since any conditional other than one having a true antecedent and a false consequent is true, it follows that *any conditional having either a false antecedent or a true consequent is true*. Thus statements such as the following would have to count as true conditionals:

**E13.** If some circles are square, then Monaco is larger than the Soviet Union. (False antecedent, false consequent.)

**E14.** If William Shakespeare was a Russian dwarf, then all circles are round. (False antecedent, true consequent.)

**E15.** If William Shakespeare wrote *Hamlet*, then Ronald Reagan was president of the United States in 1982. (True antecedent, true but unrelated consequent.)

It is perhaps surprising to discover that such strange-sounding statements as these are, according to the definition of material implication, true conditionals. Indeed, it is hard to imagine a real-life situation in which anyone would have any use for such statements. All that this means, however, is that the relation of material implication happens to hold in many imaginable statements—statements that nobody would ever think of asserting—as well as in some more ordinary ones that might be expected to occur in everyday conversation. The *logically important* link between antecedent and consequent in an ordinary-language conditional is expressed in the relation called "material implication" as defined by the above truth table. That this same logical link can be found in some unexpected places in no way diminishes its importance or usefulness in the more ordinary cases in which it plays a significant role in the structure of an argument.

In ordinary language, then, conditionals are often expressed in statements of the form "If . . . then . . ." For this reason, the most common reading of symbolic expressions of the form $p \supset q$ is "If $p$, then $q$." Ordinary-language conditionals may, however, be expressed in many other ways. Consider the statement "If the car starts, then we will go." That same conditional might be expressed in a number of ways, including the following:

**E16.** We will go if the car starts.
**E17.** We will go provided that the car starts.
**E18.** We will go on the condition that the car starts.
**E19.** That the car starts implies that we will go.
**E20.** That the car starts entails that we will go.

If we use the letter $S$ to stand for the statement "the car starts" and the letter $G$ for the statement "we will go," then any of the above could be expressed symbolically as $S \supset G$ (read "If $S$, then $G$").

There are also expressions in ordinary English that resemble conditionals in some respects but are not in fact true conditionals.

Such expressions should not be stated symbolically as statements of the form $p \supset q$. Examples of such statements are the following:

**E21.** I'm ready if you are.
**E22.** I could show you a less expensive model if you wish.
**E23.** I'd like to drive my own car if it's all right with you.

The essential clue to the presence of a conditional is the juxtaposition of two statements in such a way as to assert that if one (the antecedent) is true, then the other (the consequent) is also true. Where that clue is lacking—as in examples E21–E23—the expression should not be restated symbolically as an instance of $p \supset q$, notwithstanding the presence of such words as "if," "provided," "on condition that," and so on. As always, one must make a reasoned judgment about the *sense* of what is being asserted and proceed accordingly.

# 8.8 MATERIAL EQUIVALENCE ($\equiv$)

Two statements are said to be **materially equivalent** when they have the same truth value, that is, when either both are true or both are false. Thus a true statement is materially equivalent to any other true statement, and a false statement is materially equivalent to any other false statement. The symbol for material equivalence is the triple bar: $\equiv$. Its meaning is defined by the following truth table:

| $p$ | $q$ | $p \equiv q$ |
|-----|-----|--------------|
| T   | T   | T            |
| T   | F   | F            |
| F   | T   | F            |
| F   | F   | T            |

A statement asserting that two statements are materially equivalent is called a **biconditional** because it is equivalent to asserting that each materially implies the other. To assert "$A \equiv B$" (read "$A$ if and only if $B$") is equivalent to asserting the conjunction of $A \supset B$ and $B \supset A$. $A \equiv B$ means, therefore, that it is not the case that $A$ is true and $B$ false, nor is it the case that $B$ is true and $A$ false. That leaves two possibilities: that both $A$ and $B$ are true, or that both $A$ and $B$ are false. It is these two possibilities that are expressed in the phrase "if and only if." "$A$ if and only if $B$" means "$A$ is true if $B$ is true, and $A$ is true only if $B$ is true; otherwise $A$ is false." This statement, as was noted earlier, is equivalent to the conjunction of the statements $A \supset B$ and $B \supset A$.

Since a biconditional is nothing more than a double conditional, we should not be surprised to find that it shares many of the peculiarities of conditionals. Any true statement is materially equivalent to any other true statement, and any false statement to any other false statement. The following statements, for example, are true biconditionals:

**E24.** Ibsen wrote *Peer Gynt* if and only if ice is colder than steam. (Both component statements are true.)
**E25.** The moon is inhabited by giant mosquitoes if and only if all residents of Michigan are pygmies. (Both component statements are false.)

Once again we must bear in mind that the connection between the two parts of the statement that is of interest to logic has nothing to do with subject matter, but only with truth values. "Materially equivalent" means merely "having the same truth value." Everything else about the statement is irrelevant to its status as a biconditional.

Biconditionals are relatively uncommon in ordinary language, but they do occur. For example:

**E26.** I will go if and only if you will go with me.
**E27.** Unemployment will moderate by September only if there is an upturn in the economy; otherwise it will continue at its current level.

## EXERCISE 8.6–8.8

Write the compound statements listed below in symbolic notation, using the letters indicated for the component statements and using the symbols $\vee$, $\supset$, and $\equiv$ as appropriate.
   1. I will dive off the high board if and only if you will also. (*I, Y*)
   2. If I can keep up this pace for one more mile I will win the race. (*P, W*)
   3. If Sally receives a promotion within three months, she can rest assured that her job is secure. (*S, R*)
   4. Either you will receive a promotion within six months or you will receive a raise. (*P, R*)
   5. You will receive a promotion if and only if your supervisor believes that you have executive potential. (*P, E*)
   6. If you can hum, you can swim. (*H, S*)
   7. I will pay the bill only on the condition that you repair the motor at no additional charge. (*P, R*)
   8. If you mow the lawn, then I will trim the hedge. (*M, H*)
   9. Either you will repair the motor or I will not pay the bill. (*R, P*)
  10. If it's a red convertible, it's mine. (*C, M*)

## 8.9 SCOPE INDICATORS

Statement connectives may operate on either simple or compound statements. The negation sign, for example, may operate on compound statements of the form $p \vee q$, or $p \cdot q$ (and so on), as may all of the statement connectives. Thus it is possible to have conjunctions of disjunctions, disjunctions of conditionals, conditionals whose antecedent and consequent are both compound statements, and so on. There is, in fact, no theoretical limit to the degree of complexity that a symbolic statement may have, since even a very complex statement can be treated merely as a statement $p$ that can be negated or related by one of the other statement connectives to another statement $q$.

Suppose now that we wish to negate a compound statement of the form $p \vee q$ so as to state that the disjunction is not the case. Let the disjunction that we wish to negate be the statement $A \vee B$. We cannot negate this statement simply by prefixing the negation sign, for $\sim A \vee B$ would negate only $A$, not the disjunction $A \vee B$. $\sim A \vee B$ means "either $A$ is not the case or $B$ is the case," and that is not the statement that we are trying to symbolize. What is needed is some method of indicating that the *scope* of a given connective extends beyond the statement or statements immediately adjacent to that connective. We indicate this by the use of parentheses, brackets, and braces as **scope indicators.** To negate the disjunction $A \vee B$ we write:

$$\sim(A \vee B)$$

which means "the disjunction of $A$ and $B$ is not the case." Here are some additional examples of compound statements whose clear expression requires the use of scope indicators:

**E28.** $(A \cdot B) \supset \sim C$ (If $A$ and $B$, then not-$C$.)
**E29.** $A \cdot (B \supset \sim C)$ (Both $A$ and if $B$ then not-$C$.)
**E30.** $(A \vee B) \supset (C \equiv D)$ (If $A$ or $B$, then $C$ if and only if $D$.)
**E31.** $(A \supset B) \equiv (\sim A \vee B)$ (If $A$, then $B$ if and only if not-$A$ or $B$.)

The negation sign preceding a statement or statement variable negates only that statement or statement variable; when it precedes a scope indicator it negates the compound statement or statement form identified by that indicator. The scope of the other (i.e., binary) connectives is determined by what immediately precedes and follows them. If a connective is immediately preceded or immediately followed by a statement or statement variable, its scope in that direction includes only that statement or statement variable. If it is immediately preceded or followed by a scope indicator, its scope in that direction includes the entire compound statement or statement form identified by that indicator.

You may recall from Section 8.6 that it is customary to state exclusive disjunctions as complex expressions rather than by means of a single truth-functional connective. We can now explain how to do this. With the use of scope indicators, we can now state such disjunctions as follows:

$$\sim(p \equiv q)$$

A statement of this form asserts that it is not the case that $p$ is materially equivalent to $q$, which means that it is not the case that $p$ and $q$ have the same truth value. It is not the case, therefore, that both $p$ and $q$ are true, nor is it the case that both $p$ and $q$ are false. Thus, either $p$ must be true and $q$ false, or else $p$ must be false and $q$ true, which is precisely what is asserted by an exclusive disjunction. This statement form—the negation of a biconditional—is the most common way of symbolizing exclusive disjunctions. Another way is by means of a statement of the following form:

$(p \vee q) \cdot \sim(p \cdot q)$

As symbolic statements become more complex, it sometimes becomes necessary to use several different types of scope indicators to indicate the varying scopes of the several connectives. Suppose, for example, that we wish to express the disjunction of statements E28 and E29. We could do so as follows:

**E32.** $[(A \cdot B) \supset \sim C] \vee [A \cdot (B \supset \sim C)]$

Suppose further that we wish to express the conjunction of E31 and E32. In order to do so we have to use yet a third scope indicator, giving us the following complex statement:

**E33.** $[(A \supset B) \equiv (\sim A \vee B)] \cdot \{[(A \cdot B) \supset \sim C] \vee [A \cdot (B \supset \sim C)]\}$

Note that in E33 the scope of the first conjunction sign includes everything within the first set of brackets on one side and everything within braces on the other; the scope of the wedge in the second conjunct is the two statements within brackets on either side of the wedge; and the scope of the material implication sign in the first conjunct is the two statements within parentheses on either side of that sign.

Note also that in all of the above examples, one and only one of the binary connectives appears outside the scope indicators. This is always the case, and it is this connective that determines the basic form of the total statement. Thus E28 is a conditional, E29 a conjunction, E30 a conditional, E31 a biconditional, E32 a disjunction, and E33 a conjunction. It is also correct terminology to say that the antecedent of E28 is a conjunction, the second conjunct of E29 is a conditional, the consequent of E30 is a biconditional, and so on. It is very important for what follows, however, to be able to identify the basic form of compound statements, that is, to recognize them as sometimes quite complex instances of just five basic statement forms: negations, conjunctions, disjunctions, conditionals, and biconditionals. All sentential arguments consist of reasoning concerning statements of these five basic types.

## EXERCISES 8.9

**A.**   Refer again to the statements in Exercise 8.6–8.8. Using the indicated letters for the component statements and using statement connectives and scope indicators as appropriate, do the following:

1. Formulate a symbolic statement in which statements 1 and 2 are the conjuncts in a conjunction.

2. Formulate a symbolic statement in which statements 3 and 4 are the antecedent and consequent, respectively, of a conditional.

3. Formulate a symbolic statement in which statements 5 and 6 are the disjuncts of a disjunction.

4. Formulate a symbolic statement in which statements 7 and 8 are the components of a biconditional.

5. Negate statements 9 and 10, and formulate a symbolic statement using the resulting statements as the conjuncts of a conjunction.

**B.**   Symbolize the following statements, using the letters indicated for the component statements. Symbolize negative statements as negations of the corresponding affirmative statements (i.e., use the symbol ~).

1. If I keep these kittens I will be burdened trying to care for them, and if I get rid of them I will be lonesome. (*K, B, R, L*)

2. Either I will tell the truth and my fellows will condemn me, or I will not tell the truth and my conscience will condemn me. (*T, F, C*)

3. My fellows will condemn me if and only if I tell the truth, and my conscience will condemn me if and only if I do not tell the truth. (*F, T, C*)

4. If one works to become wealthy one is greedy, and if one works to achieve fame one is inordinately proud; moreover, one works either to become wealthy or to achieve fame. (*W, G, F, P*)

5. If Nixon told the truth about Watergate, then either John Dean's testimony is untrue or the Watergate tapes were fabricated; but John Dean's testimony is not untrue, and the Watergate tapes were not fabricated. (*T, D, F*)

6. If God has either created evil or has allowed it to arise from another source, then either he is not good or he is not omnipotent. (*C, A, G, O*)

7. We will get a balanced budget if and only if we either increase taxes or cut spending, and if we increase taxes we will lose the election in November. (*B, I, C, L*)

8. One can either study and allow one's social life to suffer or one can party and allow one's grades to suffer. (*S, L, P, G*)

9. If Michelangelo did not paint the frescoes on the ceiling of the Sistine Chapel almost singlehandedly, then the accounts of his contemporaries are mistaken and the letters that he is supposed to have written to his father are fabricated; but the accounts of his contemporaries are not mistaken, and the letters are clearly genuine. (*M, A, L*)

10. If we continue to develop nuclear energy, life-threatening nuclear

accidents will almost certainly occur, and if we do not do so we will experience an energy shortage that will seriously alter our way of life; and we either will or will not continue to develop nuclear energy. (*C, A, S*)

11. George will pass this course if and only if he answers all the questions on this test correctly, and he will graduate this June only on the condition that he passes this course. (*P, A, G*)

12. If Michelangelo carved the Florentine *David*, then neither Homer nor Rodin carved it and it is neither Greek nor French. (*M, H, R, G, F*)

13. If Michelangelo did not carve the Florentine *David*, then it is either Greek or French; but it is not either Greek or French. (*M, G, F*)

14. If the engine is in proper working condition, then either the fuel tank is empty or the fuel gauge is defective; and the engine is in proper working condition. (*E, T, G*)

15. If it rains tomorrow the roads will be slippery, and if it snows they will be impassable; and it will either rain or snow. (*R, L, S, I*)

16. Henry will stop smoking cigars only on the condition that his friends promise not to make fun of him, and if he doesn't stop smoking them his wife will divorce him. (*S, P, D*)

17. If you are destined to survive this illness the services of a doctor are unnecessary, and if not those services will be futile; and you either are or are not destined to survive this illness. (*D, U, F*)

18. If it is the case that to a student who is a lover of learning grades are unnecessary, and to one who is not a lover of learning they are ineffective, then grades are always either unnecessary or ineffective. (*L, U, I*)

19. We will have an economic recovery if and only if we have price stability and full employment. (*R, S, E*)

20. These books either do or do not teach what the Koran teaches; if the former, they are superfluous; if the latter, they are dangerous and should be burned. (*T, S, D, B*)

# 8.10 CALCULATING THE TRUTH VALUE OF COMPOUND STATEMENTS

Having now familiarized ourselves with truth tables by means of a few examples, let us pause to consider systematically how they are constructed. How do we know what columns to create in order to calculate the truth value of a compound statement in whose truth value we happen to be interested? Suppose, for example, that we wish to construct a truth table to determine under what conditions the compound statement $A \supset (B \lor C)$ is true. How shall we proceed?

The first step is to identify the statement constants and set down all of the possible relations of truth and falsity between or among them. These are the columns that appear in the truth table to the left of the vertical line. The number of horizontal rows that will be required depends on the number of statement constants: one constant requires two rows, two constants require four rows, and the number doubles with the addition of each new constant. If you examine the partial truth table below you will quickly see why. A statement can be either true or false; thus, for one statement constant, two rows exhaust all of the possibilities (the first two rows of column C below). Two statement constants yield four possibilities: the second statement may be true while the first is true, true while the first is false, false while the first is true, or false while the first is false (the first four rows of columns B and C below). If you add a third statement, the number of possibilities again doubles: that statement may be true in conjunction with each of the four possible situations just described, or it may be false in conjunction with each of those four situations. Thus, the number of horizontal rows will always be $2^n$, $n$ being the number of statement constants required to be entered into the truth table. For obvious reasons, it is advisable to enter the T's and F's left of the vertical line in some systematic way so as to make sure that one has no duplicate rows.

The statement $A \supset (B \lor C)$ has three statement constants. We need, then, a truth table having eight rows ($2^3$), as follows:

| A | B | C | |
|---|---|---|---|
| T | T | T | |
| T | T | F | |
| T | F | T | |
| T | F | F | |
| F | T | T | |
| F | T | F | |
| F | F | T | |
| F | F | F | |

The next step is to identify and enter above the horizontal line all of the elements (other than the statement constants already identified) of the compound statement whose truth value we are interested in, working from the simpler elements to the more complex elements. In the case of the statement $A \supset (B \lor C)$, we note that it is a conditional whose antecedent is the statement $A$ and whose consequent is the disjunction of statements $B$ and $C$. In order to calculate its truth value under various conditions of truth or falsity for $A$, $B$, and $C$, therefore, we need just two additional columns: one for the disjunction $B \lor C$ and one for the total statement $A \supset (B \lor C)$. We don't need a column to the right of the vertical line for the antecedent, $A$, in this case because $A$ is a statement constant for which we already have a column to the left of the vertical line. Our truth table, therefore—pending the entry of the appropriate T's and F's in the two new columns—looks like this:

| A | B | C | $B \lor C$ | $A \supset (B \lor C)$ |
|---|---|---|---|---|
| T | T | T | | |
| T | T | F | | |
| T | F | T | | |
| T | F | F | | |
| F | T | T | | |
| F | T | F | | |
| F | F | T | | |
| F | F | F | | |

All of the truth values on a given horizontal line must be consistent with each other. The truth value of any statement whose truth value has not already been determined, therefore, is calculated by reference to all other truth values on that line. Since the truth value of more complex expressions depends on the truth value of their components, one must first calculate the truth value of the components. In the above example, it is obvious that the truth value of $A \supset (B \lor C)$ depends in part on the truth value of $B \lor C$; the truth value of the latter must therefore be calculated first. This is done, line by line, by reference to the truth values of B and C. The statement $B \lor C$ is false only if B and C are both false; otherwise it is true. We can therefore calculate the truth values of $B \lor C$ under various conditions of truth and falsity of B and C as follows:

| A | B | C | $B \lor C$ | $A \supset (B \lor C)$ |
|---|---|---|---|---|
| T | T | T | T | |
| T | T | F | T | |
| T | F | T | T | |
| T | F | F | F | |
| F | T | T | T | |
| F | T | F | T | |
| F | F | T | T | |
| F | F | F | F | |

We can now calculate the truth value of the statement $A \supset (B \lor C)$ under all possible conditions of truth and falsity of A, B, and C. We know that a conditional is false only if the antecedent is true and the consequent false; otherwise it is true. The antecedent, in this case, is A, and the consequent is $(B \lor C)$. Reading the values of A from the appropriate column left of the vertical line and the values of $(B \lor C)$ as previously calculated, we complete our truth table as follows:

| A | B | C | $B \lor C$ | $A \supset (B \lor C)$ |
|---|---|---|---|---|
| T | T | T | T | T |
| T | T | F | T | T |
| T | F | T | T | T |
| T | F | F | F | F |
| F | T | T | T | T |
| F | T | F | T | T |
| F | F | T | T | T |
| F | F | F | F | T |

What our truth table shows is that the statement $A \supset (B \lor C)$ is true for all combinations of truth values of A, B, and C except the one case in which A is true and B and C are both false.

The essential steps in constructing a truth table, then, are these:

1.  Identify the statement constants (represented by upper-case letters) or statement variables (lower-case letters) in the statement or statement form to be tested.

2.  Construct a matrix setting forth all of the possible relations of truth and falsity among the statements or statement variables so identified. Remember that the number of horizontal rows must equal $2^n$, n being the number of statement constants or statement variables, and that no two rows may be identical.

3.  Identify all of the compound statement components (if any) in the statement to be tested. Create a (vertical) column for each such component.

4.  Calculate the value of each such component, working from the more simple to the more complex. Remember that all truth values on a given horizontal line must be consistent with each other. Note also that the T's and F's in a column headed by a compound statement or statement form appear directly under the principal connective in that statement.

5.  Create a column for the statement to be tested. Calculate its truth value by reference to the values determined in the previous steps.

The compound statement for which we have just constructed a truth table is, of course, a relatively simple one. The principles of truth-table construction remain the same, however, for expressions of any degree of complexity. If, for example, one wanted to construct a truth table for the somewhat more complex statement form $[A \supset$

$(B \lor C)] \cdot {\sim}A$, one would simply add a column for ${\sim}A$ and one for $[A \supset (B \lor C)] \cdot {\sim}A$, and then calculate those truth values. The result would be the following truth table:

| $A$ | $B$ | $C$ | $B \lor C$ | $A \supset (B \lor C)$ | ${\sim}A$ | $[A \supset (B \lor C)] \cdot {\sim}A$ |
|---|---|---|---|---|---|---|
| T | T | T | T | T | F | F |
| T | T | F | T | T | F | F |
| T | F | T | T | T | F | F |
| T | F | F | F | F | F | F |
| F | T | T | T | T | T | T |
| F | T | F | T | T | T | T |
| F | F | T | T | T | T | T |
| F | F | F | F | T | T | T |

If the statement $[A \supset (B \lor C)] \cdot {\sim}A$ were a component in a yet more complex statement, one would simply have to add columns to one's truth table to accommodate the additional elements of that more complex statement and, finally, the statement itself. If that more complex statement contained more than three statement constants, additional columns and rows would have to be added in the manner already discussed.

The principles of truth-table construction are, of course, exactly the same whether one is dealing with statements (the elementary components of which are statement constants) or with statement forms (the elementary components of which are statement variables). The truth table on page 173 shows, as we have seen, that the statement $A \supset (B \lor C)$ is false only if $A$ is true and $B$ and $C$ are both false; otherwise it is true. This finding pertains only to the specific statement $A \supset (B \lor C)$. That statement, however, instantiates the statement form $p \supset (q \lor r)$. Had we substituted the statement variables $p$, $q$, and $r$ for the statement constants $A$, $B$, and $C$, our truth table would have shown that any statement of the form $p \supset (q \lor r)$ is false only if $p$ is true and $q$ and $r$ are false; otherwise it is true.

## EXERCISE 8.10

Construct a truth table for each of the statement forms listed below.

1. $(p \supset q) \cdot {\sim}p$
2. $(p \supset q) \cdot {\sim}q$
3. $(p \cdot q) \lor (p \lor q)$
4. $(p \equiv q) \cdot {\sim}p$
5. $(p \lor q) \cdot {\sim}p$
6. ${\sim}(p \cdot q) \cdot p$

7. $\sim(p \equiv q) \cdot \sim p$
8. $[(p \supset q) \supset r] \cdot \sim r$
9. $[(p \cdot q) \supset r] \cdot \sim p$
10. $[p \vee (q \supset r)] \cdot \sim r$

# 8.11 TAUTOLOGIES, CONTRADICTIONS, AND CONTINGENT STATEMENTS

In defining the truth-functional connectives, we constructed truth tables showing the conditions under which a compound statement formed by a given connective is true and the conditions under which it is false. In each case, as we have seen, a compound statement so formed may be either true or false depending on the truth or falsity of the component statements.

Some compound statements, however, are true under all possible combinations of truth values of their component statements. Such statements are called **tautologies,** and are said to be "logically true," "necessarily true," or "true as a matter of logical necessity." A simple example of a tautology is any statement of the form $p \vee \sim p$—for example, "Either it is raining or it is not raining." That such a statement is true under all possible circumstances (and thus a tautology) is intuitively obvious, and is proved by the following truth table:

| $p$ | $\sim p$ | $p \vee \sim p$ |
|---|---|---|
| T | F | T |
| F | T | T |

In more complex cases the tautological character of a given statement may not be at all obvious, but may be demonstrated by the use of a truth table. Consider, for example, the statement form $(p \vee q) \vee (\sim p \vee \sim q)$. Any statement of this form is a tautology, as is evident from the following truth table:

| $p$ | $q$ | $\sim p$ | $\sim q$ | $p \vee q$ | $\sim p \vee \sim q$ | $(p \vee q) \vee (\sim p \vee \sim q)$ |
|---|---|---|---|---|---|---|
| T | T | F | F | T | F | T |
| T | F | F | T | T | T | T |
| F | T | T | F | T | T | T |
| F | F | T | T | F | T | T |

There are also compound statements that are false under all possible combinations of truth and falsity of their component statements. Such statements are called **contradictions,** and are said to be "logically false," "necessarily false," or "false as a matter of logical necessity." A simple example of a contradiction is any statement of the form $p \cdot \sim p$, the contradictory character of which is proved by the following truth table:

| $p$ | $\sim p$ | $p \cdot \sim p$ |
|-----|----------|------------------|
| T | F | F |
| F | T | F |

A more complex example of a contradiction is any statement of the form $(p \vee q) \cdot (\sim p \cdot \sim q)$. That a statement of this form is a contradiction is proved by the following truth table:

| $p$ | $q$ | $\sim p$ | $\sim q$ | $p \vee q$ | $\sim p \cdot \sim q$ | $(p \vee q) \cdot (\sim p \cdot \sim q)$ |
|-----|-----|----------|----------|------------|------------------------|-------------------------------------------|
| T | T | F | F | T | F | F |
| T | F | F | T | T | F | F |
| F | T | T | F | T | F | F |
| F | F | T | T | F | T | F |

A statement that is neither a tautology nor a contradiction is a **contingent** statement, that is, a statement that may be either true or false depending on the truth values of its component statements. Every statement is a tautology, a contradiction, or a contingent statement.

Tautologies and contradictions tell us nothing about the world. "Either it will rain tomorrow or it won't rain tomorrow" (which instantiates the tautological statement form $p \vee \sim p$), for example, tells us nothing about tomorrow's weather. But tautologies are of great logical importance nonetheless. Proofs of validity and invalidity, for example, depend on the concepts of tautology and contradiction, as we shall see in Chapter 9. The concept of logical equivalence, which is of enormous value in the assessment of complex sentential arguments, also presupposes the concept of a tautology. We shall next consider the concept of logical equivalence.

## EXERCISE 8.11

Construct a truth table for each of the statement forms below to determine whether a statement of that form is a tautology, a contradiction, or a contingent statement.

1. $(p \vee q) \cdot p$
2. $[(p \supset q) \cdot p] \supset q$

3. $[(p \supset q) \cdot \sim q] \cdot p$
4. $(p \cdot \sim q) \supset \sim (p \supset q)$
5. $(p \equiv q) \cdot q$
6. $p \supset \sim (p \vee q)$
7. $p \equiv \sim q$
8. $(p \vee q) \equiv r$
9. $(p \vee q) \supset (\sim p \supset q)$
10. $[p \cdot (\sim p \vee q)] \supset q$

# 8.12 LOGICALLY EQUIVALENT STATEMENTS

The intuitive meaning of the phrase "logically equivalent statements" is that the statements in question "have the same meaning" or "mean the same thing." In ordinary discourse, for example, one might say that the statement "The population of New York City is greater than that of Chicago" is logically equivalent to the statement "There are more people living in New York City than there are in Chicago." Moreover, it is intuitively obvious that these two statements are equivalent in such a way that they will, as a matter of logical necessity, have the same truth value: if one is true, the other will be true, and if one is false, the other will be false.

This intuitive sense of the concept of logical equivalence is preserved in the formal definition of that concept. Two statements are said to be **logically equivalent** when the assertion of their material equivalence (see Section 8.8) is a tautology. The statement form $p \vee q$, for example, is logically equivalent to the statement form $\sim(\sim p \cdot \sim q)$. The proof that these two statement forms are logically equivalent is that the statement affirming their material equivalence is a tautology, as is proved by the following truth table:

| $p$ | $q$ | $p \vee q$ | $\sim p$ | $\sim q$ | $(\sim p \cdot \sim q)$ | $\sim(\sim p \cdot \sim q)$ | $(p \vee q) \equiv \sim(\sim p \cdot \sim q)$ |
|---|---|---|---|---|---|---|---|
| T | T | T | F | F | F | T | T |
| T | F | T | F | T | F | T | T |
| F | T | T | T | F | F | T | T |
| F | F | F | T | T | T | F | T |

The importance of this concept in logic is enormous, for logically equivalent statements can always be substituted for one another in a chain of reasoning without invalidating that reasoning (just as, in the above example about the relative populations of New York City and Chicago, either statement could be substituted for the other at any time). Some techniques for testing the validity of complex arguments, as we shall see shortly, depend on the mutual substitutability of logically equivalent expressions.

For the present, however, it will be useful to note a few simple logical equivalences as a way of clarifying the logical relationships between and among the various truth-functional connectives. Assuming the definitions of the connectives as defined in Sections 8.4–8.8, all of the statement forms below are tautological, as is proved by the respective truth tables. In all cases, therefore, the statement forms that are asserted to be materially equivalent are logically equivalent statement forms:

1.   $(p \cdot q) \equiv \sim(\sim p \vee \sim q)$

| $p$ | $q$ | $p \cdot q$ | $\sim p$ | $\sim q$ | $\sim p \vee \sim q$ | $\sim(\sim p \vee \sim q)$ | $(p \cdot q) \equiv \sim(\sim p \vee \sim q)$ |
|---|---|---|---|---|---|---|---|
| T | T | T | F | F | F | T | T |
| T | F | F | F | T | T | F | T |
| F | T | F | T | F | T | F | T |
| F | F | F | T | T | T | F | T |

2.   $(p \supset q) \equiv (\sim p \vee q)$

| $p$ | $q$ | $p \supset q$ | $\sim p$ | $\sim p \vee q$ | $(p \supset q) \equiv (\sim p \vee \sim q)$ |
|---|---|---|---|---|---|
| T | T | T | F | T | T |
| T | F | F | F | F | T |
| F | T | T | T | T | T |
| F | F | T | T | T | T |

3.   $(p \supset q) \equiv \sim(p \cdot \sim q)$

| $p$ | $q$ | $p \supset q$ | $\sim q$ | $p \cdot \sim q$ | $\sim(p \cdot \sim q)$ | $(p \supset q) \equiv \sim(p \cdot \sim q)$ |
|---|---|---|---|---|---|---|
| T | T | T | F | F | T | T |
| T | F | F | T | T | F | T |
| F | T | T | F | F | T | T |
| F | F | T | T | F | T | T |

4.   $(p \equiv q) \equiv [(p \supset q) \cdot (q \supset p)]$

| $p$ | $q$ | $p \equiv q$ | $p \supset q$ | $q \supset p$ | $(p \supset q) \cdot (q \supset p)$ | $(p \equiv q) \equiv [(p \supset q) \cdot (q \supset p)]$ |
|---|---|---|---|---|---|---|
| T | T | T | T | T | T | T |
| T | F | F | F | T | F | T |
| F | T | F | T | F | F | T |
| F | F | T | T | T | T | T |

The two following logical equivalences are known as De Morgan's theorems (named after the nineteenth-century English logician

Augustus De Morgan) and are of great importance in the construction of formal proofs of validity for sentential arguments. We shall encounter them again shortly.

5.     $\sim(p \cdot q) \equiv (\sim p \lor \sim q)$

This theorem states that the negation of the conjunction of any two statements is logically equivalent to the disjunction of the negations of those statements. That this is indeed the case is proved by the following truth table:

| $p$ | $q$ | $p \cdot q$ | $\sim(p \cdot q)$ | $\sim p$ | $\sim q$ | $\sim p \lor \sim q$ | $\sim(p \cdot q) \equiv (\sim p \lor \sim q)$ |
|---|---|---|---|---|---|---|---|
| T | T | T | F | F | F | F | T |
| T | F | F | T | F | T | T | T |
| F | T | F | T | T | F | T | T |
| F | F | F | T | T | T | T | T |

6.     $\sim(p \lor q) \equiv (\sim p \cdot \sim q)$

This theorem states that the negation of the disjunction of any two statements is logically equivalent to the conjunction of the negations of those two statements. This logical equivalence is proved by the following truth table:

| $p$ | $q$ | $p \lor q$ | $\sim(p \lor q)$ | $\sim p$ | $\sim q$ | $\sim p \cdot \sim q$ | $\sim(p \lor q) \equiv (\sim p \cdot \sim q)$ |
|---|---|---|---|---|---|---|---|
| T | T | T | F | F | F | F | T |
| T | F | T | F | F | T | F | T |
| F | T | T | F | T | F | F | T |
| F | F | F | T | T | T | T | T |

Let us now bring together in one place the six examples of logical equivalence that we have just identified. They are:

1.     $(p \cdot q)$ is equivalent to $\sim(\sim p \lor \sim q)$
2.     $(p \supset q)$ is equivalent to $(\sim p \lor q)$
3.     $(p \supset q)$ is equivalent to $\sim(p \cdot \sim q)$
4.     $(p \equiv q)$ is equivalent to $[(p \supset q) \cdot (q \supset p)]$
5.     $\sim(p \cdot q)$ is equivalent to $(\sim p \lor \sim q)$
6.     $\sim(p \lor q)$ is equivalent to $(\sim p \cdot \sim q)$

This is by no means an exhaustive list of logically equivalent statements. Indeed, since statement forms (and, of course, statements) can be indefinitely complex, it is impossible in principle to create such a list. It is evident from examples 2 and 3 above, for instance, that $\sim p \vee q$ is logically equivalent to $\sim(p \cdot \sim q)$, since both of them are logically equivalent to $p \supset q$. The above list warrants a bit of study, however, for it states some of the elementary relationships among the various truth-functional connectives. Statements 1 and 2 show, for example, that we could get along without the connectives $\cdot$ and $\supset$, since both can be replaced by expressions using only the connectives $\sim$ and $\vee$. That being the case, it follows from statement 4 that the connective $\equiv$ can also be defined in terms of $\sim$ and $\vee$, for statement 2 shows that $(p \supset q) \cdot (q \supset p)$ is logically equivalent to $(\sim p \vee q) \cdot (\sim q \vee p)$, and statement 2 shows further that the latter is equivalent to $\sim[\sim(\sim p \vee q) \vee \sim(\sim q \vee p)]$. This set of relations among the various connectives is sometimes expressed by the statement that $\sim$ and $\vee$ are *primitive* connectives whereas the remaining three are *derivative* connectives. It is also possible to treat $\cdot$ as primitive in place of $\vee$; in either case, $\supset$ and $\equiv$ are derivative.

## EXERCISES 8.12

**A.** Write the compound statements below in symbolic notation, using the letters indicated. Then write a logically equivalent statement for each such statement.
*Example:*
   **0.** If it rains today, I cannot mow the lawn. ($R, M$)
   Symbolic statement: $R \supset \sim M$
   Logically equivalent statement: $\sim R \vee \sim M$
   **1.** I am old and you are young. ($O, Y$)
   **2.** That I am old and you are young is not the case. ($O, Y$)
   **3.** Either I am not seeing clearly or that is a kangaroo in my driveway. ($S, K$)
   **4.** I am not seeing clearly and that is not a kangaroo in my driveway. ($S, K$)
   **5.** I will try parachute jumping only on the condition that you will too. ($I, Y$)
   **6.** It is not the case that the senator accepted a bribe, nor was one offered. ($A, O$)
   **7.** Either the senator did not accept a bribe or else he did not know what he was doing. ($A, K$)
   **8.** I will go if you will drive. ($G, D$)
   **9.** We will go to Florida if and only if the check arrives. ($F, C$)
   **10.** That you ought to do it implies that you can do it. ($O, C$)
**B.** Assume that $\sim$ and $\cdot$ are primitive connectives and that $\vee$, $\supset$, and $\equiv$ are derivative. State the logical equivalences defining the derivative connectives in terms of the primitive ones.
*Example:*
$p \vee q$ is equivalent to $\sim(\sim p \cdot \sim q)$

# nine
# Sentential Arguments

The symbolic notation introduced in Chapter 8 is adequate to state all truth-functional sentential arguments, that is, all arguments whose validity depends on the relations of truth and falsity between and among the statements of which those arguments are composed. Such arguments, since they are deductive, are either valid or invalid. Their validity cannot be tested by any of the methods discussed thus far, however, since those methods are appropriate only for testing categorical arguments. In this chapter we shall discuss several methods for testing and proving the validity of truth-functional sentential arguments.[1]

## 9.1 STATING SENTENTIAL ARGUMENTS IN SYMBOLIC FORM

With the exception of a few elementary argument forms that have special names, sentential arguments do not have a standard form. In general, a sentential argument may have any number of premises,

---

[1] Throughout this chapter the term "sentential arguments" should be understood to mean "*truth-functional* sentential arguments."

and these premises may be stated in any order. Thus most sentential arguments contain no "major premise" or "minor premise." About the only generalizations that can be made about the forms of such arguments when they are stated symbolically are that the premises and conclusion (*a*) must be correctly stated (the symbols must be used correctly) and (*b*) must be identified as such. It is also customary to state the premises first and the conclusion last.

It will be recalled from Chapter 8 that we use upper-case letters to symbolize arguments and lower-case letters to symbolize argument forms. Upper-case letters are statement constants; they are used to symbolize statements. Lower-case letters are statement variables; they are used to symbolize statement forms. In translating ordinary-language arguments into symbols, therefore, it is appropriate to use upper-case letters, since it is specific statements that are being symbolized. If we subsequently wish to symbolize merely the form of the argument so symbolized, we may then do so by means of lower-case notation.

In translating an ordinary-language argument into symbolic form, it is advisable first to identify all of the simple statements that occur in the argument and assign an identifying letter (a statement constant) to each one. If the same statement occurs more than once in the argument, it should, of course, be assigned the same letter each time it occurs. Be careful, however, not to assign the same letter to two different statements.

Consider the following argument: "If George is a chemist, then Robert is a geologist; and if Robert is a geologist, then Gloria and Connie are both mathematicians. But Gloria is not a mathematician; therefore, George is not a chemist." Assigning the statement constant *G* to the simple statement "George is a chemist," *R* to "Robert is a geologist," *L* (not *G*, since it has already been used for another statement in the argument) to "Gloria is a mathematician," and *C* to "Connie is a mathematician," we may symbolize this argument as follows:

1. $G \supset R$
2. $R \supset (L \cdot C)$
3. $\sim L \ / \therefore \sim G$

The use of the letters *G*, *R*, *L*, and *C* is, of course, arbitrary; we chose them only because they make it easier to remember that the statements being symbolized are about George, Robert, Gloria, and Connie, respectively.

If now we wish to look at the *specific form* of this argument—a form that it of course shares with many other arguments—we may represent this form as follows:

1.   $p \supset q$
2.   $q \supset (r \cdot s)$
3.   $\sim r \mid \therefore \sim p$

The selection of $p$, $q$, $r$, and $s$ to occupy those particular positions in the argument is in a sense arbitrary—it would make no *logical* difference if one used different letters—but it is customary to use $p$ as the first statement variable, then $q$, and so on until every component statement has been assigned a variable.

Note that in symbolizing arguments and argument forms we number the premises, and we enter the conclusion on the same line as the last-stated premise, separating it from that premise with a diagonal line. The reason for stating the argument in this way is to facilitate the construction of formal proofs—a topic that we shall consider shortly (Sections 9.4–9.6).

Any sentential argument can be symbolized by means of the notation system introduced in Chapter 8. Each statement is replaced by a statement constant (or statement variable), and the logical relations between and among these statements (or statement forms) are represented by the appropriate truth-functional connectives. The result is an argument (or argument form) in which there are no words at all, but only statement constants (or statement variables) and truth-functional connectives. The tests of validity that we shall now discuss may be applied to any sentential argument or argument form correctly stated in terms of this notation system.

## EXERCISES 9.1

**A.**   Restate the following arguments symbolically, using the letters indicated:

*Example:*
0.   If John is a plumber, then either Sam is a bricklayer or Timothy is a carpenter. But Sam is not a bricklayer, nor is Timothy a carpenter. Therefore, John is not a plumber. ($J$, $S$, $T$)
   1. $J \supset (S \vee T)$
   2. $\sim S \cdot \sim T \mid \therefore \sim J$
1.   If it rains tomorrow, then either the picnic will be postponed or else it will be held indoors. The picnic will not be postponed, and it will rain tomorrow. Therefore, the picnic will be held indoors. ($R$, $P$, $I$)
2.   If it snows this week the cattle ranchers will be unhappy, and if it doesn't snow this week the skiers will be unhappy. It either will or will not snow, so either the ranchers or the skiers are going to be unhappy. ($S$, $R$, $K$)

3. If I stay on campus and study during spring vacation, I will not go home. If I do not go home, I will not be able to look for a summer job. If I am not able to look for a summer job, then either I will have no job or I will find a low-paying job later. If I have no job, I cannot go to school next year, and if I have a low-paying job I will need a loan to continue. Neither of these consequences is acceptable to me. Therefore, I will not stay on campus and study during spring vacation. (C, S, H, L, J, P, G, N)

4. If Russia intervenes in Iran, then if the United States acts to protect its interests in the Middle East, either there will be a confrontation between Russia and the United States or Israel will act as a surrogate for the United States. Israel will act as a surrogate if and only if it is absolutely assured of unlimited supplies of American weapons. If the United States meets this condition, however, the friendly Arab states will turn against the United States; the United States cannot allow that to happen. Therefore, if Russia intervenes in Iran and the United States acts to protect its interests in the Middle East, there will be a confrontation between the two superpowers. (R, U, C, I, A, F)

5. If wages continue to rise, prices will also rise and people on fixed incomes will experience increasing hardship. If wages do not continue to rise, workers at the lower end of the pay scale will never be able to afford a decent life. Wages either will or will not continue to rise, so either people on fixed incomes will experience hardship or workers at the lower end of the pay scale will not be able to afford a decent life. (R, P, H, W)

6. Either I will take a trip to Europe this summer or I will save my money and get married in September. If I do the latter, I will move to Denver. So if I don't go to Europe this summer I will move to Denver. (E, S, M, D)

7. If I buy a new car, I will be saddled with high monthly payments, and if I buy a used car I will have high repair bills. I am unwilling to do either. Therefore, I will not buy a car. (N, M, U, R)

8. Either I will go to school for the next four years or I will be working for the next four years. If I go to school, I will forfeit the income that I could have been earning but will be prepared to do what I want to do. If I work, I will have the immediate income but will lose the opportunity to have the career that I really want. I must choose, therefore, between immediate income and the career that I really want. (S, W, I, C)

9. John's father is either an architect or a builder. If he is an architect, John's mother is an interior decorator and a member of the city planning commission. If he is a builder, John's mother is either a school principal or a dentist. Therefore, if John's mother is not an interior decorator, then if she is not a school principal she is a dentist. (A, B, D, C, P, T)

10. I will attend State next year if and only if my girl friend also attends. If I attend State, then I will either major in engineering or go out for football. I have decided not to go out for football.

Therefore, if I do not major in engineering my girl friend will not attend State. (*A, G, E, F*)

**B.**   Symbolize the logical form of the above arguments, using appropriate statement variables and truth-functional connectives.

# 9.2 TESTING FOR VALIDITY: TRUTH TABLES

You will recall (Section 6.2) that to say that an argument is valid is to say that the *form* of that argument is such that the conclusion follows necessarily from the premises. A valid argument is one that instantiates a valid argument form, and a valid argument form is one in which the conclusion is logically implied by the premises.

This being the case, it follows that for every valid argument a statement of the form "If [premises], then [conclusion]" will be necessarily true, that is, a tautology. Consider, for example, the following argument form (which has a special name, **Modus Ponens**):

**1.**   $p \supset q$
**2.**   $p / \therefore q$

If this is a valid argument form, as it obviously is, then the statement form

$$[(p \supset q) \cdot p] \supset q$$

must be tautological, since it merely indicates what must be the case in order for this argument form to be valid: that if $p$ implies $q$, and if $p$ is the case, then $q$ is the case.

As we have already seen (Section 8.11), it is possible to construct a truth table to determine whether or not a given statement or statement form is tautological. That the above statement form is tautological is proved by the following truth table:

| $p$ | $q$ | $p \supset q$ | $(p \supset q) \cdot p$ | $[(p \supset q) \cdot p] \supset q$ |
|---|---|---|---|---|
| T | T | T | T | T |
| T | F | F | F | T |
| F | T | T | F | T |
| F | F | T | F | T |

Consider a second example. There is another simple argument form that has a special name—**Modus Tollens**—that may be stated as follows:

**1.**   $p \supset q$
**2.**   $\sim q / \therefore \sim p$

If this is a valid argument form, then the following statement form must be tautological:

$[(p \supset q) \cdot \sim q] \supset \sim p$

That this statement form is indeed tautological—thus proving the validity of Modus Tollens—is proved by the following truth table:

| $p$ | $q$ | $p \supset q$ | $\sim q$ | $(p \supset q) \cdot \sim q$ | $\sim p$ | $[(p \supset q) \cdot \sim q] \supset \sim p$ |
|---|---|---|---|---|---|---|
| T | T | T | F | F | F | T |
| T | F | F | T | F | F | T |
| F | T | T | F | F | T | T |
| F | F | T | T | T | T | T |

Let us now use this method to test the validity of the following argument form:

1. $p \supset q$
2. $q / \therefore p$

If this is a valid argument form, then the following statement form must be tautological:

$[(p \supset q) \cdot q] \supset p$

We test this statement form with the following truth table:

| 1 | 2 | 3 | 4 | 5 |
|---|---|---|---|---|
| $p$ | $q$ | $p \supset q$ | $(p \supset q) \cdot q$ | $[(p \supset q) \cdot q] \supset p$ |
| T | T | T | T | T |
| T | F | F | F | T |
| F | T | T | T | F |
| F | F | T | F | T |

Looking at column 5, we see that the above statement form is not tautological, as evidenced by the fact that an F appears in the third row. This argument form, therefore, is invalid.

Obviously, this method can be used to test the validity of individual arguments as well as of argument forms. Suppose, for example, that we wish to test the validity of the following argument:

1. $K \vee Z$
2. $K / \therefore \sim Z$

To test the argument, we construct a truth table to determine whether or not the statement $[(K \vee Z) \cdot K] \supset \sim Z$ is a tautology. We need, then, columns for $K$, $Z$, $K \vee Z$, $\sim Z$, $(K \vee Z) \cdot K$, and $[(K \vee Z) \cdot K] \supset \sim Z$. Our truth table looks like this:

| 1 | 2 | 3 | 4 | 5 | 6 |
|---|---|---|---|---|---|
| K | Z | $K \lor Z$ | $\sim Z$ | $(K \lor Z) \cdot K$ | $[(K \lor Z) \cdot K] \supset \sim Z$ |
| T | T | T | F | T | F |
| T | F | T | T | T | T |
| F | T | T | F | F | T |
| F | F | F | T | F | T |

Examining our truth table, we find that there is an F in column 6. This proves that the statement $[(K \lor Z) \cdot K] \supset \sim Z$ is not a tautology, and we therefore conclude that the argument is invalid.

To summarize: we can test the validity of any sentential argument by (*a*) formulating a conditional statement in which the antecedent is the conjunction of the premises of the argument and the consequent is the conclusion, and (*b*) constructing a truth table to establish the possible truth values of that conditional. If the conditional is a tautology, the argument (and any argument instantiating the same argument form) is valid; if not, the argument (and, of course, any argument of that form) is invalid.

## EXERCISES 9.2

I.  Explain how truth tables can be used to test the validity of sentential arguments.

II. Determine by means of truth tables which of the following arguments and argument forms are valid and which are invalid.

A. 1. $A \supset (B \lor C)$
   2. $\sim B$ / $\therefore C \lor \sim A$

B. 1. $M \equiv (N \cdot R)$
   2. $\sim R \supset S$ / $\therefore M \lor \sim S$

C. 1. $A \lor B$
   2. $B \lor C$ / $\therefore \sim A \supset (A \cdot C)$

D. 1. $S \lor L$
   2. $L \lor R$ / $\therefore \sim S \lor R$

E. 1. $(L \supset C) \cdot (S \supset A)$
   2. $L \cdot S$ / $\therefore C \lor A$

F. 1. $p \supset \sim q$
   2. $r \supset q$ / $\therefore p \lor r$

G. 1. $p \lor (q \cdot r)$
   2. $\sim r$ / $\therefore q$

H. 1. $p \supset (q \cdot r)$
   2. $\sim p$ / $\therefore \sim (q \cdot r)$

I. 1. $p \supset q$
   2. $\sim q$ / $\therefore \sim p$

J. 1. $p \supset q$
   2. $q \supset r$ / $\therefore p \supset r$

## 9.3 TESTING FOR VALIDITY: ABBREVIATED TRUTH TABLES

Although the truth-table method of testing for validity is completely reliable, it is not satisfactory unless the arguments are quite simple. The reason is that truth tables become increasingly complex as the number of variables increases, and one quickly reaches a point where they are too unwieldy to serve as a convenient method of testing for validity. Consider, for example, the following argument form (called the "Constructive Dilemma" argument form):

1. $(p \supset q) \cdot (r \supset s)$
2. $p \lor r / \therefore q \lor s$

In order to test the validity of this fairly simple argument form by the truth-table method, we would have to construct a truth table consisting of sixteen rows and eleven columns—a total of 176 T's and F's. Obviously, it is desirable to find a more efficient way of testing arguments for validity.

   One clue to a possible simplification of the truth-table method is to be found in the fact that only one row of a truth table is required to prove that an argument form is invalid—a row in which the premises are true and the conclusion false. Look once again, for example, at the truth table for the argument form:

1. $p \supset q$
2. $\cdot q / \therefore p$

The truth table for this argument form, you will recall, is as follows:

| 1 | 2 | 3 | 4 | 5 | |
|---|---|---|---|---|---|
| $p$ | $q$ | $p \supset q$ | $(p \supset q) \cdot q$ | $[(p \supset q) \cdot q] \supset p$ | |
| T | T | T | T | T | |
| T | F | F | F | T | |
| F | T | T | T | F | $\longleftarrow$ |
| F | F | T | F | T | |

Note that row 3 by itself is sufficient to prove that argument form invalid, for it shows that the premises could be true and the conclusion false. Suppose, then, that instead of constructing an entire truth table, we simply start with the hypothesis that the premises are true and the conclusion false, and let us then try to find some possible combination of truth values of all of the component statements (or statement forms) that will allow this to be the case. If that is a possible state of affairs—if the premises can be true and the conclusion false— the argument is invalid. If that is *not* a possible state of affairs, it is valid.

   In order to familiarize ourselves with this method, let us begin with a simple example:

1. $p \supset q$
2. $\sim p / \therefore \sim q$

Imagine a truth table that has a column for each premise and another for the conclusion. What we want to know, then, is whether the following truth-value assignments represent a possible state of affairs:

$$
\begin{array}{ccc}
(1) & (2) & (3) \\
p \supset q & \sim p & \sim q \\
\text{T} & \text{T} & \text{F}
\end{array}
$$

Working from right to left, we see that the assignment of F to $\sim q$ in column 3 requires us to assign T to $q$ in column 1, and the assignment of T to $\sim p$ in column 2 requires us to assign F to $p$ in column 1. Thus we have the following truth values:

$$
\begin{array}{ccc}
(1) & (2) & (3) \\
p \supset q & \sim p & \sim q \\
\text{F T T} & \text{T} & \text{F}
\end{array}
$$

It is clear that this *is* a possible state of affairs. We have found a consistent set of truth values for all components that results in true premises and a false conclusion, and we are therefore justified in concluding that this argument form is invalid.

Let us now use this method to test the validity of the Constructive Dilemma argument form:

**1.**   $(p \supset q) \cdot (r \supset s)$
**2.**   $p \vee r\ /\ \therefore q \vee s$

Our task is to determine whether there is a consistent set of truth values that will allow us to make the following truth-value assignments:

$$
\begin{array}{ccc}
(1) & (2) & (3) \\
(p \supset q) \cdot (r \supset s) & p \vee r & q \vee s \\
\text{T} & \text{T} & \text{F}
\end{array}
$$

Again working from right to left, we quickly see that if $q \vee s$ is false, then both $q$ and $s$ must be false. We therefore assign the truth value F to $q$ and $s$ in columns 3 and 1. We thus have the following truth values:

$$
\begin{array}{ccc}
(1) & (2) & (3) \\
(p \supset q) \cdot (r \supset s) & p \vee r & q \vee s \\
\text{F T} \quad \text{F} & \text{T} & \text{F F}
\end{array}
$$

Given these truth-value assignments, we are now forced to assign the truth value F to $p$ and $r$ in column 1, for that is the only way to preserve the value of T for each of the conjuncts $p \supset q$ and $r \supset s$ in column 1. Thus we have the following truth values:

$$
\begin{array}{ccc}
(1) & (2) & (3) \\
(p \supset q) \cdot (r \supset s) & p \vee r & q \vee s \\
\text{F T F T F T F} & \text{? T ?} & \text{F F}
\end{array}
$$

Can we still assert the truth of the premise in column 2? The answer is that we cannot. In order for $p \lor r$ to be true, at least one of the disjuncts—$p$ or $r$—must be true. But in order for $(p \supset q) \cdot (r \supset s)$ to be true, assuming the falsity of $q$ and $s$, both $p$ and $r$ must be false. It is therefore impossible to assign to the component statements a consistent set of truth values that result in true premises and a false conclusion, and we are therefore justified in concluding that this argument form is valid.

Let us now try this method on a slightly more complex example. Suppose that we wish to test the validity of the following argument form:

1.     $(p \supset q) \equiv (p \supset r)$
2.     $\sim q \; / \; \therefore (p \supset r) \equiv \sim p$

We want to know, then, whether the following assignment of truth values is possible:

$$
\begin{array}{ccc}
(1) & (2) & (3) \\
(p \supset q) \equiv (p \supset r) & \sim q & (p \supset r) \equiv \sim p \\
\text{T} & \text{T} & \text{F}
\end{array}
$$

The further assignment of truth values in this case is not so straight-forward as in the previous examples, since there are alternative ways of accommodating the provisional assignments in both column 1 and column 3. In the case of column 3, for example, the assignment of F to the biconditional is preserved if $p \supset r$ is T and $\sim p$ is F, or if $p \supset r$ is F and $\sim p$ is T. It is possible that one of these options would lead to a contradiction and that the other would not. We have no choice, therefore, but to try each possibility until we have either discovered a set of truth values for which there is no contradiction (thus proving invalidity) or established that there is no such possible set of truth values (thus proving validity).

Let us first, in order to preserve the F in column 3, assume that $p \supset r$ is F and that $\sim p$ is T. It quickly becomes evident that we cannot make this assumption, however, for to make $p \supset r$ false we must make $p$ true and $r$ false, and that is inconsistent with the assumption that $\sim p$ is true. We do not even need to look at the implications of that assumption with respect to the premises, since the assumption itself—that $p \supset r$ is false and $\sim p$ true—is self-contradictory.

But there is another possibility. The F in column 3 would also be preserved if $p \supset r$ were T and $\sim p$ were F. If $\sim p$ is F, then $p$ must be T. Following out the implications of these new assignments, we get the following truth values:

$$
\begin{array}{ccc}
(1) & (2) & (3) \\
(p \supset q) \equiv (p \supset r) & \sim q & (p \supset r) \equiv \sim p \\
\text{T T ? T T T T} & \text{T} & \text{T T T F F}
\end{array}
$$

Once again, however, there is a contradiction. Our assumption in column 3 that $p \supset r$ is T and that $\sim p$ is F requires us to assign the value T to $q$ in column 1 in order to preserve the T of the biconditional in that column, and that would contradict the assignment of T to $\sim q$ in column 2. There is, therefore, no consistent way to assign truth values to this argument form so that the premises will be true and the conclusion false. We are therefore justified in concluding that the argument form is valid.

This method of testing the validity of sentential arguments and argument forms is sometimes called the **Reductio Ad Absurdum** (meaning "reduction to an absurdity") test, because it consists in attempting to show that the supposition that the premises are true and the conclusion false leads to an absurdity, that is, a contradiction. This test, like the truth-table method from which it is derived, is a reliable method of testing the validity of sentential arguments. It is, moreover, much more efficient than the truth-table method. If one can find a consistent set of truth values that will allow the premises to be true and the conclusion false, one can confidently conclude that the argument or argument form being tested is invalid. If no such set of truth values is possible, the argument is valid.

## EXERCISES 9.3

I.  Explain how abbreviated truth tables may be used to test the validity of sentential arguments.

II. Test the validity of the following arguments and argument forms by means of abbreviated truth tables:

**A.**  1. $(A \supset B) \cdot (C \supset D)$
        2. $A \cdot \sim D \ / \therefore B \cdot C$

**B.**  1. $A \lor (B \lor C)$
        2. $\sim C \supset D \ / \therefore A \lor \sim D$

**C.**  1. $(G \cdot K) \supset P$
        2. $M \supset (S \cdot \sim P) \ / \therefore M \supset \sim (G \cdot K)$

**D.**  1. $(F \supset R) \cdot (F \lor B)$
        2. $\sim B \ / \therefore R$

**E.**  1. $(L \equiv S) \supset (W \cdot B)$
        2. $\sim (L \equiv S) \ / \therefore \sim (W \cdot B)$

**F.**  1. $p \supset (q \supset r)$
        2. $[r \lor \sim (s \equiv t)] \cdot \sim r \ / \therefore p \supset (s \equiv t)$

**G.**  1. $(p \lor q) \supset r$
        2. $\sim r \ / \therefore \sim p \cdot \sim q$

**H.**  1. $p \supset q$
        2. $q \supset r \ / \therefore r \lor \sim p$

**I.**  1. $p \supset (q \equiv r)$
        2. $r \supset (s \lor t) \ / \therefore p \supset s$

**J.**  1. $(p \lor q) \supset (r \cdot s)$
        2. $p \cdot \sim q \ / \therefore r \equiv s$

# 9.4 FORMAL PROOFS: ELEMENTARY VALID ARGUMENT FORMS

Although the tests for validity discussed above are theoretically adequate to establish the validity or invalidity of any sentential argument or argument form, it is nonetheless desirable to have at one's disposal a method that is somewhat less mechanical than either of them. The reasons are both practical and aesthetic. Truth tables, as we have already noted, are extremely unwieldy for all but the simplest of arguments, and even abbreviated truth tables become a rather complicated matter of trial and error as the options for assignments of truth values increase. More important, however, there is something aesthetically dissatisfying about a test that merely tells us that an argument is valid or invalid and reveals nothing about the internal logical structure that makes it so. The test of validity that I shall now introduce is as much a product of the quest on the part of logicians for an *elegant* test as it is for one that escapes the impracticalities of the other methods.

This new method consists in attempting to construct for any argument one wishes to assess a *formal proof of validity* by means of elementary valid argument forms (Sections 9.4 and 9.5) and logical equivalences (Sections 9.6 and 9.7). We already know, for example, that Modus Ponens is a valid argument form (see Section 9.2). Suppose, then, that we encounter the following argument:

1. $A \supset B$
2. $B \supset C$
3. $A \: / \therefore C$

The knowledge that Modus Ponens is a valid argument form enables us to prove the validity of this argument without difficulty. We can say, "Well, it's obvious from premises 1 and 3 that $B$ is the case (by Modus Ponens), and from premise 2 and $B$ it follows that $C$ is the case (again by Modus Ponens). The conclusion follows from the premises, so the argument is valid."

Although this example is a simple one, it illustrates the main feature of any formal proof of validity: such a proof attempts to show that the conclusion can be derived from the premises by means of one or more inferences that are known to be correct.

A correct inference is one that is warranted by a valid argument form. If each inference in a series is so warranted, then the entire series is warranted, and the conclusion that is drawn at the end of the series has been proved to follow from the premises.

Modus Ponens is one of just nine **elementary valid argument forms** (also called **elementary rules of inference**) used to construct formal proofs. These nine, some of which we have encountered previously, are as follows (standard abbreviations in parentheses):

## ELEMENTARY VALID ARGUMENT FORMS

**Modus Ponens (MP)**
1. $p \supset q$
2. $p \;/\; \therefore q$

**Constructive Dilemma (CD)**
1. $(p \supset q) \cdot (r \supset s)$
2. $p \lor r \;/\; \therefore q \lor s$

**Modus Tollens (MT)**
1. $p \supset q$
2. $\sim q \;/\; \therefore \sim p$

**Simplification (Simp.)**
$p \cdot q \;/\; \therefore p$
    or
$p \cdot q \;/\; \therefore q$

**Hypothetical Syllogism (HS)**
1. $p \supset q$
2. $q \supset r \;/\; \therefore p \supset r$

**Conjunction (Conj.)**
1. $p$
2. $q \;/\; \therefore p \cdot q$

**Disjunctive Syllogism (DS)**
1. $p \lor q \qquad or \qquad p \lor q$
2. $\sim p \;/\; \therefore q \qquad\quad \sim q \;/\; \therefore p$

**Addition (Add.)**
$p \;/\; \therefore p \lor q$

**Absorption (Abs.)**
$p \supset q \;/\; \therefore p \supset (p \cdot q)$

In order to use these argument forms in the construction of formal proofs, one must be so familiar with them that one can quickly recognize instances of them even in the midst of quite complicated arguments. It would be well, therefore, to take time to memorize these argument forms before you attempt to use them in the construction of proofs.

**Modus Ponens (MP)** is in some ways the most fundamental of all argument forms. If one thinks of $p$ as representing the conjunction of the premises of a deductive argument (any deductive argument) and of $q$ as the conclusion of the argument, then every valid argument instantiates Modus Ponens. You will encounter this argument form frequently in the construction of formal proofs.

Modus Ponens and the other elementary valid argument forms are easily identifiable when single statement constants take the place of statement variables. Thus such arguments as the following are quickly recognizable as instances of MP:

| | | |
|---|---|---|
| 1. $A \supset B$ | 1. $B \supset \sim L$ | 1. $\sim P \supset K$ |
| 2. $A \;/\; \therefore B$ | 2. $B \;/\; \therefore \sim L$ | 2. $\sim P \;/\; \therefore K$ |

It must be remembered, however, that a statement variable is instantiated by any correctly formed statement. Thus any two statements—no matter how complex—of which one is a conditional and the other is identical to the antecedent of the conditional will instantiate Modus Ponens. The following arguments are representative of some more complex instances of Modus Ponens that one might expect to encounter in extended arguments:

1.    $A \supset (L \vee K)$
2.    $A$ / $\therefore L \vee K$

1.    $(A \vee B) \supset (C \cdot D)$
2.    $A \vee B$ / $\therefore C \cdot D$

1.    $(F \cdot G) \supset [(A \cdot B) \vee (C \cdot D)]$
2.    $F \cdot G$ / $\therefore (A \cdot B) \vee (C \cdot D)$

Notice that in the third example the statement $F \cdot G$ appears in parentheses in the first premise but not in the second, and the statement $(A \cdot B) \vee (C \cdot D)$ appears in brackets in the first premise but not in the conclusion. The reason, of course, is that those statements are components of a conditional in their first occurrence but not in their second, and the scope indicators are needed in the conditional to eliminate ambiguity about the scope of the respective connectives.

     **Modus Tollens (MT)** is also extremely useful in the construction of formal proofs. You should be able to recognize all of the following as instances of MT:

1.    $A \supset B$
2.    $\sim B$ / $\therefore \sim A$

1.    $(B \cdot Z) \supset (R \vee G)$
2.    $\sim(R \vee G)$ / $\therefore \sim(B \cdot Z)$

1.    $(B \vee S) \supset \sim[(A \cdot B) \vee C]$
2.    $\sim\sim[(A \cdot B) \vee C]$ / $\therefore \sim(B \vee S)$

Note the double negation in statement 2 in the third example.

     Following are some typical substitution instances of **Hypothetical Syllogism (HS):**

1.    $A \supset B$
2.    $B \supset C$ / $\therefore A \supset C$

1.    $(G \cdot H) \supset (K \vee L)$
2.    $(K \vee L) \supset \sim Z$ / $\therefore (G \cdot H) \supset \sim Z$

1.    $[(A \vee B) \cdot (C \vee D)] \supset E$
2.    $E \supset \sim[L \supset (M \cdot N)]$ / $\therefore [(A \vee B) \cdot (C \vee D)] \supset \sim[L \supset (M \cdot N)]$

Any time one encounters in an argument two conditionals with a common component, it is advisable to check for the possibility of a hypothetical syllogism. If the common component is the consequent of one conditional and the antecedent of the other, the two conditionals will warrant a conclusion by HS.

**Disjunctive Syllogism (DS)** is instantiated by all of the following:

**1.** $A \lor B$
**2.** $\sim A / \therefore B$

**1.** $(A \cdot B) \lor (C \cdot D)$
**2.** $\sim(C \cdot D) / \therefore A \cdot B$

**1.** $[(K \lor L) \cdot (M \lor N)] \lor \sim(O \cdot P)$
**2.** $\sim\sim(O \cdot P) / \therefore (K \lor L) \cdot (M \lor N)$

Note once again (in the third example) the absence of the brackets in the conclusion and the double negation in the second premise.

**Absorption (Abs.)** is a way of exporting the antecedent of a conditional to the consequent of that same conditional, where it becomes one member of a conjunction. This argument form is instantiated by such arguments as the following:

$A \supset B / \therefore A \supset (A \cdot B)$

$(B \lor R) \supset (C \equiv K) / \therefore (B \lor R) \supset [(B \lor R) \cdot (C \equiv K)]$

The **Constructive Dilemma (CD)** is a very common argument form that is often present when the conclusion to be derived is a disjunction. Here are some examples:

**1.** $(A \supset B) \cdot (C \supset D)$
**2.** $A \lor C / \therefore B \lor D$

**1.** $[A \supset (C \lor R)] \cdot [(B \cdot K) \supset M]$
**2.** $A \lor (B \cdot K) / \therefore (C \lor R) \lor M$

**1.** $[(Q \lor L) \supset (A \equiv B)] \cdot [R \supset \sim(C \lor D)]$
**2.** $(Q \lor L) \lor R / \therefore (A \equiv B) \lor \sim(C \lor D)$

Note that to make an inference by CD just two things are required: a conjunction of two conditionals and a disjunction of the antecedents of those conditionals.

**Simplification (Simp.)** allows one to assert either conjunct of a conjunction independently. **Conjunction (Conj.)** is just the opposite of Simplification; it allows one to join in a conjunction any two statements that are asserted independently. Here are some examples of each:

*Simplification*

$A \cdot B / \therefore A$
$(A \equiv C) \cdot [\sim(B \lor L) \lor R] / \therefore \sim(B \lor L) \lor R$
$(K \lor R) \cdot \sim C / \therefore \sim C$

*Conjunction*

1. $A$
2. $B$ / $\therefore A \cdot B$

1. $X \vee Z$
2. $B \equiv K$ / $\therefore (X \vee Z) \cdot (B \equiv K)$

1. $L \supset Z$
2. $Z \equiv (M \vee R)$ / $\therefore (L \supset Z) \equiv [Z \cdot (M \vee R)]$

The validity of all of the above argument forms is fairly evident and can, of course, be proved by means of truth tables. The validity of the argument form called **Addition (Add.),** however, is less intuitively obvious. What Addition says is this: Any statement that is not a component of another statement can be joined in a disjunction with *any other statement whatsoever.* If $A$ is true, then $A \vee B$ is also true; if $R \supset L$ is true, then $(R \supset L) \vee K$ is true; and so on. The validity of this argument form is proved by the following truth table:

| $p$ | $q$ | $p \vee q$ | $p \supset (p \vee q)$ |
|-----|-----|------------|------------------------|
| T | T | T | T |
| T | F | T | T |
| F | T | T | T |
| F | F | F | T |

In order to make this argument form more intuitively evident, you might find it helpful to think of a concrete example. Consider the statement "The sky is blue." If that is a true statement, it is evident that all of the following statements are also true:

The sky is blue or the sky is green.
The sky is blue or the ocean is blue.
The sky is blue or the moon is made of cheese.
The sky is blue or Norway is in Africa.

As you can see, it makes no difference what statement you insert after the "or": the resulting disjunction is true if the first disjunct is true. Thus it is clear that from any asserted statement (i.e., any statement that is not a component of another statement) one can validly infer a disjunction of which one disjunct is the asserted statement and the other is any other statement whatsoever.

Addition warrants such inferences as the following:

$A$ / $\therefore A \vee B$

$K \supset L$ / $\therefore (K \supset L) \vee (B \cdot R)$
$(R \equiv M) \cdot (Z \supset L)$ / $\therefore [(R \equiv M) \cdot (Z \supset L)] \vee (Q \supset Z)$

Note well: *The elementary valid argument forms may be applied only to complete statements,* that is, only to statements that are not components of other statements. If, for example, one is given the statement $(A \cdot B) \supset C$, one cannot apply Simplification to $A \cdot B$ so as to assert $A \supset C$, or to assert $B \supset C$, nor can one apply Addition merely to a part of the statement so as to assert $[(A \lor D) \cdot B] \supset C$, or $[A \cdot (B \lor D)] \supset C$, or $(A \cdot B) \supset (C \lor D)$. One can, however, apply Addition to the complete statement $(A \cdot B) \supset C$ so as to produce the statements $[(A \cdot B) \supset C] \lor D$, $[(A \cdot B) \supset C] \lor (K \cdot L)$, and so on. This is an exceedingly important fact about the elementary valid argument forms (and, indeed, about all argument forms), and must be treated as a rule to which absolutely no exceptions are permissible.

## EXERCISES 9.4

I.  Write from memory the nine elementary valid argument forms stated on page 193, identifying each of them by name and by the appropriate abbreviation.

II.  Invent two examples of each elementary valid argument form, using statement constants of your own choosing.

III.  Each of the following arguments makes an inference that is warranted by one of the elementary valid argument forms. Identify the argument form that warrants each inference.

    **A.**  1. $B \supset Q$
          2. $R \mathbin{/} \therefore R \cdot (B \supset Q)$

    **B.**  1. $(K \cdot L) \supset (M \cdot R)$
          2. $K \cdot L \mathbin{/} \therefore M \cdot R$

    **C.**  1. $A \supset (B \lor R)$
          2. $(B \lor R) \supset (C \equiv K) \mathbin{/} \therefore A \supset (C \equiv K)$

    **D.**  $B \equiv (Z \lor R) \mathbin{/} \therefore [B \equiv (Z \lor R)] \lor (Z \supset K)$

    **E.**  1. $A \equiv (X \cdot Q)$
          2. $R \supset Z \mathbin{/} \therefore [A \equiv (X \cdot Q)] \cdot (R \supset Z)$

    **F.**  1. $(A \equiv X) \supset {\sim}(L \lor Z)$
          2. ${\sim}{\sim}(L \lor Z) \mathbin{/} \therefore {\sim}(A \equiv X)$

    **G.**  $(A \supset K) \cdot (R \lor L) \mathbin{/} \therefore A \supset K$

    **H.**  1. $(A \equiv Z) \supset [R \cdot (K \lor D)]$
          2. $A \equiv Z \mathbin{/} \therefore R \cdot (K \lor D)$

    **I.**  1. $Z \supset [(A \lor B) \cdot (C \equiv D)]$
          2. $[(A \lor B) \cdot (C \equiv D)] \supset L \mathbin{/} \therefore Z \supset L$

    **J.**  1. $(K \supset Z) \lor {\sim}(L \cdot R)$
          2. ${\sim}{\sim}(L \cdot R) \mathbin{/} \therefore K \supset Z$

    **K.**  1. $(B \cdot R) \supset (Q \cdot S)$
          2. ${\sim}(Q \cdot S) \mathbin{/} \therefore {\sim}(B \cdot R)$

    **L.**  1. $K \lor (A \equiv B)$
          2. ${\sim}K \mathbin{/} \therefore A \equiv B$

    **M.**  1. $(L \lor K) \supset [S \lor {\sim}(B \cdot S)]$
          2. $L \lor K \mathbin{/} \therefore S \lor {\sim}(B \cdot S)$

**N.** $R \supset [P \supset (K \vee Z)]$ / $\therefore R \supset \{R \cdot [P \supset (K \vee Z)]\}$

**O.** 1. $(B \cdot G) \supset (M \cdot {\sim}K)$
2. ${\sim}(M \cdot {\sim}K)$ / $\therefore {\sim}(B \cdot G)$

**P.** 1. $[(K \equiv L) \supset (A \vee B)] \cdot [D \supset (R \cdot N)]$
2. $(K \equiv L) \vee D$ / $\therefore (A \vee B) \vee (R \cdot N)$

**Q.** $(A \vee L) \cdot R$ / $\therefore [(A \vee L) \cdot R] \vee K$

**R.** 1. $(A \vee B) \supset K$
2. $(C \vee D) \supset L$ / $\therefore [(A \vee B) \supset K] \cdot [(C \vee D) \supset L]$

**S.** 1. $(M \cdot R) \vee [B \supset (L \vee {\sim}N)]$
2. ${\sim}(M \cdot R)$ / $\therefore B \supset (L \vee {\sim}N)$

**T.** 1. $[(A \vee B) \supset E] \cdot [(C \vee D) \supset F]$
2. $(A \vee B) \vee (C \vee D)$ / $\therefore E \vee F$

# 9.5 FORMAL PROOFS: USING THE ELEMENTARY VALID ARGUMENT FORMS

Only the simplest of arguments makes a single inference from one or two premises. More typically, an argument contains several premises from which one must make a *series* of inferences in order to derive the conclusion. A demonstration that the conclusion of an argument can be derived from the premises through a series of warranted inferences constitutes a **formal proof** of that argument.

In constructing formal proofs of validity it is customary to follow a certain prescribed pattern. That pattern is illustrated by the following statement of the proof stated informally on page 192:

1. $A \supset B$
2. $B \supset C$
3. $A$ / $\therefore C$
4. $B$      1, 3 MP
5. $C$      2, 4 MP

Note that the argument is stated (lines 1–3 in the above example) in the manner described in Section 9.1. One then proceeds to make the appropriate inferences, assigning a number to each new statement thus derived and justifying each inference by reference to preceding statements and the elementary valid argument form that warrants that inference. Once you have made and justified an inference, the statement thus obtained may be used to make further inferences. When you have succeeded in deriving the conclusion from the premises by a series of such inferences, you have proved that the argument is valid.

We shall now use the elementary valid argument forms to construct formal proofs of two sample arguments. In the course of developing these proofs I will point out several things about the proof-construction process that should be useful to the beginning student. There is no substitute for practice, however, if one wishes to master the process of constructing formal proofs. It is only through practice that one begins to see the less obvious logical connections in the argument and to develop sufficient familiarity with the elementary valid argument forms to recognize quickly situations to which they may be applied.

We begin with the following argument and proof:

1. $A \supset (B \lor C)$
2. $(B \lor C) \supset D$
3. $A \lor E$
4. $E \supset (F \equiv G)$
5. $\sim(F \equiv G) \ / \therefore D$
6. $A \supset D$        1, 2 HS
7. $\sim E$        4, 5 MT
8. $A$        3, 7 DS
9. $D$        6, 8 MP

In order to construct formal proofs of this kind, one must be able to pick out of the argument the statements that could serve as the premises of a valid elementary argument. In the above argument, for example, it is easy to see that statements 1 and 2 can serve as the premises of a hypothetical syllogism: both are conditionals, and the consequent of one is the antecedent of the other. They therefore warrant the inference $A \supset D$, which we then write as statement 6. To the right of statement 6 we write "1, 2 HS," which means, "The statement on this line is derived from statements 1 and 2 by means of the elementary valid argument form 'Hypothetical Syllogism.' " Next we direct our attention to statements 4 and 5. Statement 4 instantiates the statement form $p \supset q$, statement 5 the statement form $\sim q$. They therefore can serve as the premises of a Modus Tollens argument whose conclusion is the statement $\sim E$. We write this as statement 7, noting the premises and the argument form that warrant this inference as before. Statements 3 and 7 now allow us to assert $A$ by Disjunctive Syllogism (statement 8), and statements 6 and 8 give us $D$ by Modus Ponens. Thus we have derived $D$—the conclusion of the argument—from the premises by a series of steps each of which is warranted by an argument form known to be valid, and in so doing we have proved the argument to be valid.

It should be noted that in constructing our proof we are not merely drawing inferences at random: we are looking for those specific inferences that will allow us to deduce the conclusion. In the construction of such a proof it is often helpful to start with the conclusion and work back toward the premises, rather than the reverse. In the case of the above argument, for example, we could imagine a teacher (T) helping a student (S) develop a proof as follows:

T: What is the conclusion of the argument?

S: D.

T: Do you see anything in the premises that would allow you to affirm D?

S: Yes, I can see that if A were true, then D would be true—in other words, $A \supset D$.

T: Very good. Let us then write $A \supset D$ as statement 6, writing the justification for that inference off to the right in the conventional way. Now what?

S: Well, I suppose I ought to look for some way to affirm A.

T: Why?

S: Because I'm trying to find a way to establish D, and if I knew that A were true, that statement in conjunction with statement 6 would establish D by Modus Ponens.

T: Fine. Do you see any way to establish A?

S: Oh, I suppose that's what the other three premises are all about.

T: Come now, you can do better than that. *How* might you derive A from those premises?

S: Well, let's see. If I knew that E were not true, then from that fact and statement 3 I could get A as the conclusion of a Disjunctive Syllogism. Ah! Now I see it: statements 4 and 5 give me ~E by Modus Tollens. I'll make ~E statement 7, and A then follows from statements 3 and 7, as I said before, by Disjunctive Syllogism. I'll make that statement 8. And that gives me D as the conclusion of statements 6 and 8 by Modus Ponens.

T: Bravo! Now let's try some more difficult examples.

S: Please, not today. My head hurts.

Another thing to note about the above argument—and this is true of many arguments—is that it can be proved in more than one way. In constructing a formal proof, one is usually looking for *a* proof, not *the* proof, of the validity of the argument. The above argument, for example, is also shown to be valid by the following formal proof:

$$
\begin{array}{lll}
6. & \sim E & 4, 5 \text{ MT} \\
7. & A & 3, 6 \text{ DS} \\
8. & B \lor C & 1, 7 \text{ MP} \\
9. & D & 2, 8 \text{ MP}
\end{array}
$$

Is one proof better than the other? Possibly, but only in the sense that one (the first one above) is the result of a rational search strategy, whereas the other could be a result of mere trial and error, or even of luck. On the other hand, one might have followed an equally rational search strategy in developing the second proof: "What I want is $D$. I could get that from 1 and 2 if I knew $A$. I could get $A$ from 3 if I knew $\sim E$. Aha! I can get $\sim E$ from 4 and 5. So now let me retrace my steps . . ." The point, in any case, is that so far as possible one should follow a rational search strategy in constructing formal proofs, since an important reason for constructing such proofs is to try to understand *how* the conclusion follows from the premises, not merely to prove that it does.

Our next argument is slightly more difficult to prove, and illustrates further the importance of using a rational search strategy in developing one's proof. Here is the argument:

1. $A \supset (B \supset C)$
2. $(B \supset C) \supset D$
3. $(C \cdot E) \supset \sim F$
4. $\sim F \supset (B \equiv \sim G)$
5. $A \lor (C \cdot E) \: / \therefore \: D \lor (B \equiv \sim G)$

The first fact that should catch our attention as we examine this argument is that the conclusion looks like the conclusion of a Constructive Dilemma: its form is $p \lor q$. What we want, therefore, is a premise in which $D$ is the consequent of one conditional and $B \equiv \sim G$ is the consequent of another. The joining of these two conditionals in a conjunction would then give us the major premise of a Constructive Dilemma. Moreover, statement 5 looks just right to serve as the minor premise of our dilemma provided that $A$ and $C \cdot E$ are the antecedents of our two conditionals. And now the proof is easy: we can get $A \supset D$ from statements 1 and 2, and $(C \cdot E) \supset (B \equiv \sim G)$ from statements 3 and 4. The formal proof, therefore, requires just four steps:

6. $A \supset D$                                        1, 2 HS
7. $(C \cdot E) \supset (B \equiv \sim G)$               3, 4 HS
8. $(A \supset D) \cdot [(C \cdot E) \supset (B \equiv \sim G)]$   6, 7 Conj.
9. $D \lor (B \equiv \sim G)$                           8, 5 CD

Note that the key to finding a formal proof, in this example as in the previous one, is *knowing what we are looking for.* The more complex the argument that we are trying to prove, the more important it becomes not merely to begin drawing random inferences in the hope of hitting by accident on something that works. The construction of formal proofs should, so far as possible, be a matter of insight and skill, not of mere luck.

## EXERCISE 9.5

Stated below are several valid arguments, each followed by a formal proof of validity. Justify each statement in the proof, citing the appropriate preceding statement or statements and elementary valid argument form.

**A.**
1. $K \supset L$
2. $M \supset N$
3. $(L \lor N) \supset Z$
4. $K \lor M$ / $\therefore Z$
5. $(K \supset L) \cdot (M \supset N)$
6. $L \lor N$
7. $Z$

**B.**
1. $W \supset B$
2. $B \supset L$
3. $(W \cdot L) \supset C$
4. $W$ / $\therefore C$
5. $W \supset L$
6. $L$
7. $W \cdot L$
8. $C$

**C.**
1. $A \cdot (B \lor C)$
2. $A \supset \sim B$ / $\therefore C$
3. $A$
4. $\sim B$
5. $B \lor C$
6. $C$

**D.**
1. $(L \supset T) \cdot (\sim L \supset Z)$
2. $\sim T$ / $\therefore Z$
3. $L \supset T$
4. $\sim L$
5. $\sim L \supset Z$
6. $Z$

**E.**
1. $A \lor (S \equiv L)$
2. $(S \equiv L) \supset R$
3. $\sim R$ / $\therefore A$
4. $\sim (S \equiv L)$
5. $A$

**F.**
1. $B \supset V$
2. $R \supset X$
3. $(V \lor X) \supset Q$
4. $B$ / $\therefore Q$
5. $(B \supset V) \cdot (R \supset X)$
6. $B \lor R$
7. $V \lor X$
8. $Q$

**G.**
1. $(A \equiv B) \supset (C \cdot D)$
2. $(C \cdot D) \supset (R \lor Q)$
3. $(A \equiv B) \cdot [(R \supset L) \cdot (Q \supset T)]$
4. $(L \lor T) \supset X$ / $\therefore X$
5. $(A \equiv B) \supset (R \lor Q)$
6. $A \equiv B$
7. $R \lor Q$
8. $(R \supset L) \cdot (Q \supset T)$
9. $L \lor T$
10. $X$

**H.**
1. $(Z \supset H) \supset (I \supset M)$
2. $\sim (Z \supset H) \supset (P \lor Q)$
3. $\sim (I \supset M) \cdot \sim P$ / $\therefore Q$
4. $\sim (I \supset M)$
5. $\sim (Z \supset H)$
6. $P \lor Q$
7. $\sim P$
8. $Q$

**I.**
1. $(R \lor V) \equiv (X \supset Y)$
2. $[(R \lor V) \equiv (X \supset Y)] \supset (L \lor M)$
3. $Q \cdot \sim M$ / $\therefore L$
4. $L \lor M$
5. $\sim M$
6. $L$

**J.**
1. $(B \supset R) \cdot (G \supset P)$
2. $(\sim B \lor \sim G) \supset L$
3. $\sim R$ / $\therefore L$
4. $B \supset R$
5. $\sim B$
6. $\sim B \lor \sim G$
7. $L$

## 9.6 FORMAL PROOFS: LOGICALLY EQUIVALENT STATEMENTS (I)

The elementary argument forms discussed in Sections 9.4 and 9.5 do not by themselves enable us to construct formal proofs for all valid sentential arguments. Consider, for example, the following argument:

**1.** $(A \lor B) \lor C$
**2.** $\sim(B \lor C) / \therefore A$

Although this is in fact a valid argument, we cannot *prove* it to be so merely by appealing to our nine elementary valid argument forms. The problem is that our conclusion appears in the premises only as a component of another statement, and the argument forms discussed thus far provide no way for us to extract it from that context.

The key to the solution of this problem is the fact that, as we have previously noted (Section 8.12), a statement may be replaced by another *logically equivalent* statement at any time. That a statement of one form is logically equivalent to a statement of another form can be established by means of truth tables. Once an equivalence of a definite form has been established, equivalences of that form may be used in the construction of formal proofs. A list of ten such equivalences commonly used in the construction of formal proofs will be given in this section and the next.

In the case of the argument stated above, for example, the statement $(A \lor B) \lor C$ is logically equivalent to the statement $A \lor (B \lor C)$. Once we replace the first premise with its logical equivalent, the resulting argument is easily seen to be a disjunctive syllogism.

The general rule that a statement may be replaced by a logically equivalent statement at any time is called the **Principle of Replacement.** A particular type of logical equivalence that has been authorized for use in the construction of formal proofs is called a **replacement rule.**

Replacement rules are often stated as material equivalences. The **Rule of Association,** for example, states that statements of the form $p \lor (q \lor r)$ are logically equivalent to statements of the form $(p \lor q) \lor r$, and this rule is often stated as follows:

$$[p \lor (q \lor r)] \equiv [(p \lor q) \lor r].$$

To assert that two statements are logically equivalent, however, is not merely to assert that they are materially equivalent; it is to assert that the statement asserting their material equivalence is a tautology. In order to emphasize this important fact about logical equivalences, I will state them not in the above form but as follows:

$[p \lor (q \lor r)]$ is equivalent to $[(p \lor q) \lor r]$.

If one were to state this rule in words instead of symbols, it could be stated as follows: Statements of the forms $p \lor (q \lor r)$ and $(p \lor q) \lor r$ are logically equivalent; either may replace the other in any occurrence.

*The use of replacement rules in constructing formal proofs differs from that of the elementary valid argument forms in that replacement rules may be applied either to a part or to the whole of a compound statement,* whereas rules of inference may be applied only to statements that are not themselves parts of more complex statements. If one knows $P \cdot Q$, for example, one can derive $P$ by Simplification. In this case, one can correctly use this elementary valid argument form. If, however, one's premise is $(P \cdot Q) \supset R$, one cannot apply Simplification to the antecedent only so as to derive $P \supset R$. One can, however, apply a replacement rule (Commutation) to the statement $(P \cdot Q) \supset R$ so as to derive the statement $(Q \cdot P) \supset R$. This important difference between elementary valid argument forms and replacement rules must be kept clearly in mind as we proceed with our discussion of formal proofs.

Ten types of logical equivalence (i.e., ten replacement rules) are commonly used in the construction of formal proofs. Five of them will be introduced in the present section, and their uses in the construction of formal proofs will be explained. The remaining five rules will be discussed in Section 9.7.

The following replacement rules express logically equivalent statement forms. Statements of one form may be substituted for statements of a logically equivalent form at any occurrence:

1. Association (Assoc.)
   $p \lor (q \lor r)$ is equivalent to $(p \lor q) \lor r$
   $p \cdot (q \cdot r)$ is equivalent to $(p \cdot q) \cdot r$
2. Commutation (Com.)
   $p \lor q$ is equivalent to $q \lor p$
   $p \cdot q$ is equivalent to $q \cdot p$
3. Distribution (Dist.)
   $p \cdot (q \lor r)$ is equivalent to $(p \cdot q) \lor (p \cdot r)$
   $p \lor (q \cdot r)$ is equivalent to $(p \lor q) \cdot (p \lor r)$
4. Double Negation (DN)
   $p$ is equivalent to $\sim\sim p$
5. Tautology (Taut.)
   $p \lor p$ is equivalent to $p$
   $p \cdot p$ is equivalent to $p$

Let us look briefly at each of these five types of logical equivalence.

The unique value of **Association (Assoc.)** is that it enables us to change the position of the scope indicators in certain compound statements, that is, to regroup the components. We have already seen an example of how Association can be used in our proof of the argument on page 203. Note in that example that the use of the Rule of Association enables us to isolate $A$ from the compound statement $A \lor B$ and that without such isolation we would not be able to draw any inference simply about $A$.

**Commutation (Com.)** is a simple but extremely useful type of logical equivalence: it enables us to reverse the order of the conjuncts and the disjuncts in conjunctions and disjunctions, respectively. Suppose, for example, that we wish to construct a proof for the following argument:

1. $C \lor (A \lor B)$
2. $\sim(B \lor A) / \therefore C$

The proof, with the aid of Commutation, looks like this:

3. $\sim(A \lor B)$      2 Com.
4. $C$                          1, 3 DS

**Distribution (Dist.)** is a somewhat more complicated type of logical equivalence, but with a bit of pondering you should be able to see that the two statements in each pair really are equivalent. If not, you can easily demonstrate their equivalence with a truth table. One unique value of this type of equivalence is that under certain conditions it enables us to turn a conjunction into a disjunction, or a disjunction into a conjunction. Another is that when we are dealing with a statement that is either the conjunction of two disjunctions or the disjunction of two conjunctions, it enables us to isolate one conjunct or disjunct.

The use of Distribution is illustrated in the following proof:

1. $(A \lor B) \cdot (A \lor C)$
2. $\sim(B \cdot C) / \therefore A$
3. $A \lor (B \cdot C)$       1 Dist.
4. $A$                            3, 2 DS

**Double Negation (DN)** merely enables us to avoid the unnecessary complication of an increasing number of negation signs. The function of the connective $\sim$, as we know, is to negate a statement. To negate $A$, we write $\sim A$. To negate $\sim A$, we write $\sim\sim A$. Theoretically, then, the negation of $\sim\sim A$ should be $\sim\sim\sim A$, and the negation of $\sim\sim\sim A$ should be $\sim\sim\sim\sim A$, and so on to infinity. The rule of Double Negation keeps us out of this infinite regress, and allows us to substitute a statement for its double negation. Thus the number of negation signs need never exceed two.

The usefulness of Double Negation in constructing a formal proof is illustrated by the following example:

1. $\sim A \supset B$
2. $\sim B / \therefore A$
3. $\sim\sim A$          1, 2 MT
4. $A$                      3 DN

The principal value of the two instances of **Tautology (Taut.)** included in our list is that they sometimes enable us to derive a desired conclusion $p$ from a compound statement in which $p$ appears as both elements of a conjunction or a disjunction. This occurs, for example, in the following argument:

1. $A \supset B$
2. $C \supset B$
3. $A \vee C / \therefore B$
4. $(A \supset B) \cdot (C \supset B)$     1, 2 Conj.
5. $B \vee B$     4, 3 CD
6. $B$        5 Taut.

It sometimes also occurs that one is given $p$ as a premise, and one needs $p \vee p$ or $p \cdot p$ to proceed with one's proof. Here is an example:

1. $(A \supset B) \cdot (A \supset C)$
2. $A / \therefore B \vee C$
3. $A \vee A$     2 Taut.
4. $B \vee C$     1, 3 CD

## EXERCISES 9.6

I.    Write from memory the expressions that state the following types of logical equivalence: Association, Commutation, Distribution, Double Negation, Tautology.

II.    Construct truth tables to prove that the rules of Association, Commutation, Distribution, Double Negation, and Tautology do indeed express logical equivalences.

III.   Explain briefly the specific function of each of the above types of equivalence in the construction of formal proofs.

IV.   Stated below are ten valid arguments, each followed by a formal proof of validity. Justify each statement in the proof by reference to the appropriate preceding statement or statements and the appropriate elementary valid argument form or replacement rule.

A.
1. $A \vee (B \cdot C)$
2. $\sim C / \therefore A$
3. $(A \vee B) \cdot (A \vee C)$
4. $A \vee C$
5. $A$

B.
1. $A \supset B$
2. $C \supset D$
3. $C \vee A$
4. $(B \vee D) \supset R / \therefore R$
5. $(A \supset B) \cdot (C \supset D)$
6. $A \vee C$
7. $B \vee D$
8. $R$

C.
1. $A \supset [B \vee (C \vee D)]$
2. $A \cdot \sim C / \therefore B \vee D$
3. $A$
4. $B \vee (C \vee D)$
5. $B \vee (D \vee C)$
6. $(B \vee D) \vee C$
7. $\sim C$
8. $B \vee D$

D.
1. $A \vee \sim C$
2. $A \supset R$
3. $C / \therefore C \cdot R$
4. $\sim\sim C$
5. $A$

      6. $R$

      7. $C \cdot R$

**E.**   1. $(P \supset Q) \cdot (P \supset R)$

      2. $P \cdot [(R \lor Q) \supset S] \: / \therefore S \lor T$

      3. $P$

      4. $P \lor P$

      5. $Q \lor R$

      6. $R \lor Q$

      7. $(R \lor Q) \supset S$

      8. $S$

      9. $S \lor T$

**F.**   1. $(S \supset L) \cdot (F \supset L)$

      2. $(S \lor F) \cdot (L \supset M) \: / \therefore M$

      3. $S \lor F$

      4. $L \lor L$

      5. $L$

      6. $L \supset M$

      7. $M$

**G.**   1. $(C \cdot T) \lor (C \cdot M)$

      2. $\sim M \: / \therefore T \cdot (C \lor L)$

      3. $C \cdot (T \lor M)$

      4. $T \lor M$

      5. $T$

      6. $C$

      7. $C \lor L$

      8. $T \cdot (C \lor L)$

**H.**   1. $(A \lor B) \supset D$

      2. $A \lor (B \lor \sim C)$

      3. $C \: / \therefore D$

      4. $(A \lor B) \lor \sim C$

      5. $\sim\sim C$

      6. $A \lor B$

      7. $D$

**I.**   1. $(P \supset Q) \cdot (R \supset S)$

      2. $P \lor (T \cdot R)$

      3. $(Q \supset Z) \cdot \sim S \: / \therefore Z$

      4. $(P \lor T) \cdot (P \lor R)$

      5. $P \lor R$

      6. $Q \lor S$

      7. $\sim S$

      8. $Q$

      9. $Q \supset Z$

    10. $Z$

**J.**   1. $C \supset (V \lor \sim X)$

      2. $A \cdot (B \cdot C)$

      3. $X \: / \therefore V \lor R$

      4. $(A \cdot B) \cdot C$

      5. $C$

      6. $V \lor \sim X$

      7. $\sim\sim X$

      8. $V$

      9. $V \lor R$

**V.** The arguments stated below are valid. Construct a formal proof of validity for each argument, using elementary valid argument forms and replacement rules as appropriate.

**A.**   1. $B \supset (M \lor X)$

      2. $(M \lor X) \lor Q$

      3. $\sim(Q \lor X) \: / \therefore M \lor X$

**B.**   1. $M \lor N$

      2. $M \lor O$

      3. $(M \supset S) \cdot \sim(N \cdot O) \: / \therefore S$

**C.**   1. $D \cdot (M \lor J)$

      2. $\sim J \lor \sim D$

      3. $R \supset \sim M \: / \therefore \sim R$

**D.**   1. $(M \lor \sim N) \lor (R \supset Q)$

      2. $N \cdot \sim M$

      3. $R \: / \therefore Q$

**E.**   1. $(A \lor B) \cdot C$

      2. $(C \cdot A) \supset R$

      3. $\sim(B \cdot C) \: / \therefore R$

**F.**   1. $(M \cdot R) \lor (M \cdot P)$

      2. $\sim R \: / \therefore P$

**G.**   1. $(A \supset R) \cdot (A \supset P)$

      2. $(X \supset A) \cdot X \: / \therefore R \lor P$

**H.**   1. $(A \supset K) \cdot (C \supset L)$

      2. $A \lor (B \cdot C) \: / \therefore K \lor L$

**I.**   1. $(K \lor R) \supset (Z \lor \sim L)$

      2. $K \cdot L \: / \therefore Z$

**J.**   1. $M \lor (G \cdot B)$

      2. $\sim G \supset (M \supset R)$

      3. $\sim G \: / \therefore R$

# 9.7 FORMAL PROOFS: LOGICALLY EQUIVALENT STATEMENTS (II)

The remaining five logical equivalences, numbered in sequence with those discussed in Section 9.6, are as follows:

6. De Morgan's Theorems (De M.)
   $\sim(p \cdot q)$ is equivalent to $\sim p \vee \sim q$
   $\sim(p \vee q)$ is equivalent to $\sim p \cdot \sim q$
7. Exportation (Exp.)
   $(p \cdot q) \supset r$ is equivalent to $p \supset (q \supset r)$
8. Transposition (Trans.)
   $p \supset q$ is equivalent to $\sim q \supset \sim p$
9. Material Implication (Impl.)
   $p \supset q$ is equivalent to $\sim p \vee q$
   $p \supset q$ is equivalent to $\sim(p \cdot \sim q)$
10. Material Equivalence (Equiv.)
    $p \equiv q$ is equivalent to $(p \supset q) \cdot (q \supset p)$
    $p \equiv q$ is equivalent to $(p \cdot q) \vee (\sim p \cdot \sim q)$

**De Morgan's Theorems (De M.)** are enormously important in the construction of formal proofs. Note carefully what they assert. The first theorem asserts that the negation of a conjunction is logically equivalent to the disjunction of the negations of the conjuncts. The second theorem asserts that the negation of a disjunction is logically equivalent to the conjunction of the negations of the disjuncts. In constructing formal proofs, therefore, De Morgan's Theorems can be used to change certain kinds of conjunctions into logically equivalent disjunctions, and vice versa. Note, for example, the role played by De M. in the following proof:

1. $\sim(A \vee B) \supset C$
2. $\sim A$
3. $\sim B$ / $\therefore C$
4. $\sim A \cdot \sim B$      2, 3 Conj.
5. $\sim(A \vee B)$      4 De M.
6. $C$      1, 5 MP

**Exportation (Exp.)** provides a way to change the form of certain types of compound statements (those specified in the rule) so as to isolate various members of the compound, thus making them available for further logical manipulation. The following proof illustrates the use of this logical equivalence:

1. $A \supset (B \supset C)$
2. $\sim C$ / $\therefore \sim A \vee \sim B$
3. $(A \cdot B) \supset C$      1 Exp.
4. $\sim(A \cdot B)$      3, 2 MT
5. $\sim A \vee \sim B$      4 De M.

**Transposition (Trans.)** enables us to reverse the position of the

antecedent and the consequent of any conditional by merely negating
both terms. This rule is especially helpful when a conditional appears
as part of a more complex statement, since in such a case Modus
Tollens cannot be applied to derive the negation of the antecedent
from the negation of the consequent. Here is an example:

1. $\sim B \supset (A \supset C)$
2. $(\sim A \supset D) \cdot \sim B / \therefore \sim D \supset C$
3. $\sim B$                        2 Simp.
4. $A \supset C$              1, 3 MP
5. $\sim C \supset \sim A$        4 Trans.
6. $\sim A \supset D$           2 Simp.
7. $\sim C \supset D$           5, 6 HS
8. $\sim D \supset \sim\sim C$      7 Trans.
9. $\sim D \supset C$           8 DN

**Material Implication (Impl.)** is one of the most useful types of
logical equivalence in the construction of formal proofs. Note what
it does: it enables us to change certain conjunctions, disjunctions,
and conditionals into either of the other two types of compound
statement. The following proof illustrates its use:

1. $A \supset \sim B$
2. $\sim B \supset \sim C$
3. $D \lor C / \therefore \sim A \lor D$
4. $A \supset \sim C$         1, 2 HS
5. $C \lor D$              3 Com.
6. $\sim\sim C \lor D$         5 DN
7. $\sim C \supset D$          6 Impl.
8. $A \supset D$            4, 7 HS
9. $\sim A \lor D$      ·     8 Impl.

**Material Equivalence (Equiv.)** enables us to "unpack" statements that assert material equivalence into simpler statements that
may then be used in the formal proof process. A statement of Material
Equivalence—$A \equiv B$, for example—contains much more information
than appears on the surface. The restatements authorized by our two
statements of logical equivalence enable us to get at this information.
An example of the application of this type of logical equivalence
appears in the following proof:

1. $\sim A \lor (B \cdot C)$
2. $A \equiv D$
3. $\sim C / \therefore \sim D$
4. $(\sim A \lor B) \cdot (\sim A \lor C)$     1 Dist.

$$5.\ (\sim\!A \lor B) \cdot (A \supset C) \qquad \text{4 Impl.}$$
$$6.\ A \supset C \qquad\qquad\qquad \text{5 Simp.}$$
$$7.\ \sim\!A \qquad\qquad\qquad\quad \text{6, 3 MT}$$
$$8.\ (A \supset D) \cdot (D \supset A) \qquad \text{2 Equiv.}$$
$$9.\ D \supset A \qquad\qquad\qquad \text{8 Simp.}$$
$$10.\ \sim\!D \qquad\qquad\qquad\quad \text{9, 7 MT}$$

The nine elementary valid argument forms discussed in Section 9.4 together with the ten types of logical equivalence discussed in Sections 9.6 and 9.7 constitute a complete system of truth-functional logic. By this I mean that it is theoretically possible to prove the validity of any valid truth-functional argument by the use of this system. Indeed, we could eliminate some elements of the system and still be able to develop proofs for all valid truth-functional arguments. We could, for example, eliminate Modus Tollens or Transposition (but not both). Since Commutation is available to enable us to reverse the order of the constituents of any conjunction or disjunction, we also do not really need two forms of Disjunctive Syllogism or of Simplification; one form of each would suffice. The inferences involved are so intuitively obvious, however, that it seems silly not to include them in our list of authorized steps to use in the construction of formal proofs. The effect of including them is to simplify (i.e., to shorten) the proofs in which they are employed.

## EXERCISES 9.7

I.  Write from memory the expressions that state the following types of logical equivalence: De Morgan's Theorems, Exportation, Transposition, Material Implication, Material Equivalence.

II.  Construct truth tables to prove that De Morgan's Theorems, Exportation, Transposition, Material Implication, and Material Equivalence do indeed express logical equivalences.

III.  Explain briefly the function of each of the above types of equivalence in the construction of formal proofs.

IV.  Stated below are ten valid arguments, each followed by a formal proof of validity. Justify each statement in the proof by reference to the appropriate preceding statement or statements and the appropriate elementary valid argument form or replacement rule.

**A.**
1. $A \supset (B \supset \sim\!C)$
2. $A \cdot B\ /\ \therefore C \supset D$
3. $(A \cdot B) \supset \sim\!C$
4. $\sim\!C$
5. $\sim\!C \lor D$
6. $C \supset D$

**B.**
1. $A \lor [B \supset (C \supset D)]$
2. $\sim\!A\ /\ \therefore C \supset (B \supset D)$
3. $B \supset (C \supset D)$
4. $(B \cdot C) \supset D$
5. $(C \cdot B) \supset D$
6. $C \supset (B \supset D)$

**C.**
1. $V \equiv (X \supset Y)$
2. $V$ / $\therefore X \supset (Y \lor Z)$
3. $[V \supset (X \supset Y)] \cdot [(X \supset Y) \supset V]$
4. $V \supset (X \supset Y)$
5. $X \supset Y$
6. $(X \supset Y) \lor Z$
7. $(\sim X \lor Y) \lor Z$
8. $\sim X \lor (Y \lor Z)$
9. $X \supset (Y \lor Z)$

**D.**
1. $K \supset (L \lor M)$
2. $K \cdot \sim L$ / $\therefore R \supset M$
3. $K$
4. $L \lor M$
5. $\sim L$
6. $M$
7. $M \lor \sim R$
8. $\sim R \lor M$
9. $R \supset M$

**E.**
1. $A \supset (B \cdot C)$
2. $\sim B$ / $\therefore \sim A$
3. $\sim A \lor (B \cdot C)$
4. $(\sim A \lor B) \cdot (\sim A \lor C)$
5. $\sim A \lor B$
6. $\sim A$

**F.**
1. $K \supset [L \supset (M \cdot N)]$
2. $K$ / $\therefore (L \supset M) \cdot (L \supset N)$
3. $L \supset (M \cdot N)$
4. $\sim L \lor (M \cdot N)$
5. $(\sim L \lor M) \cdot (\sim L \lor N)$
6. $(\sim L \lor M) \cdot (L \supset N)$
7. $(L \supset M) \cdot (L \supset N)$

**G.**
1. $K \supset (L \cdot M)$
2. $N \supset (\sim L \lor \sim M)$
3. $(N \cdot R) \cdot (K \lor O)$ / $\therefore O$
4. $N \cdot R$
5. $N$
6. $\sim L \lor \sim M$
7. $\sim (L \cdot M)$
8. $\sim K$
9. $K \lor O$
10. $O$

**H.**
1. $(M \lor R) \supset (P \supset X)$
2. $M \cdot P$ / $\therefore (P \cdot Q) \supset X$
3. $M$
4. $M \lor R$
5. $P \supset X$
6. $\sim P \lor X$
7. $(\sim P \lor X) \lor \sim Q$
8. $\sim Q \lor (\sim P \lor X)$
9. $(\sim Q \lor P) \lor X$
10. $\sim (Q \cdot P) \lor X$
11. $(Q \cdot P) \supset X$
12. $(P \cdot Q) \supset X$

**I.**
1. $\sim A \lor [B \supset (C \cdot D)]$
2. $A$ / $\therefore B \supset D$
3. $A \supset [B \supset (C \cdot D)]$
4. $B \supset (C \cdot D)$
5. $\sim B \lor (C \cdot D)$
6. $(\sim B \lor C) \cdot (\sim B \lor D)$
7. $\sim B \lor D$
8. $B \supset D$

**J.**
1. $A \lor [(B \lor C) \supset D]$
2. $\sim A$ / $\therefore C \supset D$
3. $(B \lor C) \supset D$
4. $\sim D \supset \sim (B \lor C)$
5. $\sim D \supset (\sim B \cdot \sim C)$
6. $\sim \sim D \lor (\sim B \cdot \sim C)$
7. $D \lor (\sim B \cdot \sim C)$
8. $(D \lor \sim B) \cdot (D \lor \sim C)$
9. $D \lor \sim C$
10. $\sim C \lor D$
11. $C \supset D$

**V.** All of the arguments stated below are valid. Construct a formal proof of validity for each.

**A.**
1. $(A \cdot B) \supset C$
2. $\sim C$ / $\therefore \sim A \lor \sim B$

**B.**
1. $(M \lor O) \supset R$
2. $\sim R$ / $\therefore \sim M$

**C.**
1. $(\sim M \lor P) \lor R$
2. $M$ / $\therefore P \lor R$

**D.**
1. $X \supset \sim (R \cdot \sim Z)$
2. $X$ / $\therefore R \supset Z$

**E.**
1. $K \supset (L \supset M)$
2. $\sim M$ / $\therefore \sim K \lor \sim L$

**F.**
1. $Z \equiv L$
2. $\sim L$ / $\therefore \sim Z \lor R$

**G.**
1. $(R \supset K) \cdot (\sim R \supset Z)$
2. $\sim K$ / $\therefore Z$

**H.**
1. $R \lor (L \cdot Z)$
2. $\sim Z$ / $\therefore R$

**I.**
1. $(L \cdot M) \supset K$
2. $\sim K$ / $\therefore \sim (M \cdot L)$

**J.**
1. $(L \lor R) \supset Q$
2. $(Q \supset E) \cdot \sim E$ / $\therefore \sim R$

**K.**
1. $(B \lor S) \supset (K \equiv L)$
2. $K \cdot \sim L$ / $\therefore \sim B$

**L.** 1. $D \supset \sim(E \lor F)$
    2. $(E \lor F) \cdot (\sim D \supset R) / \therefore R$

**M.** 1. $(G \supset K) \lor \sim(L \cdot M)$
    2. $G \cdot \sim K / \therefore \sim L \lor \sim M$

**N.** 1. $L \supset (R \supset Z)$
    2. $(Z \supset K) \cdot \sim K / \therefore R \supset \sim L$

**O.** 1. $(A \supset B) \cdot (C \supset B)$
    2. $\sim B / \therefore \sim A \cdot \sim C$

**P.** 1. $(A \equiv B) \supset \sim L$

    2. $(A \supset B) \cdot (B \supset A) / \therefore L \supset K$

**Q.** 1. $Z \supset (L \supset R)$
    2. $(L \lor K) \cdot \sim K / \therefore Z \supset R$

**R.** 1. $Z \supset [(S \lor L) \supset M]$
    2. $(\sim B \lor Z) \cdot B / \therefore S \supset M$

**S.** 1. $G \equiv [(A \lor B) \supset R]$
    2. $G / \therefore B \supset R$

**T.** 1. $\sim A \lor [(K \supset L) \cdot (R \supset L)]$
    2. $A / \therefore (K \lor R) \supset L$

# 9.8 REDUCTIO AD ABSURDUM (RAA) PROOFS

An alternative proof strategy that can be used to prove the validity of any valid truth-functional sentential argument is the **Reductio Ad Absurdum (RAA)** proof. It is similar to the abbreviated truth-table method (Section 9.3) in that it attempts to show that the assumption that the premises of a given argument are true and the conclusion false leads to an absurdity, that is, a contradiction. It differs from that method, however, in that it uses the formal proof apparatus introduced in Sections 9.4–9.7 rather than the assignment of truth-table values to achieve its purpose.

If an argument is valid, it is impossible—logically impossible—for the premises to be true and the conclusion false. If, then, we make the provisional assumption that the premises are true and the conclusion false, it should be possible to show (in the case of a valid argument) that the result is a contradiction, that is, a statement of the form $p \cdot \sim p$. This is precisely what an RAA proof attempts to do.

One conventional way of stating such a proof is illustrated in the following example:

    1. $\sim A \lor (B \cdot C)$
    2. $A \equiv D$
    3. $\sim C / \therefore \sim D$

| | | |
|---|---|---|
| | 4. $\sim\sim D$ | AP |
| | 5. $D$ | 4 DN |
| | 6. $(A \supset D) \cdot (D \supset A)$ | 2 Equiv. |
| | 7. $D \supset A$ | 6 Simp. |
| RAA | 8. $A$ | 7, 5 MP |
| | 9. $\sim\sim A$ | 8 DN |
| | 10. $B \cdot C$ | 1, 9 DS |
| | 11. $C$ | 10 Simp. |
| | 12. $C \cdot \sim C$ | 11, 3 Conj. |
| | 13. $\sim D$ | 4–12 RAA |

The letters "AP" at line 4 stand for "assumed premise." In an RAA proof the assumed premise is always the negation ( = contradictory) of the statement that is to be established (usually the conclusion). That this is a Reductio Ad Absurdum proof is indicated by the bracketed line separating (in this example) lines 4–12 from the remaining lines, and the letters "RAA" to the left of that line. Within the RAA proof, the elementary valid argument forms and logical equivalences are used in exactly the same ways they are used in ordinary formal proofs. The RAA proof continues until we have succeeded in deriving a contradiction (line 12 in our example). The contradictory of the assumed premise is then justified (line 13) on the basis of the success of our RAA proof in lines 4–12.

RAA proofs can also be used to establish intermediate conclusions. One would typically use RAA in this way if, in the course of attempting to construct a formal proof in the normal manner, one were having difficulty deriving some statement that one needed for one's proof. Here is an example of such a use of RAA:

1. $K \supset (L \cdot M)$
2. $(L \vee N) \supset R$
3. $K \vee N \, / \therefore \sim L \supset R$

$$
\begin{array}{lll}
\quad\; 4. & \sim R & \text{AP} \\
\quad\; 5. & \sim (L \vee N) & \text{2, 4 MT} \\
\quad\; 6. & \sim L \cdot \sim N & \text{5 De M.} \\
\quad\; 7. & \sim N & \text{6 Simp.} \\
\text{RAA } 8. & K & \text{3, 7 DS} \\
\quad\; 9. & L \cdot M & \text{1, 8 MP} \\
10. & L & \text{9 Simp.} \\
11. & \sim L & \text{6 Simp.} \\
12. & L \cdot \sim L & \text{10, 11 Conj.} \\
13. & R & \text{4–12 RAA} \\
14. & R \vee L & \text{13 Add.} \\
15. & L \vee R & \text{14 Com.} \\
16. & \sim L \supset R & \text{15 Impl.}
\end{array}
$$

Note that the only purpose of RAA is to establish the statement that occurs immediately following the RAA proof. The above proof shows, for example, that the assumption that $R$ is false (statement 4) in conjunction with the premises of the argument leads to a contradiction (statement 12). That is all it shows. It justifies the assertion of $R$ (statement 13), nothing more. *The statements that occur in the course of an RAA proof are not available for further inferences,* since those statements are derived from the assumption—an assumption that the RAA proof has shown to be false—that the statement provisionally asserted at the beginning of the RAA proof is true.

One advantage of this method of proof is that *any* contradiction that one can produce (assuming that there is no contradiction in the premises) will prove the negation of the assumed premise with which the RAA proof begins, and if one makes enough inferences one is likely eventually to stumble upon at least one contradiction (if the argument is indeed valid). It is therefore a useful alternative to ordinary formal proofs, especially when one is having difficulty finding a proof of the other type.

## EXERCISES 9.8

I.  Explain the concept of a Reductio Ad Absurdum (RAA) proof.
II. Justify each step in the following RAA proofs:

A.  1. $(A \supset B) \cdot (C \supset B)$
    2. $(A \vee C) \cdot (B \supset D)$ / $\therefore D$
    RAA
    3. $\sim D$
    4. $B \supset D$
    5. $\sim D \supset \sim B$
    6. $\sim B$
    7. $A \vee C$
    8. $B \vee B$
    9. $B$
    10. $B \cdot \sim B$
    11. $D$

B.  1. $(A \supset B) \cdot (C \supset D)$
    2. $C \vee A$
    3. $(B \vee D) \supset R$ / $\therefore R$
    RAA
    4. $\sim R$
    5. $\sim R \supset \sim(B \vee D)$
    6. $\sim(B \vee D)$
    7. $A \vee C$
    8. $B \vee D$
    9. $(B \vee D) \cdot \sim(B \vee D)$
    10. $R$

C.  1. $X \vee (Y \cdot Z)$
    2. $\sim Z$ / $\therefore X$
    RAA
    3. $\sim X$
    4. $Y \cdot Z$
    5. $Z$
    6. $Z \cdot \sim Z$
    7. $X$

D.  1. $(A \supset N) \cdot (L \supset M)$
    2. $A$ / $\therefore N \vee M$
    RAA
    3. $\sim(N \vee M)$
    4. $\sim N \cdot \sim M$
    5. $\sim N$
    6. $A \supset N$

      7. $N$
      8. $N \cdot \sim N$
      9. $N \vee M$

**E.**  1. $(R \supset X) \cdot (R \supset Z)$
     2. $R \cdot [(Z \vee X) \supset Y] / \therefore Y \vee M$
     3. $\sim(Y \vee M)$
     4. $\sim Y \cdot \sim M$
     5. $\sim Y$
     6. $R$
RAA  7. $R \vee R$
     8. $X \vee Z$
     9. $Z \vee X$
    10. $(Z \vee X) \supset Y$
    11. $Y$
    12. $Y \cdot \sim Y$
    13. $Y \vee M$

**F.**  1. $(M \vee B) \supset R$
     2. $M \vee (B \vee \sim K)$
     3. $K / \therefore R$
     4. $\sim R$
     5. $\sim R \supset \sim (M \vee B)$
     6. $\sim(M \vee B)$
     7. $\sim M \cdot \sim B$
RAA  8. $\sim M$
     9. $B \vee \sim K$
    10. $\sim B$
    11. $\sim K$
    12. $K \cdot \sim K$
    13. $R$

**G.**  1. $F \vee (G \cdot H)$
     2. $(G \cdot \sim H) \cdot (F \supset R) / \therefore R$
     3. $\sim R$
     4. $F \supset R$
     5. $\sim F$
     6. $G \cdot H$
RAA  7. $G \cdot \sim H$
     8. $H$
     9. $\sim H$
    10. $H \cdot \sim H$
    11. $R$

**H.**  1. $L \supset [M \vee (N \vee O)]$
     2. $L \cdot \sim N / \therefore M \vee O$
     3. $\sim(M \vee O)$
     4. $\sim M \cdot \sim O$
     5. $L$
     6. $M \vee (N \vee O)$
RAA  7. $\sim M$
     8. $N \vee O$

$$9. \ \sim O$$
$$10. \ N$$
$$11. \ \sim N$$
$$12. \ N \cdot \sim N$$
$$\overline{13. \ M \vee O}$$

I.   1. $(A \supset R) \cdot (\sim A \supset L)$
    2. $\sim R \ / \therefore L$
    3. $\sim L$
    4. $\sim A \supset L$
    5. $\sim \sim A$
RAA   6. $A$
    7. $A \supset R$
    8. $R$
    9. $R \cdot \sim R$
    10. $L$

J.   1. $(A \vee Z) \supset L$
    2. $\sim L \ / \therefore \sim A$
    3. $\sim \sim A$
    4. $A$
RAA   5. $A \vee Z$
    6. $L$
    7. $L \cdot \sim L$
    8. $\sim A$

**III.**   Construct an RAA proof for each of the arguments in Exercises 9.7, Part V (pp. 211–212).

# 9.9 CONDITIONAL PROOF (CP)

One other type of formal proof that is useful in proving the validity of certain kinds of arguments is the Conditional Proof. A **Conditional Proof (CP)** can be used only to establish a conditional, that is, a statement of the form $p \supset q$. The concept of this type of proof is very simple: if the premises of an argument do indeed establish a statement of the form $p \supset q$, then those premises in conjunction with $p$ must establish $q$. In a Conditional Proof, therefore, we assume the antecedent of the conditional that we are attempting to derive as an additional premise, and attempt to derive the consequent. If we succeed, we have proved that the conditional follows from the premises alone. A Conditional Proof may be thought of as the application of the principle of Exportation to an entire argument: if $(p \cdot q) \supset r$ ($p$ being the conjunction of the premises of the argument and $q$ the antecedent of the conclusion), then $p \supset (q \supset r)$.

The following proof illustrates the application of this method:

1. $(A \lor B) \supset C$
2. $D \supset A$
3. $E \supset B$
4. $F \supset (D \lor E) / \therefore F \supset C$

CP
5. $F$ — AP
6. $D \lor E$ — 4, 5 MP
7. $(D \supset A) \cdot (E \supset B)$ — 2, 3 Conj.
8. $A \lor B$ — 7, 6 CD
9. $C$ — 1, 8 MP
10. $F \supset C$ — 5–9 CP

Although Conditional Proofs can be used only to establish conditionals, they are more useful than this limitation may seem to indicate. Like RAA proofs, they can be used to establish intermediate conclusions as well as the final conclusion of an argument. Moreover, as previously noted, certain disjunctions and conjunctions are logically equivalent to certain conditionals. Thus the above argument, for example, also establishes $\sim F \lor C$ and $\sim (F \cdot \sim C)$, both of which are logically equivalent to $F \supset C$. Had the conclusion been stated in one of these equivalent forms, we could still have used our Conditional Proof to establish $F \supset C$, and then simply added one more step to state the equivalence between $F \supset C$ and the conclusion of the argument.

The use of a Conditional Proof to establish an intermediate conclusion is illustrated by the following example:

1. $(T \lor U) \supset V$
2. $(W \supset T) \cdot (X \supset U)$
3. $Y \supset (W \lor X)$
4. $(Y \supset V) \supset Z / \therefore Z$

CP
5. $Y$ — AP
6. $W \lor X$ — 3, 5 MP
7. $T \lor U$ — 2, 6 CD
8. $V$ — 1, 7 MP
9. $Y \supset V$ — 5–8 CP
10. $Z$ — 4, 9 MP

Note well: the statement immediately following a Conditional Proof must always be a conditional whose antecedent is the assumed premise and whose consequent is the last statement of the Conditional Proof. Note also that as with RAA proofs, the statements that appear in the bracketed portion of the proof *are not* available for subsequent inferences. The sole function of a Conditional Proof is to establish the conditional that is stated immediately after the proof. Only the conditional itself is available for further inferences, as indicated by the fact that it appears outside the line that marks off the Conditional Proof.

The principal value of the method of Conditional Proof is that it sometimes enables one to prove in a few steps an argument that would otherwise require a more extended proof. Strictly speaking, the method of Conditional Proof is expendable: any argument that can be shown to be valid by a Conditional Proof can also be shown to be valid by an ordinary formal proof. CP is merely a refinement of the method of formal proof, an alternative method that one may use under certain circumstances if one chooses to do so.

## EXERCISES 9.9

I.    Explain the concept of a Conditional Proof (CP).
II.   Justify each step in the following proofs:

**A.**   1. $(A \supset K) \cdot (L \supset R)$
          2. $(A \vee L) \cdot \sim K$
          3. $R \supset M / \therefore L \supset M$

CP
          4. $L$
          5. $L \supset R$
          6. $R$
          7. $M$
          8. $L \supset M$

**B.**   1. $R \supset (L \supset Z)$
          2. $(L \vee M) \cdot \sim M / \therefore R \supset Z$
          3. $R$

CP
          4. $L \supset Z$
          5. $L \vee M$
          6. $\sim M$
          7. $L$
          8. $Z$
          9. $R \supset Z$

**C.**   1. $L \supset (\sim B \vee \sim C)$
          2. $M \supset (B \cdot C) / \therefore L \supset \sim M$
          3. $L$

CP
          4. $\sim B \vee \sim C$
          5. $\sim(B \cdot C)$
          6. $\sim M$
          7. $L \supset \sim M$

**D.**   1. $[(A \cdot B) \cdot C] \supset D$
          2. $E \supset [(C \cdot A) \cdot B] / \therefore E \supset D$
          3. $E$

CP
          4. $(C \cdot A) \cdot B$
          5. $C \cdot (A \cdot B)$
          6. $(A \cdot B) \cdot C$

        7. $D$
        8. $E \supset D$

**E.**   1. $L \vee (X \cdot {\sim}Z)$
       2. $(L \vee X) \supset (Y \vee {\sim}Z) \,/\therefore Z \supset Y$
       3. $Z$
       4. $(L \vee X) \cdot (L \vee {\sim}Z)$
       5. $L \vee {\sim}Z$
       6. ${\sim}{\sim}Z$
CP    7. $L$
       8. $L \vee X$
       9. $Y \vee {\sim}Z$
    10. $Y$
    11. $Z \supset Y$

**F.**   1. ${\sim}A \supset ({\sim}B \supset {\sim}C)$
       2. $D \supset (C \cdot {\sim}A) \,/\therefore D \supset B$
       3. $D$
       4. $C \cdot {\sim}A$
       5. ${\sim}A$
       6. ${\sim}B \supset {\sim}C$
CP    7. ${\sim}{\sim}C \supset {\sim}{\sim}B$
       8. $C \supset {\sim}{\sim}B$
       9. $C \supset B$
    10. $C$
    11. $B$
    12. $D \supset B$

**G.**   1. $(A \supset B) \vee {\sim}(C \cdot D)$
       2. $A \cdot {\sim}B \,/\therefore {\sim}C \vee {\sim}D$
       3. ${\sim}(A \cdot {\sim}B) \vee {\sim}(C \cdot D)$
       4. ${\sim}{\sim}(A \cdot {\sim}B)$
       5. ${\sim}(C \cdot D)$
       6. $C$
       7. ${\sim}C \vee {\sim}D$
CP    8. ${\sim}{\sim}C$
       9. ${\sim}D$
    10. $C \supset {\sim}D$
    11. ${\sim}C \vee {\sim}D$

**H.**   1. $W \supset B$
       2. $(W \cdot B) \supset F \,/\therefore {\sim}W \vee F$
       3. $W$
       4. $B$
CP    5. $W \cdot B$
       6. $F$
       7. $W \supset F$
       8. ${\sim}W \vee F$

**I.**   1. $(P \supset {\sim}L) \cdot (P \vee R)$
       2. $(R \supset S) \cdot (R \vee P) \,/\therefore L \supset S$
       3. $L$
       4. $P \supset {\sim}L$

CP
5. $\sim\sim L$
6. $\sim P$
7. $P \vee R$
8. $R$
9. $R \supset S$
10. $S$
11. $L \supset S$

J.
1. $A \supset [B \supset (C \vee D)]$
2. $\sim D / \therefore \sim C \supset (\sim A \vee \sim B)$
3. $(A \cdot B) \supset (C \vee D)$

CP
4. $A \cdot B$
5. $C \vee D$
6. $C$
7. $(A \cdot B) \supset C$
8. $\sim C \supset \sim(A \cdot B)$
9. $\sim C \supset (\sim A \vee \sim B)$

III. Construct a formal proof of validity for each of the following arguments, using a Conditional Proof at least once in the course of each proof.

**A.**
1. $(A \supset B) \cdot [B \supset \sim(J \cdot K)]$
2. $J / \therefore A \supset \sim K$

**B.**
1. $(J \supset K) \cdot (\sim J \supset R)$
2. $R \supset X / \therefore \sim K \supset X$

**C.**
1. $B \supset (R \vee W)$
2. $\sim R / \therefore \sim W \supset \sim B$

**D.**
1. $C \equiv (D \vee E)$
2. $\sim D / \therefore E \vee \sim C$

**E.**
1. $(B \vee W) \supset (L \vee F)$
2. $\sim L / \therefore F \vee \sim(B \vee W)$

**F.**
1. $A \vee (B \vee C)$
2. $\sim C / \therefore \sim B \supset A$

**G.**
1. $(A \cdot C) \supset \sim B$
2. $B \vee (K \cdot L)$
3. $A \supset C / \therefore \sim K \supset (\sim A \vee \sim C)$

**H.**
1. $(L \vee K) \cdot C$
2. $\sim B \supset \sim (K \cdot C)$
3. $C \supset (L \supset \sim S) / \therefore S \supset B$

**I.**
1. $[(A \vee B) \cdot C] \supset D$
2. $(C \supset D) \supset (E \supset K)$
3. $E / \therefore A \supset K$

**J.**
1. $[(P \vee Q) \cdot R] \supset L$
2. $(R \supset L) \supset (H \supset M)$
3. $H / \therefore P \supset M$

# ten
# Predicate Arguments

We have now studied two somewhat different systems of deductive logic: syllogistic logic, in which the validity of arguments depends entirely on relations of inclusion and exclusion between and among the "classes" designated by the subject and predicate terms (Chapters 5–7), and a type of symbolic logic, in which the validity of arguments depends entirely on the relations of truth and falsity between and among the component statements (Chapters 8 and 9). One might reasonably ask at this point: Is there not some way to bring these two together? Cannot the rules of right reasoning be shown to constitute *one single system* rather than two quite different and apparently unrelated systems? The answer to both questions is yes. This unified system consists, as we shall see, in a relatively simple extension of the system of symbolic logic introduced in Chapters 8 and 9.

## 10.1 LOGICAL SUBJECTS AND LOGICAL PREDICATES

It will be recalled that in traditional syllogistic logic the subject and predicate terms of statements are thought of as designating *classes* of objects: "All birds are feathered," for example, is construed to mean **221**

"All members of the class of birds are members of the class of things that are feathered," "All dogs bark" is construed to mean "All members of the class of dogs are members of the class of things that bark," and so on.

There is a certain obvious artificiality about construing statements in this way. The most natural way of understanding the above statements, for example, is simply to think of the subject birds as having the quality or characteristic of being feathered, the subject dogs as engaging in the activity of barking, and so on. In ordinary thought and discourse, we distinguish between that *about which* we are thinking or speaking—our logical subject—and that which we say or think *about* it—our logical predicate—but we do not typically conjure up classes to correspond to our subject and predicate terms. It is merely a requirement of the system of traditional logic, not of thought or reasoning itself, that we divide up the world into classes as traditional logic taught us to do.

In the unified system of logic we shall have no need for the concept of classes. We shall, however, retain the concepts of logical subject and logical predicate. A **logical subject** is merely something—anything—about which a statement is made. It may be an individual (John, this house, my hat, that theory) or a group of individuals (dogs, tools, ideas, dreams). A **logical predicate** is anything that is said about a logical subject—that it has a certain characteristic or certain characteristics (that it is red, or large, or bigger than a breadbox, or oblong and wrinkled), or that it is doing something (flying, shrinking, aging, enduring), or that it is situated in such-and-such a place (up in the sky, behind my left ear), or that something is happening to it (that it is being moved, or thrown, or interrogated), or whatever. In short, *anything that can be asserted about anything* will qualify as a logical predicate.

## 10.2 SINGULAR STATEMENTS

When the logical subject of a statement is a single identifiable individual (rather than a group or class of individuals), the result is called a singular statement. "My mother is gray-haired," "That idea is absurd," and "The main character in this story is a lovable idiot" are examples of such statements. Singular statements can be further subdivided into monadic statements (those that have one-place predicates, such as are found in the examples just given), dyadic statements (those that have two-place predicates, as in the statement "John gave the book to Charles), triadic statements (those that have three-place predicates), and so on. We shall limit our consideration to monadic singular statements.

Singular statements receive little attention in traditional logic, since *within the confines of that logic* they can be treated simply as universal statements (see Section 5.3). In actuality, of course, they are not universal statements, and in our unified system of logic we shall abandon the fiction of treating them as such. Indeed, we shall make singular statements the fundamental building blocks of this system.

In order to assimilate such statements to our symbolic system, we need a way of symbolizing logical subjects and logical predicates. We shall do this as follows. First, we shall use lower-case letters of the alphabet from *a* to *w* to stand for the logical subjects of *singular statements*. A lower-case letter used in this way is called an **individual constant.** Second, we shall use upper-case letters from *A* to *Z* (but excluding *F*, for a reason to be explained shortly) to stand for logical predicates. An upper-case letter used in this way is called a **predicate constant.** Any lower-case letter from *a* to *w* may stand for the logical subject of any singular statement, and any upper-case letter from *A* to *Z* (but excluding *F*) may be used to stand for any logical predicate. That being the case, however, whenever possible we shall as a matter of convenience select letters that will serve to remind us of the subjects and predicates that they represent: *b* for "brother," *k* for "kangaroo," *R* for "red," *T* for "tall," and so on.

To assert symbolically that a given predicate applies to a given individual, we shall then write a predicate constant followed immediately by an individual constant. Suppose, for example, that we wish to assert, "My mother is gray-haired." We assign the individual constant *m* to the logical subject, "my mother," and the predicate constant *G* to the predicate, "gray-haired." We may then express this statement symbolically as follows:

*Gm*

Note that it is standard practice to write the symbol for the predicate first. Note also that there is no symbol to represent the copula: it is simply assumed to be present in every case.

Suppose now that we wanted to assert a negative statement— for example, "My mother is *not* gray-haired," or "It is not the case that my mother is gray-haired." Our new system provides a simple way to accomplish this: just put a negation sign in front of *Gm*, like this:

~*Gm*

The resulting statement may be read either "*m* is not *G*" ("My mother is not gray-haired") or "It is not the case that *m* is *G*" ("It is not the case that my mother is gray-haired").

The most important thing to remember about this new symbolism is that lower-case letters from *a* to *w* represent *individuals*, not groups. We are going to extend our symbol system shortly in such a way as to enable us to make statements about groups as well, but it is important that we not lose sight of the fact that such expressions as *Gm* and *Ci* and *Ab* are singular statements, not collective statements.

## EXERCISES 10.1–10.2

**A.**   Identify the logical subjects and logical predicates of each of the following statements:
1.   My sister is an accountant.
2.   Old Rover is somewhat arthritic.
3.   My favorite pipe is missing.
4.   *Gone with the Wind* is not a great movie.
5.   Arizona is very dry.
6.   The best advice my father ever gave me was to save 10 percent of every dollar I earned.
7.   John's best friend did not win a gold medal in the Olympics.
8.   I'm tired.
9.   Math is not my favorite subject.
10.   This novel is quite futuristic.
**B.**   State the above sentences symbolically, using allowable and appropriate symbols for each logical subject and logical predicate.
**C.**   Make any changes necessary to turn your affirmative symbolic statements into negative ones and your negative symbolic statements into affirmative ones.

# 10.3 STATEMENT FUNCTIONS

Let us now generalize the pattern that we have observed in the symbolizing of singular statements. Let us use the letter *x* as an **individual variable,** that is, as a place holder for an indefinite number of individuals that may, each in its turn, substitute for it; and let us use the letter *F* as a **predicate variable,** that is, as a place holder for an indefinite number of logical predicates that may, each in its turn, substitute for it. (It was in order to reserve the letter *F* for this purpose that we earlier excluded it from the list of letters available to serve as predicate constants.) Thus the general pattern, or **statement form,** of all correctly formed singular statements in our new symbol system is:

*Fx*

Note that the expression $Fx$, unlike the expressions considered in Section 10.2, is not a statement. It does not affirm anything; thus it is neither true nor false. It is merely the *form* in which singular statements are to be expressed in this system. The letter $x$ is merely a place holder for a singular logical subject ($a$, $b$, . . . $w$), the letter $F$ merely a place holder for a logical predicate ($A$, $B$, $C$, and so on— but of course not $F$).

Now, if we replace the predicate variable in the expression $Fx$ with a predicate constant—that is, with an upper-case letter other than $F$—the result is what is called a **statement function**.[1] A statement function is an expression that contains at least one predicate constant conjoined with an individual variable. If, for example, we define the letter $C$ to mean "clever," then the expression $Cx$ is a statement function meaning "$x$ is clever." If we define the letter $S$ to mean "sleeping," then the expression $Sx$ is a statement function meaning "$x$ is sleeping," and so on.

A statement function, like a statement form, is neither true nor false. It is not a statement. A statement function becomes a statement, however, as soon as an individual constant is put in place of the individual variable $x$. If, for example, for the individual variable $x$ we substitute $a$, meaning "Alice" (that is, a definite person by that name), then the statement function $Sx$ ("$x$ is sleeping") becomes the statement $Sa$ ("Alice is sleeping"). This statement is true if Alice is sleeping and false if she is not. Moreover, the resulting expression will be a statement—and therefore true or false—no matter what individual constant is put in the place of $x$. If the letters $b$, $c$, and $d$ stand, respectively, for "Barbara," "this crayon," and "that doll," the result of substituting $b$, $c$, or $d$ for $x$ is in each case a statement. $Sb$ will be true or false depending on whether or not Barbara is sleeping; since crayons and dolls are incapable of (literally) sleeping, $Sc$ and $Sd$ will obviously be false.

Statement functions are sometimes called **open sentences.** They are expressions that would be indicative sentences but for the fact that they lack a subject; thus they become indicative sentences as soon as a subject is supplied. You may find it helpful to think of them in terms of an ordinary-language paraphrase, such as the following:

_____is red.

In this paraphrase, the blank serves the same purpose as the $x$ in the statement function $Rx$. The result of filling in the blank (providing a

---

[1] Statement functions are sometimes called **propositional functions.**

substitution instance for $x$) will always be a statement, and any such statement will be either true or false.

A statement function may have any degree of complexity. If, for example, we let $A$ stand for "alive," $B$ for "beautiful," $C$ for "contented," and $D$ for "dismayed," we can construct the following complex statement functions that can be easily interpreted in terms of the symbolic apparatus with which we are now familiar:

$Ax \cdot Bx$
$Ax \supset (Bx \cdot Cx)$
$(Ax \cdot Bx) \supset (Cx \lor Dx)$
$(Ax \cdot Bx) \supset (Cx \equiv {\sim}Dx)$

Familiarity with the concept of statement functions is essential to what follows.

## EXERCISE 10.3

Using symbols as indicated, restate each of the following expressions as a statement function.
*Example:* Something is blue. $Bx$.
1.  Something is tall. $(T)$
2.  If something is tall, then it is slender. $(T, S)$
3.  Something is both tall and slender. $(T, S)$
4.  If something is both tall and slender, then it is not a dachshund. $(T, S, D)$
5.  Something is a dachshund if and only if it is not a giraffe. $(D, G)$
6.  Either something is new or it is old. $(N, O)$
7.  If something is new or old, then it is not red if and only if it is yellow. $(N, O, R, Y)$
8.  Something is both old and rare, and if it is genuine it is also priceless and hard to find. $(O, R, G, P, H)$
9.  If something is old and rare, then it is not both genuine and inexpensive. $(O, R, G, I)$
10. That something has feathers indicates that it is either a bird or a fake. (Your choice)

# 10.4 UNIVERSAL STATEMENTS

A statement function becomes a universal statement when it is preceded by what is called the **universal quantifier,** which is written thus: $(x)$. The symbol $(x)$ may be read "for any $x$," "for every $x$," "for anything $x$," or "if anything is an $x$." A statement function preceded by the universal quantifier is therefore a statement asserting that the statement function in question will result in a true statement no matter what individual constant is made to substitute for $x$ in that statement function.

Suppose, for example, that the predicate constants $A$, $B$, and $C$ are defined to mean, respectively, "alert," "busy," and "cranky." Then the statement functions $Ax$, $Ax \cdot Bx$, and $Bx \vee Cx$, when preceded by the universal quantifier, acquire the following meanings:

$(x)Ax$ means "For any (anything, every) $x$, it is alert," or, more simply, "All things are alert."

$(x)(Ax \cdot Bx)$ means "For any (anything, every) $x$, $x$ is alert and $x$ is busy," or, more simply, "Everything is alert and busy."

$(x)(Bx \vee Cx)$ means "For any (anything, every) $x$, $x$ is busy or $x$ is cranky," or, more simply, "Everything is busy or cranky."

There are, however, very few things that one can usefully say about everything in the universe (including statements like the above), so universal statements of these forms are extremely rare. The sorts of universal statements that one more often encounters, and that are indeed useful in ordinary discourse, are such statements as "All birds have feathers," "No party crashers are welcome," and "All models come equipped with either standard or automatic transmission." Let us see how our new symbol system can accommodate such statements.

We shall begin with standard-form **A** and **E** statements. The first step that we must take in order to express such statements in the new system is to learn to construe them somewhat differently than traditional logic taught us to do. In the new system we must construe such statements as statements about a collection of individuals each of which is conceived as having two characteristics, one designated by the subject term and one by the predicate term. "All lions are carnivorous," for example, is to be construed as follows: "Every individual that is a lion is carnivorous," or "For every individual, if it is a lion, then it is carnivorous." Similarly, "No tigers are docile" is to be construed as follows: "Every individual that is a tiger is nondocile," or "For every individual, if it is a tiger, then it is not docile."

If we use both $F$ and $G$ as predicate variables (not constants), the statement forms for the symbolic statement of standard-form **A** and **E** statements are as follows:

**A**   $(x)(Fx \supset Gx)$
**E**   $(x)(Fx \supset \sim Gx)$

where $F$ designates the subject term and $G$ the predicate term. The above statements, therefore—the ones about the lions and the tigers—can be expressed in the language of statement functions as follows (with the predicate constants *L, C, T,* and *D* used, respectively, for "lion," "carnivorous," "tiger," and "docile"):

$(x)(Lx \supset Cx)$ (All lions are carnivorous.)
$(x)(Tx \supset \sim Dx)$ (No tigers are docile.)

Note that the *scope* of the universal quantifier $(x)$ is determined by whatever immediately follows it. If it is immediately followed by a predicate constant, the quantifier applies only to the statement function of which that predicate constant is a part. If it is immediately followed by a scope indicator, it applies to the totality of what occurs within that pair of scope indicators. In the above cases, for example, the occurrence of parentheses immediately following the universal quantifier indicates that it is the compound statement functions $Lx \supset Cx$ and $Tx \supset \sim Dx$ that are quantified, not merely $Lx$ and $Tx$. With the use of brackets, braces, double parentheses, and so on, predicate statements can become increasingly complex in the same ways that sentential statements can.

Standard-form **A** and **E** statements, then—and, of course, their logical equivalents—are expressed as hypothetical statement functions preceded by the universal quantifier. One of the important values of this notation system, however, is that it is capable of expressing statements that are not in standard form as easily as it expresses those that are. Consider, for example, the following universal statements:

"All of those invited are either straight-A students or National Merit finalists."
"Everybody at the party was drunk and a bit obnoxious."

Neither of these statements can be easily stated as standard-form categorical sentences. For our new notation, however, they present no difficulty. With *I* used for "invited," *S* for "straight-A student," and *M* for "National Merit finalist," the first statement would be stated as follows:

$(x)[Ix \supset (Sx \vee Mx)]$

And with *P* used for "everybody at the party," *D* for "drunk," and *O* for "obnoxious," the second statement would be stated like this:

$(x)[Px \supset (Dx \cdot Ox)]$

With the use of the statement connectives introduced earlier—the dot, the vee, the horseshoe, the material equivalence sign—this notation system can express complex universal statements as easily as simple ones. Thus it is a powerful and versatile tool for the statement and analysis of arguments that are inaccessible to traditional logic.

## EXERCISES 10.4

A.   Review the list of statement functions that you have prepared in response to the instructions in Exercise 10.3 (p. 226). Turn these statement functions into universal statements by placing the universal quantifier in front of each. For each resulting statement do the following:
   a.   Give a correct reading of the symbolic expression ("For every . . ." etc.).
   b.   State the meaning of the symbolic expression in ordinary English. *Example:* Something is blue, *Bx*, becomes $(x)Bx$.
      **(1)** Correct reading: "For any (every, everything, etc.) $x$, $x$ is blue."
      **(2)** Meaning: "Everything is blue."
B.   Review the table of valid argument forms in Section 6.7 (p. 127). Identify the five argument forms in that table which consist entirely of universal statements. Restate those statements in symbolic notation.

# 10.5 PARTICULAR STATEMENTS

In traditional logic, particular statements are understood as statements affirming (**I** statements) or denying (**O** statements) that at least one member of the class designated by the subject term is a member of the class designated by the predicate term. The standard forms of these two types of statements are:

**I**   Some $S$ is $P$.
**O**   Some $S$ is not $P$.

It is an important feature of particular statements that, unlike universal statements, they affirm the existence of at least one member of the class designated by the subject term: they have "existential import" (see Section 5.2). In order to formulate such statements in the language of statement functions, therefore, we need a symbol to affirm the existence of at least one individual that has the specified characteristics. The symbol used for this purpose is called the **existential quantifier,** and is written thus: $(\exists x)$. It means, "There is an $x$ such that . . ." or "An $x$ exists such that . . ." The expression $(\exists x)Rx$, for example, is a statement asserting: "There is an $x$ such that $x$ is $R$," or, more simply, "Something is $R$." ($R$ is assumed to be a predicate constant with a defined meaning.)

Consider, for example, the standard-form particular statements "Some apples are sweet" and "Some merchants are not honest." Using the predicate constants $A$, $S$, $M$, and $H$ respectively for "apples," "sweet," "merchants," and "honest," we can now express these statements as follows:

$(\exists x)(Ax \cdot Sx)$ (Read: "There is an $x$ such that $x$ is $A$ and $x$ is $S$." This is exactly
equivalent to "Some $A$ is $S$.")

$(\exists x)(Mx \cdot \sim Hx)$ (Read: "There is an $x$ such that $x$ is $M$ and $x$ is not $H$." This
is exactly equivalent to "Some $M$ is not $H$.")

As with the universal quantifier (see Section 10.4), the result of
prefixing the existential quantifier to a statement function is a
statement, an expression that has the quality of being either true or
false.

The logical relations between the universal quantifier and the
existential quantifier may be stated as follows:

$(x)Fx$ is equivalent to $\sim(\exists x)\sim Fx$
$(\exists x)Fx$ is equivalent to $\sim(x)\sim Fx$

The first equivalence asserts that a statement of the form "For every
$x$, $x$ is $F$," is logically equivalent to a statement of the form "It is not
the case that there is an $x$ such that $x$ is not $F$," or, more simply, that
a statement of the form "Everything is $F$" is logically equivalent to a
statement of the form "It is not the case that something is not $F$."
The second equivalence asserts that a statement of the form "There
is an $x$ such that $x$ is $F$" is logically equivalent to a statement of the
form "It is not the case that for every $x$, $x$ is not $F$," or, more simply,
that a statement of the form "Something is $F$" is logically equivalent
to a statement of the form "It is not the case that everything is not-
$F$." It is clear from these equivalences that the expression $(x)$ has the
same meaning as the expression $\sim(\exists x)\sim$, and the expression $(\exists x)$
has the same meaning as the expression $\sim(x)\sim$.

Using the letters $F$ and $G$ as predicate variables, we can now
represent the relations among **A, E, I,** and **O** statements as in Figure
10-1.

We should not be surprised to find that, as in the Boolean
system (see Section 5.7), corresponding **A** and **O** statements and
corresponding **E** and **I** statements are contradictories, since the new
symbol system purports to state exactly what was stated in the
Boolean interpretation of **A, E, I,** and **O** statements. From the fact
that certain kinds of universally quantified statements are the contradictories of certain kinds of existentially quantified statements,
however, some interesting results can be derived. To say that two
statements are contradictories, it will be recalled, is to say that both
cannot be true and both cannot be false. It follows, therefore, that if
the statement

$(x)(Fx \supset Gx)$

is the contradictory of

$(\exists x)(Fx \cdot \sim Gx)$,

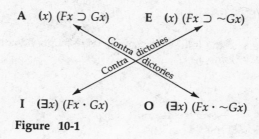

**Figure 10-1**

then the statement

$(x)(Fx \supset Gx)$

is logically equivalent to the statement

$\sim(\exists x)(Fx \cdot \sim Gx)$.

In general, a statement is logically equivalent to the denial of its contradictory. Thus, although **A, E, I,** and **O** statements are customarily expressed as I have expressed them above, the following equivalences (derived from the contradictories identified in Figure 10-1) illustrate alternative ways of expressing those same statements:

$(x)(Fx \supset Gx)$ is equivalent to $\sim(\exists x)(Fx \cdot \sim Gx)$
$(x)(Fx \supset \sim Gx)$ is equivalent to $\sim(\exists x)(Fx \cdot Gx)$
$(\exists x)(Fx \cdot Gx)$ is equivalent to $\sim(x)(Fx \supset \sim Gx)$
$(\exists x)(Fx \cdot \sim Gx)$ is equivalent to $\sim(x)(Fx \supset Gx)$

The new system can, then, be used to state exactly what was stated in the **A, E, I,** and **O** statements of traditional logic. An important advantage of the new system, however, is that it is not limited to statements that are in (or can be put into) standard form. Therefore, it can be used to express statements that cannot be conveniently expressed in traditional logic—such statements as the following (*B* stands for "black," *W* for "white"):

$(\exists x)(Bx \lor Wx)$ (Something exists that is either black or white.)
$(x)(Bx \equiv \sim Wx)$ (Everything is black if and only if it is not white.)

A further advantage of the new system is that it allows us to incorporate arguments whose validity depends on relations between subjects and predicates—the kinds of arguments treated by traditional syllogistic logic—in the powerful and versatile proof system of modern symbolic logic. Thus, it enables us to test the validity of arguments whose internal structure does not permit them to be tested by any of the methods that have thus far been discussed.

## EXERCISES 10.5

**A.** Restate the following statements in symbolic notation:
1. Some *S* is *P*.
2. Some *S* is not *P*.
3. Some *P* is *S*.
4. Some *P* is not *S*.
5. Some *S* is not non-*P*.
6. Some *P* is not non-*S*.
7. Some *S* is *P* or *Q*.
8. Some *S* is *P* and *Q*.
9. Some *S* is *P* and also either *Q* or *R*.
10. Either some *S* is *P* or some *Q* is *R*.

**B.** Restate the following statements in symbolic notation, using the letters indicated:

*Example:*
0. Some of the students in this class are quite advanced. (*S, A*)
   Symbolic restatement: $(\exists x)(Sx \cdot Ax)$.
1. Some insects are venomous. (*I, V*)
2. Some flowers are both fragrant and beautiful. (*F, R, B*)
3. Some cars have automatic transmission and some do not. (*A*)
4. Not all soldiers are courageous. (*S, C*)
5. All that glitters is not gold. (*G, O*)
6. There is a painting in this collection that is either a Rembrandt or a Goya. (*P, R, G*)
7. Space launches these days are sometimes quite routine. (*L, R*)
8. Everybody in Arizona doesn't necessarily like hot weather. (*A, L*)
9. Many skiers do only downhill skiing, whereas others prefer cross-country. (*S, D, C*)
10. Some skiers do both downhill and cross-country skiing. (*S, D, C*)

# 10.6 FORMAL PROOFS: UNIVERSAL INSTANTIATION AND UNIVERSAL GENERALIZATION

All of the elements of the formal proof apparatus introduced in Chapter 9—the nine elementary valid argument forms (Section 9.4) and the ten types of logical equivalence (Sections 9.6 and 9.7)—are also available for the formal proof of arguments involving the new symbolism insofar as the validity of those arguments depends on truth-functional relations between and among the component statements. That this apparatus is available for arguments stated in the new symbolism follows from the fact that there are no restrictions on the kinds of statements that can take the place of the *p*'s and *q*'s in the previously introduced proof system. Thus, to take a simple example, the following argument:

$Ba \supset Ca$
$Ba$
$\therefore \quad Ca$

instantiates—and is proved by—Modus Ponens no less than the arguments considered in Chapter 9 in which each component statement is represented by a single letter.

The main reason for introducing the new symbolism, however, was to enable us to get at the logic of arguments whose validity depends to some extent on the relations between subjects and predicates, not merely on the truth-functional relations between and among statements. To prove the validity of such arguments it is necessary to expand our proof apparatus to some extent.

We begin with an important reminder: that statement functions, though they resemble statements, are not statements. They cannot, therefore, serve as the premises of an argument or as steps in the proof of an argument. The statement functions that occur as a part of quantified statements can make no contribution to a truth-functional argument or proof unless some unquantified statements are derived from them, and such a proof cannot yield a quantified conclusion unless a way is provided to derive quantified statements from unquantified statements. We therefore need four new rules of inference: one pair to get us out of and into universally quantified statements, and a second pair to do the same for existentially quantified statements. We shall consider the first pair in this section, the second pair in the next.

Consider the argument "All students are brilliant, and Cathy is a student; therefore, Cathy is brilliant." This argument is obviously valid (albeit not sound), and could be symbolically represented as follows:

$(x)(Sx \supset Bx)$
$Sc$
$\therefore \quad Bc$

In order to *prove* the validity of this argument, however, we need some way of deriving a useful statement (i.e., one that is useful for purposes of proof) from the statement function $Sx \supset Bx$ in the first premise—a rule that will enable us to state that Cathy is one of the $x$'s instantiating that statement function. There is such a rule, called the **Rule of Universal Instantiation** (abbreviated **UI**), and it is stated thus: *From a universally quantified statement function, one can infer any of its substitution instances.*

Let $r$ represent any individual whatsoever. Then we may say that UI, which should be understood as a new rule of inference or elementary valid argument form, states the following:

$(x)(Fx)$
$\therefore$ $Fr$

Let us pause to consider exactly what UI is saying. The premise—$(x)(Fx)$—states that for anything whatsoever, it is $F$. It follows, therefore, that $r$ (an arbitrarily selected individual) is $F$, since $r$ is an individual constant that can take the place of the individual variable $x$. Moreover, since $r$ is an arbitrarily selected individual, it follows that any other individual constant that one might introduce instead of $r$ would also yield a valid inference.

With the help of this new rule, we can now prove the above argument as follows:

1. $(x)(Sx \supset Bx)$
2. $Sc$ / $\therefore$ $Bc$
3. $Sc \supset Bc$     1 UI
4. $Bc$          3, 2 MP

UI allows the uniform substitution of *any individual constant* for the individual variable in a universally quantified statement function. Thus, if we are given the universally quantified statement function

$(x)(Ax \supset Bx)$

we may infer such statements as the following:

$Aa \supset Ba$
$Ab \supset Bb$
$Ac \supset Bc$
$Ad \supset Bd$

UI does not allow us to infer merely a portion (i.e., merely the antecedent or the consequent) of the conditional—for example, $Aa$, or $Ab$, or $Bc$, or $Bd$. Indeed, any nontrivial statement that can be established directly by the correct use of UI will almost certainly be a compound statement. Singular statements can also be derived by UI from universally quantified statements of the form $(x)Fx$; but since anything that one can assert about *everything* is almost certain to be trivial, the result will almost certainly be a trivial singular statement.

The Rule of Universal Instantiation (UI) enables us to derive unquantified statements from universally quantified statement functions. The **Rule of Universal Generalization (UG)** serves just the opposite purpose: it enables us to derive universally quantified statement functions from certain *unquantified* statements. UG may be stated as follows: *From the presumed truth of an arbitrarily selected substitution instance of a statement function, one can infer the universal quantification of that statement function.*

Let *y* represent an arbitrarily selected individual. The Rule of Universal Generalization may then be stated as follows:

$Fy$
$\therefore \ (x)(Fx)$

The essential points to bear in mind in using this rule are (*a*) that *y* is always introduced into a proof by means of UI, and (*b*) that *y*, when introduced into the proof process in this way, signifies *any individual that instantiates the universally quantified statement function in question.* (It was in order to reserve it for this purpose that *y* was excluded from the list of letters available to serve as individual constants.) The letter *y* is what might be called a "universal" or "surrogate" individual constant. It represents all of the individual constants that can be used to instantiate any given universally quantified statement function, and whatever can be asserted of it can be asserted of any individual constant that instantiates that statement function. One might almost say that a *y* statement is a quantified universal statement expressed in the form of an unquantified singular statement.

Consider, for example, the argument "All professors are scholars, and all scholars are poverty-stricken; therefore all professors are poverty-stricken." Using the letters *P*, *S*, and *T* for, respectively, "professors," "scholars," and "poverty-stricken," we may now state and prove this argument as follows:

1. $(x)(Px \supset Sx)$
2. $(x)(Sx \supset Tx) \ / \therefore \ (x)(Px \supset Tx)$
3. $Py \supset Sy$                     1 UI
4. $Sy \supset Ty$                     2 UI
5. $Py \supset Ty$                     3, 4 HS
6. $(x)(Px \supset Tx)$              5 UG

Note the general strategy: we derive unquantified statements from the quantified premises, then we derive an unquantified version of the conclusion (containing the individual constant *y*) using the proof apparatus with which we are already familiar, and last we translate the conclusion back into a quantified statement. The same general strategy will be found useful in dealing with arguments of greater complexity.

## EXERCISES 10.6

**A.** Derive one unquantified statement from each of the following quantified statements by means of UI:

1. $(x)Bx$
2. $(x)(Ax \cdot Bx)$
3. $(x)(Cx \supset Dx)$
4. $(x)(Ax \lor Bx)$
5. $(x)[Kx \supset (Lx \lor Mx)]$
6. $(x)[Ex \lor (Gx \cdot Kx)]$
7. $(x)[Rx \supset (Sx \cdot Tx)]$
8. $(x)(Px \equiv {\sim}Qx)$
9. $(x)[Lx \supset {\sim}(Mx \lor Nx)]$
10. $(x)[{\sim}Ex \supset {\sim}(Bx \lor Ux)]$

**B.** Assume that whenever the individual constant $y$ appears in the statements below, it has been derived from a quantified statement by means of UI. Derive quantified statements from the following unquantified statements by means of UG *whenever it is legitimate to do so:*

1. $Sa$
2. $Sa \cdot Sb$
3. $Sy \cdot Ty$
4. $Sy \supset (Ty \lor Ry)$
5. $Ky \supset (Rm \cdot Tm)$
6. $Ay \supset By$
7. $(Ay \supset By) \cdot (Ky \supset Ly)$
8. $Ya \supset Yb$
9. $Ay \supset {\sim}(Cy \lor Ry)$
10. $My \lor (Ty \equiv Qy)$

# 10.7 FORMAL PROOFS: EXISTENTIAL INSTANTIATION AND EXISTENTIAL GENERALIZATION

The **Rule of Existential Instantiation (EI)** provides a way to derive unquantified statements from existentially quantified statement functions. This rule may be stated as follows: From an existentially quantified statement function one can infer any one substitution instance provided that the individual constant selected has not been used previously in the argument or its proof.

This rule may be schematically represented as follows:

$(\exists x)(Fx)$

$\therefore \quad Fz$

Consider the argument "No capitalists are Bolsheviks, and some Argentinians are capitalists, therefore some Argentinians are not Bolsheviks." With $C$ used for "capitalists," $B$ for "Bolsheviks," and $A$ for "Argentinians," this argument might be stated and, with the help of EI, proved in part as follows:

1. $(x)(Cx \supset {\sim}Bx)$
2. $(\exists x)(Ax \cdot Cx) \ / \therefore (\exists x)(Ax \cdot {\sim}Bx)$
3. $Aj \cdot Cj$            2 EI
4. $Cj$                3 Simp.
5. $Cj \supset {\sim}Bj$         1 UI

| | |
|---|---|
| 6. $\sim Bj$ | 5, 4 MP |
| 7. $Aj$ | 3 Simp. |
| 8. $Aj \cdot \sim Bj$ | 7, 6 Conj. |

At this point, however, we are stymied. It is intuitively obvious that line 8 in our proof constitutes a substitution instance of the conclusion that we are attempting to establish, but we have no way to get from line 8 to our conclusion. Suppose, for example, that $j$ is a specific individual—Juan, let us say—who is an Argentinian and not a Bolshevik. Then it is the case that there is at least one individual who is an Argentinian and not a Bolshevik, which is the conclusion that we are trying to establish. What we need is a rule that allows us to draw this generalized statement from our specific statement— a rule, that is, that allows us to infer from the statement "Juan is an Argentinian who is not a Bolshevik" that "someone is an Argentinian who is not a Bolshevik." Happily, that is the exact purpose of the **Rule of Existential Generalization (EG),** which is stated thus: From any true substitution instance of a statement function one can infer the existential quantification of that function. This rule may be stated paradigmatically as follows:

$Fz$
$\therefore \ (\exists x)(Fx)$

With the help of EG, we can now complete our proof as follows:

9. $(\exists x)(Ax \cdot \sim Bx)$     8 EG

The four new rules of inference that we have now discussed— two related to universally quantified statement functions and two to existentially quantified statement functions—enable the construction of formal proofs for any predicate argument consisting of more complex statements—for example, statements containing relational predicates—are beyond the scope of this book.

## EXERCISES 10.7

**A.** Derive one unquantified statement from each of the following quantified statements by means of EI:

1. $(\exists x)Ax$
2. $(\exists x)(Sx \cdot Px)$
3. $(\exists x)(Rx \lor Lx)$
4. $(\exists x)(Lx \equiv Mx)$
5. $(\exists x)[Bx \cdot (Cx \lor Dx)]$
6. $(\exists x)(Ax \cdot \sim Bx)$
7. $(\exists x)[Bx \cdot \sim(Cx \lor Dx)]$
8. $(\exists x)[Kx \cdot (Lx \equiv \sim Mx)]$
9. $(\exists x) \sim (Sx \cdot Tx)$
10. $(\exists x)[\sim Px \cdot \sim(Qx \lor Rx)]$

**B.** Derive a quantified statement from each of the following unquantified statements by means of EG whenever it is appropriate to do so:

1. $Sa$
2. $Sa \cdot Sb$
3. $Sr \cdot Tr$
4. $Sr \supset (Tr \lor Rr)$
5. $Kr \supset (Rm \cdot Tm)$

6. $Ar \supset Br$
7. $(Ar \supset Br) \cdot (Kr \supset Lr)$
8. $Ya \supset Yb$
9. $Ar \supset \sim(Cr \lor Rr)$
10. $Mr \lor (Tr \equiv Qr)$

# 10.8 APPLYING THE SYSTEM: STANDARD-FORM CATEGORICAL SYLLOGISMS

It will be recalled that of the 256 possible forms of SFC syllogism, only 15 are valid according to the canons of modern logic (see Section 6.8). With the proof apparatus now at our disposal it is possible to construct formal proofs of these argument forms—an exercise that is perhaps a bit redundant but that provides useful practice in the application of the proof apparatus to arguments known in advance to be valid. Proofs of three of the fifteen argument forms listed in Section 6.8 are presented here. The remaining twelve are identified in the exercises at the end of this section.

Let us begin with **AAA-1:** all $M$ is $P$ and all $S$ is $M$, therefore all $S$ is $P$. Since **AAA-1** involves only universal statements, the only new rules required for its proof are UI and UG. Stated symbolically, this argument form and its proof are as follows:

1. $(x)(Mx \supset Px)$
2. $(x)(Sx \supset Mx) \ / \therefore (x)(Sx \supset Px)$
3. $My \supset Py$                1 UI
4. $Sy \supset My$                2 UI
5. $Sy \supset Py$                4, 3 HS
6. $(x)(Sx \supset Px)$         5 UG

Next we consider **EIO-2:** no $P$ is $M$ and some $S$ is $M$, therefore some $S$ is not $P$. Since in this case one premise is universal and one particular, both UI and EI are required to give us the unquantified statements needed for our proof. Note also that in order to use the same individual constant for both premises it is necessary to instantiate the particular premise first, since we cannot use an individual constant used previously in the argument or its proof. **EIO-2** may be stated and proved as follows:

1. $(x)(Px \supset \sim Mx)$
2. $(\exists x)(Sx \cdot Mx) \ / \therefore (\exists x)(Sx \cdot \sim Px)$

| | |
|---|---|
| 3. $Sy \cdot My$ | 2 EI |
| 4. $Py \supset \sim My$ | 1 UI |
| 5. $My$ | 3 Simp. |
| 6. $\sim\sim My$ | 5 DN |
| 7. $\sim Py$ | 4, 6 MP |
| 8. $Sy$ | 3 Simp. |
| 9. $Sy \cdot \sim Py$ | 8, 7 Conj. |
| 10. $(\exists x)(Sx \cdot \sim Px)$ | 9 EG |

For our third example, let us consider **IAI-3:** some $M$ is $P$ and all $M$ is $S$, therefore some $S$ is $P$. This argument form and its proof may be stated symbolically as follows:

| | |
|---|---|
| 1. $(\exists x)(Mx \cdot Px)$ | |
| 2. $(x)(Mx \supset Sx)$ / $\therefore$ $(\exists x)(Sx \cdot Px)$ | |
| 3. $Ma \cdot Pa$ | 1 EI |
| 4. $Ma \supset Sa$ | 2 UI |
| 5. $Ma$ | 3 Simp. |
| 6. $Sa$ | 4, 5 MP |
| 7. $Pa$ | 3 Simp. |
| 8. $Sa \cdot Pa$ | 6, 7 Conj. |
| 9. $(\exists x)(Sx \cdot Px)$ | 8 EG |

The proofs of the remaining twelve valid forms of SFC syllogism present no new difficulties.

## EXERCISES 10.8

**A.** Using UI and UG as appropriate, construct formal proofs for the following SFC syllogisms:

**1.** No $M$ is $P$.
All $S$ is $M$.

$\therefore$ No $S$ is $P$.

**3.** All $P$ is $M$.
No $S$ is $M$.

$\therefore$ No $S$ is $P$.

**2.** No $P$ is $M$.
All $S$ is $M$.

$\therefore$ No $S$ is $P$.

**4.** All $P$ is $M$.
No $M$ is $S$.

$\therefore$ No $S$ is $P$.

**B.** Using EI, UI, and EG as appropriate, construct formal proofs for the following SFC syllogisms:

**1.** All $M$ is $P$.
Some $S$ is $M$.

$\therefore$ Some $S$ is $P$.

**2.** All $P$ is $M$.
Some $S$ is not $M$.

$\therefore$ Some $S$ is not $P$.

3. No $M$ is $P$.
   Some $M$ is $S$.
   ∴ Some $S$ is not $P$.

4. No $P$ is $M$.
   Some $M$ is $S$.
   ∴ Some $S$ is not $P$.

5. No $M$ is $P$.
   Some $S$ is $M$.
   ∴ Some $S$ is not $P$.

6. All $M$ is $P$.
   Some $M$ is $S$.
   ∴ Some $S$ is $P$.

7. Some $M$ is not $P$.
   All $M$ is $S$.
   ∴ Some $S$ is not $P$.

8. Some $P$ is $M$.
   All $M$ is $S$.
   ∴ Some $S$ is not $P$.

# 10.9 APPLYING THE SYSTEM: PREDICATE ARGUMENTS OF GREATER COMPLEXITY

Let us now apply our proof system to a few arguments of somewhat greater complexity—arguments that could not be proved by any of the methods discussed in earlier chapters. We shall begin with arguments stated in symbolic form, and shall then proceed to arguments stated in ordinary language.

Consider the following argument:

1. $(x)$ $[Hx \supset (Mx \lor Px)]$
2. $(\exists x)$ $(Hx \cdot {\sim}Px)$ / ∴ $(\exists x)(Hx \cdot Mx)$

Our first task is to restate the premises in a nonquantified form. Substituting $a$ for $x$ in both premises, we get the following:

3. $Ha \cdot {\sim}Pa$      2 EI
4. $Ha \supset (Ma \lor Pa)$      1 UI

The proof then proceeds exactly as if we were dealing with $p$'s and $q$'s (or $A$'s, $B$'s, and $C$'s) except for the final step, in which we translate our conclusion back into the language of quantified statements:

5. $Ha$      3 Simp.
6. $Ma \lor Pa$      4, 5 MP
7. ${\sim}Pa$      3 Simp.
8. $Ma$      6, 7 DS
9. $Ha \cdot Ma$      5, 8 Conj.
10. $(\exists x)(Hx \cdot Mx)$      9 EG

The selection of the individual variable *a* to substitute for the individual constant *x* in the above case is, of course, arbitrary. We could have used *b, c, d*, or any other lower-case letter from *a* to *w*, as discussed in Section 10.2. Remember that in developing proofs for arguments containing quantified statements it is imperative always to instantiate the existentially quantified premise(s) first. When the conclusion of an argument is a quantified universal statement, however, the selection of an individual constant to instantiate the premises is not arbitrary, since only a statement containing the individual constant *y* can yield (by means of UG) such a statement. In constructing formal proofs, therefore, one must pay close attention to the kind of conclusion one is attempting to establish, and proceed accordingly. This point is illustrated in the following argument and its proof:

| | | |
|---|---|---|
| 1. | $(x)[(Gx \cdot Qx) \supset Px]$ | |
| 2. | $(x)[Px \supset (Mx \lor Ax)]$ / | |
| | $\therefore (x)[\sim(Mx \lor Ax) \supset (\sim Gx \lor \sim Qx)]$ | |
| 3. | $(Gy \cdot Qy) \supset Py$ | 1 UI |
| 4. | $Py \supset (My \lor Ay)$ | 2 UI |
| 5. | $(Gy \cdot Qy) \supset (My \lor Ay)$ | 3, 4 HS |
| 6. | $\sim(My \lor Ay) \supset \sim(Gy \cdot Qy)$ | 5 Trans. |
| 7. | $\sim(My \lor Ay) \supset (\sim Gy \lor \sim Qy)$ | 6 De M. |
| 8. | $(x)[\sim(Mx \lor Ax) \supset (\sim Gx \lor \sim Qx)]$ | 7 UI |

The only new complication that arises when we attempt to apply our proof system to arguments that occur in ordinary language is that we must be very sure that our symbolic statement of the argument is correct. Unfortunately, there are no rules that can guarantee the correctness of such symbolic formulations. One must simply pay close attention to the *sense* of the argument, noting what is being offered as premises and what as the conclusion, and then restate that argument in appropriate symbolic language.

Consider, for example, the following argument: "All Iranians who are not loyal to the late shah are either Muslim fanatics or communists. This man, however, is neither a Muslim fanatic nor a communist. Therefore, either he is a non-Iranian or else he is loyal to the late shah." Using the predicate constants *I, L, M,* and *C* to stand, respectively, for "Iranian," "loyal to the late shah," "Muslim fanatic," and "communist," this argument may be stated symbolically and proved as follows:

1. $(x)[(Ix \cdot \sim Lx) \supset (Mx \lor Cx)]$
2. $(\exists x)(\sim Mx \cdot \sim Cx)$ / $\therefore (\exists x)(\sim Ix \lor Lx)$

| | |
|---|---|
| 3. $\sim Ma \cdot \sim Ca$ | 2 EI |
| 4. $(Ia \cdot \sim La) \supset (Ma \vee Ca)$ | 1 UI |
| 5. $\sim(Ma \vee Ca)$ | 3 De M. |
| 6. $\sim(Ia \cdot \sim La)$ | 4, 5 MT |
| 7. $\sim Ia \vee \sim\sim La$ | 6 De M. |
| 8. $\sim Ia \vee La$ | 7 DN |
| 9. $(\exists x)(\sim Ix \vee Lx)$ | 8 EG |

Some arguments in ordinary language are especially susceptible to misinterpretation. Among them are arguments containing the expressions "not all" ("Not all Republicans are conservative"), "none but" ("None but the poor truly know the despair of poverty"), "only" ("Only invitees may come"), and "always" ("Cacti are always prickly"). Special care must be taken in the restatement of such arguments (see Section 5.4). Here is an example: "Only Republicans are invited to this banquet. All Republicans are not wealthy and conservative, however, for although only invitees will attend, some will attend who are not wealthy." Clearly there are many *wrong* ways to symbolize this argument. Correctly restated, paying due attention to the apparent intention of the speaker, the argument looks like this (with *R* for "Republicans," *I* for "invitees," *W* for "wealthy," *C* for "conservative," and *A* for "attendees"):

1. $(x)(Ix \supset Rx)$
2. $(x)(Ax \supset Ix)$
3. $(\exists x)(Ax \cdot \sim Wx) / \therefore (\exists x)[Rx \cdot \sim(Wx \cdot Cx)]$

This argument is valid, and can be proved as follows:

| | |
|---|---|
| 4. $Ad \cdot \sim Wd$ | 3 EI |
| 5. $Id \supset Rd$ | 1 UI |
| 6. $Ad \supset Id$ | 2 UI |
| 7. $Ad$ | 4 Simp. |
| 8. $Ad \supset Rd$ | 6, 5 HS |
| 9. $Rd$ | 8, 7 MP |
| 10. $\sim Wd$ | 4 Simp. |
| 11. $\sim Wd \vee \sim Cd$ | 10 Add. |
| 12. $\sim(Wd \cdot Cd)$ | 11 De M. |
| 13. $Rd \cdot \sim(Wd \cdot Cd)$ | 9, 12 Conj. |
| 14. $(\exists x)[Rx \cdot \sim(Wx \cdot Cx)]$ | 13 EG |

With the addition of UI, UG, EI, and EG our proof apparatus is capable of proving the validity of any valid predicate argument, no matter how complex, provided that its component statements (premises and conclusion) are expressed in monadic statements.

Predicate arguments containing nonmonadic (dyadic, triadic, etc.) statements require additional rules for their proof, and are beyond the scope of this book. Reductio Ad Absurdum and Conditional Proofs (see Sections 9.8 and 9.9) also require certain restrictions when used in the proofs of predicate arguments and should not be used by persons who are unfamiliar with those restrictions.

## EXERCISES 10.9

**A.**   Construct a formal proof of validity for each of the following arguments:
1. $(x)[Kx \supset (Lx \cdot Mx)]$
   $(\exists x)(Nx \cdot \sim Lx)$ / $\therefore$ $(\exists x)(Nx \cdot \sim Kx)$
2. $(x)[Px \supset (Qx \cdot Rx)]$
   $(\exists x)[Tx \cdot \sim(Qx \vee Rx)]$ / $\therefore$ $(\exists x)(Tx \cdot \sim Px)$
3. $(x)(Lx \supset Mx)$
   $(x)[Mx \supset \sim(Qx \cdot Tx)]$ / $\therefore$ $(x)[Qx \supset (\sim Tx \vee \sim Lx)]$
4. $(x)[Jx \supset (Ax \equiv Rx)]$
   $(\exists x)(Jx \cdot \sim Ax)$ / $\therefore$ $(\exists x)(Jx \cdot \sim Rx)$
5. $(\exists x)(Ax \cdot Sx)$
   $(x)[Sx \supset (Tx \vee Rx)]$ / $\therefore$ $(\exists x)[Ax \cdot (\sim Tx \supset Rx)]$
6. $(x)[Ax \supset (Bx \vee Cx)]$
   $(x)(Cx \supset Dx)$
   $(x)\sim Dx$ / $\therefore$ $(x)(Ax \supset Bx)$
7. $(x)(Hx \supset Sx)$
   $(x)(Sx \supset Qx)$
   $(\exists x)(Ex \cdot \sim Qx)$ / $\therefore$ $(\exists x)(Ex \cdot \sim Hx)$
8. $(x)(Jx \supset Kx)$
   $(x)(Rx \supset \sim Kx)$
   $(\exists x)(Tx \cdot Rx)$ / $\therefore$ $(\exists x)(Tx \cdot \sim Jx)$
9. $(x)(Wx \supset Bx)$
   $(x)[Bx \supset (Qx \vee Sx)]$
   $(\exists x)(Wx \cdot \sim Sx)$ / $\therefore$ $(\exists x)(Wx \cdot Qx)$
10. $(x)[Ax \supset (Bx \vee Cx)]$
    $(x)(Bx \equiv Cx)$
    $(\exists x)(Dx \cdot \sim Bx)$ / $\therefore$ $(\exists x)(Dx \cdot \sim Ax)$

**B.**   Restate the following arguments in symbolic notation and construct a formal proof for each.
1. All ducks are birds, and all birds are feathered; therefore, all ducks are feathered. (D, B, R)
2. All birds are two-legged, and two-legged things are never reptilian, so no birds are reptilian. (B, T, R)
3. Only those who travel frequently know the boredom of spending most of one's waking hours on airplanes. Since frequent travelers never talk about their travels, however, those who do talk are not the ones who know the boredom of air travel. (Q, B, T)
4. No residents of Michigan are perfect, and anybody who lives in

Saginaw is a resident of Michigan, so anybody who lives in Saginaw is imperfect. (*M, P, S*)

5. All Pontiacs are comfortable-riding automobiles, but none of the cars in the motor pool are comfortable to ride in, so it is obvious that none of the cars in the pool are Pontiacs. (*P, C, M*)

6. None of the pilots on this list are over fifty years of age. To qualify as a senior citizen, however, one must be at least sixty-five years old, so it is clear that none of these pilots are senior citizens. (*P, O, S*)

7. All of the members of this class are either freshmen or juniors. The students in North Dorm, however, are all seniors. Obviously, if one is a senior one is neither a freshman nor a junior. Thus, none of the students in this class live in North Dorm. (*M, R, J, S, N*)

8. All citizens are both voters and taxpayers. None of the people in this group are voters, however, so it is clear that they are not citizens. (*C, V, T, G*)

9. All philanthropists are both wealthy and generous. Misers, however, are not generous, so misers never become philanthropists. (*P, W, G, M*)

10. Nobody can be simultaneously both old and young, or both rich and poor. All of the members of my club, however, are old and poor. Thus, none of them is either young or rich. (*N, O, Y, R, P, C*)

# 10.10 PROVING INVALIDITY

All of the predicate arguments that we have considered thus far have been valid, and our task has been merely to prove validity in each case by means of a formal proof. Normally, however, one does not know in advance whether an argument that one is assessing is valid or not. Indeed, one of the principal aims of logic is to provide methods for testing the validity of arguments, that is, methods for finding out whether or not a given argument is valid. If one is able to construct a formal proof for a given argument, that of course proves the argument to be valid; but the fact that one has *not* been able to construct a formal proof for a given argument does not prove that argument to be invalid, since it may be that with further effort such a proof could be found. It is desirable, therefore, that we have a method to determine conclusively whether or not an argument is valid.

It will be recalled that by means of an abbreviated truth table it is possible to construct a conclusive test for the validity of sentential arguments (see Section 9.3). In applying this test, we attempt to assign truth values in such a way as to make the premises of the argument true and the conclusion false. If this is a possible state of affairs—if it is possible for the premises to be true and the conclusion false—the argument is invalid; if not, it is valid. If, therefore, we could restate predicate arguments truth-functionally, we could then use this test to determine validity in the case of these arguments as well. That is precisely the strategy that we shall employ.

A universally quantified statement is logically equivalent to a truth-functional statement affirming the conjunction of all of its substitution instances:

$(x)(Ax \supset Bx)$ is equivalent to $[(Aa \supset Ba) \cdot (Ab \supset Bb) \cdot (Ac \supset Bc) \ldots \text{etc.}]$

If, for example, the above expression is assumed to symbolize the statement "All artichokes are beautiful," then we could theoretically affirm the same statement by saying in turn of every individual in the universe, "If this is an artichoke, then it is beautiful."

An existentially quantified statement is logically equivalent to a truth-functional statement affirming the disjunction of all of its substitution instances:

$(\exists x)(Ax \cdot Bx)$ is equivalent to $[(Aa \cdot Ba) \lor (Ab \cdot Bb) \lor (Ac \cdot Bc) \ldots \text{etc.}]$

If some artichokes are beautiful, then it must be the case that $a$ or $b$ or $c$ or *something* is an artichoke and is beautiful.

The problem with such restatements, of course, is that the "etc." represents an enormously large number of individuals—every possible logical subject in the universe—and as a practical matter it is obviously impossible to complete the list. We need some way to limit the number of substitution instances that have to be enumerated in our restatement. This limitation, if it is to be useful, must be small enough to permit its use in an abbreviated truth table, yet large enough to guarantee that a finding of validity or invalidity can be relied upon.

The smallest number of substitution instances that will guarantee the reliability of a finding of validity or invalidity is $2^n$, where $n$ is the number of predicate constants in the statement being restated. Thus, a statement containing one predicate constant requires two substitution instances, one containing two predicate constants requires four, one containing three requires eight, and so on. Needless to say, the method becomes increasingly unwieldy as the number of predicate constants increases.

Let us now use this method to test the validity of the following argument: "All human beings are mortal, and some mortals are brilliant, therefore some human beings are brilliant." Symbolically, this argument may be stated as follows:

$(x)(Hx \supset Mx)$
$(\exists x)(Mx \cdot Bx) / \therefore (\exists x)(Hx \cdot Bx)$

If we now set this argument out in the manner explained in Section 10.3, we get the following:

*Premise 1*
  $(x)(Hx \supset Mx)$

*Premise 2*
  $(\exists x)(Mx \cdot Bx)$

*Conclusion*
  $(\exists x)(Hx \cdot Bx)$

Since each of the three statements contains two predicate constants, a reliable test for validity requires that a truth-functional restatement in each case contain four substitution instances. Adding these restatements (or **expansions,** as they are more properly called) to our abbreviated truth table, we get the following:

*Premise 1*
  $(x)(Hx \supset Mx)$
  $(Ha \supset Ma) \cdot (Hb \supset Mb) \cdot (Hc \supset Mc) \cdot (Hd \supset Md)$

*Premise 2*
  $(\exists x)(Mx \cdot Bx)$
  $(Ma \cdot Ba) \vee (Mb \cdot Bb) \vee (Mc \cdot Bc) \vee (Md \cdot Bd)$

*Conclusion*
  $(\exists x)(Hx \cdot Bx)$
  $(Ha \cdot Ba) \vee (Hb \cdot Bb) \vee (Hc \cdot Bc) \vee (Hd \cdot Bd)$

In order to prove invalidity we need to show that it is possible for the premises to be true and the conclusion false. Let us start with the conclusion. In order for it to be false, every one of the disjuncts must be false. In order for that to be the case, at least one of each pair of conjuncts must be false. Let us assume, then, that the first member of each pair—*Ha, Hb, Hc,* and *Hd*—is false, and the other member of each pair true. Assigning these truth values to all occurrences of each statement, we get the following results:

*Premise 1*
  $(x)(Hx \supset Mx)$
  $(Ha \supset Ma) \cdot (Hb \supset Mb) \cdot (Hc \supset Mc) \cdot (Hd \supset Md)$
    F           F           F           F

*Premise 2*
   $(\exists x)(Mx \cdot Bx)$
   $(Ma \cdot Ba) \lor (Mb \cdot Bb) \lor (Mc \cdot Bc) \lor (Md \cdot Bd)$
      T                 T                   T                   T

*Conclusion*
   $(\exists x)(Hx \cdot Bx)$
   $(Ha \cdot Ba) \lor (Hb \cdot Bb) \lor (Hc \cdot Bc) \lor (Hd \cdot Bd)$
    F  F  T          F  F  T          F  F  T          F  F  T

Is it now possible to assign truth values to the remaining statements, consistent with the values that have already been assigned, in such a way as to preserve the truth of the premises? It is. There is nothing to prevent us from assigning the value T to all of the remaining statements, in which case all of the conditionals in premise 1 and all of the conjunctions in premise 2 will be true. We then have the following truth values:

*Premise 1*
   $(x)(Hx \supset Mx)$
   $(Ha \supset Ma) \cdot (Hb \supset Mb) \cdot (Hc \supset Mc) \cdot (Hd \supset Md)$
    F  T  T       T   F  T  T       T   F  T  T       T   F  T  T

*Premise 2*
   $(\exists x)(Mx \cdot Bx)$
   $(Ma \cdot Ba) \lor (Mb \cdot Bb) \lor (Mc \cdot Bc) \lor (Md \cdot Bd)$
    T  T  T       T   T  T  T       T   T  T  T       T   T  T  T

*Conclusion*
   $(\exists x)(Hx \cdot Bx)$
   $(Ha \cdot Ba) \lor (Hb \cdot Bb) \lor (Hc \cdot Bc) \lor (Hd \cdot Bd)$
    F  F  T   F       F  F  T   F       F  F  T   F       F  F  T

Since we have now shown that it is possible for the premises of our argument to be true and the conclusion false, we have proved conclusively that the argument is invalid. Thus it is clear that our inability to construct a formal proof of validity (assuming we had tried) is in this case due not to lack of effort or skill but rather to the fact that, since the argument is invalid, no such proof is possible.

This method is theoretically competent to establish conclusively the validity or invalidity of any predicate argument whose component statements are expressed in monadic sentences, regardless of the degree of complexity of that argument. In practice, however, the method becomes burdensomely complicated to use except with relatively simple arguments—arguments that contain no more than four premises, and premises that contain no more than three predicate constants. It is nonetheless a valuable weapon to have in one's logical arsenal for occasions when one suspects that the reason one has been unable to construct a formal proof of validity for a given argument may be that the argument is in fact invalid.

## EXERCISES 10.10

**A.** Restate the following statements truth-functionally, using the minimum number of substitution instances necessary to ensure that if they were used in an abbreviated truth table, a finding of validity or invalidity would be reliable.
 1. $(x)(Rx \supset Lx)$
 2. $(x)[Kx \supset (Mx \lor Nx)]$
 3. $(x)Dx$
 4. $(x)(Dx \lor Ax)$
 5. $(x)[Ax \supset (Bx \cdot {\sim}Cx)]$
 6. $(\exists x)Ax$
 7. $(\exists x)(Cx \cdot Dx)$
 8. $(\exists x)[Ax \cdot (Cx \lor Dx)]$
 9. $(\exists x)[(Ax \lor Bx) \cdot (Cx \lor Dx)]$
 10. $(\exists x)[Kx \cdot (Lx \equiv Mx)]$

**B.** Determine which of the following arguments are valid and which are invalid by means of abbreviated truth tables:
 1. $(x)(Ax \supset Bx)$
    $(\exists x)(Bx \cdot Cx)$ / $\therefore$ $(x)(Ax \supset Cx)$
 2. $(x)(Ax \lor Cx)$
    $(\exists x){\sim}Ax$ / $\therefore$ $(\exists x)Cx$
 3. $(\exists x)(Kx \cdot Lx)$
    $(x)[Lx \supset (Mx \lor Nx)]$ / $\therefore$ $(\exists x)(Kx \cdot Mx)$
 4. $(x)(Lx \supset Qx)$
    $(x)[Qx \supset (Px \lor Mx)]$ / $\therefore$ $(x)[Lx \supset ({\sim}Px \supset Mx)]$
 5. $(x)(Dx \lor Ax)$
    $(\exists x){\sim}Dx$ / $\therefore$ $(\exists x)Ax$
 6. $(x)[Cx \supset (Dx \cdot Zx)]$
    $(\exists x)(Nx \cdot {\sim}Dx)$ / $\therefore$ $(\exists x)(Nx \cdot {\sim}Cx)$
 7. $(x)[Rx \supset (Sx \cdot Tx)]$
    $(\exists x)[Zx \cdot {\sim}(Sx \lor Tx)]$ / $\therefore$ $(\exists x)(Zx \cdot {\sim}Rx)$
 8. $(x)(Dx \supset Zx)$
    $(x)[Zx \supset {\sim}(Qx \cdot Tx)]$ / $\therefore$ $(x)[Qx \supset (Tx \cdot Dx)]$
 9. $(x)[Bx \supset (Ix \equiv Gx)]$
    $(\exists x)(Bx \cdot {\sim}Ix)$ / $\therefore$ $(\exists x)(Bx \cdot {\sim}Gx)$
 10. $(\exists x)(Kx \cdot Sx)$
    $(x)[Sx \supset (Tx \cdot Rx)]$ / $\therefore$ $(\exists x)[Kx \cdot (Tx \supset Rx)]$

# INDUCTION AND
# SCIENTIFIC METHOD

# eleven
# An Introduction to Induction

Inductive arguments differ from deductive arguments in three important ways. First, it is impossible for the premises of a correct (valid) deductive argument to be true and the conclusion false. A correct inductive argument may, however, have true premises and a false conclusion (though it goes without saying that one ordinarily does not intend such an outcome). Second, the conclusion of a valid deductive argument cannot assert anything that is not asserted in the premises, whereas the conclusion of an inductive argument always asserts more than what is asserted in the premises. Third, the addition of further relevant premises (more evidence) to a correct inductive argument increases or decreases the probability that its conclusion is true, whereas nothing comparable occurs in the case of deductive arguments.

Notwithstanding the fact that inductive arguments lack the logical necessity of deductive arguments, much of our reasoning is inductive rather than deductive. Inductive reasoning may be uncertain, risky, and prone to error, but we quite literally cannot get along without it. All of our reasoning concerning matters that go beyond our immediate experience—our conclusions about the past, about the future, about unobserved members of a class, and so on—is **251** inductive. It is desirable, therefore, that we understand what we are doing when we reason inductively, and that we master the logic involved well enough to be able to distinguish between correct and incorrect inductive arguments.

## 11.1 INDUCTIVE ARGUMENTS

An inductive argument is defined as any argument for which it is claimed that the premises provide evidence making it more or less probable (but not certain) that the conclusion is true. If it is claimed that the premises offer conclusive evidence in support of the conclusion—that the conclusion follows from the premises as a matter of logical necessity—then the argument is not inductive but deductive.

Contrary to what many people believe, it is not true that inductive arguments always proceed from the particular to the universal—nor, as we have seen, do deductive arguments always proceed from the universal to the particular. Some inductive arguments reason from particular premises to a universal conclusion, others from particular premises to a particular conclusion, and yet others from universal premises to a universal conclusion. The differences between inductive and deductive arguments have nothing to do with the universality or particularity of premises or conclusions. The differences derive solely from the different relations that exist between the premises and the conclusions of the two types of argument. If it is claimed that the conclusion follows necessarily from the premises, the argument is deductive. If it is claimed only that the premises make the conclusion more or less probable, the argument is inductive.

Inductive arguments can be conveniently classified according to the types of conclusions that they attempt to establish. These conclusions are of four basic types: causal theories, empirical generalizations, theoretical hypotheses, and specific alleged matters of fact (including predictions).

Causal theories, as the name implies, are theories about causes. The following statements all express causal theories:

**E1.** The outbreak of food poisoning that followed our staff picnic last Friday was caused by spoiled ham.
**E2.** Pneumonia is caused by a virus.
**E3.** The solar system is the result of an enormous explosion that occurred billions of years ago.

Note the differences: E1 purports to identify a specific cause of a specific effect of limited scope, E2 asserts a general theory about the type of entity that allegedly causes all occurrences of the phenomenon called "pneumonia," and E3 asserts a one-of-a-kind cause of an enormous number of observable phenomena. The logical questions are: What kind of theory is a causal theory, and by what reasoning are such theories established? These questions will be discussed in Chapter 13.

An **empirical generalization** is a general statement about a class of objects made on the basis of observation of some members of that class. An empirical generalization concerning all members of a class is called a **universal generalization.** "All crows are black" is a well-worn example of such a statement.[1] An empirical generalization of the form "*n* percent of _____ is _____" is called a **statistical generalization.** The results of political polls—"54 percent of the voters plan to vote for Reagan," for example—illustrate this type of conclusion. The logical question is: By what reasoning do we proceed from the premises to the universal or statistical generalization? This question will be discussed in Chapter 14.

A **theoretical hypothesis** is a theory of broad scope that purports to explain (in a sense of "explains" yet to be specified) a wide range of phenomena, including many empirical generalizations. The wave theory of light, the general theory of gravitation, and the atomic theory are examples of theoretical hypotheses. It is characteristic of such hypotheses that (*a*) they are not observably instantiated in concrete instances (i.e., you cannot observe that light beam 1 is wavelike, light beam 2 is wavelike, and so on) and (*b*) they typically affirm the existence of unobserved entities (waves, atoms, gravitational force). They are not, therefore, empirical generalizations. The logical questions are: What kind of statements are they, and by what kind of reasoning are they established? These questions also will be discussed in Chapter 14.

Specific alleged matters of fact are such statements as "The tank is empty," "The butler did it," and "There will be rain tomorrow" (assuming in each case that one is making the statement without having actually *observed* the empty tank, the butler's act, or—obviously—tomorrow's rain). Clearly, we sometimes make such statements on the basis of remote evidence: the motor stopped, the butler had both a motive and an opportunity to commit the crime, the atmospheric conditions are similar to those that have often preceded rain in the past, and so on. The logical question is: By what reasoning do we support such statements? This question will be discussed in both Chapter 13 and Chapter 14.

---

[1] Negative universal statements also may be universal empirical generalizations according to this definition. The evidence supporting the statement "All crows are black" would equally support the statement "No crows are nonblack."

# 11.2 INDUCTIVE STRENGTH

In constructing deductive arguments, one aims to construct arguments that are *valid*. In constructing inductive arguments, one aims to construct arguments that are *strong*. Let us examine the concept of inductive strength.

To say that an argument is inductively strong is to say that the premises, if true, make it highly probable (though not logically certain) that the conclusion is true. Inductive strength is directly proportional to the probability that the conclusion is true given only those premises. Evidently, then, probability theory is relevant to the logic of induction. Just how it is relevant will be explored shortly.

Note that validity and invalidity are mutually exclusive qualities, whereas inductive strength and inductive weakness are complementary qualities. If an argument is valid, then it is 100 percent certain that it is not invalid. If, however, there is a 99 percent probability that the conclusion of an argument is true if the premises are true, then there is also a 1 percent probability that the conclusion is false if the premises are true. Thus we arrive at yet another definition of an inductive argument: an argument whose conclusion follows from its premises with a probability greater than 0 percent but less than 100 percent—or, as it is more commonly expressed, an argument whose conclusion follows from its premises with a probability greater than 0 but less than 1.

The intuitive meaning of the concept of inductive strength may be clarified by a consideration of some sample arguments. Consider the following argument:

Fifty-one of the 100 members of the U.S. Senate are Republicans.
In twenty-seven votes on tax matters over the past two years, the Republican senators have unanimously supported the president's position.
The Senate will vote tomorrow on a tax bill.

∴ The Senate vote tomorrow will support the president's position.

One's intuitive judgment would certainly have to be that this is a fairly strong argument. If you were going to bet on the outcome of tomorrow's Senate vote—given only the information contained in the above premises—you would be wise to bet that the vote will favor the president's position. Given these premises (and only these), it is quite probable that the vote will go the president's way, and correspondingly improbable that it will go against him.

Suppose now that we acquire some additional information

relevant to our argument, which we state in the following new premises:

Two former Republican senators have recently declared themselves to be independents because they are opposed to the president's tax policies.
No Democrats have indicated support for the president's position.

Given these new additional premises, the probability that the conclusion is true—that is, the probability that "the Senate vote tomorrow will support the president's position"—is greatly reduced. The argument containing the new premises has less inductive strength than the earlier argument. It is, as we say, a weaker argument.

Inductive strength is a quality of arguments, not a measure of the probable truth of the premises considered by themselves or of the conclusion considered by itself. It is a measure of the degree to which the premises support the conclusion. The following argument, for example, is inductively strong:

Ten million people are or have been residents of Amarillo, Texas.
No resident of Amarillo, Texas, has ever died before reaching the age of 100.
My grandmother is a resident of Amarillo, Texas.

∴ My grandmother will live to be 100.

This is an inductively strong argument because it is highly probable that the conclusion is true *if the premises are true*. But it is, of course, highly improbable that the first two premises are true.

The fact that the conclusion of an argument is probably true does not guarantee that the argument is inductively strong. Consider, for example, the following argument:

I have interviewed 400 Californians during the past three months.
None of the people whom I interviewed knew Abraham Lincoln personally.

∴ Nobody who is living today knew Abraham Lincoln personally.

The conclusion is, of course, almost certainly true, but these premises provide little support for it. The argument is inductively weak, notwithstanding the fact that both the premises and the conclusion may be true.

Inductive strength then, is a measure of the degree to which the premises of an inductive argument support its conclusion. In assessing the inductive strength of an argument we ask: What is the probability that the conclusion is true *given only these premises*? If the probability is high, the argument is inductively strong; if low, it is weak.

## EXERCISES 11.1–11.2

**A.** Listed below are several inductive arguments. Identify the conclusion of each argument, and state whether the conclusion is a causal theory, an empirical generalization, a theoretical hypothesis, or a specific alleged matter of fact.

1. The phases exhibited by the planet Venus are not those that one would expect if Venus and the sun revolve around the earth, but are those one would expect if both Venus and the earth revolve around the sun. The latter theory also explains the fact that the apparent size of Venus varies over time, as if it is nearer to the earth at some times than it is at others. Thus we may conclude that Venus and the earth revolve around the sun.

2. The frequency of lung cancer in persons who have smoked a pack or more of cigarettes daily for twenty years is eight times greater than it is for nonsmokers. The relation between cigarette smoking and lung cancer is clear and undeniable.

3. Professor Softouch has not given a student a failing grade in the last twenty years. Therefore, I am confident that I will get a passing grade in his course.

4. I have made an extensive study of chickens. I have examined thousands of chickens of many different breeds, and I can report that all of the adult males that I have examined have combs and that none of the adult females that I have examined do. I conclude, therefore, that all adult male chickens have combs, and that no adult female chickens have combs.

5. Having studied birds for some time, I note that all chickens have wings, all turkeys have wings, all canaries, robins, sparrows, and meadowlarks have wings—in short, all species of birds that I have had occasion to observe have wings. I conclude that all birds have wings.

6. The sky is hazy tonight, and there is a ring around the moon. It will rain tomorrow.

7. Do you hear that sound? There must be a squirrel in the attic.

8. Good heavens! The front door is standing open, the dresser drawers have all been pulled out, and our TV is missing. We've been robbed!

9. It's Friday. No doubt Smith will be home late tonight—when the bars close, that is.

10. There is no opening in the septum of the human heart. There are, however, valves in the veins that permit the blood in the veins to flow only toward the heart. The blood in the arteries is notably brighter in color than that in the veins. It is evident,

therefore, that the blood is constantly being circulated through the body, flowing away from the heart via the arteries and returning to it via the veins.

B.   Explain the concept of inductive strength as a quality of inductive arguments. Construct an example of an argument that you think is inductively strong, and one of an argument that you think is inductively weak.

C.   Make an estimate of the inductive strength of each of the inductive arguments in part A of these exercises, classifying each argument as very strong, strong, weak, or very weak.

# 11.3 THE STATUS OF INDUCTIVE LOGIC

You will recall that logic was defined as "the science of distinguishing between correct and incorrect reasoning or arguments" (Section 1.6.) In the case of deductive arguments, the criterion for distinguishing between correct and incorrect arguments is very precise: valid arguments are correct and invalid arguments are incorrect. Moreover, the techniques for determining whether or not an argument is valid are well established and noncontroversial. Deductive logic is an advanced and highly sophisticated science.

Such is not the case with inductive logic. Inductive arguments are not valid or invalid; they have various degrees of inductive strength. A science of inductive logic, if it existed, should provide noncontroversial methods of measuring the inductive strength of arguments and noncontroversial rules for constructing inductively strong arguments. Unfortunately, such a science does not exist. Indeed, it is a matter of dispute whether such a science is even possible. What does exist is a set of intuitive beliefs about induction which it is generally assumed must eventually be incorporated into a scientific inductive logic (if there is to be one), plus some parts of a system of inductive logic that have been worked out with varying degrees of precision. The goal of putting these intuitions and partial subsystems together into a complete system of scientific induction is being actively pursued by a number of logicians at the present time.

The intuitive beliefs about induction on which there is fairly widespread agreement may be summarized as follows:

1.   An empirical generalization becomes increasingly probable as the number of observed positive instances increases, provided there are no negative instances. (The more black crows that have been observed, the more probable it is that the statement

"All crows are black" is true, provided that no nonblack crows have been observed.)

2. The greater the number of observed similarities between two objects or types of objects, the greater the probability that they will prove to be similar also with respect to further qualities that have not yet been observed. (There is a greater number of similarities between chimpanzees and human beings than there is between horses and human beings. Given this fact, it is more probable that a disease-combating drug that is effective in chimpanzees will be effective in human beings than that a disease-combating drug that is effective in horses will be effective in human beings.)

3. If a given type of phenomenon can be accounted for by two or more hypotheses, the disproof of one hypothesis increases the probability of the truth of the remaining hypothesis or hypotheses. (The disproof of the corpuscular theory of light makes it more probable that the wave theory is true.)

4. No matter how much evidence there may be in support of a given hypothesis, if that hypothesis yields consequences that are clearly contrary to fact, the hypothesis is false. (If the Ptolemaic theory implies that the observed size of the planet Venus should remain constant, and if Venus as observed through a sufficiently powerful telescope appears to change in size over time, then the Ptolemaic theory is false.)

5. If a theoretical hypothesis yields predictions of phenomena that would not have been expected in the absence of that hypothesis, and if those predictions are subsequently confirmed, the probability of the truth of the hypothesis is thereby increased. (The probability of the truth of Einstein's general theory of relativity was increased by the observation—contrary to what would have been expected on the basis of prevailing physical theory before Einstein's hypothesis—that, as predicted by the theory, light rays bend when they pass through a strong gravitational field.)

Whatever the general rules of inductive inference may eventually turn out to be—if, indeed, they are ever successfully formulated—it seems clear that they must somehow incorporate the insights embodied in these (and perhaps other) common-sense intuitions. In the absence of clearly formulated rules, such intuitions as these must often guide us as we attempt to reason from the particular facts of experience to the generalizations and hypotheses by which we seek to cast those facts into some kind of intelligible pattern.

Two divisions of inductive logic are fairly well developed at the present time: probability theory and the theory of causal inferences.

We shall look first at probability theory, since it is relevant to all kinds of inductive inferences (Chapter 12). We shall then proceed to a consideration of the logic of causal inferences (Chapter 13), and shall conclude with a consideration of empirical generalizations and theoretical hypotheses (Chapter 14).

# twelve
# Probability

Modern probability theory had a rather interesting beginning. The mathematician-philosopher Blaise Pascal (1623–1662), during an uncharacteristic period of worldliness, spent some time frequenting the gambling houses of Paris with his friend the Chevalier de Mère. In the course of these visits Pascal reportedly became intrigued with such questions as "What is the probability of getting a seven on a single roll of a pair of dice?" and "What are the conditions of a reasonable wager?" Pascal's inquiries into these and similar questions led to an exchange of letters with another mathematician, Pierre de Fermat (1601–1665). The foundations of modern probability theory were laid in the correspondence between Pascal and Fermat. History does not record whether the gambling fortunes of the Chevalier de Mère improved as a result of his friend's discoveries concerning the laws of probability.

Probability theory provides rules according to which the probability of certain compound statements can be precisely calculated provided that one knows (or assumes) the probability of their components. What, for example, is the probability of getting two heads on two successive tosses of a fair coin? Probability theory **260** provides a rule (called the Special Conjunction Rule) according to which it can be calculated that the probability is $\frac{1}{4}$, or 25 percent. That a given coin is a "fair" coin—that is, one so constructed that neither heads nor tails is favored—is, of course, a question of fact that is beyond the scope of probability theory. In calculating probabilities one must assume fair coins, unloaded dice, and—with respect to examples drawn from playing cards—honest dealers. Probability theory deals for the most part with *mathematical* probability under ideal conditions.

# 12.1 THE CONCEPT OF PROBABILITY

The concept of probability is more obscure than one might suppose. We all use the word "probable" and its variants ("probably," "improbably," "probability," etc.) from time to time, and we presumably have some idea of what we mean by them. We make such statements as the following:

**E1.** It is highly probable that the Yankees will win the American League pennant this year.

**E2.** In an inductively strong argument, the conclusion is probably true if the premises are true.

**E3.** The probability of rain today is very low.

These examples illustrate two important characteristics of the concept of probability. The first is that we sometimes speak of the probability of an *event* (E1 and E3) and sometimes of the probability of a *statement* (E2). Second, probability is a matter of degree: events (or statements) are said to have a high (low) probability, to be very probable (improbable), and so on.

What, exactly, does it mean to assert that something is *probable?* This question has been answered in three ways. Let us briefly consider them.

The first view to be considered is what may be called the possibility theory.[1] With respect to any specific future event, according to this theory, one can theoretically specify a set of equipossible events, some of which would constitute occurrences of the event in question and some of which would not. Let us call an event that would constitute an occurrence of the event in question a "favorable" event, and let us call an event that would not constitute an occurrence of such an event an "unfavorable" event. (Note that "favorable" means only an occurrence of an event of the type whose probability

---

[1] The terminology throughout this section follows that of Georg Henrik von Wright in *A Treatise on Induction and Probability* (London: Routledge & Kegan Paul, 1951).

is in question. If one is discussing the probability of getting a speeding ticket, for example, then getting a ticket is a "favorable" event in this sense of the word, no matter how unfavorable it may be in other respects. This particular example will come up later.) According to the **possibility theory,** the probability of an event consists in the ratio of the number of possible favorable events to the total set of equipossible events, favorable and unfavorable. If there are two equipossible events, as in the tossing of a coin, then the ratio of favorable events (heads, let us say) to the total set of possible events is 1:2. According to the possibility theory, this arithmetical ratio is the *meaning* of any statements that may be made about the probability of tossing heads. If there are 52 equal possibilities, as in the drawing of a card from a standard 52-card deck, then 13 of them are favorable to the specified event of drawing a spade. The ratio of 13 to 52 is 1:4, and this ratio—according to the possibility theory—is what is meant by saying that there is such-and-such a "probability" of drawing a spade.

According to this theory, every statement regarding the probability of an event is, at least covertly, a statement about arithmetical ratios. Such phrases as "high probability," "low probability," "small chance," and "great likelihood" are simply ways of informally specifying *approximate* ratios in situations in which we lack the information to specify the actual ratio. We don't know the actual arithmetical ratio that expresses the probability that the Yankees will win the pennant, for example, so instead we make statements like E1. The essential point, in any case, is that according to this theory, probability statements are always, at bottom, statements about the ratio of the number of favorable events to the total number of equipossible events.

A second theory concerning probability is the **frequency theory.** According to this theory, probability statements are essentially statistical summaries: they report the proportion of favorable occurrences to total occurrences (favorable plus unfavorable) in the past as the basis for expectations concerning the future. On this view, the statement "The probability of tossing heads on a single toss of a fair coin is 1:2" means something like this: "In a large number of tosses of coins in the past, approximately half have resulted in heads and half in tails. Thus the ratio of heads to total tosses is approximately 1:2."

Like the possibility theory, the frequency theory requires that probability statements that are not expressed as ratios be construed as informal specifications of approximate ratios. Thus a statement like E3, for example, should be understood as an imprecise way of saying, "In many past cases in which weather conditions have been similar to today's weather conditions, rain has occurred in $n_1$ out of

$n_2$ cases [e.g., 1 out of 20] or less." Once again, then, probability statements are to be understood as expressing arithmetical ratios, but according to the frequency theory the ratios are to be understood as summaries of empirical information rather than as proportions of ideal possibilities.

It follows from either of the above theories that it is reasonable to have varying degrees of confidence regarding the occurrence of various future events, depending on the ratios that one believes to be applicable. Suppose, for example, that you are going to draw one card at random from a standard 52-card deck. How confident would you be regarding each of the following?

E4. The card drawn will be something other than the ace of spades.
E5. The card drawn will be red.
E6. The card will be the ace of spades.

Clearly, there is *some* sense in which one can say that a reasonable person would have quite a high degree of confidence (albeit not absolute certainty) in the case of E4, less confidence in the case of E5, and very little confidence in the case of E6. It appears, then, that there is some correlation between the arithmetical ratios produced by both of the theories we have discussed and the degree of confidence that a reasonable person would have concerning the occurrence of an event to which those ratios are applicable.

This correlation has led to the formulation of a third theory of probability, the **psychological theory**. According to this theory, the probability of an event is what might be called rational credence: it is the degree of confidence that a reasonable person would have in the occurrence of an event, given everything that person knows that is in any way relevant to the occurrence of that event. Sometimes, as in the tossing of coins and the drawing of cards, one's degree of confidence may be governed almost entirely by one's knowledge of the mathematical odds involved (though one must assume that the coin is a fair coin and that the deck is not stacked). At other times, as in predicting the weather, one's degree of confidence is governed by one's past experience regarding the kind of weather that has tended to occur under such-and-such conditions. Consider the statement "It will not rain here for the next sixty minutes." One might be very confident that this prediction would prove true if the sun were currently shining and there were no clouds in the sky. One would be less confident if it were currently beginning to cloud over, still less confident if one could also hear thunder in the distance, and so on. Now according to the psychological theory, this varying degree of confidence regarding a possible future event is the very meaning of the term "probability." "It is highly probable that *p*" means "I am very confident that *p*"; "It is unlikely that *p*" means "I am very uncertain that $p$," and so on—$p$ being in each case a statement asserting the occurrence of some event in the future.

It is possible that the term "probability" is ambiguous—that it means all of the above, and that we use it in some contexts with one meaning and in other contexts with another. In ideal situations of chance—tossing coins, drawing cards at random, and so on—the possibility theory seems highly plausible. When the ratio of favorable outcomes to total equipossible outcomes cannot be calculated, but when past experience in similar situations appears to provide some guidance regarding what the future will bring, the frequency theory seems more adequate. The fact that varying degrees of confidence is apparently a common element in all situations involving probability is the principal consideration in favor of the psychological theory. The fact that confidence cannot be measured, however, whereas probability sometimes can, is an argument against that theory.

Fortunately, probability theory enables us to calculate the probability of certain kinds of complex events no matter which view we adopt about what probability "really is." Indeed, even the psychological theory—though acknowledging that confidence cannot be measured—accepts numerical ratios as somehow corresponding to varying "degrees of confidence" in a certain outcome. And since both of the other two theories define probability in terms of such ratios (although they disagree about what it is that we are counting when we establish those ratios), it is clear that they have an interest in a general theory of probability worked out in terms of such ratios. This part of probability theory, called the **calculus of probability,** is wholly noncontroversial.

Probability is typically expressed either as a fraction ($\frac{1}{4}$, $\frac{1}{6}$, $\frac{4}{5}$, and so on) or as a decimal equivalent of a fraction (.25, .167, .8, and so on). A statement that is certainly false (for example, a self-contradiction) has a probability of 0. A statement that is certainly true (for example, a tautology) has a probability of 1. A statement that is neither certainly false nor certainly true has a probability between 0 and 1. The exact *meaning* of the statement "Event $A$ has a probability of $\frac{1}{4}$" depends, of course, on which of the above-mentioned theories is correct.

As previously noted, it is possible to speak of probability in terms of either the probability of the occurrence of *events* or the probability of the truth of *statements*. Which meaning one adopts is purely a matter of convenience, since the probability of an event's occurrence will always be exactly the same as the probability of the truth of the statement affirming the occurrence of that event. Since logic is concerned with arguments, however, and arguments consist of statements, we shall normally speak of the probability of the truth of statements. We shall, moreover, adopt a simple notation for doing so. If we want to state "The probability that statement $A$ is true is $\frac{1}{4}$," we shall write as follows:

$P(A) = \frac{1}{4}$

We shall also use certain of the logical connectives introduced in Chapter 8—namely, the dot ($\cdot$), the vee ($\vee$), and the tilde ($\sim$). You should, then, be able to read and understand such expressions as the following:

$P(p \cdot \sim p) = 0$
$P(p \vee \sim p) = 1$

The first statement affirms that the probability of any statement asserting the conjunction of a statement and its contradictory is 0; the second affirms that the probability of any statement asserting the disjunction of a statement and its contradictory is 1. If you are not clear about the exact meanings of the connectives used in these expressions, you should review Sections 8.4–8.6 before proceeding further.

# 12.2 DETERMINING INITIAL PROBABILITIES

The calculus of probability provides rules for the calculation of the probability of certain compound statements given the probabilities of their components. In order to make these calculations, then, one needs first to determine the probabilities of the components. If it is known, for example, that the probability of the Yankees' winning the pennant in a given year is $\frac{1}{4}$, and that the probability of the Orioles' winning the pennant in that year is $\frac{1}{5}$, the calculus of probability provides a formula whereby we can calculate the probability that *one or the other* will win the pennant. The calculus of probability does not tell us, however, how to determine that the probability of the Yankees' winning is $\frac{1}{4}$ and that the probability of the Orioles' winning is $\frac{1}{5}$. The problem of how to do so is called *the problem of determining initial probabilities.*

When one is dealing with situations of pure chance in which all of the relevant possibilities are known, the determination of initial probabilities is relatively easy. It is obvious, for example, that the probability of tossing heads on a single toss of a fair coin is $\frac{1}{2}$, that the probability of drawing the ace of spades in a random draw from a standard 52-card deck is $\frac{1}{52}$, and so on. That is why coin tosses and random draws are used so often (in this book and elsewhere) in discussions of probability theory: they avoid the sticky problem of determining initial probabilities. But in most of the real-life situations in which we have to make estimates of probability, the odds cannot be so easily determined. Real-life estimates of probability typically have to do with such questions as the following:

**Q1.** What is the probability of getting a speeding ticket if I drive at an average speed of 65 miles per hour on the Pennsylvania Turnpike from Philadelphia to Pittsburgh?

**Q2.** What is the probability of being able to get along for one more year with this old car if I spend $400 on a repair job?

**Q3.** What is the probability of getting an acceptable summer job in Montana if I hitchhike there in June without any leads?

How does one determine probability in such cases?

Note that one's theory about what probability is (as discussed in Section 12.1) does not provide an answer to this question. Consider, for example, Q1. Suppose that one holds the possibility theory: that theory provides no way to calculate the ratio of favorable outcomes (getting a ticket) to the total number of equipossible outcomes, since we don't have any way of determining the number of unfavorable outcomes. (We don't know how many cards are in that deck.) Suppose, alternatively, that one holds the frequency theory: if in the past we had made a large number of trips between Philadelphia and Pittsburgh at an average speed of 65 miles per hour, and had received some number of speeding tickets, we of course could make a probability statement based on that evidence. But the point of asking Q1 is presumably to help us decide whether it is worth it to exceed the speed limit on the trip. One asks Q1 in the hope of avoiding one's first ticket on such a trip, not in order to summarize one's findings during a series of trial runs. What one is trying to decide in asking Q1 is whether it is reasonable to risk the possibility of a fine in order to gain an hour or so of time. If one judges the probability of getting a ticket to be very low, and if the time to be gained is for some reason very important, one may decide that it is a reasonable wager. If one judges the probability of getting a ticket to be quite high, and if there is no special reason to arrive an hour or so earlier than one otherwise would, one will presumably conclude that it is a poor wager. It is even more evident that the psychological theory yields no estimates of initial probability.

How, then, do we make such estimates in concrete cases? To be sure, we do not ordinarily express those estimates in precise mathematical form. But we do say things like "I think there is a high probability that I would get a ticket," "I think it is unlikely that I could get an acceptable summer job in Montana," and so on. How do we arrive at such statements?

The answer appears to be something like the following. Whenever we make a probability statement in which the probability is not deduced by means of the calculus of probability from other probability statements, we are implicitly framing for ourselves an inductive argument whose conclusion is the statement in question and whose premises are statements reporting everything that we know or believe that is in any way relevant to that conclusion. The probability that we assign to that statement, then, depends on the inductive strength of the implicit argument of which it is the conclusion. The inductive strength of any such argument is an objective fact about that argument, just as validity is an objective fact about deductive arguments. Different individuals might correctly assign different estimates of probability to the same statement (conclusion), however, since each of them would be affirming that statement on the basis of somewhat different premises (i.e., each would be deriving it from his or her own relevant knowledge and beliefs.).

The problem with trying to illustrate this account of initial probabilities is that in any real-life case the list of statements reporting everything that we know or believe that is relevant to a given conclusion would be so enormously long and, in a sense, indefinite that it would be impossible in principle to make it complete. Everything that one knows or believes that is *in any way* relevant to an estimate of probability in a concrete case might well include a large proportion of everything that one knows or believes. Consider, for example, Q2—a typical real-life question if there ever was one. Some (but only some) of the statements that might function as premises in an implicit argument leading to the conclusion "If I get the repair job, the car will last at least one more year without further major expense" are these:

The car is eight years old.
Eight-year-old cars tend to have problems.
They're not making cars like they used to.
I spent over $350 on repairs last year.
The tires are badly worn; they may not last another year.
I once read a book that presented convincing evidence that car makers deliberately make cars in such a way that they will have to be replaced in a few years.
Several people I know who have owned this make of car have had major problems after the car passed 50,000 miles. This one has nearly 70,000 miles on it already.
The mechanic says that so far as he can tell, there's nothing else wrong with it.
The mechanic has been quite reliable in the past.
The last car of this make that I owned went over 100,000 miles.
. . . and so on.

It is not surprising that in cases like this one does not attempt to express the probability of the conclusion in terms of an arithmetical ratio.

This account of how initial possibilities are determined can be illustrated much more easily in the simpler case of estimating the probability of, say, drawing an ace on a random draw from a standard 52-card deck. Once again, everything that one knows or believes that is relevant to the conclusion is to be thought of as constituting the premises of an inductive argument whose conclusion is the statement "The card drawn will be an ace." In this case, however, one can specify precisely the knowledge or beliefs that are relevant to the conclusion:

1. The cards have been thoroughly shuffled; each card has the same chance of being drawn as any other card in the deck.
2. The number of cards in the deck is 52.
3. Exactly 4 of the cards are aces.

Given these premises, the conclusion—that the card drawn will be an ace—follows with a probability of $\frac{1}{13}$. Change premise 3—let it state instead that 26 cards are black, or 13 cards are clubs, or 20 cards are even-numbered—and other conclusions can be drawn ("The card drawn will be black"; "The card drawn will be a club"; "The card drawn will be even-numbered"), each with a probability that can be stated with mathematical precision.

If the view here presented—that estimates of probability are essentially conclusions of inductive arguments whose premises are statements reporting everything that we know or believe that is in any way relevant to that conclusion—is correct, then the only logically important difference between estimating the probability that one's car will last another year and estimating the probability of drawing a certain card is that in the one case we cannot state everything that is relevant to determining the probability of the conclusion and in the other case we can. Because of this difference, in the one case we can express the probability of the conclusion only imprecisely ("There is an outside chance that the car will last another year," "It is quite likely that it will last another year," and so on), whereas in the other case we can state the probability of the conclusion with mathematical precision.

The question as to how initial probabilities are determined is a difficult one, and not all logicians would accept the above account. The calculus of probability is not dependent on any particular theory regarding initial probabilities, however. The calculus of probability requires only that initial probabilities be determined *somehow or other*, since its formulas concern relations between components whose separate probabilities are presumed to be known.

## EXERCISES 12.1–12.2

**A.** Explain the three concepts of probability discussed in Section 12.1.

**B.** Restate the following probability statements in ordinary language:
*Example:*

0. $P(A \cdot B) = \frac{1}{4}$ Answer: The probability that statements A and B are both true is $\frac{1}{4}$.
1. $P(A \lor B) = \frac{1}{2}$
2. $P(A \lor \sim B) = \frac{2}{3}$
3. $P[A \cdot (B \lor C)] = \frac{4}{5}$
4. $P[A \lor (B \cdot C)] = \frac{2}{7}$
5. $P(A \cdot \sim A) = 0$
6. $P(A \lor \sim A) = 1$
7. $P \sim [A \cdot (B \lor C)] = \frac{4}{9}$
8. $P[A \cdot (B \lor \sim C)] = \frac{5}{11}$
9. $P[A \cdot (\sim B \lor \sim C)] = \frac{6}{7}$
10. $P[A \cdot (\sim B \cdot C)] = \frac{5}{12}$

**C.** Estimate the probability of each of the following statements, stating your estimates either as fractions or as decimal equivalents.

1. Snow will fall in Siberia at least once next winter.
2. A child will be born in New York City on Christmas Day in the year 2000.
3. Automobiles capable of achieving 100 miles per gallon will be in general use by the year 2000.
4. No major war involving the United States will occur before the end of this century.
5. The budget of the United States government will be balanced for four consecutive years sometime before the year 2000.
6. An individual who becomes a pack-a-day smoker at age 20 will incur lung cancer before he or she is 60 years old.
7. A commercial airline crash will occur next year.
8. A president of the United States will die in office within the next twenty years.
9. A life-threatening earthquake will occur in California within the next six months.
10. The sun's fuel will eventually be depleted, and the sun will cease to give sufficient heat and light to sustain life on earth.

# 12.3 THE SPECIAL CONJUNCTION RULE

As previously stated, the calculus of probability provides formulas for calculating the probability of certain compound statements given the probabilities of their components. These formulas are stated in a series of simple rules. Because of the difficulty of determining initial probabilities in real-life situations, I shall illustrate each rule with familiar examples involving tossed coins, random draws from a deck of cards, and so on. It should be remembered, however, that the rules of the calculus are equally applicable to *any* component statements whose probabilities have been assigned.

We begin with what is called the **Special Conjunction Rule.** Let us suppose that a probability has been assigned to each of two events, A and B. Let us assume further that the occurrence of one has no effect on the occurrence of the other. What is the probability that both events will occur? We know, for example, that the probability of getting a 5 on a single roll of an unloaded die is $\frac{1}{6}$. We know further that getting a 5 on one roll of a die does not affect the probability of getting a 5 on a second roll. What, then, is the probability of getting 5s on *two successive* rolls of a single unloaded die? The Special Conjunction Rule enables us to make the calculation required to answer this question. The rule may be stated as follows:[2]

$P(p \cdot q)^1 = P(p) \times P(q)$

The probability of getting a 5 on the first roll (A) is $\frac{1}{6}$, and the probability of getting a 5 on the second roll (B) is also $\frac{1}{6}$. Applying the Special Conjunction Rule, we calculate as follows:

$P(A \cdot B) = P(A) \times P(B)$
$P(A \cdot B) = \frac{1}{6} \times \frac{1}{6} = \frac{1}{36}$

The Special Conjunction Rule may be used to calculate the probability of a conjunction *whenever the events asserted in each of the conjuncts are independent of each other*, that is, when the occurrence of one event has no influence on the occurrence or nonoccurrence of the other. Each roll of a single die, for example, is independent of every other roll. Thus we can apply the Special Conjunction Rule to calculate the probability of getting a specific result on two successive rolls of a single die. When the conjuncts are not mutually independent, however, the Special Conjunction Rule cannot be used.

Consider a second example. What is the probability of drawing two aces in succession from a standard 52-card deck if the first card drawn is replaced and the deck thoroughly reshuffled after the first draw? The probability of drawing an ace on each draw is $\frac{1}{13}$. The probability of drawing two aces, then, is calculated as follows:

$P(A_1 \cdot A_2) = P(A_1) \times P(A_2)$
$P(A_1 \cdot A_2) = \frac{1}{13} \times \frac{1}{13} = \frac{1}{169}$

Now consider a real-life example. What is the probability that

---

[2] The expression "$P(p \cdot q)$" means "the probability of the conjunction of $p$ and $q$ when the occurrence or nonoccurrence of the event asserted by $p$ has no effect on the probability of the event asserted by $q$, and the occurrence or nonoccurrence of the event asserted by $q$ has no effect on the probability of the event asserted by $p$."

it will snow in Minneapolis and in Boston on January 14, 1997? Obviously, in order to do this calculation we must first assign a probability to each of the components. Let us suppose that we have checked the weather records of both cities since 1900, and have discovered that in Minneapolis the record shows snow on January 14 one year out of seven, and in Boston the record shows snow on that date two years out of thirteen. Taking the past record as the best available way of estimating future probabilities, we may calculate as follows:

$$P(M \cdot B) = P(M) \times P(B)$$
$$P(M \cdot B) = \tfrac{1}{7} \times \tfrac{2}{13} = \tfrac{2}{91}$$

We conclude, then, that the probability that it will snow in Minneapolis and in Boston on January 14, 1997, is $\tfrac{2}{91}$.

# 12.4 THE GENERAL CONJUNCTION RULE

What is the probability of drawing aces in two successive draws from a shuffled deck of cards if the first card drawn is *not* replaced before the second draw? In this case we cannot apply the Special Conjunction Rule since the two events are not mutually independent: if an ace is drawn on the first draw, the probability of getting an ace on the second draw is reduced by a small quantity and the probability of getting something other than an ace is increased by the same quantity.

The rule for making the calculation in such cases is called the **General Conjunction Rule.** In order to state this rule precisely, we need to understand the concept of contingent probability. Let A mean "an ace is drawn on the first draw," and let B mean "an ace is drawn on the second draw." We are interested in the probability of B only on the condition that A has occurred, since only on that condition can two aces be drawn in succession. This probability is expressed as P(B given A)—that is, the probability of B if A is true. With this concept, the General Conjunction Rule can now be stated as follows:

$$P(p \cdot q) = P(p) \times P(q \text{ given } p)$$

Since there are 52 cards in the deck, 4 of which are aces, it is clear that $P(A) = \tfrac{4}{52} = \tfrac{1}{13}$. But what is the probability of B if an ace is drawn on the first draw? It is not the same as the probability of A, for (a) there are now only 51 cards from which the draw will be made, and (b) if the first card drawn was an ace, then only three of the remaining cards are aces. Thus, the probability of (B given A) is

$\frac{3}{51} = \frac{1}{17}$. We may now calculate the probability of the conjunction of $A$ and $B$ as follows:

$P(A \cdot B) = P(A) \times P(B \text{ given } A)$
$P(A \cdot B) = \frac{1}{13} \times \frac{1}{17} = \frac{1}{221}$

The General Conjunction Rule may be used to calculate the probability of any conjunction, since if the conjuncts are mutually independent, the probability of ($q$ given $p$) will be the same as the probability of $q$. In the case of mutually independent conjuncts, however, the simpler Special Conjunction Rule may be used, whereas in any case involving nonindependent conjuncts the General Conjunction Rule *must* be used.

## EXERCISES 12.3–12.4

**A.** Answer the following questions, using the Special Conjunction Rule.
*Example:* What is the probability of getting heads on two successive tosses of a fair coin? Answer: The probability of getting heads on each toss is $\frac{1}{2}$. Therefore:
$P(H_1 \cdot H_2) = P(H_1) \times P(H_2)$
$P(H_1 \cdot H_2) = \frac{1}{2} \times \frac{1}{2} = \frac{1}{4}$

1. What is the probability of getting a head and a tail (in that order) on two successive tosses of a fair coin?
2. What is the probability of throwing a pair of 3s on a single throw of two unloaded dice?
3. What is the probability of throwing a pair of 6s on a single throw of two unloaded dice?
4. You are to make two draws from a shuffled deck of bridge cards (52 cards in all), replacing the first card drawn and reshuffling before making your second draw.
   a. What is the probability of drawing two queens?
   b. What is the probability of drawing two spades?
   c. What is the probability of drawing an ace on draw 1 and a club on draw 2?
   d. What is the probability of drawing two red cards?
   e. What is the probability of drawing two face cards?
   f. What is the probability of drawing two even-numbered cards?
   g. What is the probability of drawing an ace on draw 1 and an even-numbered card on draw 2?
   h. What is the probability of drawing the ace of spades on draw 1 and a face card on draw 2?
   i. What is the probability of drawing two even-numbered cards above 5?
   j. What is the probability of drawing the ace of hearts and the king of diamonds (in that order)?
5. The weather service states that on a given date there is a 40 percent

chance of rain in San Francisco and a 60 percent chance of rain in Seattle. What is the probability of rain in both San Francisco and Seattle on that date?

**B.** Answer the following questions, using the General Conjunction Rule:

1. You are to draw two cards from a standard deck of bridge cards, but this time you are not to replace the first card drawn.

   **a.** What is the probability of drawing an ace on draw 1 and a face card on draw 2?

   **b.** What is the probability of drawing two red cards?

   **c.** What is the probability of drawing a red card on draw 1 and a black card on draw 2?

   **d.** What is the probability of drawing two even-numbered cards?

   **e.** What is the probability of drawing two clubs?

2. The lead-off batter on a certain baseball team has a batting average of .320. The next batter in the line-up has a batting average of .290, but being a noted clutch hitter he bats .340 when another runner is on base. What is the probability that both batters will get hits in successive turns at bat?

3. Someone, in a burst of generosity, has given you a bag containing 50 red and 50 green jelly beans. You select one at random and eat it, then you select a second at random and eat it as well.

   **a.** What is the probability that both of the jelly beans you selected were green?

   **b.** What is the probability that both of the jelly beans you selected were red?

   **c.** What is the probability that the jelly beans you selected were of the same color?

   **d.** What is the probability that the first one was green and the second red?

   **e.** What is the probability that one (either) was red and the other green?

# 12.5 THE EXCLUSIVE DISJUNCTION RULE

Sometimes we are interested not in the probability that two events will occur in combination, but rather in the probability that *one or the other* of two events will occur. To calculate the probabilities in such cases we use either the Exclusive Disjunction Rule or the General Disjunction Rule.

The **Exclusive Disjunction Rule** may be used only when the disjuncts are mutually exclusive, that is, when the truth of one implies the falsehood of the other. Such a statement can be expressed symbolically in either of the following ways:

$$\sim(p \equiv q) \qquad or \qquad (p \lor q) \cdot (\sim p \lor \sim q)$$

Using the first of these logically equivalent expressions, we may now state the Exclusive Disjunction Rule as follows:

$$P{\sim}(p \equiv q) = P(p) + P(q)$$

That is to say, if $p$ and $q$ are mutually exclusive possibilities, then the probability that *one or the other* (but not both) will occur is equal to the probability that $p$ will occur plus the probability that $q$ will occur.

Consider once again the tossing of a fair coin. Let $H$ equal "It will fall heads," and let $T$ equal "It will fall tails." Clearly, in this case one statement must be true and one false. The probability of $H$ is $\frac{1}{2}$ and the probability of $T$ is $\frac{1}{2}$. Therefore, according to the Exclusive Disjunction Rule, $P(H \vee T) = \frac{1}{2} + \frac{1}{2} = 1$. This result is, of course, consistent with the common-sense observation that the coin must fall either heads or tails.[3]

Consider another example. An ordinary deck of bridge cards has been thoroughly shuffled, and we are to draw one card. What is the probability that the card we draw will be an ace ($A$) or a face card ($F$)? The probability of drawing an ace $= \frac{4}{52} = \frac{1}{13}$. The probability of drawing a face card $= \frac{12}{52} = \frac{3}{13}$. Therefore, according to the Exclusive Disjunction Rule:

$$P(A \vee F) = P(A) + P(F) = \frac{1}{13} + \frac{3}{13} = \frac{4}{13}$$

This, again, is consistent with our intuitive judgment that, since there are 16 cards in the deck that fit the description "ace or face," the probability of drawing one of those cards is $\frac{16}{52} = \frac{4}{13}$.

The Exclusive Disjunction Rule does not apply, however, when the alternatives are not mutually exclusive. Suppose, for example, that the probability that it will rain in Miami tomorrow is 80 percent ($\frac{4}{5}$), and the probability that it will rain in New York City tomorrow is 50 percent ($\frac{1}{2}$). If we tried to apply the Exclusive Disjunction Rule in this case, we would get the result that the probability that it will rain either in Miami or in New York City tomorrow is 130 percent ($\frac{13}{10}$), which is absurd. The Exclusive Disjunction Rule is applicable only when the disjuncts are mutually exclusive, that is, only when the truth of one excludes the possibility of the truth of the other. Since the occurrence of rain in Miami does not exclude the possibility that it may also rain in New York City, and vice versa, the Exclusive Disjunction Rule does not apply.

---

[3] For purposes of this calculation we ignore the infinitesimally small probability that the coin will fall *neither* heads nor tails, but on its edge.

**12.6** THE GENERAL DISJUNCTION RULE

In order to calculate the probability of a disjunction when the disjuncts are *not* mutually exclusive, we must use the **General Disjunction Rule**. This rule may be stated as follows:

$$P(p \lor q) = P(p) + P(q) - P(p \cdot q)$$

That is to say, the probability of a disjunction is equal to the sum of the probabilities of the disjuncts minus the probability of their joint occurrence. The probability of their joint occurrence is, of course, calculated by means of the appropriate conjunction rule (see Sections 12.3 and 12.4).

Let us consider a simple problem that can be solved by means of this rule. What is the probability of drawing a club (C) or an ace (A) on a random draw from a standard 52-card deck? According to the General Disjunction Rule, we would calculate this probability as follows:

$$P(C \lor A) = P(C) + P(A) - P(C \cdot A)$$
$$P(C \lor A) = \tfrac{13}{52} + \tfrac{4}{52} - \tfrac{1}{52} = \tfrac{16}{52} = \tfrac{4}{13}$$

Note that this result is consistent with our common-sense observation that there are 16 cards in the deck—13 clubs plus 3 aces that are not clubs—that fit the definition "a club or an ace." In order to avoid counting the ace of clubs twice, however, we must subtract the card that is both a club and an ace; otherwise we would get the erroneous result that the probability of getting a club or an ace on a single draw is $\tfrac{17}{52}$. This is exactly what is accomplished when we subtract the probability of the conjunction of the two disjuncts ($\tfrac{13}{52} \times \tfrac{4}{52} = \tfrac{1}{52}$).

We can now solve the problem concerning the probability of rain in Miami *or* New York City on a given date on the supposition that the probability of rain in Miami (M) is $\tfrac{4}{5}$ and that of rain in New York City (N) is $\tfrac{1}{2}$. The solution is as follows:

$$P(M \lor N) = P(M) + P(N) - P(M \cdot N)$$
$$P(M \lor N) = \tfrac{8}{10} + \tfrac{5}{10} - \tfrac{4}{10} = \tfrac{9}{10}$$

We conclude, therefore, that if there is an 80 percent probability of rain in Miami on a given date and a 50 percent probability of rain in New York City on the same date, then the probability of rain in Miami *or* New York City (i.e., at least one, and possibly both) is 90 percent.

The General Disjunction Rule can be used for all disjunctions, exclusive or inclusive, since in the case of an exclusive disjunction, $P(p \cdot q)$ will always be 0. Thus in the case of an exclusive disjunction,

$P(p) + P(q)$ is exactly the same as $P(p) + P(q) - P(p \cdot q)$. For exclusive disjunctions, however, one may use the simpler Exclusive Disjunction Rule, but for disjunctions in which the disjuncts are not mutually exclusive one must use the General Disjunction Rule.

## 12.7 THE NEGATION RULE

We already know (Section 8.11) that any statement of the form $p \lor \sim p$ is a tautology, that is, a statement that is true regardless of the truth value of $p$. Any statement of the form $p \lor \sim p$, therefore, has a probability of 1. A statement of the form $p \lor \sim p$, however, is an exclusive disjunction. Since $P(p \lor \sim p) = 1$, it follows that $P(p) + P(\sim p) = 1$, from which it also follows that $P(\sim p) = 1 - P(p)$. This last formula is called the **Negation Rule**. It enables us to calculate the probability of the negation of any statement whose probability is known.

Let us return to our example concerning the probability of drawing an ace or a face card in a random draw from a shuffled deck (Section 12.3). What is the probability of *not* drawing an ace or a face card in a single draw? Having calculated the probability of drawing an ace or a face card ($A \lor F$) as $\frac{4}{13}$, we can easily calculate the negation of this outcome as follows:

$P(A \lor F) = \frac{4}{13}$
$P\sim(A \lor F) = 1 - P(A \lor F)$
$P\sim(A \lor F) = 1 - \frac{4}{13} = \frac{9}{13}$

Thus, the probability of drawing a card other than an ace or a face card is $\frac{9}{13}$.

## EXERCISES 12.5–12.7

A.  Answer the following questions using the Exclusive Disjunction Rule.
    1.  You are to roll a single unloaded die. What is the probability of rolling:
        a.  a 2 or a 6?
        b.  an even number or a 3?
        c.  a 1 or a number greater than 3?
        d.  an odd number or an even number other than 6?
        e.  an odd number or an even number?
    2.  You are to make a random draw from a standard 52-card deck of bridge cards. What is the probability of drawing:
        a.  a red face card or a black ace?
        b.  a red face card or a black face card?

    **c.** an even-numbered card or an ace?

    **d.** an odd-numbered red card or a black card?

    **e.** a black face card or the queen of hearts?

  **3.** A certain quarterback is noted for his passing game. His statistics on pass plays are as follows: 40 percent completions, 52 percent incompletions, 5 percent interceptions, and 3 percent sacks. On a given pass play, what is the probability of:

    **a.** an incompletion or an interception?

    **b.** an interception or a sack?

    **c.** a completion or an incompletion?

    **d.** a completion or an interception?

    **e.** an incompletion or a sack?

**B.**  Answer the following questions using the General Disjunction Rule.

  **1.** Lefty Smith and Slugger Jones are about to take their turns at bat. Lefty's batting average is .260, Slugger's is .340. What is the probability that Lefty or Slugger will get a hit in his turn at bat?

  **2.** There is a 60 percent probability of rain on Monday and an 80 percent probability of rain on Tuesday. What is the probability of rain on Monday or Tuesday?

  **3.** Joe and Fred are enrolled in the same course. Joe has already ensured a passing grade, and there is a probability of .95 that Fred will also pass. What is the probability that Joe or Fred will pass?

  **4.** Margo and Virginia both entered a lottery to win a free trip to London. Margo has learned that she has been eliminated, but Virginia is among 100 finalists, of whom 2 will be randomly selected as winners. What is the probability that Margo or Virginia will be a winner?

  **5.** You are to roll a pair of unloaded dice. On a single roll, what is the probability of rolling:

    **a.** an even number or a number above 6?

    **b.** a double or a number above 6?

    **c.** an odd number or a number greater than 4 and less than 10?

    **d.** a 7 or an odd number above 7?

    **e.** a double or a 4?

**C.**  Calculate the probability of $\sim R$ for each of the indicated probabilities of $R$:

| | |
|---|---|
| **1.** $P(R) = .97.$ | **6.** $P(R) = \frac{4}{5}$ |
| **2.** $P(R) = .45.$ | **7.** $P(R) = \frac{81}{131}$ |
| **3.** $P(R) = .83.$ | **8.** $P(R) = \frac{9}{17}$ |
| **4.** $P(R) = .91.$ | **9.** $P(R) = \frac{12}{19}$ |
| **5.** $P(R) = .35.$ | **10.** $P(R) = \frac{107}{313}$ |

# 12.8 PROBABILITY IN REAL-LIFE SITUATIONS

The probabilities that can be calculated according to the rules discussed in Sections 12.3–12.7 may be summarized as follows:

| IF YOU KNOW OR ASSUME: | THEN YOU CAN CALCULATE: | BY MEANS OF: |
|---|---|---|
| 1. The probability of $p$ and of $q$ when $p$ and $q$ are mutually independent | The probability of $(p \cdot q)^1$ | The Special Conjunction Rule |
| 2. The probability of $p$ and of $q$ whether or not $p$ and $q$ are mutually independent | The probability of $(p \cdot q)$ | The General Conjunction Rule |
| 3. The probability of $p$ and of $q$ when $p$ and $q$ are mutually exclusive | The probability of $\sim(p \equiv q)$ | The Exclusive Disjunction Rule |
| 4. The probability of $p$ and of $q$ whether or not $p$ and $q$ are mutually exclusive | The probability of $(p \lor q)$ | The General Disjunction Rule |
| 5. The probability of $p$ | The probability of $\sim p$ | The Negation Rule |

Admittedly, most of the examples that I have chosen to illustrate the above rules have been drawn from situations in which one can see more or less directly what the probabilities are. The value of such examples, however, lies precisely in their simplicity: they help us understand the rules that they exemplify, and they provide an intuitive validation of those rules. Once we have considered a few examples dealing with thrown dice, tossed coins, random draws from a deck of cards, and so on, we cannot seriously doubt that *if* we know or assume the probabilities of some statements, we can calculate the probabilities of certain other statements (conjunctions, disjunctions, negations) of which those statements are components. The rules of probability, in short, provide *some* help in finding our way about in a world in which most of the statements that we wish to assert—tautologies being the only indisputable exceptions—are, at best, only more or less probable.

Let us now apply the appropriate rules to a pair of real-life situations.

Situation 1: A young married couple has a son who is one year old. They do not plan to have any more children. The father is 30 years of age, the mother 25. For planning purposes they wish to determine the probability that both parents will survive until their child reaches age 21. Their problem, therefore, may be stated as follows: What is the joint probability that the father will survive to age 50, the mother to age 45, and the child to age 21? They consult a mortality table and learn that the probability that a 30-year-old white American male will survive to age 50 is .934; the probability that a 25-year-old white American female will survive to age 45 is

.956; and the probability that a one-year-old white American male will survive to age 21 is .985. Applying the Special Conjunction Rule, they calculate the probability that both parents will survive for an additional 20 years as follows ($F$ = father will live to age 50, $M$ = mother will live to age 45):

$P(F \cdot M) = P(F) \times P(M)$
$P(F \cdot M) = .934 \times .956 = .893$

or approximately $\frac{9}{10}$. The probability that the parents will survive until their one-year-old child is 21 years of age can now be calculated as follows ($S$ = son will survive to age 21):

$P[(F \cdot M) \cdot S] = P(F \cdot M) \times P(S)$
$P[(F \cdot M) \cdot S] = .893 \times .985 = .879$

or approximately $\frac{22}{25}$. Obviously, there is also a probability of approximately $\frac{3}{25}$ that at least one of the three will not survive an additional 20 years.

Can any practical consequences be drawn from these calculations? Yes. The finding that the probability that all three family members will survive until the child is 21 years of age is about $\frac{22}{25}$ (88 percent) might, for example, influence important decisions in such areas as insurance plans, the family budget, vacation plans (current enjoyment versus deferred enjoyment), and so on.

Situation 2: An entrepreneur is considering opening a retail store to sell and service computers for use by small businesses and private individuals. His research indicates that the success of the proposed venture depends on (a) the availability of at least $100,000 in capital, (b) securing franchises to sell and service at least three different makes of computer, and (c) the nonappearance of another microcomputer store within a five-mile radius during the first two years of operation. What is the probability of the proposed venture's success?

It is obvious that in this case there is nothing corresponding to a mortality table that our entrepreneur can consult in order to determine the probabilities of the individual conditions. He must therefore simply *estimate* the initial probabilities in order to set up his problem in mathematical form. He does so, assigning the following probabilities:

1.  The probability of raising at least $100,000 in capital ($C$) is .90.
2.  The probability of securing franchises to sell and service at least three makes of computers ($F$) is .95.
3.  The probability that no competition will appear within a five-mile radius during the first two years of operation ($\sim O$) is estimated at .80.

The initial probabilities, therefore, are estimated as follows:

$P(C) = .90.$
$P(F) = .95.$
$P(\sim O) = .80.$

The probability of the proposed venture's success can now be calculated as the probability of the joint occurrence of $C$ and $F$ and $\sim O$. Thus:

$P[(C \cdot F) \cdot \sim O] = [P(C) \times P(F)] \times P(\sim O)$
$P[(C \cdot F) \cdot \sim O] = .90 \times .95 \times .80 = .684$

or approximately $\frac{2}{3}$.

Note, however, that this calculation of the probability of success is subject to error at two points. First, the entrepreneur's identification of the factors essential to success may be in error. It may be, for example, that the success of the proposed venture also depends, say, on a 50 percent annual increase in the market for small computers during the first three years of operation, and that this in turn requires an average annual decrease of 10 percent in the retail price of computers during the same period. Second, the entrepreneur's estimate of the initial probabilities may be in error. Different assumptions on either of these points would, of course, yield a different conclusion regarding the probability of the proposed venture's success.

Most real-life applications of probability theory involve estimates similar to those required in our computer-store example. Probability theory does not remove guesswork from human planning; it merely helps us to identify the points where we have no choice but to do some educated guessing, and it teaches us how to calculate certain other probabilities that follow from our initial estimates. This is perhaps a less spectacular result than we might have wished for, but it is all that probability theory can give us at the present stage of its development.

# thirteen
# Causal Arguments

Many of the arguments that we employ in everyday reasoning as well as in certain kinds of scientific inquiry are *causal* arguments, that is, arguments in which it is stated in the conclusion that something *x* is the *cause* of something else *y*. In this chapter we shall analyze the logic of such arguments.

## 13.1 WHY WE SEEK CAUSES

There are four principal purposes for which we may be interested in identifying the causes of phenomena. One purpose is quite simply to satisfy our curiosity. We may stare in awe at the astonishing spectacle of the so-called Northern Lights, and may become so curious about the cause or causes of this celestial display that we are moved to consult an encyclopedia or a book on astronomy to find an answer to our question. Or we may read about the periodic self-destructive behavior of lemmings, and may begin to speculate about the possible cause of this phenomenon that seems to us so contrary to nature. The twinkling of stars, the migration of birds, the turning of leaves in autumn, the varying shapes of clouds—any phenomenon that **281** catches our attention can become an object of curiosity and can launch us on a search for causes, a search that may take us far beyond the confines of our present knowledge. Curiosity is a powerful stimulus to inquiry and reasoning about causes.

A second purpose for which we sometimes attempt to identify causes is to acquire the power to produce certain desired effects, the power to make things happen. An economist may note, for example, that worker productivity in Japan is on the rise, and may pose the question "Why is this occurring?" The economist is asking a causal question: What is the *cause* (or what are the *causes*) of the rise in worker productivity in Japan? Other questions of this type are: Why do the residents of _____ live to an average age of 97? Why are there so few alcohol-related auto accidents in Sweden? Why has Germany produced so many of the world's great composers? In each case, the supposition is that if we could identify the causes, we might be able to produce similar effects in another setting. Knowledge of causes is the kind of knowledge that justifies the saying that knowledge is power.

A third purpose for which we sometimes want to identify causes is just the opposite of the previous one: to acquire the power to prevent certain *un*desired effects from occurring—in short, to make things *stop* happening. Medical diagnosis consists largely of this kind of search for causes: the patient has such-and-such symptoms (the effects), and the diagnostician wants to know what is *causing* those symptoms in order, if possible, to eliminate them by eliminating the cause. Mechanics search for causes for similar reasons, as do plumbers, appliance repairers, counselors, accident investigators, and—at one time or another—all of us. To know what causes a phenomenon is, at least sometimes, to know how to prevent it. (Not always, however. It was known that poliomyelitis is caused by a particular virus long before Dr. Jonas Salk was able to perfect the vaccine that has virtually eliminated this crippling disease.)

A fourth reason for trying to identify causes is to enable us to establish responsibility for something that has happened. Clearly, we assume that human beings are sometimes causal agents, and not infrequently we want to know *who* is the agent-cause in order to know who should be praised or blamed, rewarded or punished, for the act. "Who left the door unlocked?"; "Who drove over the lawn?"; "Who rescued the child from drowning?"; "Who painted that marvelous picture?" are questions aimed at the identification of causes in order properly to ascribe praise or blame.

## EXERCISE 13.1

State the purpose or purposes for which someone might reasonably be interested in identifying the causes of the following phenomena:

1. The rusting of automobiles.
2. Acne.
3. Shooting stars.
4. The migration of birds.
5. The emergence of genius.
6. Inflation.
7. Magnetism.
8. The low birth rate in Ireland.
9. The failure of all except three students on the first midterm in Chemistry 101.
10. The awarding of a lucrative state contract to the governor's son-in-law.
11. The decline in church membership from 1970 to 1980.
12. A sudden increase in the incidence of lung cancer.
13. A marked change in the personality and behavior of a member of one's family.
14. The natural occurrence of petroleum in some parts of the world and not others.
15. The biting of fish at some times and not at others.
16. The unhealthy appearance of one's lawn.
17. A pain in one's hip.
18. The double image that one gets by pressing one's finger gently against an eyeball.
19. The bearing of an apple tree some years but not others.
20. The whining of one's dog at 2:00 A.M.

# 13.2  THE CONCEPT OF CAUSALITY

At the intuitive level, most of us probably think of a cause simply as "that which produces an effect," or "that which makes something occur." This intuitive notion is all right as far as it goes, but unfortunately it does not take us very far toward an understanding of causality. Suppose, for example, that my house has been struck by lightning and has burned down. Which of the following events would you identify as the "cause" of the fire?

1. The presence of oxygen plus heat of such temperature as to ignite the materials of which my house was constructed.
2. The failure of the contractor who built my house to install a lightning rod.
3. My failure to instruct the contractor to install a lightning rod.
4. My ignorance regarding the importance of having a lightning rod—or, alternatively, my negligence in not having one installed.
5. The conductivity of moist air, in the absence of which the lightning could not have reached my house.
6. The occurrence of lightning at that particular place and time.

7.   The occurrence of weather conditions in the absence of which lightning would not have occurred.
8.   The multitude of preconditions, mostly unknown, that brought about those weather conditions.
9.   All of the above.

One is tempted to choose number 9—"All of the above"—for there does indeed seem to be some sense in which each of these possible "causes" might have played a role in the burning down of my house. In what sense, then, in each case? Are there, perhaps, different kinds of causes? The answer is that there are. Let us try to sort them out.

We may distinguish, first, between **remote** causes and **proximate** causes. It may be, for example, that the eruption of Mount St. Helens contributed to the weather conditions that resulted in the fateful bolt of lightning that ignited my house. Indeed, we may think of a sequence or chain of causes, as follows:

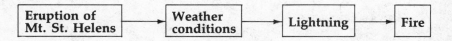

The proximate cause of the fire, then, was the occurrence of an extremely high temperature in the presence of oxygen, the proximate cause of the lightning was the weather conditions, a proximate cause of these weather conditions was the eruption of Mount St. Helens, and the eruption of Mount St. Helens presumably had its proximate causes as well. A proximate cause is that cause in a given sequence of causes that immediately precedes the event whose cause we are interested in determining. With respect to that same event, all causes in the sequence that precede the proximate cause are remote causes.

Second, we may distinguish between **tractable** causes and **intractable** causes. To say that causes of a certain kind are tractable is to say that the state of human knowledge and technology enables us to intervene in a causal sequence in such a way as to influence subsequent events in that sequence—to make certain things happen or not happen. In the above causal sequence, for example, we do not call anyone to task for allowing Mount St. Helens to erupt, or the weather conditions to develop, or lightning to occur, because we assume that the current state of science and technology is such that we are not able to do anything about the causes of those events. The causes of those events are intractable. But we do know about lightning rods, and we know that a building is less likely to be set on fire by a bolt of lightning if it has one. We can therefore control—to some extent, at least—the burning down of buildings even if lightning does occur. Lightning is to some extent a tractable cause, one in a sequence of causes that is to some extent subject to human intervention.

If human intervention would have been sufficient to prevent an undesirable event (such as the burning down of my house), we typically ask whether any particular human being might reasonably have been expected to intervene in the requisite way. If the answer is affirmative (e.g., I for not ordering a lightning rod, or the contractor for not installing one), then we have identified a human agent who is appropriately blamed—not, strictly speaking, for causing the event, but for failing to prevent it. If a human being does intervene in a sequence of events that appears to be leading toward an undesirable result (for example, a passer-by rescues a drowning child), we typically praise that person—not, again, for causing something to happen, but for preventing something from happening. If, however, the natural course of events is tending toward a desirable result, we regard it as blameworthy to intervene (i.e., to prevent the desirable result from occurring), and we regard it as praiseworthy not to do so.

Third, we may distinguish between causes in the sense of necessary conditions and causes in the sense of sufficient conditions. To say that event $A$ is a **necessary condition** for the occurrence of event $B$ is to say that the nonoccurrence of $A$ guarantees the nonoccurrence of $B$. An adequate air supply to one's lungs, for example, is a necessary condition for life for air-breathing creatures like us. Therefore, if for any reason a human being is deprived of an adequate air supply—as when one drowns, for example—life ceases. It is in this sense that we (or perhaps a coroner) may say that lack of an adequate air supply—or drowning—was the cause of death in some particular instance, even if the proximate cause of the drowning was some careless or malicious act by another human being.

To say that event $A$ is a **sufficient condition** for the occurrence of event $B$ is to say that the occurrence of $A$ guarantees the occurrence of $B$, or, more simply, that whenever $A$ occurs, $B$ also occurs. The occurrence of a flame, for example, is a sufficient condition for an increase in the temperature of the air immediately adjacent to the flame. It is in this sense of "cause" that someone might say that the cause of the overheating of the house was the continuous burning of the furnace, even though the proximate cause of the continuous burning of the furnace may have been, say, a malfunctioning thermostat.

If event $A$ is a necessary condition for the occurrence of event $B$, then the occurrence of $B$ guarantees the prior or contemporaneous occurrence of $A$. The occurrence of fire, for example, guarantees the presence of oxygen. We may therefore reason from the occurrence of any event to the occurrence of anything that is known to be a necessary condition for events of that type.

It is also the case that if $A$ is a necessary condition for $B$, then the nonoccurrence of $A$ is a sufficient condition for the nonoccurrence of $B$. This fact may also be expressed as follows: if $A$ is a necessary condition for $B$, then $\sim A$ is a sufficient condition for $\sim B$.

If event $A$ is a sufficient condition for the occurrence of event $B$, then the nonoccurrence of $B$ guarantees the nonoccurrence of $A$. If my house has not burned down, for example, then it is evident that it has not been subjected to extremely high temperatures in the presence of oxygen. Thus we may reason from the nonoccurrence of any event to the nonoccurrence of anything known to be a sufficient condition for the occurrence of events of that type.

Events of a given type may have several necessary conditions. The occurrence of fire, for example, has at least three necessary conditions: the presence of a combustible substance, the occurrence of a sufficiently high temperature to ignite that substance, and the presence of oxygen. If any one of those conditions is not fulfilled, fire does not occur.

Events of a given type may also have several sufficient conditions. A very large downpour of rain, for example, may be a sufficient condition for the occurrence of a flood in a given locale, but so also may the rapid melting of snow or the breaking of a dam. A particular flood will, of course, have its own particular sufficient conditions, but the sufficient conditions of flood $F_1$ may be different from the sufficient conditions of floods $F_2$, $F_3$, and so on.

Given all of these distinctions, it is evident that the question "What was the *cause* of event $X$?" may be answered in a variety of ways, and that the appropriate answer depends on the questioner's interest in asking the question. If the questioner is interested in knowing which of several possible proximate causes resulted in a particular fire, it is appropriate to give such answers as "lightning," "smoking in bed," "electrical malfunction," "arson," and so on, and inappropriate to recite the necessary and/or sufficient conditions for the occurrence of fires in general. (It would be inappropriate in this case to say, for example, "The fire was caused by the subjection of a combustible material to a high temperature in the presence of oxygen.") If the questioner is interested in establishing human responsibility for a given event (i.e., who caused it or failed to prevent it?), the distinction between tractable and intractable causes is of principal importance. Finally, if one is interested in determining the causal laws governing the occurrence of certain types of events, or in identifying the proximate cause in a case in which the relevant causal laws are known, the distinction between necessary and sufficient conditions is of principal importance.

## EXERCISE 13.2

Analyze the following statements, using, as appropriate, the distinctions between proximate and remote causes, tractable and intractable causes, and necessary and sufficient conditions:

1. Death was caused by a blow to the head.
2. The revolution was caused by a long list of grievances, the latest of which was a severe food shortage.
3. The power outage in New England resulted from the OPEC oil embargo.
4. The jeering of the crowd made him angry.
5. His anger caused him to speak rashly.
6. His rash speech cost him the election.
7. The jeering of the crowd caused him to lose the election.
8. The derailment occurred because the switchman neglected to throw a switch.
9. The crash resulted from faulty brakes.
10. The brakes failed because of a design defect.
11. The company elected not to acknowledge the design defect because of the high cost that it would incur.
12. The crash was caused by corporate avarice.
13. Cigarette smoking causes lung cancer.
14. Migraine headaches are sometimes caused by the eating of certain foods.
15. Ocean tides are caused by the gravitational pull of the moon.
16. Overwork gave him ulcers.
17. His poor eyesight resulted from too much reading with inadequate light.
18. His poor study habits and lack of effort resulted in his flunking out of school.
19. Her desire to get away from home drove her to a disastrous early marriage.
20. The improved appearance of the lawn resulted from an increase of nitrogen in the soil.

# 13.3 THE SEARCH FOR CAUSES

The first philosopher to attempt a systematic summary of the principles of reasoning concerning causes was John Stuart Mill (1806–73), who identified five "methods" to be used in experimental inquiry. These five—Mill's methods—are the Method of Agreement, the Method of Difference, the Joint Method of Agreement and Difference, the Method of Residues, and the Method of Concomitant Variation. Subsequent analysis[1] has demonstrated, however, that Mill's sum-

---

[1] See especially Georg Henrik von Wright, *A Treatise on Induction and Probability* (London: Routledge & Kegan Paul, 1951).

mary of the principles of causal reasoning is both redundant and incomplete: it is redundant because the Method of Residues and the Method of Concomitant Variation are unnecessary if one employs the other methods, and it is incomplete because it fails to identify two additional methods that are sometimes employed in the search for causes. Acknowledging logic's debt to Mill for his pioneering work in this area, we shall nonetheless discuss the principles of causal inquiry from a more contemporary perspective. Moreover, in accordance with the practice of most contemporary logicians, we shall analyze those principles primarily in terms of the distinction between necessary and sufficient conditions.

## 13.4 THE DIRECT METHOD OF AGREEMENT

The **Direct Method of Agreement** is a method for identifying necessary conditions for events of a given type.[2] The method consists in (a) identifying what one believes to be some possible necessary conditions for events of that type, and (b) examining a number of events of the type in question in an attempt to determine whether events of that type are always preceded or accompanied by one (or more) of the possible necessary conditions previously identified. If so, and if no counterexamples are discovered after a sufficiently large number of cases have been examined, one is justified in concluding (with some degree of confidence) that the possible necessary condition thus identified is indeed a necessary condition for the event in question.

Suppose, for example, that a medical researcher is attempting to determine the cause of postpartum depression (psychological depression following childbirth). Obviously, giving birth is itself a necessary condition for postpartum depression, but that is not the "cause" the researcher is looking for. What the researcher wants to know is: What physiological phenomenon occurs in some but not all instances of childbirth and is present in every case of postpartum depression? If this question could be answered, and if the necessary condition thus identified should turn out to be tractable, it would then be possible to treat postpartum depression, that is, to eliminate the malady by removing a necessary condition for it.

The researcher's first step is to identify some possible necessary conditions for postpartum depression. Let us suppose that, on the basis of his or her knowledge of the physiological changes associated

---

[2] Mill writes of this method simply as the "Method of Agreement." We term it the "Direct Method of Agreement" to distinguish it from the "Inverse Method of Agreement," which Mill did not discuss.

with pregnancy and childbirth, the researcher theorizes that the depression is caused by an excess or deficit of some hormone. The researcher identifies, let us say, five hormones that he or she thinks might be causally related to postpartum depression, and begins to collect data on women who are experiencing such depression. After studying ten cases, the researcher finds the following results ($-$ indicates a deficit of a given hormone, $+$ indicates an excess of a given hormone, $Y$ indicates that the condition is present, $N$ that it is not present):

| | | | | | Hormone | | | | | |
|---|---|---|---|---|---|---|---|---|---|---|
| Case | $A-$ | $B-$ | $C-$ | $D-$ | $E-$ | $A+$ | $B+$ | $C+$ | $D+$ | $E+$ |
| 1 | Y | N | N | Y | Y | N | Y | N | N | N |
| 2 | Y | N | N | Y | Y | N | Y | Y | Y | N |
| 3 | N | Y | N | Y | Y | Y | Y | Y | N | N |
| 4 | Y | Y | N | Y | Y | N | N | Y | N | Y |
| 5 | N | Y | Y | Y | N | N | N | N | Y | Y |
| 6 | Y | N | N | Y | N | N | N | Y | N | N |
| 7 | N | Y | N | Y | N | N | N | Y | Y | N |
| 8 | Y | N | N | Y | Y | Y | N | Y | N | Y |
| 9 | Y | N | N | Y | Y | N | Y | N | Y | Y |
| 10 | Y | N | Y | Y | N | Y | Y | Y | N | N |

It is apparent that if one of the ten candidates identified by the researcher is indeed the "cause" (i.e., a necessary condition) of postpartum depression, that candidate must be $D-$ (a deficit of hormone $D$), since that is the only condition that is present in all ten cases. There is, of course, no way for our researcher to be sure in advance that any of the candidates identified really is a necessary condition for postpartum depression, and after collecting data on only ten cases he or she is not likely to be very confident that a deficit of hormone $D$ is in fact a necessary condition. If no counter-examples were discovered in a hundred cases, our researcher's confidence in the result would increase, and that confidence would continue to grow as the number of confirming cases increased with no counterexamples.

The search for causes becomes more complicated when one considers the possibility that the "necessary condition" that one is seeking may turn out to be a disjunction, that is, *any one* of two or more conditions. In the summary of findings regarding postpartum depression, for example, $D-$ (a deficit of hormone $D$) is not the only condition that is present in all the cases: $(A- \lor B-)$—a deficit of hormone $A$ or hormone $B$—is also present in all ten cases. "The" cause of a given type of illness may turn out to be not one thing but *one of several*, no one of which is present in all cases. The "necessary condition" for the result, in such cases, is the disjunction of the various events *at least one* of which has been found to precede or accompany every occurrence of the type of event whose cause is being sought.

The Direct Method of Agreement is a method for seeking an *unvarying antecedent or concomitant* of some phenomenon or class of events. It is the method that we often employ when we seek to identify the causes of undesirable phenomena in order to gain the power to prevent them from occurring.

## EXERCISES 13.3–13.4

**A.** State which of the following must be the case if $A$ is a necessary condition for $B$:
  1. Whenever $A$ occurs, $B$ occurs.
  2. Whenever $A$ fails to occur, $B$ fails to occur.
  3. Whenever $B$ occurs, $A$ has occurred.
  4. Whenever $B$ fails to occur, $A$ has failed to occur.

**B.** On the basis of your general knowledge, state what you believe to be the necessary conditions for phenomena of the following types:
  1. A dented fender.
  2. A bruise.
  3. A touchdown (in football).
  4. A high grade-point average throughout four years of college.
  5. Being overweight.
  6. A snowstorm.
  7. A suntan.
  8. Suffocation.
  9. Playing major league baseball.
  10. Becoming a lawyer.

**C.** Consider the following summary of information regarding some possible necessary conditions for phenomenon $Z$:

| | Condition | | | | | | | | | | Phenomenon |
|---|---|---|---|---|---|---|---|---|---|---|---|
| Case | $A$ | $B$ | $C$ | $D$ | $E$ | $F$ | $G$ | $H$ | $I$ | $J$ | $Z$ |
| 1 | Y | N | Y | Y | N | N | N | Y | N | Y | Y |
| 2 | Y | N | N | Y | N | Y | N | Y | N | N | Y |
| 3 | N | Y | Y | Y | N | Y | N | Y | Y | Y | Y |
| 4 | N | Y | N | Y | Y | N | N | Y | Y | Y | Y |
| 5 | Y | N | Y | Y | Y | N | N | N | Y | Y | Y |
| 6 | Y | N | N | Y | Y | Y | N | N | N | N | Y |
| 7 | N | Y | Y | Y | N | Y | N | N | N | Y | Y |
| 8 | N | Y | N | Y | N | N | N | Y | N | N | Y |
| 9 | Y | N | Y | Y | N | N | N | Y | Y | N | Y |
| 10 | N | Y | N | Y | Y | Y | N | N | Y | N | Y |

On the basis of the above information, which of the following candidates remain as possible necessary conditions for $Z$?

1. $A$        6. $D$
2. $B$        7. $\sim D$
3. $A \vee B$        8. $E \vee F$
4. $C$        9. $G$
5. $C \vee E$        10. $\sim G$

# 13.5 THE INVERSE METHOD OF AGREEMENT

If we wish to eliminate an undesirable phenomenon, it is sufficient to identify any tractable necessary condition for that phenomenon, since the removal of a necessary condition will automatically eliminate that for which it is a necessary condition. For this purpose, the Method of Direct Agreement is appropriate. If, however, we wish to know the "cause" of a certain type of phenomenon in order to acquire the power to *produce* phenomena of that type—to make them occur—it is not enough merely to identify a necessary condition, for a necessary condition may not by itself guarantee the occurrence of the desired phenomenon. (For example, the presence of oxygen is a necessary condition for the occurrence of fire, but the presence of oxygen does not by itself guarantee the occurrence of fire.) In order to be able to produce a given type of phenomenon at will, we need to identify a tractable *sufficient* condition, a condition whose occurrence guarantees the occurrence of the desired phenomenon. The **Inverse Method of Agreement** is used in searching for sufficient conditions.[3]

I stated earlier (Section 13.2) that if $A$ is a sufficient condition for $B$, then the relationship between $A$ and $B$ is such that the nonoccurrence of $B$ guarantees the nonoccurrence of $A$. (This should be intuitively obvious. If $A$ is a sufficient condition for $B$, then whenever $A$ occurs, $B$ will also occur. It follows, therefore, that if $B$ does not occur, $A$ has not occurred.) In searching for a sufficient condition for $B$, therefore, we search for some event that *fails to occur whenever B fails to occur.*

Suppose, for example, that it is discovered that, contrary to a national trend, the students in certain high schools have steadily increased their performance on national standardized tests over a ten-year period. The question to be researched is: Why has this occurred? What is the cause—or what are the causes—of this "bucking-the-trend" phenomenon? The cause that is being sought in such a case is a sufficient condition, one that is present in these cases but absent in all cases in which test scores have failed to improve. The

---

[3] Mill does not discuss this method.

research proceeds by (a) collection of data on the schools that have recorded increasing test scores, (b) identification of the characteristics that these schools have in common, and (c) collection of data on a number of schools that have not had increasing test scores to determine whether any of the characteristics identified in step b are uniformly absent from these latter schools.

Let A, B, C, D, and E be selected characteristics shared by all of the schools that have increasing test scores. Then the preliminary results of the research might be summarized as follows (Y signifies that a given characteristic is present, N that it is not present):

| | | | Characteristic | | |
|---|---|---|---|---|---|
| Case | A | B | C | D | E |
| 1 | N | Y | Y | N | N |
| 2 | N | Y | Y | N | N |
| 3 | Y | N | Y | N | Y |
| 4 | Y | N | Y | N | Y |
| 5 | Y | N | Y | N | Y |
| 6 | N | Y | Y | N | N |
| 7 | Y | N | Y | N | Y |
| 8 | N | Y | Y | N | N |
| 9 | N | Y | Y | N | N |
| 10 | Y | N | Y | N | Y |

From these results, one could conclude that if A, B, C, D, or E is a sufficient condition for improved test scores, then D is that sufficient condition, since the nonoccurrence of D regularly accompanies the nonoccurrence of improved scores. If this hypothesis were to be supported by a study of many more schools, and if the absence of D was always found in conjunction with the absence of improving test scores, one's confidence in the correctness of this conclusion would increase.

In searching for sufficient causes, however, we must reckon with the possibility that *a combination of two or more events*, rather than some single event, constitutes a sufficient cause. It may be, for example, that a combination of a four-year requirement in math and English, daily drill on fundamentals, and the use of certain specified textbooks are *all* required to produce rising test scores. If that is the case, then the presence of just one of these conditions will not be sufficient to bring about the desired result. The data in the above table, for example, support the hypothesis that $[(A \lor B) \cdot D]$ is the sufficient condition that is being sought. As more and more data are collected, each candidate hypothesis can be tested. Eventually, if we are lucky, we may succeed in identifying a sufficient condition, a condition that is *always* followed by the desired result.

To summarize: One typically seeks sufficient conditions for the purpose of making a desired result occur, and the method for seeking such conditions is the Inverse Method of Agreement. As with the Direct Method of Agreement, our ability to use the knowledge thus gained to influence the course of events requires that those conditions be tractable. If a necessary condition identified by the Direct Method of Agreement is intractable, then we cannot use our knowledge of that condition to prevent the occurrence of that for which it is a necessary condition; similarly, if a sufficient condition identified by the Inverse Method of Agreement is intractable, our knowledge of that condition will not enable us to produce the event for which it is a sufficient condition.

## EXERCISES 13.5

A. State which of the following must be the case if *A* is a sufficient condition for *B*:
   1. Whenever *A* occurs, *B* occurs.
   2. Whenever *A* fails to occur, *B* fails to occur.
   3. Whenever *B* occurs, *A* has occurred.
   4. Whenever *B* fails to occur, *A* has failed to occur.
B. On the basis of your general knowledge, state two sufficient conditions for each of the following:
   1. Flunking out of school.
   2. Scoring (football).
   3. Scoring (baseball).
   4. Getting a speeding ticket.
   5. Becoming a parent.
   6. Moving a car.
   7. Removing a tree.
   8. Breaking a window.
   9. Getting out of debt.
   10. Relieving boredom.
C. Review the information in item C on page 290, but assume that *Z* has not occurred (i.e., assume that column *Z* has all *N*'s instead of *Y*'s). On the basis of the information in the table, which of the following might be sufficient conditions for *Z*?

| | | | | |
|---|---|---|---|---|
| 1. *A* | 3. $A \lor B$ | 5. $\sim D$ | 7. $\sim G$ | 9. *H* |
| 2. *B* | 4. *D* | 6. *G* | 8. $\sim D \cdot G$ | 10. $I \lor J$ |

# 13.6 THE DOUBLE METHOD OF AGREEMENT

A given type of event may be both a necessary and a sufficient condition for the occurrence of another type of event. That is to say, events of types *A* and *B* may be related in such a way that events of type *B* are always preceded or accompanied by events of type *A* (thus proving that *A* is a *necessary* condition for *B*), and events of type *A* are always followed by or accompanied by events of type *B* (thus proving that *A* is a *sufficient* condition for *B*). Since the Direct Method of Agreement is appropriate for seeking necessary conditions and the Inverse Method of Agreement is appropriate for seeking sufficient conditions, both methods must be used in combination to determine that a given type of event is both a necessary and a sufficient condition for the occurrence of another type of event.

Suppose, for example, that a new disease breaks out in a certain locale, and it is desired to know what causes it. Blood samples are taken from a number of people suffering from the disease, and several microorganisms suspected of being possible causes (necessary conditions) of the disease are noted. The results of these tests are tabulated as follows (*Y* indicates that a given microorganism was detected in the blood sample, *N* that it was not):

| | Microorganism | | | | | Disease |
| Case | *A* | *B* | *C* | *D* | *E* | *Z* |
|---|---|---|---|---|---|---|
| 1 | Y | N | Y | N | N | Y |
| 2 | N | Y | Y | N | N | Y |
| 3 | Y | Y | Y | Y | Y | Y |
| 4 | N | N | Y | Y | N | Y |
| 5 | N | N | Y | N | Y | Y |
| 6 | Y | Y | Y | Y | Y | Y |
| 7 | N | Y | Y | Y | N | Y |
| 8 | Y | N | Y | N | Y | Y |
| 9 | Y | Y | Y | N | Y | Y |
| 10 | N | N | Y | N | N | Y |

It is evident from the above information that if one of these five microorganisms is a necessary condition for the occurrence of the disease, microorganism *C* is the one, since it is the only one that is present in all ten cases. If additional cases confirm the hypothesis, one's confidence that *C* really is a necessary condition will increase, and one will begin to look for ways to destroy the microorganism in order to effect a cure.

Suppose now that a medical researcher resolves to develop a vaccine that it is hoped will prevent the occurrence of the disease, and that in the course of so doing he or she needs to be able to produce the disease in human volunteers. This raises a further question: Is microorganism *C*, which has been shown to be a *necessary* condition for the occurrence of the disease, also a *sufficient* condition? Our researcher proceeds by studying the blood samples of several healthy people—people not afflicted with the disease—and finds the following:

| Case | Microorganism | | | | | Disease |
| | A | B | C | D | E | Z |
|------|---|---|---|---|---|---------|
| 1  | Y | N | N | Y | N | N |
| 2  | Y | N | N | Y | Y | N |
| 3  | N | Y | N | Y | N | N |
| 4  | N | Y | N | Y | Y | N |
| 5  | N | Y | N | N | N | N |
| 6  | Y | Y | N | N | Y | N |
| 7  | N | N | N | N | Y | N |
| 8  | Y | N | N | Y | N | N |
| 9  | N | Y | N | N | N | N |
| 10 | Y | N | N | Y | N | N |

The above information warrants the tentative conclusion that microorganism C is a sufficient condition for the occurrence of the disease, since, in all cases examined, the nonoccurrence of the disease is accompanied by the absence of this microorganism. If this conclusion is confirmed by additional cases, and if no conflicting cases appear (i.e., the presence of microorganism C in a blood sample taken from a healthy patient), our researcher's confidence in the correctness of the conclusion will increase, and he or she will reasonably expect that an injection of microorganism C into the bloodstream of a healthy person will be followed by the occurrence of the disease in that person.

The **Double Method of Agreement,** then, is a method for identifying a type of event that is both a necessary and a sufficient condition for the occurrence of another type of event.[4] It consists in the successive application of the Method of Direct Agreement and the Method of Inverse Agreement to the relevant data. If the condition thus identified is tractable, its identification confers the power both to prevent and to bring about that of which it is the condition.


# EXERCISE 13.6

Consider the following summary of findings concerning some possible conditions for phenomenon Z:

---

[4] Since Mill did not discuss the Inverse Method of Agreement, he of course did not discuss the Double Method of Agreement, which presupposes the Inverse Method.

| | | | | Condition | | | | | Phe-nom-enon |
|---|---|---|---|---|---|---|---|---|---|
| Case | A | B | C | D | E | F | G | H | Z |
| 1 | Y | N | Y | N | Y | Y | N | N | Y |
| 2 | N | N | Y | N | Y | Y | N | Y | Y |
| 3 | Y | Y | Y | N | Y | Y | Y | Y | Y |
| 4 | N | Y | Y | N | Y | N | Y | N | Y |
| 5 | Y | N | Y | N | Y | N | N | N | Y |
| 6 | N | N | Y | N | Y | N | N | Y | Y |
| 7 | N | Y | Y | N | Y | Y | N | N | Y |
| 8 | N | Y | Y | N | N | Y | Y | Y | N |
| 9 | N | Y | N | Y | N | N | Y | Y | N |
| 10 | N | N | Y | Y | N | N | Y | N | N |
| 11 | N | N | N | N | N | N | Y | N | N |
| 12 | N | Y | Y | N | N | Y | Y | Y | N |
| 13 | N | Y | N | Y | N | Y | Y | Y | N |
| 14 | N | N | Y | Y | N | N | Y | N | N |
| 15 | N | N | N | N | N | N | Y | Y | N |

1.  Identify any candidate on the above list that might be a necessary condition for Z.
2.  Identify any candidate on the above list that might be a sufficient condition for Z.
3.  Identify any candidate on the above list that might be both a necessary and a sufficient condition for Z.

# 13.7 THE METHOD OF DIFFERENCE

If one wishes to know the cause of some particular type of event in order to acquire the power to make events of that type occur, all that is needed is to identify *any one* tractable sufficient condition for such events. The Inverse Method of Agreement is an appropriate method of inquiry in such cases. Sometimes, however, we are interested in identifying the unique cause of a particular event—the cause, for example, of a particular airplane crash, or of the collapse of a particular building. The object of our search, once again, is a sufficient condition—a condition whose occurrence is sufficient to account for the event in question—not, obviously, for the purpose of acquiring the ability to make similar events occur, but rather for the purpose of fixing responsibility or, in some cases, of simply satisfying our curiosity. The method of inquiry appropriate in such cases is called the **Method of Difference.**[5]

---

[5] This is one of Mill's five original methods.

Let us suppose that an elevated walkway has collapsed, with resultant serious human injury and death. The question is: What caused this disaster? There are, after all, thousands of elevated walkways in the world, and most of them do not collapse. Why, then, did this one collapse? How was this case *different* from the otherwise similar cases in which a collapse did not occur?

The inquiry proceeds by (*a*) identifying the characteristics of noncollapsing walkways (i.e., identifying the necessary conditions for durability of walkways) and (*b*) attempting to determine which of those conditions was absent in the present case. The sufficient condition (cause) of the collapse, then, was the absence of the necessary condition to be identified in this way. (Remember: If $A$ is a necessary condition for $B$, then $\sim A$ is a sufficient condition for $\sim B$).

Theoretically, the Method of Difference proceeds as if one collected data more or less at random on the characteristics of noncollapsing walkways, and then attempted to determine which of those characteristics was present in all cases of noncollapsing walkways but absent in the present case. In practice, of course, one proceeds somewhat differently. On the basis of the relevant engineering principles, one assumes a list of necessary conditions for durable walkways: they must be designed to carry a weight of $n_1$ pounds, constructed to such-and-such specifications, not subjected to a weight greater than $n_2$ pounds, and so on. These are the conditions that one assumes will be exemplified in all noncollapsing walkways, and the absence of some one of them is presumed to be the cause (sufficient condition) of the collapse of the walkway under investigation.

One's findings might be schematically summarized as follows ($Z$ means collapse, $\sim Z$ means noncollapse):

|  | **Characteristic** | | | | | |
| Case | A | B | C | D | E | Result |
| --- | --- | --- | --- | --- | --- | --- |
| 0 | Y | Y | Y | N | Y | Z |
| All others | Y | Y | Y | Y | Y | $\sim Z$ |

The absence of condition D, then, is presumed to be the cause—the sufficient condition—of the collapse of the walkway.

It should not be assumed that the Method of Difference is applicable only when one is seeking the cause (sufficient condition) of an undesired or unfortunate event. It is equally applicable when the outcome is desirable—for example, a patient recovers from a disease previously thought to be incurable, or someone invents a golf club that enables the user to achieve drives 20 percent longer than he or she is able to achieve with conventional clubs. In these cases, too, one asks: How is this case different from otherwise similar cases? What is the *sufficient condition* that was present in this case but absent in those relevantly similar cases where the result was not the same?

The Method of Difference differs from the Inverse Method of Agreement in the following way: the Inverse Method of Agreement has as its goal the identification of the sufficient condition or conditions of all events of a given type, whereas the Method of Difference seeks to discover the unique cause—sufficient condition—of a unique occurrence, a specific event that has occurred at some particular time and place. What caused *this walkway* to collapse? What caused *this patient* to recover? What causes *this particular golf club* to yield longer drives? The Method of Difference is a method for seeking answers to such questions.

The Method of Difference is the method of inquiry employed in such areas as accident investigations, medical diagnosis, mechanical troubleshooting, and coronary inquests. It is also the method that one would employ if one were seeking to account for the unusually high achievement of the children in a given family, the longevity of people who live in a certain community, the high gasoline mileage of a certain automobile, or the remarkable number of first-rate musicians (or artists or scientists) who have emerged from a certain locale. Note that in all cases one is *comparing* the case under investigation with similar cases that have had a different result in order to determine, if possible, the sufficient condition that accounts for the unique event whose cause is being sought.

## EXERCISES 13.7

A. A light aircraft has to make an emergency landing because the engine suddenly stops running. Explain how the Method of Difference would be used to seek the cause of the malfunction.

B. The students in a certain school have an absentee rate three times greater than those of any other school in the city. Explain how the Method of Difference would be used to investigate this phenomenon.

C. Explain how the Method of Difference is employed in medical diagnosis.

D. An inventor creates an automobile that achieves 80 miles per gallon in ordinary highway driving. Explain how the Method of Difference would be used to determine how it achieves these results.

E. Explain the difference or differences between the Method of Difference and the Inverse Method of Agreement.

# 13.8 THE JOINT METHOD OF AGREEMENT AND DIFFERENCE

The **Joint Method of Agreement and Difference,** like the Double Method of Agreement (see Section 13.6), is a method for identifying an event that is both a necessary and a sufficient condition for another event.[6] It differs from the Double Method of Agreement, however, in that the event for which a necessary and sufficient condition is being sought is a specific occurrence rather than an exemplar of events of a certain type. It consists in the successive application of the Method of Difference and the Direct Method of Agreement to the relevant data.

To illustrate the application of this method, let us imagine the following situation. A young boy, Robert, is observed by his parents to be growing much faster than his peers. Robert is examined by a pediatrician and given a series of tests, and by the Method of Difference (see Section 13.7) it is determined that the probable cause (sufficient condition) of his rapid growth rate is an excess of a certain hormone being secreted by an overactive pituitary gland. Medication is administered to slow down the activity of this gland, and Robert's growth rate returns to normal.

The pediatrician, however, wants to know more about the phenomenon that she has just observed. She wants to know whether an abnormally rapid growth rate is *always* preceded by an excess of this particular hormone, that is, whether such excess is a necessary condition for an excessive growth rate as well as a sufficient condition in the present case. She therefore reads up on the subject and discovers that in twenty out of twenty cases of abnormal growth, including both male and female patients, the hormone excess was present. She concludes, therefore, that an excess of this hormone is probably a necessary condition for the occurrence of accelerated growth.

The Joint Method of Agreement and Difference, then, is a method for determining two things: (a) that event A is a sufficient condition for event B, and (b) that an event of type A is a necessary condition for an event of type B.

## EXERCISES 13.8

A.  Explain the reasoning involved in any application of the Joint Method of Agreement and Difference.

---

[6] This is one of Mill's five original methods.

**B.** Using the Joint Method of Agreement and Difference, state the conclusion, if any, that might be drawn from the following summary of information regarding some possible necessary and/or sufficient conditions for Z:

| | Condition | | | | | |
|---|---|---|---|---|---|---|
| Case | *A* | *B* | *C* | *D* | *E* | Result |
| 0 | Y | N | Y | Y | Y | ~Z |
| 1–5 | Y | Y | Y | Y | Y | Z |
| 6–10 | Y | N | Y | Y | Y | ~Z |

# 13.9 THE METHOD OF RESIDUES

The **Method of Residues,** which Mill regarded as a distinct type of experimental inquiry, is in fact only a modified version of the Method of Difference. We shall discuss it briefly because of its historical interest as one of Mill's five original methods of experimental inquiry. Mill's statement of the Method of Residues is as follows:

> Subduct from any phenomenon such part as is known by previous inductions to be the effect of certain antecedents, and the residue of the phenomenon is the effect of the remaining antecedents.[7]

A favorite example of the supposed application of this method has long been the investigations that led to the discovery of the planet Neptune. The orbits of the known planets had been calculated in accordance with the theories of Sir Isaac Newton, and on the basis of these calculations it was assumed that astronomers could predict the exact location of any planet at any moment in time. This assumption proved to be correct in the case of all of the planets except Uranus, whose actual orbit varied from the calculated orbit by an amount too great to be attributed to errors in observation. A young French astronomer, Urbain Jean Joseph Leverrier, hypothesized that the deviation in the orbit of Uranus was caused by the gravitational pull of another and heretofore unknown planet beyond the orbit of Uranus. Leverrier recommended that astronomers look for the new planet in a certain location suggested by his calculations, and within a short time the planet—subsequently named Neptune—was discovered in almost exactly the location that Leverrier had specified.

---

[7] John Stuart Mill, *A System of Logic* (London: Longmans, Green, 1930), 1:460. (This book was first published in 1843.)

Mill presumably would have loved this example, for it clearly is the sort of thing he had in mind in formulating the Method of Residues. *Most* of the orbit of Uranus could be calculated on the basis of the combined gravitational pull of the sun and the interior planets; what remained to be accounted for—the "residue"—required another cause. If, therefore, one takes the entire orbit of Uranus as the phenomenon whose causes are to be identified, it does appear as if one needs something like the Method of Residues to guide one's inquiry. If, however, one simply identifies the *deviation of Uranus from its expected orbit* as the phenomenon that is to be explained, it is clear that the necessary and/or sufficient conditions of this phenomenon can be investigated by the methods previously discussed. The Method of Residues, therefore, is not a new and different method for the identification of necessary and sufficient conditions (causes). It is merely a method for identifying that part of a complex phenomenon whose necessary and/or sufficient conditions must be sought by the methods appropriate for the identification of such conditions.

# 13.10 THE METHOD OF CONCOMITANT VARIATION

The **Method of Concomitant Variation,** like the Method of Residues, is of primarily historical interest as one of Mill's five original methods of experimental inquiry. It does not justify any inferences that are not covered by the methods previously discussed. Mill's formulation of this method is as follows:

> Whatever phenomenon varies in any manner whenever another phe-
> nomenon varies in some particular manner, is either a cause or an
> effect of that phenomenon, or is connected with it through some fact
> of causation.[8]

Mill's own favorite example of the application of this method was the reasoning that led to the conclusion that ocean tides are caused by the gravitational pull of the moon. Mill observes that we cannot remove the moon in order to determine whether by so doing we have eliminated the tides as well, nor can we show that the presence of the moon is the only phenomenon that accompanies tidal action. What we can show, Mill argues, is that *the tides vary as the moon varies,* and it is this "concomitant variation" that proves that tidal action is "connected . . . through some fact of causation" with the

---

[8] Ibid., p. 464.

apparent revolution of the moon around the earth every twenty-four hours and fifty minutes.

Upon reflection, however, it is clear that one does not need this allegedly new method in order to infer a causal link between the moon and the tides. In bodies of water sufficiently large to exhibit a measurable tidal action, a high tide occurs twice every twenty-four hours and fifty minutes. Repeated observation makes it evident that at each such high tide one of two things is the case: either the moon is at its closest position to the location where the high tide occurs (let us call this event $C$), or else it is at its farthest remove from that location (let us call this event $F$). Clearly, by the application of the Direct Method of Agreement one can in this case conclude that ($C \lor F$) is a necessary condition for the occurrence of high tides. A similar analysis can be applied to any example in which "concomitant variation" may be observed.

# 13.11 EVALUATION OF THE METHODS

It has long been recognized that John Stuart Mill was excessively optimistic about the results that could be achieved by the careful application of the methods of experimental inquiry. Mill seems to have believed that his five methods, if rigorously followed, would lead to the discovery of all causal connections that are capable of being known by us, and also to the proof of true causal connections previously thought, on whatever grounds, to exist. Indeed, he seems to have believed that in identifying and formulating the five methods he had accomplished for inductive logic something comparable to what Aristotle had accomplished for deductive logic in formulating the rules of validity for syllogisms; and in this belief he was, of course, mistaken. His list of rules to govern inquiry concerning causes, as we have seen, was both incomplete and redundant, and even with the revisions that we have noted these methods are not and cannot be the universal instrument for inquiry that Mill hoped and expected that they would become.

All of the methods are essentially ways of eliminating possible necessary or sufficient conditions until—if one is lucky—only one such condition remains. The basic principles of elimination are just two: If $A$ can occur and not be followed by $B$, then $A$ is not a sufficient condition for $B$; and if $B$ can occur without being preceded or accompanied by $A$, then $A$ is not a necessary condition for $B$. In order to apply any of the methods successfully, therefore, we must first set up a list of candidates—a list of possible necessary or sufficient conditions—among which the condition being sought is presumed to be present. The methods, however, provide no guidance in setting up this list. In retrospect, the method for discovering the cause of malaria may appear to have been incredibly simple: a list of possible antecedents was tested, and it was discovered by the Double Method of Agreement that people contracted malaria if and only if they were bitten by a certain type of mosquito. But how could it be known in advance that "being bitten by a certain type of mosquito" belonged on the list? The answer is that it couldn't—just as we do not currently know how to construct an exhaustive list of possible causes of various types of cancer or of crib death or of spontaneous abortion (miscarriage) or of numerous other maladies. In a real-life search for causes, we construct our lists of possible causes on the basis of our general knowledge of the phenomenon in question: we assume, for example, that cancer probably is caused by a malfunctioning physiological system, or by a virus, or by a chemical agent, and so on, and we assume that it is not caused by an increase in the sheep population in China, or by variations in the mean temperature at the North Pole, or by billions of other events that have occurred and are occurring elsewhere in the universe. If we are lucky enough to get the real cause—a real necessary or sufficient condition—on our list, the methods will indeed guide us in the process of identifying that cause. If not, they will not aid us in identifying additional candidates to be tested.

Even if we have, on the basis of our general knowledge of a phenomenon, constructed a reasonable list of possible necessary or sufficient conditions, and even if by the careful application of the appropriate method we have identified what we believe to be a necessary or a sufficient condition (or both) for the occurrence of phenomena of that type, we can never be absolutely certain that our conclusion is correct. We may have observed 1,000 cases in which an event of type *A* was uniformly followed by an event of type *B*, and on the basis of these observations we may have confidently concluded that *A* is a sufficient condition for *B*—only to discover in case 1,001 that an event of type *A* is not followed by an event of type *B*. The discovery of causes—of the necessary and sufficient conditions that mark regularities in the flow of events that make up the world of our experience—is a far more complicated and uncertain affair than John Stuart Mill seems to have realized.

A further defect of Mill's methods is that they fail to allow a role for comprehensive theories, whereas in any rational search for causes such theories clearly are of great importance. The importance of theories is illustrated by the previously cited example of the discovery of Neptune: given the Galilean theories of motion and the Newtonian theory of gravitation, there *had* to be another planet affecting the orbit of Uranus. It was not, in this case, the repeated observation of Neptune in conjunction with the perturbation of the orbit of Uranus that led to the conclusion that Neptune was "causing" the perturbation; rather, it was the actual behavior of Uranus in contrast to the predicted behavior that led to the discovery of the additional planet that, if the theory was correct, had to be influencing the path of Uranus around the sun. Indeed, it is precisely on the basis of theories—that is, general principles of explanation believed to be applicable to phenomena of a certain type—that we identify the candidates that may eventually turn out to be the causes—the necessary or sufficient conditions—that we are seeking. Were it not for the presumed relevance of certain theories, medical researchers would not know whether to search for germs or unfavorable constellations or witches' spells in their efforts to identify the causes of diseases.

The methods for experimental inquiry described above are not, therefore, the infallible guides to the discovery of causes that Mill thought he had found. In reasoning concerning causes, as in all inductive reasoning, there is no infallible guide. The methods for experimental inquiry can, however, increase the probability that the conclusions we reach when we inquire concerning causes are true. In that more humble role, they serve us well.

# 13.12 PROBABILITY AND CAUSAL REASONING

Probability is involved in our reasoning about causes at a number of points. Let us identify them and see what inferences may be drawn from our earlier discussion of probability (Chapter 12).

The first step in the identification of the causes of an event, as we have seen, is the construction of a list of *possible* causes, that is, antecedent events that we have some reason to think might be necessary or sufficient conditions (or both) for the occurrence of such an event. Now since anything that has ever happened anywhere in the universe is an antecedent event in relation to anything that is happening now, there must be some way of narrowing down the field of candidates. This narrowing of the field of candidates is done on the basis of our total fund of knowledge, beliefs, and explanatory theories. Let us call our knowledge, beliefs, and theories our *assumptions*. Then we may say that the first element of probability that enters into our search for causes is reflected in the following question: What is the probability that the assumptions in terms of which we have identified some possible causes of a given phenomenon are true? If the theory that the relative position of the planets at the moment of one's birth affects one's fortunes throughout life is correct, then it makes sense to investigate astronomical phenomena as clues to the destinies of individuals; if not, it does not make sense—that is, astronomical events do not then belong on a list of possible causes of human fortune or misfortune. If the theory that disease is sometimes caused by microbes is correct, then it makes sense to include viruses and bacteria on one's list of possible causes of certain kinds of disease; if not, it does not make sense. Clearly, our assumptions have much to do with what we are prepared to consider as possible causes of any phenomenon. People once believed as sincerely in the "evil spirit" theory of disease as most people today believe in the microbe theory.

There is, of course, no general answer to the question about the probability of the truth of our assumptions. We have acquired them from many sources—parents, teachers, textbooks, experience, to name but a few—and all are capable of being mistaken. Some we have tested, others we have not. Some will stand the test of time, others will eventually have to be modified or abandoned. In the meantime, they are all we have. If we do not use them, we have no basis for identifying any possible causes, and our search for causes cannot get under way. What probability theory tells us about these assumptions is simply that their probability is less than 1, that is, they are uncertain. To whatever extent the truth of our assumptions is in doubt, the possible causes identified on the basis of those assumptions must also be in doubt. (Imagine two witch doctors debating about whether a given type of illness is caused by one, two, three, or a multitude of evil spirits.)

Second, even if we are reasonably sure of the truth of a given set of assumptions, the adequacy of those assumptions to explain a given phenomenon may remain uncertain. The microbe theory of disease, for example, does not explain all diseases: it only explains those diseases that are caused by microbes. A researcher may therefore, on the basis of well-established theories, pursue a line of investigation—test various microbes as possible necessary or sufficient conditions for the occurrence of a certain disease, for example—that leads to no positive results because the assumptions being employed, though true, are the wrong ones. Again, probability theory cannot tell us *how* probable it is that the assumptions we are making are relevant to the present case; it can only tell us that that probability is less than 1. The possibility of error on this score is a second reason why a carefully drawn list of possible causes may nonetheless fail to include the cause we are seeking to identify.

Third, one's search for causes may go astray because of errors in measurement or observation. Simple observation is notoriously subject to error, and even the most sophisticated measuring devices measure whatever they measure only within certain ranges of probable error. We can, for example, measure the distance between the surface of the earth and the surface of the sun with a high degree of accuracy, but not to the nearest millimeter. In analyzing data for evidence of some necessary or sufficient condition of the phenomenon in question, therefore, we must always reckon with the possibility of errors in the data—errors resulting from faulty observation, insufficiently sensitive measuring devices, or malfunctioning equipment. We can reduce the probability of such error by maintaining rigorous research procedures—using multiple measuring devices, for example, and having more than one observer recording the data— but we cannot totally eliminate it. The probability that any set of research data is completely accurate is always less than 1.

Finally, no matter how many instances we may have observed in which a phenomenon of type $A$ is uniformly followed by a phenomenon of type $B$—thus leading us to conclude that $A$ is (probably) a sufficient condition for $B$—it is always possible that $A$ is a sufficient condition for $B$ only in conjunction with certain other relevant conditions that we have failed to note, and that in the absence of those conditions $A$ will not be followed by $B$. The probability of our conclusion will presumably be relative to the care with which we have gathered and analyzed our data, the number of instances we have observed, and so on. That probability, however, can never reach 100 percent. The probability that there are no exceptions to the regularity that we have observed is always less than 1.

The probability of any statement of the form "$A$ is a necessary (or sufficient) condition for $B$" is therefore the product of four constituent probabilities:

1.   The probability that the assumptions in terms of which we identify the possible necessary or sufficient conditions are correct.
2.   The probability that these assumptions are relevant to the phenomenon being investigated.
3.   The probability that our data are free from error.
4.   The probability that there are no unobserved exceptions to the observed regularity.

Obviously, the higher the probability on each of these critical points, the higher the probability of a true conclusion. A probability of $\frac{9}{10}$ on each point yields a probability of approximately $\frac{2}{3}$ for our conclusion ($\frac{9}{10} \times \frac{9}{10} \times \frac{9}{10} \times \frac{9}{10}$). A probability of $\frac{99}{100}$ on each point yields a conclusion having a probability of approximately $\frac{24}{25}$ (96 percent). When we search for causes, therefore, it is not enough merely to apply the appropriate method for experimental inquiry. It is equally important to be as certain as possible that our assumptions are both true and relevant, that our data are accurate, and that the observed cases are representative of the phenomenon we are studying. Otherwise our conclusion, though justified by the data, will have such a low probability that it will not be useful for any of the purposes for which we seek to identify the causes of phenomena.

# fourteen
# Empirical Generalizations and Theoretical Hypotheses

The ultimate goal of science is to achieve an understanding of natural processes that is so complete that everything that occurs can be understood as an instance of the relevant laws of nature. The laws of nature, however, are of several different kinds, and the reasoning by which these laws are established varies from one kind to another. In this chapter we shall consider several types of such laws, and shall attempt to elucidate the reasoning involved in the establishment of each.

## 14.1 OBSERVATION STATEMENTS

Any statement that is to qualify as a law of nature must be logically connected in some way to statements of a very elementary type called observation statements. An **observation statement** is a statement that purports to report an actual observation by some observer at some particular place and time. An observation statement is what in popular parlance might be called an "eyewitness report." With respect to observation statements it is always appropriate to ask: Who made the alleged observation? When was it made? Where was it made? Under what conditions was it made? Examples of such statements are: "There was a bright flash in the sky," "A dog barked," and "The barometer showed 29.97 inches of mercury."

Although observation statements can be formulated purely in terms of sense experience ("I had a bright-flash-in-the-sky sort of visual sensation"), they typically are stated in ways that involve a certain amount of interpretation of that sense experience. All of the following, for example, would qualify as observation statements:

1.   I had a bright-flash-in-the-sky sort of visual sensation.
2.   There was a bright flash in the sky.
3.   There was a flash of lightning in the sky.

Note, however, that the more interpretive the statement, the greater the likelihood of error. The observer who sincerely reports a bright-flash-in-the-sky sort of visual sensation is not likely to be mistaken about what he or she reports. Statement 2 introduces a possibility of error, however, since "a bright-flash-in-the-sky sort of visual sensation" might be caused by something other than an actual bright flash in the sky—for example, a blow on the head, or artificial stimulation (or malfunction) of the optic nerve. Statement 3 is even more subject to error, since what an observer believes to be a flash of lightning may in fact be a flash of light from some other source (a malfunctioning transformer, for example).

It is largely because of the possibility of error by a single observer that the principle of intersubjective verifiability is so important in scientific inquiry. If a physicist in Helsinki reports having observed a certain phenomenon under such-and-such laboratory conditions, then it should be possible for a physicist in Moscow or Berkeley or Tokyo to duplicate those conditions and, by so doing, to duplicate the phenomenon. If other physicists find that under the prescribed conditions the predicted phenomenon does not occur, they will probably—justifiably—conclude that their colleague in Helsinki is mistaken about what he thinks he observed.

Notwithstanding the possibility of error, however, observation statements are the building blocks of the entire edifice of scientific knowledge. The loftiest scientific theory as well as the humblest must, in the final analysis, justify itself in terms of the observation statements that it was invoked to explain. Broadly speaking, the logic of scientific inquiry is concerned with the logical relations between scientific theories and the observation statements to which those theories are logically relevant.

## EXERCISE 14.1

Identify the statements in the following list that, under the appropriate circumstances (i.e., if affirmed by an actual observer), would qualify as observation statements:

1. Everybody in Nebraska roots for the Cornhuskers.
2. Both of my sisters are blondes.
3. It is cloudy today.
4. There is a birch tree in the front yard across the street from my home.
5. Apples are sweet.
6. Holidays are depressing.
7. My car is blue.
8. My brother often loses his temper.
9. The seven crows sitting on a tree in that cornfield are black.
10. My feet are cold.
11. It is snowing.
12. The Boeing 707 is a reliable aircraft.
13. This microcomputer has 64K of internal memory.
14. This car holds five passengers.
15. The traffic is heavy today.
16. There was a loud sound.
17. The sky is clear.
18. Fraternity parties are fun.

# 14.2 UNIVERSAL EMPIRICAL GENERALIZATIONS

What is observed in sense experience is particular facts: that this piece of ice is cold, this flame is hot, this ripe strawberry is sweet, and so on. It is facts such as these that are reported in observation statements. Over a period of time, however, we sometimes note certain regularities, or recurring facts, in what we observe. We note, for example, that every piece of ice that we touch is cold, every flame that we encounter is hot, every ripe strawberry that we taste is sweet, and we sum up such observations in such statements as the following:

All ice is cold.
All flames are hot.
All ripe strawberries are sweet.

Such statements are called universal empirical generalizations. A **universal empirical generalization** is a statement ascribing to all members of a class a characteristic that has been observed to be present in all members of the class thus far observed. Such a statement is called *universal* for the obvious reason that it asserts something about all members of the subject class. It is called a *generalization* because it involves "generalizing" from the observed cases to all cases. It is an *empirical* generalization because it is about empirical entities, that is, entities that present themselves to sense experience (with or without the aid of scientific instruments).

The logical process by which we arrive at such generalizations seems, at first sight, to be quite simple. It appears that the reasoning goes like this:

Ripe strawberry no. 1 is sweet.
Ripe strawberry no. 2 is sweet.
Ripe strawberry no. 3 is sweet.

.
.
.

Ripe strawberry no. *n* is sweet.

∴  All ripe strawberries are sweet.

But suppose we ask: How many sweet ripe strawberries must one taste before one can be sure that *all* ripe strawberries are sweet? The answer would appear to be "All of them"—and that, of course, is impossible. Can we, then, be reasonably sure of our conclusion on the basis of having observed (tasted, in this case) some smaller sample? Only, it would appear, if we have reason to believe (*a*) that some uniformities exist in the class of objects about which we are making our assertion and (*b*) that the sample we have observed is representative of the total class of objects of which it is a sample. Unfortunately, both statements are exceedingly difficult (if not impossible) to establish without the use of circular reasoning. We cannot know that some uniformities exist without having established the existence of at least one uniformity, and we cannot know that our sample is representative without knowing something about the total class of which it is supposed to be representative. This is the so-called Problem of Induction, and despite the efforts of many philosophers, it remains to this day one of the most baffling problems in philosophy.[1]

The procedure of reasoning from observed instances to a generalization based on those instances is called **induction by simple enumeration,** and notwithstanding the difficulty of justifying the procedure, it is clear that we do in fact employ it, and rather frequently. All of the homely, everyday regularities that we take so much for granted—that objects thrown into the air come down again, that boiling water evaporates, that the leaves fall in autumn, that the sun gives light and warmth, and so on—seem clearly to have been

---

[1] The Problem of Induction is a meta-logical problem and thus will not be discussed further here. For a fuller discussion of the problem see William H. Halverson, *A Concise Introduction to Philosophy*, 4th ed. (New York: Random House, 1981), pp. 67–99.

established by such inductions. Without them the world would appear to us as a bewildering series of utterly novel events.

It is evident that, at best, a universal empirical generalization is a probable assertion: no matter how many instances of a phenomenon may have been observed, it is always theoretically possible that the next instance will be an exception to what has previously been observed. (For example, the next crow that one sees may be white.) It seems reasonable to ask, therefore, whether there are any general rules governing induction by simple enumeration, rules whose observance will increase the probability that the conclusions of such inductions will be true. The answer is that there are. The rules are these:

*Rule 1:* The probability of a generalization depends in part on the type of phenomenon about which the generalization is made. Phenomena of a type that has yielded reliable inductions in the past are more likely to yield reliable new inductions than phenomena for which this is not the case.

*Rule 2:* For any given type of phenomenon, the probability of the generalization increases as the number of observed instances increases (assuming that no negative instances have been observed).

*Rule 3:* For any given type of phenomenon, the probability of the generalization increases as the representativeness of the sample increases.

Rule 1 calls attention to variations in the known law-abidingness of various types of phenomena. We have encountered enough surprises in tasting foods to know that a red, ripe appearance is no guarantee that something will be sweet to the taste, and so, no matter how many sweet-tasting ripe strawberries we may have tasted, we will always be wary of the statement "All ripe strawberries are sweet." Phenomena of this type (i.e., the taste of foods) have not yielded reliable inductions in the past, and so we do not place much confidence in a new induction concerning a phenomenon of this type. Inductions about the boiling and freezing of water, and indeed many types of natural processes, however, have in the past proved to be reliable, and so we make new inductions about phenomena of these types with much greater confidence that the observed regularity will hold for the unobserved cases as well.

Rule 2 takes account of the previously stated common-sense view (Section 11.3) that the probability of an inductive generalization varies directly with the number of observations on which that generalization is based. Note, however, that this rule applies only to inductions concerning a given type of phenomenon; it does not apply in such a way as to enable us to compare the strength of an induction concerning a phenomenon of one type with that of an induction concerning a phenomenon of another type. If I have observed a million black crows (and no nonblack ones), for example, I can be more confident that all crows are black than if I have observed just ten, or a hundred, or a thousand; but I may, nonetheless, be more confident that the statement "Pure water freezes at 0 degrees C." is true without exception after experimenting with only a few samples, since this is a type of phenomenon that has yielded reliable inductions in the past (Rule 1). Rule 2 states, in effect, that the probability of an empirical generalization increases as the favorable evidence increases (provided there are no counterexamples). Generalizations concerning some types of phenomena (weather patterns, for example) require much more evidence to reach a given level of probability than generalizations concerning other types of phenomena, however.

Rule 3 makes the important point that the probability of an empirical generalization is influenced by the degree of similarity between the observed sample and the total class of objects or phenomena concerning which the generalization is made. Children, for example, are human beings, but generalizations based on the observation of children (for example, that they cry when angry) cannot be safely affirmed of the whole class of human beings, since children are not representative of the whole. Similarly, one cannot safely make statements about the gas mileage or durability of all Buicks on the basis of one's experience with a single Buick, or about the temperament of all dogs on the basis of the observed behavior of one's six-month-old spaniel.

The probability of an empirical generalization cannot be precisely calculated by any existing formula. It must, therefore, simply be estimated. Attention to the above-stated rules will increase the probability of our generalizations, but that is all; and every empirical generalization, however well supported by evidence, is subject to possible contradiction by future observations.

## EXERCISES 14.2

A. Define the terms "universal empirical generalization" and "induction by simple enumeration."
B. State and briefly explain the three rules governing induction by simple enumeration.
C. Give five examples of universal empirical generalizations.

# 14.3 STATISTICAL GENERALIZATIONS

**Statistical generalizations** are similar to universal empirical generalizations in a number of ways. They are, of course, based on the facts of observation, and are established by induction from observed samples. They differ, however, in that they affirm a statistical regularity rather than an alleged universal empirical truth.

Consider, for example, the phenomenon of twinning in sheep. A sheep rancher knows that each year a certain fairly predictable proportion of his ewes will produce twins, though he cannot predict which of them will do so in any given year. The occurrence of such-and-such a number of twin births out of a hundred in sheep is an observed statistical regularity, and the assertion of such a regularity is a statistical generalization. Statistical generalizations are statements of the form "Among sheep, *n* births out of every hundred are twins."

Statistical generalizations, like universal empirical generalizations, are probable assertions, and their probability is governed by the same three rules (Section 14.2). Because the representativeness of the observed sample is especially important in making statistical generalizations, the science of statistics has developed sophisticated techniques for securing what is called a "scientific random sample" of any population. As in the case of universal empirical generalizations, the probability of a statistical generalization can only be estimated.

## EXERCISES 14.3

A. Explain the difference between a statistical generalization and a universal empirical generalization.
B. Give five examples of statistical generalizations.

# 14.4 EMPIRICAL LAWS

Empirical generalizations (either universal or statistical) that purport to describe unvarying features of the natural world are termed **empirical laws.** An empirical law, then, is a universal or statistical generalization about the natural world. It is a type of natural law or "law of nature."

Empirical laws assert certain uniformities in the observable features of the natural world. By "observable features" I mean those features of the natural world that are directly present in sense experience (such things as color, taste, smell, size, sound, motion) or detectable with the aid of appropriate scientific instruments (craters on the moon, blood cells, bacteria, and so on). Empirical laws may or may not be incorporated within some larger theoretical framework (see Section 14.5), but even if they are, they remain, in a sense, independent of that framework. Because of this independence, empirical laws that are well supported by empirical evidence may in fact survive the collapse of the theories in which they are sometimes incorporated. Indeed, by virtue of the fact that they stand in this close relation to the facts as actually observed, they are the most secure elements in the entire edifice of empirical knowledge. The atomic theory may or may not pass the test of time, but numerous lower-level empirical laws that are currently understood in terms of that theory—such as the laws governing various chemical reactions— are unlikely to be overturned by any challenge to the atomic theory.

Empirical laws differ from common-sense generalizations only in the greater precision with which they are formulated. It is a common-sense generalization that the farther you are away from a light source, the less light you receive from it; it is an empirical law that the intensity of the light received by an object varies inversely with the square of its distance from the light source. It is a common-sense generalization that a low-density object—an inflated balloon, for example—is more difficult to submerge in a fluid than an object of higher density, such as a piece of wood. It is an empirical law (known as the Archimedean law of buoyancy) that a fluid buoys up a body immersed in it with a force equal to the weight of the fluid displaced by the body. It is a common-sense generalization that the melting point of lead is higher than that of ice. It is an empirical law that the melting points of ice and of lead are 0 degrees C. and 327 degrees C., respectively.

It is an important characteristic of empirical laws that they are testable by means of a direct appeal to empirical facts. That pure water freezes at 0 degrees C. can be tested by subjecting samples of pure water to the appropriate temperature and observing whether or not it freezes. That water evaporates when it is boiled can be tested by boiling several samples of water and observing whether or not the quantity is reduced in each case. An empirical law is a generalization about some observable state of affairs in the physical world, and such a law is true if and only if the world really is as the law affirms it to be.

With respect to their logical status, empirical laws are simply empirical generalizations, either universal (as in the case of Galileo's laws of falling bodies) or statistical (as with Mendel's laws of heredity). Like all empirical generalizations, they are probable, not certain. No matter how much favorable evidence may have been gathered in support of a given law, it is always possible (logically possible) that some future observation will contradict it. That empirical laws normally have a very high probability is due principally to two things: the fact that the generalizations that we call empirical laws typically concern phenomena that in the past have yielded reliable inductions (see Section 14.2, Rule 1) and the extreme care with which the scientific community tests any generalization that is put forward as an empirical law. The confidence of the scientific community in the truth of any generalization put forward as an empirical law is, in general, proportional to the effort that has been made to disprove that generalization. Only those claimants that are able to survive science's best efforts to prove them false are accepted as empirical laws.

Although empirical laws can be verified only with some degree of probability (albeit a very high degree), they can be conclusively disproved. The empirical law that the planets orbit in perfect circles around the sun, for example, was conclusively disproved by Johannes Kepler, who demonstrated that planetary orbits are elliptical. The empirical law that freely falling heavy objects accelerate more rapidly than freely falling light objects was conclusively disproved by Galileo, who demonstrated that freely falling objects on the surface of the earth accelerate at a constant rate (32.16 feet per second per second) regardless of their weight.

Clearly, many of the laws that come to mind when one hears the phrase "scientific law" have the status of empirical laws. Laws describing the properties of the chemical elements, the freezing and boiling points of various liquids, or the acceleration of freely falling bodies are examples of such laws. What they chiefly have in common is the fact that they purport to describe uniformities in the observable features of the natural world. An empirical law states a generalization that purports to be accurately descriptive of the relevant facts observed to date, a generalization that will—if it is indeed a law of nature—continue to be accurately descriptive of similar phenomena in the future.

## EXERCISES 14.4

A.   Define the terms "common-sense generalization," "empirical law," and "observable feature of the natural world."

B.   What does it mean to say that empirical laws are testable by means of a direct appeal to empirical facts?

C.   Which of the following are properly classified as empirical laws?
1.   All crows are black.
2.   Pure water freezes at 32 degrees C.
3.   Most Catholics are Democrats.
4.   Atmospheric pressure decreases as altitude increases.
5.   At a given altitude, the annual mean temperature decreases as one proceeds from the equator toward the North Pole.
6.   The offspring of blue-eyed parents are blue-eyed.
7.   Lions are carnivorous.
8.   One out of every seven students in college today is seeking a degree in engineering.

9.  The planets circumnavigate the sun in elliptical orbits.
10. Light travels at a velocity of 186,000 miles per second.

# 14.5 THEORETICAL HYPOTHESES

If empirical laws are defined as universal or statistical generalizations that affirm certain uniformities in the observable features of the natural world, then it is clear that not all laws of nature are of this type. Consider, for example, the law of gravitation, which states that all natural bodies are mutually attracted in direct proportion to the products of their masses and in inverse proportion to the square of the distance between their centers. Obviously this law, first formulated by Sir Isaac Newton, is not an empirical generalization. Indeed, the alleged mutual attraction cannot be precisely measured in any specific instance. One cannot measure the mutual attraction between, say, two apples (placed, perhaps, at various distances from each other), or between the earth and the moon, or between Venus and the sun. Therefore, the law cannot be a summing up of a series of observations, each of which exemplifies the stated law (as, for example, the law about the boiling point of water sums up what has been observed in case 1, case 2, case 3, and so on).

The law of gravitation is representative of a class of laws called **theoretical hypotheses.** Other examples of such laws are the wave theory of light, the atomic theory, and the theory of relativity.

Theoretical hypotheses differ from empirical laws in a number of ways. First, and most important, they posit unobserved entities. Gravitation, for example, is an alleged force that cannot be seen, heard, tasted, touched, or smelled. We can, of course, feel the weight of our own bodies pressing downward toward the earth, but before Newton it had not occurred to anyone to explain this fact of everyday experience in terms of a general hypothesis that at the same time explains a wide range of other phenomena as well. Similarly, light waves and atoms are unobserved entities whose assumed existence aids in the understanding and explanation of certain phenomena. The positing of unobserved entities is a defining characteristic of theoretical hypotheses.

Second, unlike empirical laws, theoretical hypotheses cannot be verified directly. You can boil some water and observe the temperature at which boiling occurs to verify the empirical law that water boils at 100 degrees C., but you cannot examine a ray of light to see whether it is made up of waves, nor can you analyze a sample of a substance to see if it contains any atoms. The verification of theoretical hypotheses must therefore be indirect.

Third, theoretical hypotheses are broader in scope than empirical laws; they purport to explain a wider range of phenomena. The law of the acceleration of freely falling bodies—an empirical law—explains the phenomenon of the acceleration of bodies falling unimpeded in a vacuum at or near the surface of the earth. The theory of gravitation, however, explains that and numerous additional phenomena, from the orbital behavior of the planets to the ebb and flow of the tides and the slight variations in the measured weight of an object at various points on the earth's surface. One superficial indication of this difference is the fact that empirical laws can usually be formulated in a single statement, whereas theoretical hypotheses often require for their complete statement a number—sometimes a very large number—of interrelated statements.

Since theoretical hypotheses are not empirical generalizations, and thus are clearly not established by induction from observed instances, two interesting questions arise: how are such hypotheses generated, and, once they have been proposed, how are they verified?

The answer to the first question appears to be that there are no rules for the creation of theoretical hypotheses. Such hypotheses are created by a leap of imagination, a brilliant guess that a certain kind of previously undetected order lies behind the observed phenomena. The creator of a new hypothesis starts with an intimate knowledge of the relevant phenomena, including a knowledge of the existing empirical laws relevant to those phenomena, and perhaps a conviction that those phenomena and those laws must hang together in some more comprehensive way than has thus far been discerned. But the imaginative leap from these homely, earthbound facts and mundane empirical generalizations to the hypothesis that puts everything in its place—that leap is not bound by any rule. The capacity to make such leaps is what distinguishes the true geniuses of science—Copernicus, Galileo, Kepler, Newton, Einstein, and a handful of others—from the more routinely capable researchers to whom it remains to work out many of the lower-level generalizations that are explained by the more inclusive theories.

Consider, for example, the Copernican theory that the sun, not the earth, is the center of the region of the universe in which the earth is located. The truth of the matter is that there were no facts known at the time of Copernicus that could not be explained by the Ptolemaic theory (the theory that the earth is at rest in the center of the universe, and that the sun and all other heavenly bodies revolve around it). Copernicus was troubled, however, by the *complexity* of the geocentric theory. It seemed to him that a correct understanding of the system of the universe should be somehow simpler than the received theory, and he set about the task of finding that simpler theory. But how did he hit upon the twin insights that the earth revolves upon its axis once every twenty-four hours, and that the earth and the other planets move in orbits around the sun? That is the question to which there is no answer. He did; that is all that one can say. That is all that one can ever say with respect to the creation of theoretical hypotheses.

The *verification* of theoretical hypotheses, however, does proceed according to statable rules. We can therefore speak of a logic of verification with respect to such hypotheses. The Copernican hypothesis may once again serve as our example. Once the theory had been proposed, its verification required at least the following steps:

1. It had to be shown that the hypothesis is consistent with the known relevant facts.
2. It had to be shown that other consequences deducible from the hypothesis also are consistent with the facts of experience.

As a matter of historical fact, the discussion of the Copernican hypothesis did revolve largely around these two points—although, as is well known, most of Copernicus' contemporaries were unwilling to have the issue decided purely on this basis. The authority of ancient men, particularly Aristotle, was not easily laid aside. Copernicus was able to show without much difficulty, however, that his theory accounted in a relatively simple way for such things as the perceived motions of the planets, the daily rising and setting of the sun, the annual changes in the seasons as the earth pursues its orbit around the sun, and so on. Indeed, Copernicus was able to show that his theory accounted more satisfactorily than the geocentric theory for the perceived motions of the planets, for he was able to dispense completely with the theory of "epicycles"—the peculiar aberrations in the perceived paths of the planets resulting from (as we now know) changes in the relative positions of the earth and the several planets as they pursue their respective orbits around the sun. Some of Copernicus' critics argued that the Copernican theory is inconsistent with the fact that we directly perceive the motion of the sun, moon, planets, and stars around the earth, to which Copernicus and his defenders of course replied that that is exactly how we should expect the heavens to look if, as the theory claimed, the earth is revolving on its axis. The Copernicans were able to grasp—as most of their critics were not—the concept of the relativity of motion.

Copernicus' critics also argued, however, that the heliocentric theory implies the following consequences, all of which are contrary to the observed facts:

1. A strong wind should be blowing steadily from east to west.
2. A stone thrown straight upward into the air should not come straight down again, but should come down some distance to

the west (the surface of the earth having moved eastward during the time the stone was in the air).

3.  The relative positions of the fixed stars should appear to vary from time to time as they are viewed from different positions during the earth's alleged orbit around the sun.

Copernicus was able to answer the first two objections without much difficulty. No east-to-west wind is to be expected as a result of the earth's rotation on its axis, he argued, for everything on the earth—including the air that surrounds it—revolves with it. For the same reason—that is, because it shares in the earth's motion—a stone thrown straight upward into the air appears to come straight down again. With respect to the third objection, however, Copernicus himself was admittedly puzzled. He shared the common opinion of his day concerning the size of the universe, and according to that opinion the distances between the various heavenly bodies were assumed to be only a tiny fraction (about 5 percent) of what they are now known to be. On this assumption Copernicus had to admit that there should have been an observed difference in the pattern of the fixed stars from one time of the year to another, and it was evident to everyone that no such difference could be seen. Copernicus' critics regarded this as decisive evidence against the theory; Copernicus himself regarded it as a problem to be solved. The problem eventually was solved with the realization that the fixed stars are many times farther away from the earth than had been supposed, so far that the expected differences in the observed pattern are too small to be discerned.

I stated earlier that the verification of a theoretical hypothesis requires at least two steps: a demonstration that the hypothesis is consistent with the known relevant facts—that is, that it explains the facts that it was invented to explain—and, second, a demonstration that any additional consequences deducible from the hypothesis are also consistent with the observed facts. To the extent that a hypothesis stands up to these two criteria, it is said to be "verified" or "corroborated."

What, then, was the status of the Copernican hypothesis at the time that it appeared to be in conflict with the observed facts regarding the pattern of the fixed stars? Was it verified or not? The answer, of course, is that it was partly verified: to the extent that it satisfactorily explained the relevant facts, it was verified, but to the extent that it appeared to be in conflict with certain facts, it remained unverified. Indeed, had the hypothesis proved to be in irreconcilable conflict with the facts, even its supporters would have had to conclude that the hypothesis was in error.

It might seem that it should be a relatively simple matter to determine whether or not a theoretical hypothesis is in irreconcilable conflict with the facts, but in actuality it is not, for two reasons. First, the alleged consequences of a given hypothesis may or may not be validly deducible from that hypothesis. Copernicus and his critics disagreed, as we have seen, about what could be deduced from the heliocentric theory. The reason that such disagreement is possible is that the most important alleged consequences of a theoretical hypothesis typically do not follow deductively from that hypothesis alone, but only from that hypothesis *in conjunction with certain other assumptions or beliefs that may or may not be true.* Copernicus' critics, for example, assumed a certain theory of motion (the so-called impetus theory), and the Copernican hypothesis in conjunction with that theory did indeed imply certain consequences that were inconsistent with the observed facts. In replying to his critics, Copernicus was in fact challenging the impetus theory of motion—a theory that was eventually to be overturned by the work of Galileo. Second, one's reading of the facts may be in error. With the technology available in Copernicus' time, for example, highly accurate astronomical observation was not possible. Thus it might plausibly have been argued that the reason that the expected changes in the pattern of the fixed stars were not observed was simply that those changes were too small to be observed with the instruments available at the time. Accuracy of measurement is always a matter of degree, and perfect accuracy is seldom if ever attained.

It follows, therefore, that theoretical hypotheses are neither conclusively verified nor conclusively disproved by the two tests that we have been discussing. That a given hypothesis explains all of the known relevant facts does not conclusively verify the hypothesis, for a number of hypotheses may be invented that will do that. That certain consequences apparently deducible from the hypothesis are in conflict with the observed facts does not conclusively disprove that hypothesis, since some other assumption that is being made in conjunction with the hypothesis in question may lead to the contrary-to-fact conclusion, or one's reading of the facts may be in error. The progressive verification of a theoretical hypothesis is therefore a matter of trial and error—of attempting to deduce testable consequences and then trying to determine whether the facts conform to it—and the task is in principle never finally completed. Long-held and well-substantiated theories have been overturned more than once in the history of science, and there is no reason to suppose that all of the theoretical hypotheses currently held by the scientific community will survive future discoveries.

Nevertheless, theoretical hypotheses constitute some of the most important elements in any body of knowledge. The hypotheses prevailing at any given time are the most general truths—or supposed truths—about the world that have been achieved to date, and they generate the questions that may lead inquiring minds on toward yet more adequate hypotheses. Moreover, although such hypotheses cannot be *conclusively* verified or disproved, they can, of course, sometimes be verified or disproved with a high degree of probability. And finally, even when a hypothesis turns out to be probably false in its original formulation, it may survive in some form in the hypothesis that takes its place. As Albert Einstein once wrote, "No fairer destiny could be allotted to any [hypothesis], than that it should of itself point out the way to the introduction of a more comprehensive theory, in which it lives on as a limiting case."[2]

## EXERCISES 14.5

**A.** Review the definition of "empirical law." Explain why one cannot classify the law of gravitation as such a law.

**B.** State three important differences between empirical laws and theoretical hypotheses.

**C.** How are theoretical hypotheses generated? How are they verified?

**D.** Defend two of the following statements:
1. Theoretical hypotheses are conclusively verifiable.
2. Theoretical hypotheses are not conclusively verifiable.
3. Theoretical hypotheses are conclusively disprovable.
4. Theoretical hypotheses are not conclusively disprovable.

# 14.6 REVOLUTIONARY HYPOTHESES

From time to time in the history of science a theoretical hypothesis may be advanced that, if true, appears to require a substantial revision of prevailing theories and beliefs. Such a hypothesis is called a **revolutionary hypothesis.** The Copernican hypothesis was such a one, for much of medieval science was tied up with the geocentric theory. Other revolutionary hypotheses are the theory of evolution, the general theory of relativity, and the Heisenberg principle of indeterminacy.

Since a revolutionary hypothesis is merely a theoretical hypothesis, albeit one that appears to have unusually far-reaching consequences, one might assume that it would be evaluated in the same way as any other theoretical hypothesis, that is, according to the two criteria stated in Section 14.5. In practice, however, it is evident that

---

[2] Albert Einstein, *Relativity: The Special and General Theory*, trans. Robert W. Lawson (New York: Crown, 1961), p. 77. (Originally published in German in 1916.)

a third criterion comes into play in the evaluation of such hypotheses, and indeed in the evaluation of all theoretical hypotheses. That third criterion is this: Is the proposed hypothesis consistent with other well-established empirical laws and theoretical hypotheses, that is, with the existing body of knowledge?

An objection immediately comes to mind: may it not be that the new hypothesis is right, and that the existing body of knowledge (at least to the extent that it is incompatible with the new hypothesis) is wrong? Of course. But the fact that a theoretical hypothesis is consistent with the existing body of knowledge (or what is taken for knowledge) is, in general, presumptive evidence in favor of that hypothesis, and apparent inconsistency is presumptive evidence against it. It is reasonable to demand more convincing evidence in support of a hypothesis that requires us to give up or revise a large portion of our previous body of knowledge than of one that does not.

Consider a pair of contrasting examples. Suppose that a medical researcher were to uncover evidence indicating that a certain type of cancer is caused by a virus. Presumably, such a proposal would be received with equanimity by the scientific community, for it would require no major change in the existing body of knowledge. There is nothing revolutionary about the idea of a disease being caused by a virus, and if the researcher's findings were verified by other researchers, the proposal would eventually be accepted, which is to say that it would become a part of the prevailing body of knowledge. Such a proposal, we might say, is an innocuous candidate for admission to the previously existing body of knowledge. But now suppose that a research physicist comes up with findings that lead him or her to conclude—and to propose for general accceptance—that atoms do not exist. Obviously, if such a proposal were to be accepted it would wreak havoc with current physical theory, and would require major changes in numerous other sciences as well. Such a proposal, therefore, would not be accepted without extremely convincing evidence, evidence so strong as to outweigh all the evidence that has been amassed in support of the atomic theory.

How strong must the evidence be before it is reasonable to accept a revolutionary hypothesis, even at the cost of giving up some portion (perhaps a very large portion) of the previously existing body of knowledge? Obviously, no general answer to this question can be given. If a major portion of the existing body of knowledge is at stake, and if the new hypothesis is of limited scope (i.e., one that, if true, explains few phenomena), it would be reasonable to demand very convincing evidence before accepting the new hypothesis. If the opposite is the case—if the old hypotheses are of limited scope, and if the new hypothesis promises to assist in the explanation of many phenomena (including, perhaps, some that were not well understood in terms of the old hypotheses)—then one might reasonably demand less convincing evidence.

History has judged rather harshly those contemporaries of Copernicus and Galileo and others whose theories posed a radical challenge to the body of knowledge existing at the time their respective theories were put forward. Perhaps the realization that these theories were truly revolutionary, and that it is reasonable to demand very convincing proof of such theories, can lead us toward a somewhat fairer verdict. In retrospect we can, of course, see that Copernicus and Galileo were right and their critics were wrong, and those who resisted their theories appear from our vantage point to have been mere obscurantists who were stubbornly unwilling to let the issues be decided on the basis of the evidence. In the final analysis, however, the hypotheses that are supported by the most convincing evidence do prevail. The critics of Copernicus and Galileo were obviously wrong in rejecting hypotheses that we now know beyond a reasonable doubt to be true, but in demanding extremely convincing evidence for the new theories before giving up vast portions of the existing body of knowledge they were essentially right. Truly revolutionary hypotheses are undoubtedly rare in the history of science, but when they are put forward it is appropriate that they be held to a stricter test than hypotheses that merely augment what is already known.

## EXERCISES 14.6

A. What, exactly, is a revolutionary hypothesis? How does such a hypothesis differ from other theoretical hypotheses?

B. Identify from the following list at least two hypotheses with which you are familiar, and state why you think they were or were not revolutionary when they were first proposed:

1. The theory of the evolution of species.
2. The theory that the solar system originated in a gigantic cosmic explosion ("big bang") some billions of years ago.
3. The general theory of relativity.
4. The theory that light is wavelike rather than corpuscular in nature.
5. The theory that there is intelligent life elsewhere in the universe.
6. The theory that the earth is spherical rather than flat.
7. The theory that the heart is a pump, and that the blood circulates throughout the body.
8. The theory that human beings are merely complex organisms no part of which survives after death.
9. The theory that gravity is a basic force that operates throughout the universe.
10. The theory that the earth is surrounded by a "sea of air" whose

weight accounts for such phenomena as the functioning of pumps, the variations in barometric readings at various altitudes, and the discomfort that one feels in one's ears as one goes up or down a mountain.

# 14.7  SCIENCE AND PSEUDOSCIENCE

It is evident from the preceding discussion that scientific theories may be true or false, and that their truth or falsity often is not knowable with absolute certainty. The geocentric theory is a scientific theory that we now believe to be false, the heliocentric theory one that we now believe to be true. Both, however, are clearly scientific theories. By virtue of what, then, are they called "scientific" theories, and how are they different from what we may call "pseudoscientific" theories—nonscientific theories masquerading as scientific theories? How, for example, are the geocentric and heliocentric theories different from such pseudoscientific theories as the "evil spirit" theory of disease and the astrological theory of human destiny?

It might seem that the answer to our question is relatively simple: scientific theories are supported by the facts, whereas pseudoscientific theories are not. But this answer will not do for a number of reasons. First, it is not the case that pseudoscientific theories are not supported by any facts. In the case of astrology, for example, one can always find human beings whose life experience has been roughly consistent with what astrology would predict for someone born under this or that sign of the zodiac. A believer in astrology, therefore, could point to the life experience of such people as evidence in support of that theory in precisely the same way that the proponent of a genuine scientific theory cites evidence in support of the latter theory. Second, as we have seen (Section 14.6), the facts available at a given time do not always clearly support one theory in preference to another. Indeed, a number of theories can usually be invented to explain any given body of facts; some of these theories might be scientific and others not. Third, pseudoscientific theories often are formulated in such a way as to fit the facts *no matter what the facts may be*. For all of these reasons, the fact that a theory is—or at least appears to be—supported by some facts is no guarantee that it is scientific.

Let us consider a second possibility. Perhaps what distinguishes a scientific theory from a pseudoscientific theory is the fact that the former is theoretically capable of being disproved by the facts, whereas the latter is not. A scientific theory, we might say, is specific: it states that the facts are thus and not so, and if the facts turn out to be otherwise, the theory is judged to be false. A pseudoscientific theory, on the other hand, is pliable: it purports to be about the facts, but no conceivable set of facts is ever allowed to prove the theory false. No matter what may be the actual life experience of a person born under the sign of Leo, for example, the various statements that constitute the theory of astrology are so flexible and indefinite as to be capable of assimilating and, in a sense, "accounting for" that life experience. Thus the theory of astrology is shown to be pseudo-scientific.

Although this proposal has much to commend it, it does not provide an entirely satisfactory criterion for distinguishing between scientific and pseudoscientific theories. The reason that it is not entirely satisfactory is that, as we have seen (Section 14.5), theoretical hypotheses—some of the most important elements in any system of scientific knowledge—are not capable of being conclusively disproved. Thus we are in danger of stating our criterion in such a way as to classify all theoretical hypotheses as pseudoscientific, and of course not all of them are.

We can avoid ruling out theoretical hypotheses if we state our criterion as follows: A theory is scientific if and only if it is possible to state the kind of evidence that would *count against* it, that is, would tend to disprove it. Thus, although theoretical hypotheses cannot be conclusively disproved, they nonetheless qualify as scientific hypotheses inasmuch as they do imply certain consequences that are subject to empirical verification. If the expected consequences failed to materialize, this failure would count against the hypothesis, although—for reasons that we have already discussed—such a finding would not conclusively disprove the theory.

Consider, for example, the theory that the mercury in an inverted closed tube immersed in a dish of mercury (i.e., the mercury in a barometer) is forced upward into the tube by the weight of a column of air pressing down on the mercury in the dish. Is this a scientific theory or not? According to our criterion, we must decide this question by asking another: Are there any facts that would count against the theory? The answer is that there are. Since the column of air pressing down on the mercury in the dish is longer and therefore presumably heavier at a low altitude than at a higher altitude, the mercury should rise higher in the tube at the bottom of a mountain than at the top. If tests showed that this expected result did not occur, that fact would count against the theory. Moreover, since an ordinary water pump evidently operates on the same principle, by comparing the specific gravities of mercury and water we should be able to calculate the maximum vertical distance that water can be pumped at one time. If it were to be shown that water could in fact be pumped a greater vertical distance than the theory says is possible, this fact, too, would count against the theory. So, according to our criterion, the theory that we are considering is a scientific theory.

Now consider a second example. There are people who believe that some kinds of illness are caused by demon possession. Is this a scientific theory according to our criterion? Again we ask: are there any facts that would count against the theory? Evidently not. The theory yields no predictions, and thus specifies no consequences that could be contradicted by the facts. If the patient dies and the autopsy reveals no demons in the body of the deceased, that fact does not count against the theory because demons are said to be invisible. If the patient recovers, no residual evidence of demons is to be expected because the demons have, of course, departed. There are *no* facts that would count against the theory, much less prove it to be false. Thus, according to our criterion, the demon-possession theory of illness, whatever else it may be, is not a scientific theory.

Pseudoscientific theories should not be confused with genuine scientific theories that turn out to be false (or at least apparently so). The theory of the spontaneous generation of insects from decaying substances, for example—a theory that Aristotle unfortunately endorsed—is a scientific theory that was not discredited until the seventeenth century. That it is a scientific theory, however, and not a pseudoscientific theory, is evident, according to our criterion, from the fact that empirical evidence did indeed count against it, and led eventually to its abandonment. The same is true of the Ptolemaic cosmology, the impetus theory of motion, Galen's theory of the function of the blood in human and animal bodies, the corpuscular theory of light, and many other theories that have been abandoned in favor of others. In contrast to all of these, the theories associated with astrology, fortunetelling, and pop psychology are shown by our criterion to be pseudoscientific because no facts can be specified that would count against them. They are unassailable by the facts precisely because, although it appears otherwise, they really do not make factual claims—which, no doubt, is what makes them so seductive.

## EXERCISES 14.7

**A.**   State the criterion proposed above for distinguishing between scientific theories and pseudoscientific theories.

**B.**   According to the proposed criterion, identify each of the theories listed below as either scientific or pseudoscientific:

   **1.**   The theory that the earth came into existence approximately 6,000 years ago.

   **2.**   The theory that acquired characteristics can be passed on to one's progeny.

3. The theory that the earth is flat.
4. The theory that prayer changes things.
5. The theory that events in human history, like events in nature, occur in accordance with unchanging laws (sometimes called the theory of historical determinism).
6. The theory of evolution.
7. The theory that, barring an accident, the length of a person's life can be predicted from the "life line" that appears on his or her palm.
8. The theory that the universe contains "black holes" in which matter is so concentrated that even light cannot escape from them (as a consequence of which they cannot be seen).
9. The theory that human life first appeared in Mesopotamia.
10. The theory that soldiers who survive a battle are the beneficiaries of divine protection.

# appendix a
# Brain-Stretcher Clues

The following clues should set you on the right track toward the solution of these logical puzzles. If you find that the clues are not adequate, you will have to get help from your instructor—who can, of course, solve them all without difficulty!

## 1. TWIN SOULS

Capitals stand for men, the corresponding lower-case letters for their wives. (1) B's wife had never met A. (2) D's wife is younger than B's. (3) C's wife is younger than a's husband. (4) There was one double wedding. (5) By 1, B did not marry a, therefore married c or someone younger. . . . Can you carry on from here?

## 2. THE WISE FOOL

Who could not possibly answer, "The God of Truth," to the first question? Who could not possibly answer, "The God of Diplomacy," to the second question? The rest is easy.

**329**

# 3. YOU CAN'T TELL THE TEACHERS WITHOUT A PROGRAM

First identify the English teacher. The English teacher is a man, therefore not Arthur, Bascomb, or Conroy. He is the oldest of the six, therefore not Furness. He has taught the longest of the six, therefore cannot be Eggleston. That leaves Duval as the English teacher. It follows, of course, that Duval does not teach economics, French, history, Latin, or mathematics.

Let's summarize the information obtained thus far in a matrix:

| TEACHER | ECON | ENGLISH | FRENCH | HIST | LATIN | MATH |
|---------|------|---------|--------|------|-------|------|
| Arthur |  | O |  |  |  |  |
| Bascomb |  | O |  |  |  |  |
| Conroy |  | O |  |  |  |  |
| Duval | O | X | O | O | O | O |
| Eggleston |  | O |  |  |  |  |
| Furness |  | O |  |  |  |  |

Now start working on the relative ages of the teachers. Eggleston is older than Furness, Furness is the French teacher's father, Arthur is older than the Latin teacher. Eggleston does not teach economics or French, Furness does not teach French, Arthur does not teach Latin. You take it from there.

# 4. IF IT'S TUESDAY

This problem, like problem 3, calls for a matrix. Set it up like this, using X's to indicate that the language is spoken, O's to indicate that it is not:

| SPEAKER | ENGLISH | FRENCH | GERMAN | ITALIAN |
|---------|---------|--------|--------|---------|
| John | O |  |  |  |
| Peter |  |  |  |  |
| Jacob |  |  | X |  |
| William |  |  | O |  |

Now let's start drawing some inferences. Since Jacob speaks German, he cannot speak French. Since Peter and Jacob need an interpreter to converse with each other, Peter evidently cannot speak

German. Since John cannot speak both French and German, he must speak either French and Italian or German and Italian. In either case he speaks Italian, so we can add that to our matrix.

What else do we know? We know that John has one language in common with Peter and one with Jacob, that Jacob has one language in common with William, that John, Peter, and William do *not* have a language in common, and that one language is shared by three speakers—from which it follows also that one language must be spoken by only one of the four (since each speaks just two languages).

Find a hypothesis that fits these facts.

# 5. THE LINEUP

Each man makes just three statements, and we are told that exactly one statement made by each is false. In the case of Watts, for example, one of the following must be the case:

Statement 1 is false, and statements 2 and 3 are true.
Statement 2 is false, and statements 1 and 3 are true.
Statement 3 is false, and statements 1 and 2 are true.

Each of these possibilities has certain implications that can be conveniently summarized in what is called a truth table (see Section 9.2). Assigning numbers 1–3 to the statements made by Watts, numbers 4–6 to the statements made by Rogers, and numbers 7–9 to the statements made by O'Neil, we get the following outline for a truth table:

| WATTS | | | ROGERS | | | O'NEIL | | |
|---|---|---|---|---|---|---|---|---|
| 1 | 2 | 3 | 4 | 5 | 6 | 7 | 8 | 9 |
| F | T | T | | | | | | |
| T | F | T | | | | | | |
| T | T | F | | | | | | |

What follows if we assume that statement 1 is false and statements 2 and 3 are true (row 1 in the truth table)? Well, for one thing, statement 5 must be false, for it is inconsistent with statement 3. But then statements 4 and 6 must be true. That is not possible, however, for statement 4 contradicts statement 2. Therefore, the supposition that statement 1 is false and statements 2 and 3 true (row 1 in our truth table) must be incorrect. Now try row 2 and, if necessary, row 3. Then, by elimination, you should have no trouble determining that—Ah, but of course you would rather figure that out for yourself, wouldn't you?

# appendix b
# Solutions to Selected Exercise Items

Solutions are given below for all *even-numbered* exercise items to which objective answers are possible. In the case of items identified by letter rather than by number, solutions are provided for alternate items B, D, F, and so on. In some cases, representative solutions are given for items to which alternative solutions would be equally correct.

## EXERCISES 1.1–1.3

2. *Premises:* Inflation is caused by an excess of money in circulation. An excess of money in circulation is caused by deficit spending by government.
   *Conclusion:* Inflation is caused by deficit spending by government.
   *Type:* Deductive.

4. *Premises:* Recent tests indicate that the Rabbit gives the best mileage of any car sold in this country. My new car is a Rabbit, whereas my old one was not a Rabbit.
   *Conclusion:* My new car will give me better mileage than my old one.
   *Type:* Inductive.

6. *Premises:* The individual who is elected homecoming queen on any campus in any particular year is the most beautiful girl on that campus. On one campus, a heifer was once elected homecoming queen.
   *Conclusion:* The heifer was the most beautiful girl on campus that year.
   *Type:* Deductive.

8. *Premises:* Most of the people who have ever worked with computers are still living. That most of the people in a given category are still living indicates that what they are doing is good for their health (assumed premise).
   *Conclusion:* Working with computers is good for one's health.
   *Type:* Deductive.

10. *Premises:* In the past, the frequency of nuclear accidents has increased as the number of nuclear power plants has increased. In ten years, there will be twice as many nuclear power plants as there are today.
    *Conclusion:* The frequency of nuclear accidents will increase.
    *Type:* Inductive.

## EXERCISES 1.4–1.7

A. Logical implication:
   2. c, d, e, h, i, j
   4. c, e, f, h, i, j
B. Probable inferences:
   Probable inferences are to some extent a matter of judgment. These are suggested as reasonable possibilities:
   2. The Smiths' house had been burglarized. Presumption of determinate fact.
   4. The boy in question had not burglarized the Smiths' house. Presumption of determinate fact.
   6. Team A will win the pennant. None of the above.
   8. The average weight of defensive tackles in the NFL is greater than that of American adult males generally. Empirical generalization.
   10. The males of this species are on the average heavier than the females, and the males make a sound not made by the females. Empirical generalizations.

## EXERCISE 2.1

2. Informative
4. Informative, expressive
6. Informative, expressive
8. Informative
10. Informative

## EXERCISE 2.2

**2.**   Not in a metalanguage.
**4.**   Not in a metalanguage.
**6.**   Not in a metalanguage.
**8.**   Metalanguage. Restatement: "Firm" means "stubborn."
**10.**  Metalanguage. Restatement: The definition of "crab" as "ill-tempered person" is thought to derive from the behavior of the marine animal of that name.

## EXERCISES 2.3–2.4

Open-ended. Solutions not provided.

## EXERCISE 3.1

**2.**   A person's conscience may speak clearly.
The dictates of a person's conscience may be in conflict with the law.
The dictates of a person's conscience may be in conflict with those of somebody else's conscience.
Some person's conscience may assert that he or she should be a conscientious objector.
Another person's conscience may assert that one ought not to tolerate conscientious objectors.
If one is a conscientious objector, then one knows that the conscience of someone who asserts that one ought not to tolerate conscientious objectors is mistaken.
The voice of conscience is not the voice of God.
The voice of conscience is the voice of a finite, limited human being living at a particular time and in a particular place.
The voice of conscience is not infallible.
The dictates of conscience need to be examined by critical, reflective thought.
The dictates of conscience, if unexamined, are likely to be mere prejudice.
**4.**   The following problems exist: widespread unemployment and underemployment, poor housing, and poor education.
Black people are denied equal access to and use of public accommodations and services.
The latter is a result of racial discrimination on the part of white people.
Black people do not have adequate access to medical facilities.
Black people suffer injustices in the courts.
Black people are the victims of repressive police practices.
The Black Power movement has an obligation to find solutions to the above problems.
**6.**   The possibilities confronting us are few.

The possibilities confronting us can be ascertained.

One possibility is that we continue on our present course.

If we continue on our present course, the result will be either thermonuclear war or severe human pathology.

Another possibility is that we attempt to change our present course by force or revolution.

If we do this, the result will be violence and dictatorship.

A third possibility is to humanize the system.

This third possibility would result in an enhancement of human well-being and growth and the preservation of the central elements of the second Industrial Revolution.

8. Some human beings eat little and see heaven.

Some human beings drink much and see snakes.

There is no objective basis to distinguish between the above-mentioned two groups of human beings.

Both of the above-mentioned groups are in an abnormal physical condition.

Both of the above-mentioned groups have abnormal perceptions.

Normal perception has some correspondence with fact.

The correspondence of normal perception with fact is essential to its usefulness in the struggle for life.

There is nothing about abnormal perception that requires that it correspond to the facts.

The testimony of abnormal perception is not more credible than that of normal perception.

10. That a thing is done once proves decisively that it can be done.

Doing a thing once is sometimes difficult.

To prove that a thing cannot be done requires that one claim that each and every possible way of doing it has been tried and failed.

The latter claim is bold.

## EXERCISE 3.2

Premises (P) and conclusions (C) of arguments:

2. **P:** All experience is absolutely individual in its existence.
   **P:** (All) intrinsic good is experience.
   **C:** All intrinsic good is individual.

4. **P:** All states of consciousness are caused by molecular changes of the brain substance.
   **P:** No state of consciousness is the cause of change in the motion of the matter of an organism.
   **C:** Mental conditions are merely the symbols in consciousness of the changes that take place automatically in an organism.

6. **P:** Personality is a matter of organization.
   **P:** This organization is effected by means of causal laws.
   **P:** These causal laws depend on the body.
   **C:** Personality cannot survive the disintegration of the body.

8.  **P:**  The British bullied the Iranians for decades.
    **P:**  The CIA joined British intelligence in organizing the 1953 coup.
    **C:**  The Iranians often had reason to be suspicious of foreigners.
10. **P:**  Science predicts.
    **C:**  Science is useful and can serve as a rule of action.

## EXERCISE 3.3

**B.  Principal argument:**
  **P:**  If a university cooperates with the Selective Service system, it thereby strengthens the draft system.
  **P:**  If a university refuses to cooperate, it thereby hurts or weakens the draft system.
  **P:**  It must do one or the other (this is assumed), and neither is value-neutral.
  **C:**  A university cannot adopt a value-neutral stance vis-à-vis government policy.

  **Subargument:**
  **P:**  Public refusal to cooperate with Selective Service would harm the government more than quiet cooperation would help it.
  **P:**  The strength of one's reasons for acting in a given way should be commensurate with the seriousness of the presumed consequences of one's actions (assumed premise).
  **C:**  Refusal to cooperate could be justified only if there are stronger reasons for opposition than there are for cooperation.

## EXERCISE 3.4

**B.**  The constituent statements are identified on page 34.
  **Principal argument:**
  **P:**  All thinking and honest people desire a scientific democratic approach to politics, economy, and culture (assumed premise).
  **P:**  Freedom of thought would guarantee the feasibility of a scientific democratic approach to politics, economy, and culture.
  **P:**  Nothing other than freedom of thought would guarantee the feasibility of a scientific democratic approach to politics, economy, and culture.
  **P:**  Freedom of thought is threatened by mass culture, certain ideologies, governmental dogmatism, and ideological censorship.
  **P:**  One should oppose that which threatens an essential condition of what one desires (assumed premise).
  **C:**  All thinking and honest people should oppose mass culture, certain ideologies, governmental dogmatism, and ideological censorship.

## EXERCISES 4.1–4.4

**B.**  Fallacies:
  **2.**  **a.** Fallacy: Appeal to pity.
    **b.** That a student is about to be dismissed from school and that his or her mother is a widow are irrelevant to the question of whether or not the student received the grade that he or she deserved in a particular course.
  **4.**  **a.** Fallacy: Argument against the person (circumstantial).
    **b.** Senator Smith's arguments against gun control legislation deserve to be considered on their own merits, notwithstanding the support given him by the American Rifle Association.
  **6.**  **a.** Fallacy: Appeal to authority.
    **b.** Abraham Lincoln has no special credentials that make him an authority in matters of ethics.
  **8.**  **a.** Fallacy: Appeal to pity.
    **b.** The facts adduced by the attorney are irrelevant to the guilt or innocence of the defendant.
  **10.**  **a.** Fallacy: Argument against the person (abusive).
    **b.** That the governor has not paid taxes for the past three years is not relevant to the question of whether or not taxes need to be raised in order to maintain governmental services at their present level.
  **12.**  **a.** Fallacy: Appeal to popular sentiment.
    **b.** Statements about "excessive profit of the owners" and "high salaries of management" are obviously addressed to the sentiments of union members, and contribute nothing to a rational consideration of the causes of inflation.
  **14.**  **a.** Fallacy: Appeal to authority.
    **b.** Presidents have no special credentials that make them authorities with respect to religion.
  **16.**  **a.** Fallacy: Argument against the person (*tu quoque*).
    **b.** That the second candidate has been charged with drunk driving is irrelevant to the defense of the first candidate against the claim that his or her conviction for income tax evasion makes him or her unfit to hold public office.
  **18.**  **a.** Fallacy: Appeal to force.
    **b.** That a TV station is vulnerable to punitive governmental action is irrelevant to the veracity of its newscasts.
  **20.**  **a.** Fallacy: Biased sample.
    **b.** The students on any one campus are not likely to be representative of all college students.

## EXERCISES 4.5

**B.**  Fallacies:
  **2.**  **a.** Fallacy: Begging the question.
    **b.** The speaker is assuming that the person accused of a crime is

a criminal—that is, guilty—which is precisely the point that needs to be established whenever someone is accused of having committed a crime.

4.  a. Fallacy: Genetic fallacy.
    b. That the practice of treating frostbite with snow originated among "poor and ignorant people" is irrelevant to the question as to whether or not it is an effective treatment.

6.  a. Fallacy: False cause (*post hoc*).
    b. That frost regularly precedes the turning of the leaves does not prove that it causes the turning.

8.  a. Fallacy: Begging the question (circular argument).
    b. That a critic recognizes the superiority of Mozart's music is offered as evidence that the critic is competent, and the unanimous opinion of "competent critics" so defined is offered as evidence in support of the superiority of Mozart's music.

10. a. Fallacy: False cause (*post hoc*).
    b. That the increase in the incidence of tuberculosis coincides with the increase in the importation of bananas does not prove that there is a causal link between the two.

12. a. Fallacy: Begging the question (circular argument).
    b. That one is a true believer is offered as evidence that one will not die, and that someone has died is offered as evidence that he or she was not a true believer.

14. a. Fallacy: Irrelevant conclusion.
    b. That libraries are, in general, a good thing does not support the proposition that a particular university should establish a program in library science.

16. a. Fallacy: Complex question.
    b. It is assumed that dislike for any of the assigned articles is attributable to some defect in the reader's character.

18. a. Fallacy: Begging the question (sort of).
    b. The question is whether the man who wishes to cash a check is who he says he is, or, more generally, whether he is trustworthy. The friend is offered to vouch for his identity, but since the friend is unknown to the teller, it would be reasonable to trust the statement of the friend only on the supposition that the man who wishes to cash the check is trustworthy—in which case the friend's testimony would be irrelevant.

20. a. Fallacy: False cause (*post hoc*).
    b. The alleged correlation between television viewing time and declining test scores does not establish a causal link between the two.

# EXERCISES 4.6–4.7

B.  Fallacies:

2.  a. Fallacy: Quotation out of context.

    b. In its original context it is clear that the statement "Render unto Caesar that which is Caesar's" did not mean "Do absolutely anything that the government orders you to do."

4.  a. Fallacy: Quotation out of context.

    b. Taken in context, Jefferson's words are hostile to religion. The visitor, reading the italicized words without knowing the context, misunderstood Jefferson's meaning.

6.  a. Fallacy: Accent.

    b. The reporter is laying undue stress on the word "public."

8.  a. Fallacy: Equivocation.

    b. The word "ass" can mean a four-legged animal (the Duke's intended meaning) or a fool (even a duke!).

10.  a. Fallacy: Composition.

    b. From the fact that each person's happiness is a good to that person one cannot infer that the general happiness is a good to the aggregate of all persons.

12.  a. Fallacy: Quotation out of context.

    b. The context makes it clear that the original statement was not a decree or prediction that all efforts to eliminate poverty are doomed to failure.

14.  a. Fallacy: Amphiboly.

    b. "How do you like $x$?" can mean "Do you like $x$ or don't you?" or it can mean "Do you prefer $x$ this way or that way?" The person answering the question assumed the first meaning, whereas the questioner obviously intended the second.

16.  a. Fallacy: Composition.

    b. From the fact that each of several colors is beautiful it does not follow that the composite result of all of those colors taken together will be beautiful.

18.  a. Fallacy: Quotation out of context.

    b. Considered in context, the reviewer's comments were uncomplimentary to the book in question. As quoted, however, they appear to be complimentary.

20.  a. Fallacy: Amphiboly.

    b. This is, of course, a silly example of amphiboly. The statement "[The sheikh] leaves his chauffeur-driven Mercedes wrapped in a flowing white robe" obviously means that the sheikh, not the Mercedes, is thus wrapped. The grammar of the statement does, however, permit the other interpretation.

## EXERCISE 5.1

($S$ = subject class; $P$ = predicate class; $CS$ = complement of subject class; $CP$ = complement of predicate class; $V$ = copula; $EC$ = empty class.)

2.  $S$: college presidents; $P$: illiterate people; $CS$: non-(college presidents); $CP$: non-(illiterate people); $V$: are; $EC$: none.

4.  $S$: college graduates; $P$: underemployed workers; $CS$: non-(college graduates); $CP$: non-(underemployed workers); $V$: are; $EC$: none.

6. *S:* people who can leap tall buildings in a single bound; *P:* superpeople; *CS:* non-(people who can leap tall buildings in a single bound); *CP:* nonsuperpeople; *V:* are; *EC:* people who can leap tall buildings in a single bound; superpeople.

8. *S:* congressmen; *P:* vote getters; *CS:* noncongressmen; *CP:* non-(vote getters); *V:* are; *EC:* none.

10. *S:* nonsupporters of the ERA; *P:* fair-minded people; *CS:* supporters of the ERA; *CP:* non-(fair-minded people); *V:* are; *EC:* none.

12. *S:* noncitizens; *P:* people whose primary loyalty is to the country from which they came; *CS:* citizens; *CP:* non-(people whose primary loyalty is to the country from which they came); *V:* are; *EC:* none.

14. *S:* ping-pong players; *P:* people who love pizza and beer; *CS:* non-(ping-pong players); *CP:* nonlovers of pizza and beer; *V:* are; *EC:* none.

16. *S:* people who are frightened by absurdities; *P:* nonphilosophers; *CS:* non-(people who are frightened by absurdities); *CP:* philosophers; *V:* are; *EC:* none.

18. *S:* people who drive westward at sundown; *P:* people who cannot see in bright sunshine without sunglasses; *CS:* non-(people who drive westward at sundown); *CP:* non-(people who cannot see in bright sunshine without sunglasses); *V:* are; *EC:* none.

20. *S:* Martians; *P:* two-headed creatures; *CS:* non-Martians; *CP:* non-(two-headed creatures); *V:* are; *EC:* Martians; two-headed creatures.

## EXERCISE 5.2

2. Universal negative.
4. Particular affirmative.
6. Universal affirmative.
8. Universal affirmative.
10. Universal negative.
12. Particular affirmative.
14. Universal affirmative.
16. Universal affirmative.
18. Particular affirmative.
20. Universal affirmative.

## EXERCISES 5.3–5.4

A. A, E, I, and O statements:

| 2. E | 6. A | 10. E | 14. A | 18. I |
|------|------|-------|-------|-------|
| 4. I | 8. A | 12. I | 16. A | 20. A |

B. Restatements in standard form.
(*Note:* Any of the logical equivalents of the statements listed below would also constitute correct solutions to this exercise. See Section 5.6.)

2. Some Democrats are not persons who support massive welfare spending. (**O**)
4. All persons who arrive by six o'clock in the morning are persons who will receive free admission. (**A**)
6. Some things in life that are certain are things other than death and taxes. (**I**)
8. Some distinguished-looking people are tall. (**I**)
10. No people are machines. (**E**)
12. All ducks are swimmers. (**A**)
14. All people are people who are entitled to their day in court. (**A**)
16. Some readers of our local newspaper are people who are badly misinformed about current events. (**I**)
18. All people who live in glass houses are people who should not throw stones. (**A**)
20. Some people who earn good grades are not people who are naturally brilliant. (**O**)

## EXERCISES 5.5

**A.** Distributed and undistributed terms (*S:D* means "subject term is distributed"; *P:U* means "predicate term is undistributed"; etc.):

| | | | | | |
|---|---|---|---|---|---|
| 2. | *S:D, P:D* | 8. | *S:D, P:U* | 14. | *S:D, P:U* |
| 4. | *S:U, P:U* | 10. | *S:D, P:D* | 16. | *S:D, P:U* |
| 6. | *S:D, P:U* | 12. | *S:U, P:U* | 18. | *S:U, P:U* |
| | | | | 20. | *S:D, P:U* |

**B.** Open-ended.

## EXERCISES 5.6–5.7

**A.** Logical equivalents:
1. Following are the converses of all even-numbered statements on pages 87–88 that have logically equivalent converses:
   (2) No illiterate people are college presidents.
   (4) Some underemployed workers are college graduates.
   (10) No fair-minded people are nonsupporters of the Equal Rights Amendment.
   (12) Some people whose primary loyalty is to the country from which they came are noncitizens.
   (18) Some people who cannot see in bright sunshine without sunglasses are people who drive westward at sundown.
2. Following are the contrapositives of all even-numbered statements on pages 87–88 that have logically equivalent contrapositives:
   (6) All nonsuperpeople are non-(people who can leap tall buildings in a single bound).
   (8) All non-(vote getters) are noncongressmen.
   (14) All nonlovers of pizza and beer are non-(ping-pong players).

      **(16)** All philosophers are non-(people who are frightened by absurdities).

      **(20)** All non-(two-headed creatures) are non-Martians.

  **3.** Following are the obverses of all even-numbered statements on pages 87–88:

      **(2)** All college presidents are literate people.

      **(4)** Some college graduates are not non-(underemployed workers).

      **(6)** No people who can leap tall buildings in a single bound are nonsuperpeople.

      **(8)** No congressmen are non-(vote getters).

      **(10)** All nonsupporters of the ERA are non-(fair-minded people).

      **(12)** Some noncitizens are not non-(people whose primary loyalty is to the country from which they came).

      **(14)** No ping-pong players are nonlovers of pizza and beer.

      **(16)** No people who are frightened by absurdities are philosophers.

      **(18)** Some people who drive westward at sundown are not people who can see in bright sunshine without sunglasses.

      **(20)** No Martians are non-(two-headed creatures).

  **4.** Following are other logical equivalents of all even-numbered statements on pages 87–88. The statements given are the converse of the obverse for **A** and **O** statements, and the obverse of the converse for **E** and **I** statements:

      **(2)** All illiterate people are non-(college presidents).

      **(4)** Some underemployed workers are not non-(college graduates).

      **(6)** No nonsuperpeople are people who can leap buildings in a single bound.

      **(8)** No non-(vote getters) are congressmen.

      **(10)** All fair-minded people are supporters of the ERA.

      **(12)** Some people whose primary loyalty is to the country from which they came are not citizens.

      **(14)** No nonlovers of pizza and beer are ping-pong players.

      **(16)** No philosophers are people who are frightened by absurdities.

      **(18)** Some people who cannot see in bright sunshine without sunglasses are not people who do not drive westward at sundown.

      **(20)** No non-(two-headed creatures) are Martians.

**B.** On the assumption that the statements on pages 87–88 are true, the following statements must be false:

    **2.** Some college presidents are illiterate people.

    **4.** No college graduates are underemployed workers.

    **6.** Some people who can leap buildings in a single bound are not superpeople.

    **8.** Some congressmen are not vote getters.

   **10.** Some nonsupporters of the ERA are fair-minded people.

   **12.** No noncitizens are people whose primary loyalty is to the country from which they came.

   **14.** Some ping-pong players are not lovers of pizza and beer.

   **16.** Some people who are frightened by absurdities are not non-philosophers.

18. No people who drive westward at sundown are people **who** cannot see in bright sunshine without sunglasses.
20. Some Martians are not two-headed creatures.

## EXERCISES 5.8

**A.** Venn diagrams.
   **1.** Statements on pages 87–88:
      **(2)** No college presidents are illiterate people.

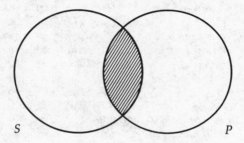

      **(4)** Some college graduates are underemployed workers.

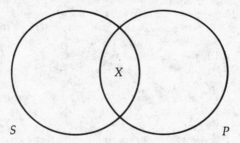

      **(6)** All people who can leap tall buildings in a single bound **are** superpeople.

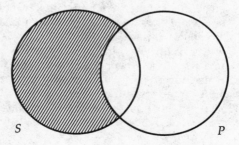

**(8)** All congressmen are vote getters.

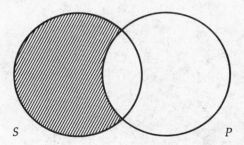

**(10)** No nonsupporters of the ERA are fair-minded people.

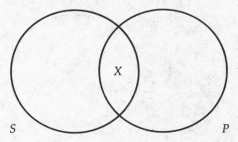

**(12)** Some noncitizens are people whose primary loyalty is to the country from which they came.

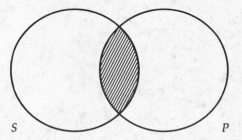

**(14)** All ping-pong players are lovers of pizza and beer.

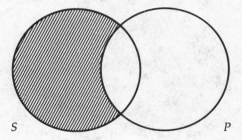

**(16)** All people who are frightened by absurdities are nonphilos-ophers.

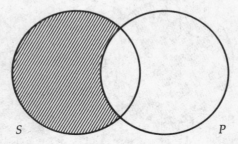

**(18)** Some people who drive westward at sundown are people who cannot see in bright sunshine without sunglasses.

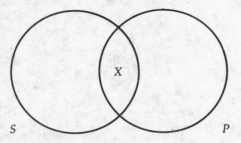

**(20)** All Martians are two-headed creatures.

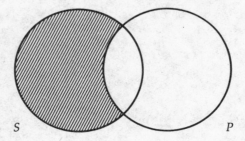

**2.** Obverse of statements on pages 87–88:
**(2)** All college presidents are literate people.

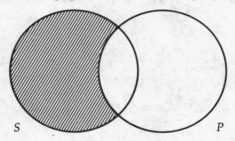

**(4)** Some college graduates are not non-(underemployed workers).

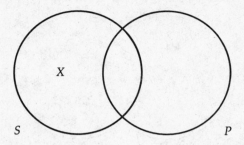

**(6)** No people who can leap tall buildings in a single bound are nonsuperpeople.

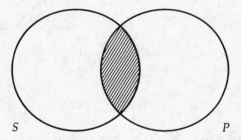

**(8)** No congressmen are non-(vote getters).

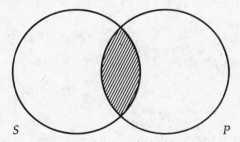

**(10)** All nonsupporters of the ERA are non-(fair-minded people).

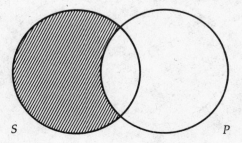

**(12)** Some noncitizens are not non-(people whose primary loyalty is to the country from which they came).

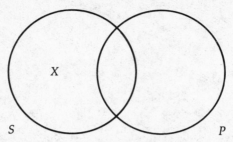

**(14)** No ping-pong players are nonlovers of pizza and beer.

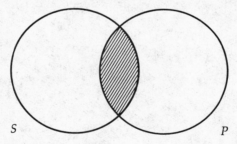

**(16)** No people who are frightened by absurdities are philosophers.

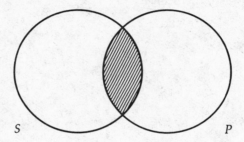

**(18)** Some people who drive westward at sundown are people who cannot see in bright sunshine without sunglasses.

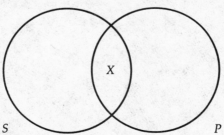

**(20)** No Martians are non-(two-headed creatures).

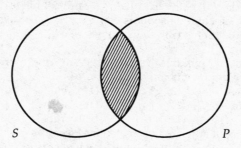

**B.** Open-ended.


# EXERCISE 6.1

**a.** Major, minor, and middle terms (Maj = major term; Min = minor term; Mid = middle term):

**(2)** Maj = pilots, Min = people who have taken flying lessons, Mid = people who are legally blind.

**(4)** Maj = (things that are) bad for one's waistline, Min = desserts, Mid = high-calorie foods.

**(6)** Maj = fish, Min = dogs, Mid = animals that bark.

**(8)** Maj = members of the legislature, Min = people who are qualified to hold office, Mid = people who have been duly elected.

**(10)** Maj = (people who) will not live to be a hundred, Min = students who successfully complete this course, Mid = students who will receive a grade of *S* in the course.

**(12)** Maj = great music, Min = rock and roll music, Mid = (music that is) uplifting.

**(14)** Maj = (things that) should be regarded as dangerous, Min = pilots of UFO's, Mid = extraterrestrial beings.

**(16)** Maj = philosophers, Min = people, Mid = people who are frightened by absurdities.

**(18)** Maj = college graduates, Min = congressmen, Mid = semiliterate people.

**(20)** Maj = (things that) should be avoided at all costs, Min = future wars, Mid = (things that) have the potential of annihilating the human race.

**b.** Major and minor premises (Maj = major premise, Min = minor premise):

**(2)** Maj: No pilots . . . Min: Some people . . .

**(4)** Maj: High-calorie foods . . . Min: Desserts . . .

**(6)** Maj: No fish . . . Min: Dogs . . .

**(8)** Maj: All members . . . Min: Some people . . .

**(10)** Maj: Some students . . . Min: All students . . .

    **(12)** Maj: All great . . . Min: Some rock . . .
    **(14)** Maj: All extraterrestrial . . . Min: All pilots . . .
    **(16)** Maj: No philosophers . . . Min: Some people . . .
    **(18)** Maj: Some college graduates . . . Min: Some semiliterate people . . .
    **(20)** Maj: Anything that has . . . Min: Any future war . . .

**c.** Are the arguments in standard form?

| | | | | | | | |
|---|---|---|---|---|---|---|---|
| **(2)** Yes | | **(8)** Yes | | **(14)** No | | **(20)** No | |
| **(4)** No | | **(10)** No | | **(16)** No | | | |
| **(6)** No | | **(12)** Yes | | **(18)** Yes | | | |

**d.** Why arguments are not in standard form:
    **(4)** None of the constituent statements is in standard form.
    **(6)** The minor premise is not in standard form.
    **(10)** The minor premise is stated first.
    **(14)** The major premise is not in standard form (it is lacking a copula). Also, the minor premise is stated first.
    **(16)** The minor premise is stated first.
    **(20)** None of the constituent statements is in standard form. Also, the minor premise is stated first.

## EXERCISES 6.2

**A.** Syllogisms 8, 10, 12, and 18 are invalid. The remaining even-numbered syllogisms are valid.

**B.** The invalid syllogisms are, of course, unsound. Whether the premises of the valid syllogisms are true, thus making those syllogisms sound, is a matter of judgment.

## EXERCISES 6.3

**A.** Moods and figures of syllogisms in standard form:

| | | | |
|---|---|---|---|
| **(2)** EIO-2. | | **(12)** AII-2. | |
| **(4)** Not in standard form. | | **(14)** Not in standard form. | |
| **(6)** Not in standard form. | | **(16)** Not in standard form. | |
| **(8)** AOO-4. | | **(18)** III-4. | |
| **(10)** Not in standard form. | | **(20)** Not in standard form. | |

**B.** Restatement in standard form of syllogisms not in standard form; mood and figure of each:

    **(4)** All high-calorie foods are foods that are bad for one's waistline.
    All desserts are high-calorie foods.

    ∴ All desserts are foods that are bad for one's waistline. **(AAA-1)**

    **(6)** No fish are animals that bark.
    All dogs are animals that bark.

    ∴ No dogs are fish. **(EAE-2)**

(10)   Some students who will receive a grade of $S$ in the course are people who will not live to be a hundred.
All students who successfully complete this course are students who will receive a grade of $S$ in the course.

∴ Some students who successfully complete this course are people who will not live to be a hundred. **(IAI-1)**

(14)   All extraterrestrial beings are beings that should be regarded as dangerous.
All pilots of UFO's are extraterrestrial beings.

∴ All pilots of UFO's are beings that should be regarded as dangerous. **(AAA-1)**

(16)   No philosophers are people who are frightened by absurdities.
Some people are people who are frightened by absurdities.

∴ Some people are not philosophers. **(EIO-2)**

(20)   All events that will have the potential of annihilating the human race are events that should be avoided at all costs.
All future wars are events that will have the potential of annihilating the human race.

∴ All future wars are events that should be avoided at all costs. **(AAA-1)**

C.   Schematic arguments:

**EIO-2**
No $P$ is $M$.
Some $S$ is $M$.

∴ Some $S$ is not $P$.

**AOO-4**
All $P$ is $M$.
Some $M$ is not $S$.

∴ Some $S$ is not $P$.

**AAA-4**
All $P$ is $M$.
All $M$ is $S$.

∴ All $S$ is $P$.

**AEO-2**
All $P$ is $M$.
No $S$ is $M$.

∴ Some $S$ is not $P$.

**EIO-3**
No $M$ is $P$.
Some $M$ is $S$.

∴ Some $S$ is not $P$.

**IEO-2**
Some $P$ is $M$.
No $S$ is $M$.

∴ Some $S$ is not $P$.

# EXERCISE 6.4

This exercise is open-ended. The criteria for an effective proof of invalidity by this method are stated in the instructions.

## EXERCISES 6.5

**A.**   Open-ended.
**B.**   Invalid syllogisms (**A** = axiom of validity that a syllogism fails to satisfy, **F** = the fallacy that results from failing to satisfy that axiom):

   **2.**   A: The middle term must be distributed at least once.
      F: Undistributed middle term.
   **4.**   A: The middle term must be distributed at least once.
      F: Undistributed middle term.
   **6.**   A: If the conclusion is particular, at least one premise must be particular.
      F: Existential fallacy.
   **8.**   A: If a term is distributed in the conclusion, it must also be distributed in the premises.
      F: Illicit major.
  **10.**   A: If the conclusion is particular, at least one premise must be particular.
      F: Existential fallacy.
  **12.**   A: If a term is distributed in the conclusion, it must also be distributed in the premises.
      F: Illicit minor.
  **14.**   A: The middle term must be distributed at least once.
      F: Undistributed middle term.
  **16.**   A: If the conclusion is particular, at least one premise must be particular.
      F: Existential fallacy.
  **18.**   A: The middle term must be distributed at least once.
      F: Undistributed middle term.
  **20.**   A: If a term is distributed in the conclusion, it must also be distributed in the premises.
      F: Illicit minor.
**C.**   Testing for validity by means of axioms of validity:
   **2.**   Invalid.
      Fallacy: Illicit major.
   **4.**   Invalid.
      Fallacy: Undistributed middle term.
   **6.**   Valid.
   **8.**   Valid.
  **10.**   Valid.

## EXERCISES 6.6

**A.**   Venn diagrams for syllogisms on pages 120–121:

2.  $S$ = atheists; $P$ = Russians; $M$ = Christians.

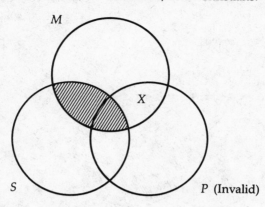

4.  $S$ = Republicans; $P$ = supporters; $M$ = conservatives.

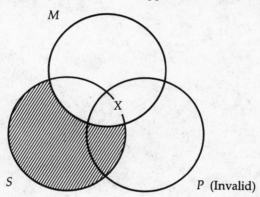

6.  $S$ = people despised; $P$ = fanatics; $M$ = sincere people.

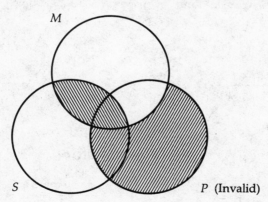

8. $S$ = residents of Jones Hall; $P$ = college students; $M$ = people who can read.

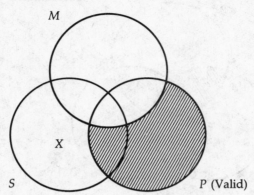

10. $S$ = sugar-free foods; $P$ = desserts; $M$ = high-calorie foods.

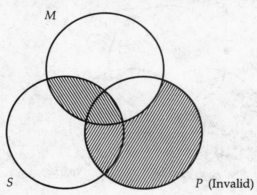

**B.** Testing argument forms by means of Venn diagrams:

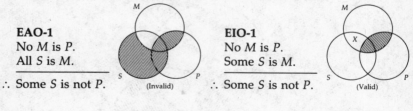

**EAO-1**
No $M$ is $P$.
All $S$ is $M$.
───────────
∴ Some $S$ is not $P$.

**EIO-1**
No $M$ is $P$.
Some $S$ is $M$.
───────────
∴ Some $S$ is not $P$.

**AEO-2**
All $P$ is $M$.
No $S$ is $M$.
───────────
∴ Some $S$ is not $P$.

**EIO-2**
No $P$ is $M$.
Some $S$ is $M$.
───────────
∴ Some $S$ is not $P$.

**OAO-3**
Some *M* is not *P*.
All *M* is *S*.
_____
∴ Some *S* is not *P*.

(Valid)

**EIO-3**
No *M* is *P*.
Some *M* is *S*.
_____
∴ Some *S* is not *P*.

(Valid)

**EAE-4**
No *P* is *M*.
All *M* is *S*.
_____
∴ No *S* is *P*.

(Invalid)

**EIO-4**
No *P* is *M*.
Some *M* is *S*.
_____
∴ Some *S* is not *P*.

(Valid)

## EXERCISES 6.7

**A.**  Determining validity of arguments on pages 120–121 (Exercises 6.5) by reference to the table of valid argument forms:

**(2)**  Some *P* is *M*
No *M* is *S*.
_____
∴ Some *S* is not *P*.
**IEO-4 (invalid)**

**(4)**  Some *M* is *P*.
All *S* is *M*.
_____
∴ Some *S* is *P*.
**IAI-1 (invalid)**

**(6)**  All *P* is *M*.
No *M* is *S*.
_____
∴ No *S* is *P*.
**AEE-4 (valid)**

**(8)**  All *P* is *M*.
Some *S* is not *M*.
_____
∴ Some *S* is not *P*.
**AOO-2 (valid)**

**(10)**  All *P* is *M*.
No *M* is *S*.
_____
∴ No *S* is *P*.
**AEE-4 (valid)**

**B.**  Determining validity of argument forms on page 126 by reference to the table of valid argument forms:

AII-2: Invalid          AEO-4: Invalid
AEE-2: Valid            IAI-4: Valid
AEO-2: Invalid          EAE-4: Invalid
EIO-2: Valid            EIO-4: Valid

**C.**  Venn diagrams verifying validity of argument forms on page 127:

**EAE-1**
No *M* is *P*.
All *S* is *M*.
_____
∴ No *S* is *P*.

**EIO-1**
No *M* is *P*.
Some *S* is *M*.
_____
∴ Some *S* is not *P*.

**EAE-2**
No *P* is *M*.
All *S* is *M*.
───────
∴ No *S* is *P*.

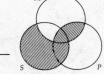

**EIO-2**
No *P* is *M*.
Some *S* is *M*.
───────
∴ Some *S* is not *P*.

**IAI-3**
Some *M* is *P*.
All *M* is *S*.
───────
∴ Some *S* is *P*.

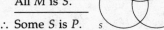

**OAO-3**
Some *M* is not *P*.
All *M* is *S*.
───────
∴ Some *S* is not *P*.

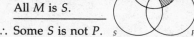

**IAI-4**
Some *P* is *M*.
All *M* is *S*.
───────
∴ Some *S* is *P*.

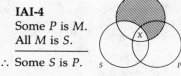

# EXERCISE 7.1

2.  All swimmers are sun lovers, and some Californians are swimmers; therefore, some Californians are sun lovers.
4.  No rotten things are tasty, and some apples are rotten; therefore, some apples are not tasty.
6.  No birds are four-legged animals, and some pets are birds; therefore, some pets are not four-legged animals.
8.  No astronauts are martyrs, and some saints are martyrs, so some saints are not astronauts.
10. In standard form.

# EXERCISE 7.2

(The arguments in this exercise could be put into standard form in a number of ways. The following restatements are provided as a model.)

2.  All 700-pound gorillas are animals that sleep where they please.
    Priscilla the gorilla is a 700-pound gorilla.
    ───────
    ∴ Priscilla the gorilla is an animal that sleeps where she pleases.

4.  All persons who tell lies are persons who will get their due.
    Molly is a person who tells lies.
    ───────
    ∴ Molly is a person who will get her due.

6. All times when I have consumed more than one drink within an hour are times when I have gotten a headache.
   This time is a time when I have consumed more than one drink within an hour.

   ∴ This time is a time when I will get a headache.

8. All things that go up are things that eventually must come down.
   All prices are things that go up.

   ∴ All prices are things that eventually must come down.

10. All persons who say that I am not honest are liars.
    All witnesses for the prosecution are persons who say that I am not honest.

    ∴ All witnesses for the prosecution are liars.

12. All persons with good sense are persons who know that you cannot spend your way to prosperity.
    Some Americans are persons with good sense.

    ∴ Some Americans are persons who know that you cannot spend your way to prosperity.

14. All times when a jury has reached a verdict of innocent are times when they look the accused in the eye when they enter the courtroom.
    This time is not a time when they look the accused in the eye when they enter the courtroom.

    ∴ This time is not a time when a jury has reached a verdict of innocent.

16. All preventable diseases are diseases that it is inexcusable to allow people to die from.
    Polio is a preventable disease.

    ∴ Polio is a disease that it is inexcusable to allow people to die from.

18. All adorable things are lovable.
    Some small children are adorable.

    ∴ Some small children are lovable.

20. All network television shows are shows that have frequent interruptions for commercials.
    All shows that have frequent interruptions for commercials are things that I do not enjoy.

    ∴ All network television shows are things that I do not enjoy.

## EXERCISE 7.3

### Set A

(In most cases, there is more than one way by which an argument may be reduced to three terms. One such way is given for each argument.)

2. a. Eliminate synonym: Some melodies are unsingable.
   b. No change: All songs are melodies.
   c. Obvert: Some songs are unsingable.
4. a. Obvert: All truths are inherently comprehensible.
   b. Obvert: Some things not easily grasped by the slow-witted are truths.
   c. No change: Some things not easily grasped by the slow-witted are comprehensible.
6. a. Obvert: All nonreaders are college students.
   b. Obvert: All two-year-olds are nonreaders.
   c. No change: No two-year-olds are college students.
8. a. Obvert: No astronauts are martyrs.
   b. No change: Some saints are martyrs.
   c. Obvert: Some saints are not astronauts.
10. a. Obvert: No out-of-date checks are things of value.
    b. Obvert: Some things of value are negotiable.
    c. No change: Some negotiable things are not out-of-date checks.

### Set B

12. a. No change: All *P* is *M*.
    b. Obvert: No *S* is *M*.
    c. Obvert: No *S* is *P*.

14. a. Obvert: All *P* is *M*.
    b. Obvert: No *M* is *S*.
    c. Obvert: No *S* is *P*.

16. a. No change: No *M* is *P*.
    b. Contrapositive: All *S* is *M*.
    c. Obvert: No *S* is *P*.

18. a. No change: Some *M* is *P*.
    b. Obvert: All *M* is *S*.
    c. Obvert: Some *S* is *P*.

20. a. Obvert: Some *M* is not *P*.
    b. Contrapositive: All *M* is *S*.
    c. No change: Some *S* is not *P*.

## EXERCISE 7.4

2. All families that buy a new Cadillac every year or so are wealthy.
   The Jones family is a family that buys a new Cadillac every year or so.

   ∴ The Jones family is wealthy.

4. All professors from whom Dumb Dora got an *A* are easy graders.
   Professor Jones is a professor from whom Dumb Dora got an *A*.

   ∴ Professor Jones is an easy grader.

6. All restaurants to which Uncle George takes Aunt Tillie for dinner are low-priced.
   Sam's Steak House is a restaurant to which Uncle George took Aunt Tillie for dinner.

   ∴ Sam's Steak House is low-priced.

8. All sick people for whom many people are praying are people who will soon get well.
   Jimmy is a sick person for whom many people are praying.

   ∴ Jimmy is a sick person who will soon get well.

10. All persons admitted to medical school are strong students.
    Gretchen is a person admitted to medical school.

    ∴ Gretchen is a strong student.

## EXERCISES 7.5

A. Restating soriteses in standard form.
   (Statements are given a letter identifier for later reference.)
   2. a. All delectable things are things that one would serve to one's guests.
      b. No things that burn one's tongue are delectable.
      c. All spicy things are things that burn one's tongue.
      d. Some sausages are spicy.

      e. ∴ Some sausages are not things that one would serve to one's guests.

   4. a. All Arthurian legends are fictitious.
      b. No stories in this book are fictitious.
      c. Some incredible tales are stories in this book.
      d. Some true-life adventures are incredible tales.

      e. ∴ Some true-life adventures are not Arthurian legends.

6.  a.  All conceited people are obnoxious.
    b.  All mathematicians are conceited.
    c.  All occupants of this room are mathematicians.
    d.  Some occupants of this room are bookworms.

    e.  ∴ Some bookworms are obnoxious.

8.  a.  No contented cows are bad-tempered.
    b.  Some animals in this corral are bad-tempered.
    c.  All animals in this corral are cows.
    d.  All cows are bovine animals.

    e.  ∴ Some bovine animals are not contented cows.

10. a.  No loquacious people are unwelcome guests at a cocktail party.
    b.  All cab drivers are loquacious.
    c.  All inhabitants of this apartment building are cab drivers.
    d.  Some Egyptians are inhabitants of this apartment building.

    e.  ∴ Some Egyptians are not unwelcome guests at a cocktail party.

B.  Venn diagrams.
    Each sorites is restated with the intermediate conclusion or conclusions supplied. The Venn diagram tests the last syllogism in the series.
2.  a.  All delectable things are things that one would serve to one's guests.
    b.  No things that burn one's tongue are delectable.
    b'. (No conclusion can validly be drawn from these premises. The argument, therefore, is invalid.)
4.  a.  All Arthurian legends are fictitious.
    b.  No stories in this book are fictitious.

    b'. ∴ No stories in this book are Arthurian legends. (AEE-2)

    b'. No stories in this book are Arthurian legends.
    c.  Some incredible tales are stories in this book.

    c'. ∴ Some incredible tales are not Arthurian legends. (EIO-1)

    c'. Some incredible tales are not Arthurian legends.
    d.  Some true-life adventures are incredible tales.

    e.  ∴ Some true-life adventures are not Arthurian legends.

S = true-life adventures   Some M is not P.
P = Arthurian legends       Some S is M.
M = incredible tales        ─────────────────
                            ∴ Some S is not P.

(Invalid)

## EXERCISE 7.6

### Set A

2.  All sailors are persons who have a girl in every port.
    All my brothers are sailors.

    ∴ All my brothers are persons who have a girl in every port. (Valid)

4.  Some good-tasting things are not conducive to health.
    Some medicines are not good-tasting.

    ∴ Some medicines are not conducive to health. (Invalid. At least one premise must be affirmative.)

6.  All times when I do my best work are forenoon times.
    No times when I have class are forenoon times.

    ∴ No times when I have class are times when I do my best work. (Valid)

8.  All likable people are generous.
    Some people of wealth are generous.

    ∴ Some people of wealth are likable people. (Invalid. Middle term must be distributed at least once.)

10. All things that are in our memory are accessible to our consciousness.
    All things that we have experienced are things that are in our memory.

    ∴ All things that we have experienced are accessible to our consciousness. (Valid)

### Set B

(In most cases, more than one correct restatement is possible. A single correct restatement is given here for each argument.)

2.  All large birds are birds that do not live on honey.
    All birds that do not live on honey are dull in color.
    No hummingbirds are dull in color.

    ∴ No hummingbirds are large birds. (Valid)

4.  All incompetent people are inexperienced.
    All people who are always blundering are incompetent.
    Jenkins is a person who is always blundering.

    ∴ Jenkins is inexperienced. (Valid)

6.  All colored flowers are scented.
    All flowers grown in the open air are colored.
    All flowers that I like are flowers grown in the open air.

    ∴ No flowers that I like are scented. (Invalid. If a term is distributed in the conclusion, it must also be distributed in the premises.)

8.  All "cousins" of our cook are people who love cold mutton.
    All people who eat supper with our cook are "cousins" of our cook.
    All policemen on this beat are people who eat supper with our cook.
    All poets are policemen on this beat.
    All men with long hair are poets.
    All people who have not been in prison are men with long hair.
    Amos Judd is a person who has not been in prison.

    ∴ Amos Judd is a person who loves cold mutton. (Valid)

10. No easy soriteses are soriteses that make my head ache.
    All soriteses at which I grumble are soriteses that make my head ache.
    All soriteses that I cannot understand are soriteses at which I grumble.
    All soriteses that are not arranged in regular order, like those I am used to, are soriteses that I cannot understand.
    This sorites is a sorites that is not arranged in regular order, like those I am used to.

    ∴ This sorites is not an easy sorites. (Valid)

## EXERCISES 8.1

A.  Open-ended.
B.  Categorical and sentential arguments.
    2.  Sentential.
    4.  Sentential.
    6.  Sentential.
    8.  Categorical
    10. Sentential.

## EXERCISE 8.4–8.5

2.  $D \cdot P$
4.  $C \cdot \sim K$
6.  $J \cdot M$
8.  $G \cdot P$
10. $S \cdot \sim A$

## EXERCISE 8.6–8.8

2.   $P \supset W$
4.   $P \vee R$
6.   $H \supset S$
8.   $M \supset H$
10.  $C \supset M$

## EXERCISES 8.9

**A.**   2.  $(S \supset R) \supset (P \vee R)$
       4.  $(P \equiv R) \equiv (M \supset H)$
**B.**   2.  $(T \cdot F) \vee (\sim T \cdot C)$
       4.  $[(W \supset G) \cdot (F \supset P)] \cdot (W \vee F)$
       6.  $(C \vee A) \supset (\sim G \vee \sim O)$
       8.  $(S \cdot L) \vee (P \cdot G)$
      10.  $[(C \supset A) \cdot (\sim C \supset S)] \cdot (C \vee \sim C)$
      12.  $M \supset [(\sim H \cdot \sim R) \cdot (\sim G \cdot \sim F)]$
      14.  $[E \supset (T \vee G)] \cdot E$
      16.  $(S \equiv P) \cdot (\sim S \supset D)$
      18.  $[(L \supset U) \cdot (\sim L \supset I)] \supset (U \vee I)$
      20.  $(T \vee \sim T) \cdot \{(T \supset S) \cdot [\sim T \supset (D \cdot B)]\}$

## EXERCISE 8.10

2.

| $p$ | $q$ | $\sim q$ | $p \supset q$ | $(p \supset q) \cdot \sim q$ |
|---|---|---|---|---|
| T | T | F | T | F |
| T | F | T | F | F |
| F | T | F | T | F |
| F | F | T | T | T |

4.

| $p$ | $q$ | $\sim p$ | $p \equiv q$ | $(p \equiv q) \cdot \sim p$ |
|---|---|---|---|---|
| T | T | F | T | F |
| T | F | F | F | F |
| F | T | T | F | F |
| F | F | T | T | T |

6.

| $p$ | $q$ | $p \cdot q$ | $\sim(p \cdot q)$ | $\sim(p \cdot q) \cdot p$ |
|---|---|---|---|---|
| T | T | T | F | F |
| T | F | F | T | T |
| F | T | F | T | F |
| F | F | F | T | F |

**8.**

| $p$ | $q$ | $r$ | $p \supset q$ | $(p \supset q) \supset r$ | $\sim r$ | $[(p \supset q) \supset r] \cdot \sim r$ |
|---|---|---|---|---|---|---|
| T | T | T | T | T | F | F |
| T | T | F | T | F | T | F |
| T | F | T | F | T | F | F |
| T | F | F | F | T | T | T |
| F | T | T | T | T | F | F |
| F | T | F | T | F | T | F |
| F | F | T | T | T | F | F |
| F | F | F | T | F | T | F |

**10.**

| $p$ | $q$ | $r$ | $q \supset r$ | $p \vee (q \supset r)$ | $\sim r$ | $[p \vee (q \supset r)] \cdot \sim r$ |
|---|---|---|---|---|---|---|
| T | T | T | T | T | F | F |
| T | T | F | F | T | T | T |
| T | F | T | T | T | F | F |
| T | F | F | T | T | T | T |
| F | T | T | T | T | F | F |
| F | T | F | F | F | T | F |
| F | F | T | T | T | F | F |
| F | F | F | T | T | T | T |

# EXERCISE 8.11

**2.**

| $p$ | $q$ | $p \supset q$ | $(p \supset q) \cdot p$ | $[(p \supset q) \cdot p] \supset q$ |
|---|---|---|---|---|
| T | T | T | T | T |
| T | F | F | F | T |
| F | T | T | F | T |
| F | F | T | F | T |

Tautology.

**4.**

| $p$ | $q$ | $\sim q$ | $p \cdot \sim q$ | $p \supset q$ | $\sim(p \supset q)$ | $(p \cdot \sim q) \supset \sim(p \supset q)$ |
|---|---|---|---|---|---|---|
| T | T | F | F | T | F | T |
| T | F | T | T | F | T | T |
| F | T | F | F | T | F | T |
| F | F | T | F | T | F | T |

Tautology.

**6.**

| $p$ | $q$ | $p \vee q$ | $\sim(p \vee q)$ | $p \supset \sim(p \vee q)$ |
|---|---|---|---|---|
| T | T | T | F | F |
| T | F | T | F | F |
| F | T | T | F | T |
| F | F | F | T | T |

Contingent statement.

8.

| $p$ | $q$ | $r$ | $p \lor q$ | $(p \lor q) \equiv r$ |
|---|---|---|---|---|
| T | T | T | T | T |
| T | T | F | T | F |
| T | F | T | T | T |
| T | F | F | T | F |
| F | T | T | T | T |
| F | T | F | T | F |
| F | F | T | F | F |
| F | F | F | F | T |

Contingent statement.

10.

| $p$ | $q$ | $\sim p$ | $\sim p \lor q$ | $p \cdot (\sim p \lor q)$ | $[p \cdot (\sim p \lor q)] \supset q$ |
|---|---|---|---|---|---|
| T | T | F | T | T | T |
| T | F | F | F | F | T |
| F | T | T | T | F | T |
| F | F | T | T | F | T |

Tautology.


# EXERCISES 8.12

**A.**   Logically equivalent expressions. (Other logically equivalent expressions are possible in each case.)

    **2.  a.** $\sim(O \cdot Y)$     **b.** $\sim O \lor \sim Y$

    **4.  a.** $\sim S \cdot \sim K$     **b.** $\sim(S \lor K)$

    **6.  a.** $\sim A \cdot \sim O$     **b.** $\sim(A \lor O)$

    **8.  a.** $D \supset G$     **b.** $\sim D \lor G$   *or*   $\sim(D \cdot \sim G)$

    **10.  a.** $O \supset C$     **b.** $\sim O \lor C$   *or*   $\sim(O \cdot \sim C)$

**B.**   Defining $\lor$, $\supset$, and $\equiv$ in terms of $\sim$ and $\cdot$.

    **2.** The expression $p \supset q$ is equivalent to $\sim(p \cdot \sim q)$.


# EXERCISES 9.1

**A.**   Symbolic restatement of arguments.

    **(2)  1.** $(S \supset R) \cdot (\sim S \supset K)$

        **2.** $S \lor \sim S / \therefore R \lor K$

    **(4)  1.** $R \supset [U \supset (C \lor I)]$

        **2.** $I \equiv A$

        **3.** $A \supset F$

        **4.** $\sim F / \therefore (R \cdot U) \supset C$

    **(6)  1.** $E \lor (S \cdot M)$

        **2.** $(S \cdot M) \supset D / \therefore \sim E \supset M$

    **(8)  1.** $S \lor W$

        **2.** $S \supset (\sim I \cdot C)$

        **3.** $W \supset (I \cdot \sim C)$ / $\therefore \sim(I \cdot C)$

**(10)**  **1.** $A \equiv G$

        **2.** $A \supset (E \vee F)$

        **3.** $\sim F$ / $\therefore \sim E \supset \sim G$

**B.**    Logical form of above arguments.

    **(2)**  **1.** $(p \supset q) \cdot (\sim p \supset r)$

        **2.** $p \vee \sim p$ / $\therefore q \vee r$

    **(4)**  **1.** $p \supset [q \supset (r \vee s)]$

        **2.** $s \equiv t$

        **3.** $t \supset u$

        **4.** $\sim u$ / $\therefore (p \cdot q) \supset r$

    **(6)**  **1.** $p \vee (q \cdot r)$

        **2.** $(q \cdot r) \supset s$ / $\therefore \sim p \supset r$

    **(8)**  **1.** $p \vee q$

        **2.** $p \supset (\sim r \cdot s)$

        **3.** $q \supset (r \cdot \sim s)$ / $\therefore \sim(r \cdot s)$

   **(10)**  **1.** $p \equiv q$

        **2.** $p \supset (r \vee s)$

        **3.** $\sim s$ / $\therefore \sim r \supset \sim q$

## EXERCISES 9.2

**I.**   Open-ended.

**II.**   Testing for validity by means of truth tables.

**B.**

| M | N | R | S | N·R | M≡(N·R) | ~R | ~R⊃S | ~S | M∨~S | [M≡(N·R)]·(~R⊃S) | {[M≡(N·R)]·(~R⊃S)}⊃(M∨~S) |
|---|---|---|---|-----|---------|----|------|----|------|------------------|---------------------------|
| T | T | T | T | T | T | F | T | F | T | T | T |
| T | T | T | F | T | T | F | T | T | T | T | T |
| T | T | F | T | F | F | T | T | F | T | F | T |
| T | T | F | F | F | F | T | F | T | T | F | T |
| T | F | T | T | F | F | F | T | F | T | F | T |
| T | F | T | F | F | F | F | T | T | T | F | T |
| T | F | F | T | F | F | T | T | F | T | F | T |
| T | F | F | F | F | F | T | F | T | T | F | T |
| F | T | T | T | T | F | F | T | F | F | F | T |
| F | T | T | F | T | F | F | T | T | T | F | T |
| F | T | F | T | F | T | T | T | F | F | T | F |
| F | T | F | F | F | T | T | F | T | T | F | T |
| F | F | T | T | F | T | F | T | F | F | T | F |
| F | F | T | F | F | T | F | T | T | T | T | T |
| F | F | F | T | F | T | T | T | F | F | T | F |
| F | F | F | F | F | T | T | F | T | T | F | T |

The argument is invalid.

## EXERCISES 9.2 (Continued)

**D.**

| S | L | R | S∨L | L∨R | (S∨L)·(L∨R) | ~S | ~S∨R | [(S∨L)·(L∨R)]⊃(~S∨R) |
|---|---|---|-----|-----|-------------|----|------|----------------------|
| T | T | T | T | T | T | F | T | T |
| T | T | F | T | T | T | F | F | F |
| T | F | T | T | T | T | F | T | T |
| T | F | F | T | F | F | F | F | T |
| F | T | T | T | T | T | T | T | T |
| F | T | F | T | T | T | T | T | T |
| F | F | T | F | T | F | T | T | T |
| F | F | F | F | F | F | T | T | T |

The argument is invalid.

**F.**

| p | q | r | ~q | p⊃~q | r⊃q | (p⊃~q)·(r⊃q) | p∨r | [(p⊃~q)·(r⊃q)]⊃(p∨r) |
|---|---|---|----|------|-----|--------------|-----|----------------------|
| T | T | T | F | F | T | F | T | T |
| T | T | F | F | F | T | F | T | T |
| T | F | T | T | T | F | F | T | T |
| T | F | F | T | T | T | T | T | T |
| F | T | T | F | T | T | T | T | T |
| F | T | F | F | T | T | T | F | F |
| F | F | T | T | T | F | F | T | T |
| F | F | F | T | T | T | T | F | F |

The argument is invalid.

## EXERCISES 9.2 (Continued)

**H.**

| p | q | r | q · r | p ⊃ (q · r) | ~p | [p ⊃ (q · r)] · ~p | ~(q · r) | {[p ⊃ (q · r)] · ~p} ⊃ ~(q · r) |
|---|---|---|-------|-------------|----|--------------------|----------|---------------------------------|
| T | T | T | T | T | F | F | F | T |
| T | T | F | F | F | F | F | T | T |
| T | F | T | F | F | F | F | T | T |
| T | F | F | F | F | F | F | T | T |
| F | T | T | T | T | T | T | F | F |
| F | T | F | F | T | T | T | T | T |
| F | F | T | F | T | T | T | T | T |
| F | F | F | F | T | T | T | T | T |

The argument is invalid.

**J.**

| p | q | r | p ⊃ q | q ⊃ r | (p ⊃ q) · (q ⊃ r) | p ⊃ r | [(p ⊃ q) · (q ⊃ r)] ⊃ (p ⊃ r) |
|---|---|---|-------|-------|-------------------|-------|--------------------------------|
| T | T | T | T | T | T | T | T |
| T | T | F | T | F | F | F | T |
| T | F | T | F | T | F | T | T |
| T | F | F | F | T | F | F | T |
| F | T | T | T | T | T | T | T |
| F | T | F | T | F | F | T | T |
| F | F | T | T | T | T | T | T |
| F | F | F | T | T | T | T | T |

The argument is valid.

## EXERCISES 9.3

II.   Testing for validity by means of abbreviated truth tables. Each row except the last row in each set represents a set of truth values derived from the truth values assigned in the preceding rows. The last row in each set is a summary of the truth values assigned in the preceding rows in that set. A contradiction is indicated by a question mark. Except for the initial assignment of T to the premises and F to the conclusion, arbitrary assignments of truth values are enclosed in parentheses.

**B.**   $A \vee (B \vee C)$     $\sim C \supset D$     $A \vee \sim D$
      T                 T         F
                                            F    F
   F                        T
        T       T
      T   F
F T   T T F     T   T T     F F F

The argument form is invalid.

**D.**   $(F \supset R) \cdot (F \vee B)$     $\sim B$     $R$
           T                T     F
     T F     T F
    ?        ?
   ? T F T ? T F     T     F

The argument form is valid.

**F.**   $p \supset (q \supset r)$    $r \vee \sim (s \equiv t)$    $\sim r$    $p \supset (s \equiv t)$
      T              T              T    F
  T       F       F       F           T      F
     T         T
     F          (T)   (F)           (T)   (F)
T T   F T F     F T T T F   F     T    T F T F   F

The argument form is invalid.

**H.**   $p \supset q$     $q \supset r$     $r \vee \sim p$
    T           T          F
                     F      F   F
T
     ?      ?
T T   ?     ? T F     F F F

The argument form is valid.

**J.**     $(p \lor q) \supset (r \cdot s)$          $p \cdot \sim q$          $r \equiv s$
                    T                                    T                     F
      T                                          T   T
            F
         T               T
                       ?   ?                                    ?     ?
      T  T  F  T  ?  T  ?          T  T  T          ?  F  ?

The argument form is valid.


# EXERCISES 9.4

  **I.**   See page 193.
  **II.**  Open-ended.
  **III.** Justification of inferences.
     **B.**  Modus Ponens.
     **D.**  Addition.
     **F.**  Modus Tollens.
     **H.**  Modus Ponens.
     **J.**  Disjunctive Syllogism.
     **L.**  Disjunctive Syllogism.
     **N.**  Absorption.
     **P.**  Constructive Dilemma.
     **R.**  Conjunction.
     **T.**  Constructive Dilemma.


# EXERCISE 9.5

Justification of formal proofs.
**B.**    1. $W \supset B$
      2. $B \supset L$
      3. $(W \cdot L) \supset C$
      4. $W \; / \therefore C$
      5. $W \supset L$     1, 2 HS
      6. $L$         5, 4 MP
      7. $W \cdot L$      4, 6 Conj.
      8. $C$        3, 7 MP

**D.**    1. $(L \supset T) \cdot (\sim L \supset Z)$
      2. $\sim T \; / \therefore Z$
      3. $L \supset T$       1 Simp.
      4. $\sim L$        3, 2 MT
      5. $\sim L \supset Z$    1 Simp.
      6. $Z$        5, 4 MP

**F.**   1. $B \supset V$
    2. $R \supset X$
    3. $(V \lor X) \supset Q$
    4. $B$ / $\therefore Q$
    5. $(B \supset V) \cdot (R \supset X)$     1, 2 Conj.
    6. $B \lor R$                       4 Add.
    7. $V \lor X$                  5, 6 CD
    8. $Q$                        3, 7 MP

**H.**   1. $(Z \supset H) \supset (I \supset M)$
    2. $\sim(Z \supset H) \supset (P \lor Q)$
    3. $\sim(I \supset M) \cdot \sim P$ / $\therefore Q$
    4. $\sim(I \supset M)$         3 Simp.
    5. $\sim(Z \supset H)$        1, 4 MT
    6. $P \lor Q$               2, 5 MP
    7. $\sim P$                   3 Simp.
    8. $Q$                       6, 7 DS

**J.**   1. $(B \supset R) \cdot (G \supset P)$
    2. $(\sim B \lor \sim G) \supset L$
    3. $\sim R$ / $\therefore L$
    4. $B \supset R$             1 Simp.
    5. $\sim B$                 4, 3 MT
    6. $\sim B \lor \sim G$        5 Add.
    7. $L$                      2, 6 MP

# EXERCISES 9.6

**I.**   See page 204.
**II.**   Truth tables.
Commutation (disjunction)

| $p$ | $q$ | $p \lor q$ | $q \lor p$ | $(p \lor q) \equiv (q \lor p)$ |
|-----|-----|------------|------------|--------------------------------|
| T | T | T | T | T |
| T | F | T | T | T |
| F | T | T | T | T |
| F | F | F | F | T |

Commutation (conjunction)

| $p$ | $q$ | $p \cdot q$ | $q \cdot p$ | $(p \cdot q) \equiv (q \cdot p)$ |
|-----|-----|-------------|-------------|----------------------------------|
| T | T | T | T | T |
| T | F | F | F | T |
| F | T | F | F | T |
| F | F | F | F | T |

Double Negation

| $p$ | $\sim p$ | $\sim\sim p$ | $p \equiv \sim\sim p$ |
|---|---|---|---|
| T | F | T | T |
| F | T | F | T |

**III.**  Open-ended. See pages 204–206.

**IV.**  Justification of formal proofs.

**B.**  
1. $A \supset B$  
2. $C \supset D$  
3. $C \lor A$  
4. $(B \lor D) \supset R \,/\,\therefore R$  
5. $(A \supset B) \cdot (C \supset D)$      1, 2 Conj.  
6. $A \lor C$                3 Taut.  
7. $B \lor D$                5, 6 CD  
8. $R$                  4, 7 MP  

**D.**  
1. $A \lor \sim C$  
2. $A \supset R$  
3. $C \,/\,\therefore C \cdot R$  
4. $\sim\sim C$        3 DN  
5. $A$          1, 4 DS  
6. $R$          2, 5 MP  
7. $C \cdot R$       3, 6 Conj.  

**F.**  
1. $(S \supset L) \cdot (F \supset L)$  
2. $(S \lor F) \cdot (L \supset M) \,/\,\therefore M$  
3. $S \lor F$              2 Simp.  
4. $L \lor L$              1, 3 CD  
5. $L$                4 Taut.  
6. $L \supset M$             2 Simp.  
7. $M$                6, 5 MP  

**H.**  
1. $(A \lor B) \supset D$  
2. $A \lor (B \lor \sim C)$  
3. $C \,/\,\therefore D$  
4. $(A \lor B) \lor \sim C$       2 Assoc.  
5. $\sim\sim C$           3 DN  
6. $A \lor B$            4, 5 DS  
7. $D$              1, 6 MP  

**J.**  
1. $C \supset (V \lor \sim X)$  
2. $A \cdot (B \cdot C)$  
3. $X \,/\,\therefore V \lor R$  
4. $(A \cdot B) \cdot C$      2 Assoc.  
5. $C$            4 Simp.

    6. $V \lor \sim X$        1, 5 MP
    7. $\sim\sim X$           3 DN
    8. $V$                6, 7 DS
    9. $V \lor R$          8 Add.

**V.**  Formal proofs. (Alternative proofs are possible in all cases.)

**B.**  1. $M \lor N$
    2. $M \lor O$
    3. $(M \supset S) \cdot \sim(N \cdot O)$ / $\therefore S$
    4. $(M \lor N) \cdot (M \lor O)$    1, 2 Conj.
    5. $M \lor (N \cdot O)$        4 Dist.
    6. $\sim(N \cdot O)$          3 Simp.
    7. $M$              5, 6 DS
    8. $M \supset S$            3 Simp.
    9. $S$              8, 7 MP

**D.**  1. $(M \lor \sim N) \lor (R \supset Q)$
    2. $N \cdot \sim M$
    3. $R$ / $\therefore Q$
    4. $M \lor [\sim N \lor (R \supset Q)]$    1 Assoc.
    5. $\sim M$            2 Simp.
    6. $\sim N \lor (R \supset Q)$      4, 5 DS
    7. $N$              2 Simp.
    8. $\sim\sim N$            7 DN
    9. $R \supset Q$          6, 8 DS
   10. $Q$              9, 3 MT

**F.**  1. $(M \cdot R) \lor (M \cdot P)$
    2. $\sim R$ / $\therefore P$
    3. $M \cdot (R \lor P)$        1 Dist.
    4. $R \lor P$          3 Simp.
    5. $P$            4, 2 DS

**H.**  1. $(A \supset K) \cdot (C \supset L)$
    2. $A \lor (B \cdot C)$ / $\therefore K \lor L$
    3. $(A \lor B) \cdot (A \lor C)$      2 Dist.
    4. $A \lor C$          3 Simp.
    5. $K \lor L$          1, 4 CD

**J.**  1. $M \lor (G \cdot B)$
    2. $\sim G \supset (M \supset R)$
    3. $\sim G$ / $\therefore R$
    4. $M \supset R$          2, 3 MP
    5. $(M \lor G) \cdot (M \lor B)$      1 Dist.
    6. $M \lor G$          5 Simp.
    7. $M$              6, 3 DS
    8. $R$              4, 7 MP

## EXERCISES 9.7

**II.**   Truth tables.
Exportation

| $p$ | $q$ | $r$ | $p \cdot q$ | $(p \cdot q) \supset r$ | $q \supset r$ | $p \supset (q \supset r)$ | $[(p \cdot q) \supset r] \equiv [p \supset (q \supset r)]$ |
|---|---|---|---|---|---|---|---|
| T | T | T | T | T | T | T | T |
| T | T | F | T | F | F | F | T |
| T | F | T | F | T | T | T | T |
| T | F | F | F | T | T | T | T |
| F | T | T | F | T | T | T | T |
| F | T | F | F | T | F | T | T |
| F | F | T | F | T | T | T | T |
| F | F | F | F | T | T | T | T |

Material Implication (first form)

| $p$ | $q$ | $p \supset q$ | $\sim p$ | $\sim p \vee q$ | $(p \supset q) \equiv (\sim p \vee q)$ |
|---|---|---|---|---|---|
| T | T | T | F | T | T |
| T | F | F | F | F | T |
| F | T | T | T | T | T |
| F | F | T | T | T | T |

Material Implication (second form)

| $p$ | $q$ | $p \supset q$ | $\sim q$ | $p \cdot \sim q$ | $\sim(p \cdot \sim q)$ | $(p \supset q) \equiv \sim(p \cdot \sim q)$ |
|---|---|---|---|---|---|---|
| T | T | T | F | F | T | T |
| T | F | F | T | T | F | T |
| F | T | T | F | F | T | T |
| F | F | T | F | F | T | T |

**IV.**   Justification of formal proofs.

**B.**   1. $A \vee [B \supset (C \supset D)]$
2. $\sim A$ / $\therefore$ $C \supset (B \supset D)$
3. $B \supset (C \supset D)$         1, 2 DS
4. $(B \cdot C) \supset D$         3 Exp.
5. $(C \cdot B) \supset D$         4 Com.
6. $C \supset (B \supset D)$         5 Exp.


**D.**   1. $K \supset (L \vee M)$
2. $K \cdot \sim L$ / $\therefore$ $R \supset M$
3. $K$         2 Simp.
4. $L \vee M$         1, 3 MP
5. $\sim L$         2 Simp.

    6. *M*                 4, 5 DS
    7. *M* ∨ ~*R*         6 Add.
    8. ~*R* ∨ *M*         7 Com.
    9. *R* ⊃ *M*          8 Impl.

**F.**    1. *K* ⊃ [*L* ⊃ (*M* · *N*)]
    2. *K* / ∴ (*L* ⊃ *M*) · (*L* ⊃ *N*)
    3. *L* ⊃ (*M* · *N*)         1, 2 MP
    4. ~*L* ∨ (*M* · *N*)         3 Impl.
    5. (~*L* ∨ *M*) · (~*L* ∨ *N*)     4 Dist.
    6. (~*L* ∨ *M*) · (*L* ⊃ *N*)     5 Impl.
    7. (*L* ⊃ *M*) · (*L* ⊃ *N*)      6 Impl.

**H.**    1. (*M* ∨ *R*) ⊃ (*P* ⊃ *X*)
    2. *M* · *P* / ∴ (*P* · *Q*) ⊃ *X*
    3. *M*               2 Simp.
    4. *M* ∨ *R*          3 Add.
    5. *P* ⊃ *X*          1, 4 MP
    6. ~*P* ∨ *X*         5 Impl.
    7. (~*P* ∨ *X*) ∨ ~*Q*     6 Add.
    8. ~*Q* ∨ (~*P* ∨ *X*)     7 Com.
    9. (~*Q* ∨ ~*P*) ∨ *X*     8 Assoc.
   10. ~(*Q* · *P*) ∨ *X*      9 De M.
   11. (*Q* · *P*) ⊃ *X*      10 Impl.
   12. (*P* · *Q*) ⊃ *X*      11 Com.

**J.**    1. *A* ∨ [(*B* ∨ *C*) ⊃ *D*]
    2. ~*A* / ∴ *C* ⊃ *D*
    3. (*B* ∨ *C*) ⊃ *D*       1, 2 DS
    4. ~*D* ⊃ ~(*B* ∨ *C*)     3 Trans.
    5. ~*D* ⊃ (~*B* · ~*C*)     4 De M.
    6. ~~*D* ∨ (~*B* · ~*C*)     5 Impl.
    7. *D* ∨ (~*B* · ~*C*)       6 DN
    8. (*D* ∨ ~*B*) · (*D* ∨ ~*C*)    7 Dist.
    9. *D* ∨ ~*C*          8 Simp.
   10. ~*C* ∨ *D*         9 Com.
   11. *C* ⊃ *D*          10 Impl.

**V.**    Formal proofs. (Alternative proofs are possible in all cases.)
**B.**    1. (*M* ∨ *O*) ⊃ *R*
    2. ~*R* / ∴ ~*M*
    3. ~*R* ⊃ ~(*M* ∨ *O*)     1 Trans.
    4. ~(*M* ∨ *O*)        3, 2 MP
    5. ~*M* · ~*O*         4 De M.
    6. ~*M*             5 Simp.

**D.**    1. *X* ⊃ ~(*R* · ~*Z*)
    2. *X* / ∴ *R* ⊃ *Z*

    3. ~(R · ~Z)    1, 2 MP
    4. ~R ∨ ~~Z    3 De M.
    5. ~R ∨ Z    4 DN
    6. R ⊃ Z    5 Impl.

**F.**    1. Z ≡ L
       2. ~L / ∴ ~Z ∨ R
       3. (Z ⊃ L) · (L ⊃ Z)    1 Equiv.
       4. Z ⊃ L    3 Simp.
       5. ~Z    4, 2 MT
       6. ~Z ∨ R    5 Add.

**H.**    1. R ∨ (L · Z)
       2. ~Z / ∴ R
       3. (R ∨ L) · (R ∨ Z)    1 Dist.
       4. R ∨ Z    3 Simp.
       5. R    4, 2 DS

**J.**    1. (L ∨ R) ⊃ Q
       2. (Q ⊃ E) · ~E / ∴ ~R
       3. Q ⊃ E    2 Simp.
       4. ~E    2 Simp.
       5. ~Q    3, 4 MT
       6. ~(L ∨ R)    1, 5 MT
       7. ~L · ~R    6 De M.
       8. ~R    7 Simp.

**L.**    1. D ⊃ ~(E ∨ F)
       2. (E ∨ F) · (~D ⊃ R) / ∴ R
       3. E ∨ F    2 Simp.
       4. ~~(E ∨ F)    3 DN
       5. ~D    1, 4 MT
       6. ~D ⊃ R    2 Simp.
       7. R    6, 5 MP

**N.**    1. L ⊃ (R ⊃ Z)
       2. (Z ⊃ K) · ~K / ∴ R ⊃ ~L
       3. Z ⊃ K    2 Simp.
       4. ~K    2 Simp.
       5. ~Z    3, 4 MT
       6. (L · R) ⊃ Z    1 Exp.
       7. ~(L · R)    6, 5 MT
       8. ~L ∨ ~R    7 De M.
       9. ~R ∨ ~L    8 Com.
   10. R ⊃ ~L    10 Impl.

**P.**    1. (A ≡ B) ⊃ ~L
       2. (A ⊃ B) · (B ⊃ A) / ∴ L ⊃ K

3. $A \equiv B$      2 Equiv.
4. $\sim L$      1, 3 MP
5. $\sim L \vee K$      4 Add.
6. $L \supset K$      5 Impl.

**R.**
1. $Z \supset [(S \vee L) \supset M]$
2. $(\sim B \vee Z) \cdot B \,/\, \therefore S \supset M$
3. $\sim B \vee Z$      2 Simp.
4. $B$      2 Simp.
5. $\sim\sim B$      4 DN
6. $Z$      3, 5 DS
7. $(S \vee L) \supset M$      1, 6 MP
8. $\sim(S \vee L) \vee M$      7 Impl.
9. $M \vee \sim(S \vee L)$      8 Com.
10. $M \vee (\sim S \cdot \sim L)$      9 De M.
11. $(M \vee \sim S) \cdot (M \vee \sim L)$      10 Dist.
12. $M \vee \sim S$      11 Simp.
13. $\sim S \vee M$      12 Com.
14. $S \supset M$      13 Impl.

**T.**
1. $\sim A \vee [(K \supset L) \cdot (R \supset L)]$
2. $A \,/\, \therefore (K \vee R) \supset L$
3. $\sim\sim A$      2 DN
4. $(K \supset L) \cdot (R \supset L)$      1, 3 DS
5. $(\sim K \vee L) \cdot (R \supset L)$      4 Impl.
6. $(\sim K \vee L) \cdot (\sim R \vee L)$      5 Impl.
7. $(L \vee \sim K) \cdot (\sim R \vee L)$      6 Com.
8. $(L \vee \sim K) \cdot (L \vee \sim R)$      7 Com.
9. $L \vee (\sim K \cdot \sim R)$      8 Dist.
10. $L \vee \sim(K \vee R)$      9 De M.
11. $\sim(K \vee R) \vee L$      10 Com.
12. $(K \vee R) \supset L$      11 Impl.

# EXERCISES 9.8

I.      Open-ended.
II.      Justification of Reductio Ad Absurdum proofs.

**B.**
1. $(A \supset B) \cdot (C \supset D)$
2. $C \vee A$
3. $(B \vee D) \supset R \,/\, \therefore R$

RAA
4. $\sim R$      AP
5. $\sim R \supset \sim(B \vee D)$      3 Trans.
6. $\sim(B \vee D)$      5, 4 MP
7. $A \vee C$      2 Com.
8. $B \vee D$      1, 7 CD
9. $(B \vee D) \cdot \sim(B \vee D)$      8, 6 Conj.
10. $R$      4–9 RAA

**D.**  1. $(A \supset N) \cdot (L \supset M)$
    2. $A\ /\ \therefore N \vee M$
    3. $\sim(N \vee M)$         AP
    4. $\sim N \cdot \sim M$       3 De M.
RAA  5. $\sim N$            4 Simp.
    6. $A \supset N$         1 Simp.
    7. $N$            6, 2 MP
    8. $N \cdot \sim N$        7, 5 Conj.
    9. $N \vee M$        3–8 RAA

**F.**  1. $(M \vee B) \supset R$
    2. $M \vee (B \vee \sim K)$
    3. $K\ /\ \therefore R$
    4. $\sim R$             AP
    5. $\sim R \supset \sim(M \vee B)$   1 Trans.
    6. $\sim(M \vee B)$      5, 4 MP
    7. $\sim M \cdot \sim B$     6 De M.
RAA  8. $\sim M$           7 Simp.
    9. $B \vee \sim K$      2, 8 DS
   10. $\sim B$          7 Simp.
   11. $\sim K$         9, 10 DS
   12. $K \cdot \sim K$     3, 11 Conj.
   13. $R$          4–12 RAA

**H.**  1. $L \supset [M \vee (N \vee O)]$
    2. $L \cdot \sim N\ /\ \therefore M \vee O$
    3. $\sim(M \vee O)$      AP
    4. $\sim M \cdot \sim O$     3 De M.
    5. $L$            2 Simp.
    6. $M \vee (N \vee O)$   1, 5 MP
    7. $\sim M$           4 Simp.
RAA  8. $N \vee O$       6, 7 DS
    9. $\sim O$           4 Simp.
   10. $N$           8, 9 DS
   11. $\sim N$         2 Simp.
   12. $N \cdot \sim N$     10, 11 Conj.
   13. $M \vee O$      3–12 RAA

**J.**  1. $(A \vee Z) \supset L$
    2. $\sim L\ /\ \therefore \sim A$
    3. $\sim\sim A$         AP
    4. $A$            3 DN
RAA  5. $A \vee Z$       4 Add.
    6. $L$            1, 5 MP
    7. $L \cdot \sim L$      6, 2 Conj.
    8. $\sim A$         3–7 RAA

**III.** Reductio ad Absurdum proofs. (Alternative proofs are possible in all cases.)

**B.**
1. $(M \lor O) \supset R$
2. $\sim R$ / ∴ $\sim M$
    3. $\sim\sim M$         AP
    4. $M$             3 DN
RAA   5. $M \lor O$      4 Add.
    6. $R$            1, 5 MP
    7. $R \cdot \sim R$      6, 2 Conj.
    8. $\sim M$        3–7 RAA

**D.**
1. $X \supset \sim(R \cdot \sim Z)$
2. $X$ / ∴ $R \supset Z$
    3. $\sim(R \supset Z)$       AP
    4. $\sim(R \cdot \sim Z)$     1, 2 MP
    5. $\sim R \lor \sim\sim Z$    4 De M.
RAA   6. $\sim R \lor Z$      5 DN
    7. $R \supset Z$       6 Impl.
    8. $(R \supset Z) \cdot \sim(R \supset Z)$   7, 3 Conj.
    9. $R \supset Z$       3–8 RAA

**F.**
1. $Z \equiv L$
2. $\sim L$ / ∴ $\sim Z \lor R$
    3. $\sim(\sim Z \lor R)$      AP
    4. $\sim\sim Z \cdot \sim R$     3 De M.
    5. $Z \cdot \sim R$       4 DN
RAA   6. $(Z \supset L) \cdot (L \supset Z)$   1 Equiv.
    7. $Z \supset L$       6 Simp.
    8. $Z$           5 Simp.
    9. $L$           7, 8 MP
    10. $L \cdot \sim L$     9, 2 Conj.
    11. $\sim Z \lor R$    3–10 RAA

**H.**
1. $R \lor (L \cdot Z)$
2. $\sim Z$ / ∴ $R$
    3. $\sim R$      AP
    4. $L \cdot Z$    1, 3 DS
RAA   5. $Z$        4 Simp.
    6. $Z \cdot \sim Z$  5, 2 Conj.
    7. $R$        3–6 RAA

**J.**
1. $(L \lor R) \supset Q$
2. $(Q \supset E) \cdot \sim E$ / ∴ $\sim R$
    3. $\sim\sim R$      AP
    4. $R$         3 Simp.
    5. $Q \supset E$   2 Simp.
    6. $\sim E$      2 Simp.
RAA   7. $\sim Q$      5, 6 MT

|       |                                    |                 |
|-------|------------------------------------|-----------------|
| 8.    | $\sim(L \vee R)$                   | 1, 7 MT         |
| 9.    | $\sim L \cdot \sim R$              | 8 De M.         |
| 10.   | $\sim R$                           | 9 Simp.         |
| 11.   | $R \cdot \sim R$                   | 4, 10 Conj.     |
| 12.   | $\sim R$                           | 3–11 RAA        |

**L.**
1.  $D \supset \sim(E \vee F)$
2.  $(E \vee F) \cdot (\sim D \supset R) \, / \therefore R$

RAA
3.  $\sim R$  AP
4.  $\sim D \supset R$  2 Simp.
5.  $\sim\sim D$  4, 3 MT
6.  $D$  5 DN
7.  $\sim(E \vee F)$  1, 6 MP
8.  $E \vee F$  2 Simp.
9.  $(E \vee F) \cdot \sim(E \vee F)$  8, 7 Conj.
10. $R$  3–9 RAA

**N.**
1.  $L \supset (R \supset Z)$
2.  $(Z \supset K) \cdot \sim K \, / \therefore R \supset \sim L$

RAA
3.  $\sim(R \supset \sim L)$  AP
4.  $\sim\sim(R \cdot \sim\sim L)$  3 Impl.
5.  $\sim\sim(R \cdot L)$  4 DN
6.  $Z \supset K$  2 Simp.
7.  $\sim K$  2 Simp.
8.  $\sim Z$  6, 7 MT
9.  $(L \cdot R) \supset Z$  1 Exp.
10. $\sim(L \cdot R)$  9, 8 MT
11. $R \cdot L$  5 DN
12. $L \cdot R$  11 Com.
13. $(L \cdot R) \cdot \sim(L \cdot R)$  12, 10 Conj.
14. $R \supset \sim L$  3–13 RAA

**P.**
1.  $(A \equiv B) \supset \sim L$
2.  $(A \supset B) \cdot (B \supset A) \, / \therefore L \supset K$

RAA
3.  $\sim(L \supset K)$  AP
4.  $\sim\sim(L \cdot \sim K)$  3 Impl.
5.  $L \cdot \sim K$  4 DN
6.  $L$  5 Simp.
7.  $A \equiv B$  2 Equiv.
8.  $\sim L$  1, 7 MP
9.  $L \cdot \sim L$  6, 8 Conj.
10. $L \supset K$  3–9 RAA

**R.**
1.  $Z \supset [(S \vee L) \supset M]$
2.  $(\sim B \vee Z) \cdot B \, / \therefore S \supset M$
3.  $\sim(S \supset M)$  AP
4.  $\sim\sim(S \cdot \sim M)$  3 Impl.
5.  $S \cdot \sim M$  4 DN

| | | |
|---|---|---|
| | 6. $\sim B \vee Z$ | 2 Simp. |
| | 7. $B$ | 2 Simp. |
| | 8. $\sim\sim B$ | 7 DN |
| RAA | 9. $Z$ | 6, 8 DS |
| | 10. $(S \vee L) \supset M$ | 1, 9 MP |
| | 11. $S$ | 5 Simp. |
| | 12. $S \vee L$ | 11 Add. |
| | 13. $M$ | 10, 12 MP |
| | 14. $\sim M$ | 5 Simp. |
| | 15. $M \cdot \sim M$ | 13, 14 Conj. |
| | 16. $S \supset M$ | 3–15 RAA |

| | | |
|---|---|---|
| **T.** | 1. $\sim A \vee [(K \supset L) \cdot (R \supset L)]$ | |
| | 2. $A \: / \therefore (K \vee R) \supset L$ | |
| | 3. $\sim[(K \vee R) \supset L]$ | AP |
| | 4. $\sim\sim A$ | 2 DN |
| | 5. $(K \supset L) \cdot (R \supset L)$ | 1, 4 DS |
| | 6. $(\sim K \vee L) \cdot (R \supset L)$ | 5 Impl. |
| | 7. $(\sim K \vee L) \cdot (\sim R \vee L)$ | 6 Impl. |
| | 8. $(L \vee \sim K) \cdot (\sim R \vee L)$ | 7 Com. |
| RAA | 9. $(L \vee \sim K) \cdot (L \vee \sim R)$ | 8 Com. |
| | 10. $L \vee (\sim K \cdot \sim R)$ | 9 Dist. |
| | 11. $L \vee \sim(K \vee R)$ | 10 De M. |
| | 12. $\sim(K \vee R) \vee L$ | 11 Com. |
| | 13. $(K \vee R) \supset L$ | 12 Impl. |
| | 14. $[(K \vee R) \supset L] \cdot \sim[(K \vee R) \supset L]$ | 13, 3 Conj. |
| | 15. $(K \vee R) \supset L$ | 3–14 RAA |

# EXERCISES 9.9

**II.** Justification of formal proofs.

| | | |
|---|---|---|
| **B.** | 1. $R \supset (L \supset Z)$ | |
| | 2. $(L \vee M) \cdot \sim M \: / \therefore R \supset Z$ | |
| | 3. $R$ | AP |
| | 4. $L \supset Z$ | 1, 3 MP |
| CP | 5. $L \vee M$ | 2 Simp. |
| | 6. $\sim M$ | 2 Simp. |
| | 7. $L$ | 5, 6 DS |
| | 8. $Z$ | 4, 7 MP |
| | 9. $R \supset Z$ | 3–8 CP |

| | | |
|---|---|---|
| **D.** | 1. $[(A \cdot B) \cdot C] \supset D$ | |
| | 2. $E \supset [(C \cdot A) \cdot B] \: / \therefore E \supset D$ | |
| | 3. $E$ | AP |
| | 4. $(C \cdot A) \cdot B$ | 2, 3 MP |
| CP | 5. $C \cdot (A \cdot B)$ | 4 Assoc. |
| | 6. $(A \cdot B) \cdot C$ | 5 Com. |
| | 7. $D$ | 1, 6 MP |
| | 8. $E \supset D$ | 3–7 CP |

**F.**
1. $\sim A \supset (\sim B \supset \sim C)$
2. $D \supset (C \cdot \sim A) \; / \therefore D \supset B$

CP
3. $D$ — AP
4. $C \cdot \sim A$ — 2, 3 MP
5. $\sim A$ — 4 Simp.
6. $\sim B \supset \sim C$ — 1, 5 MP
7. $\sim\sim C \supset \sim\sim B$ — 6 Trans.
8. $C \supset \sim\sim B$ — 7 DN
9. $C \supset B$ — 8 DN
10. $C$ — 4 Simp.
11. $B$ — 9, 10 MP
12. $D \supset B$ — 3–11 CP

**H.**
1. $W \supset B$
2. $(W \cdot B) \supset F \; / \therefore \sim W \vee F$

CP
3. $W$ — AP
4. $B$ — 1, 3 MP
5. $W \cdot B$ — 3, 4 Conj.
6. $F$ — 2, 5 MP
7. $W \supset F$ — 3–6 CP
8. $\sim W \vee F$ — 7 Impl.

**J.**
1. $A \supset [B \supset (C \vee D)]$
2. $\sim D \; / \therefore \sim C \supset (\sim A \vee \sim B)$
3. $(A \cdot B) \supset (C \vee D)$ — 1 Exp.

CP
4. $A \cdot B$ — AP
5. $C \vee D$ — 3, 4 MP
6. $C$ — 5, 2 DS
7. $(A \cdot B) \supset C$ — 4–6 CP
8. $\sim C \supset \sim(A \cdot B)$ — 7 Trans.
9. $\sim C \supset (\sim A \vee \sim B)$ — 8 De M.

**III.** Formal proofs using CP. (Alternative proofs are possible in all cases.)

**B.**
1. $(J \supset K) \cdot (\sim J \supset R)$
2. $R \supset X \; / \therefore \sim K \supset X$

CP
3. $\sim K$ — AP
4. $J \supset K$ — 1 Simp.
5. $\sim J$ — 4, 3 MT
6. $\sim J \supset R$ — 1 Simp.
7. $R$ — 6, 5 MP
8. $X$ — 2, 7 MP
9. $\sim K \supset X$ — 3–8 CP

**D.**
1. $C \equiv (D \vee E)$
2. $\sim D \; / \therefore E \vee \sim C$

CP
3. $C$ — AP
4. $[C \supset (D \vee E)] \cdot [(D \vee E) \supset C]$ — 1 Equiv.
5. $C \supset (D \vee E)$ — 4 Simp.

| | |
|---|---|
| 6. $D \lor E$ | 5, 3 MP |
| 7. $E$ | 6, 2 DS |
| 8. $C \supset E$ | 3–7 CP |
| 9. $\sim C \lor E$ | 8 Impl. |
| 10. $E \lor \sim C$ | 10 Com. |

**F.**
1. $A \lor (B \lor C)$
2. $\sim C$ / $\therefore \sim B \supset A$
3. $(A \lor B) \lor C$    1 Assoc.
4. $A \lor B$    3, 2 DS

CP
5. $\sim B$    AP
6. $A$    4, 5 DS

7. $\sim B \supset A$    5–6 CP

**H.**
1. $(L \lor K) \cdot C$
2. $\sim B \supset \sim (K \cdot C)$
3. $C \supset (L \supset \sim S)$ / $\therefore S \supset B$

CP
4. $S$    AP
5. $C$    1 Simp.
6. $L \supset \sim S$    3, 5 MP
7. $\sim\sim S$    4 DN
8. $\sim L$    6, 7 MT
9. $L \lor K$    1 Simp.
10. $K$    9, 8 DS
11. $K \cdot C$    10, 5 Conj.
12. $\sim\sim(K \cdot C)$    11 DN
13. $\sim\sim B$    2, 12 MT
14. $B$    13 DN

15. $S \supset B$    4–14 CP

**J.**
1. $[(P \lor Q) \cdot R] \supset L$
2. $(R \supset L) \supset (H \supset M)$
3. $H$ / $\therefore P \supset M$

CP
4. $P$    AP
5. $(P \lor Q) \supset (R \supset L)$    1 Exp.
6. $P \lor Q$    4 Add.
7. $R \supset L$    5, 6 MP
8. $H \supset M$    2, 7 MP
9. $M$    8, 3 MP

10. $P \supset M$    4–9 CP

# EXERCISES 10.1–10.2

**A.** Logical subjects and logical predicates. (The word or phrase preceding the comma is the logical subject, the word or phrase following the comma is the logical predicate.)

  **2.** Old Rover, arthritic.

    **4.** *Gone with the Wind,* a great movie.

    **6.** The best advice my father ever gave me, save 10 percent of every dollar I earned.

    **8.** I, tired.

    **10.** This novel, quite futuristic.

**B.** Symbolic statements. (The selection of certain letters to represent certain logical subjects and predicates is arbitrary.)

    **2.** *Ar.*

    **4.** *~Gg.*

    **6.** *Sb.*

    **8.** *Ti.*

    **10.** *Qn.*

**C.**  **2.** *~Ar.*

    **4.** *Gg.*

    **6.** *~Sb.*

    **8.** *~Ti.*

    **10.** *~Qn.*

# EXERCISE 10.3

    **2.** $Tx \supset Sx.$

    **4.** $(Tx \cdot Sx) \supset {\sim}Dx.$

    **6.** $Nx \lor Ox.$

    **8.** $(Ox \cdot Rx) \cdot [Gx \supset (Px \cdot Hx)].$

    **10.** $Hx \supset (Bx \lor Kx).$ (Remember: *F* may not be used as a predicate constant.)

# EXERCISES 10.4

**A.** Interpretation of universal statements.

    **2.** $(x) \; Tx \supset Sx.$

      **a.** For any (every, everything, etc.) *x*, if *x* is tall, then *x* is slender.

      **b.** All tall things are slender things.

    **4.** $(x) \; (Tx \cdot Sx) \supset {\sim}Dx.$

      **a.** For any (every, everything, etc.) *x*, if *x* is tall and slender, then it is not a dachshund.

      **b.** If anything is tall and slender, then it is not a dachshund.

    **6.** $(x) \; Nx \lor Ox.$

      **a.** For any (every, everything, etc.) *x*, either *x* is new or *x* is old.

      **b.** Everything is either new or old.

    **8.** $(x) \; (Ox \cdot Rx) \cdot [Gx \supset (Px \cdot Hx)].$

      **a.** For any (every, everything, etc.) *x*, *x* is old and rare, and if it is genuine it is also priceless and hard to find.

      **b.** Everything is old and rare, and if it is genuine it is also priceless and hard to find.

    **10.** $(x) \; Hx \supset (Bx \lor Kx).$

   **a.** For any (every, everything, etc.) *x*, if *x* has feathers, then it is either a bird or a fake.
   **b.** Everything that has feathers is either a bird or a fake.
**B.**  Symbolic statement of valid SFC arguments.
   **2. EAE-1**  (*x*) *Mx* ⊃ ~*Px*
             (*x*) *Sx* ⊃ *Mx*
        ∴  (*x*) *Sx* ⊃ ~*Px*
   **4. EAE-2**  (*x*) *Px* ⊃ ~*Mx*
             (*x*) *Sx* ⊃ *Mx*
        ∴  (*x*) *Sx* ⊃ ~*Px*

# EXERCISES 10.5

**A.**  Particular statements in symbolic notation.
   **2.**  (∃*x*) (*Sx* · ~*Px*)
   **4.**  (∃*x*) (*Px* · ~*Sx*)
   **6.**  (∃*x*) (*Px* · *Sx*)
   **8.**  (∃*x*) [*Sx* · (*Px* · *Qx*)]
   **10.**  [(∃*x*) (*Sx* · *Px*)] ∨ [(∃*x*) (*Qx* · *Rx*)]
**B.**  **2.**  (∃*x*) [*Fx* · (*Rx* · *Bx*)]
   **4.**  (∃*x*) (*Sx* · ~*Cx*)
   **6.**  (∃*x*) [*Px* · (*Rx* ∨ *Gx*)]
   **8.**  (∃*x*) (*Ax* · ~*Lx*)
   **10.**  (∃*x*) [*Sx* · (*Dx* · *Cx*)]

# EXERCISES 10.6

**A.**  Application of Universal Instantiation. (The selection of individual constants is in all cases arbitrary.)
   **2.**  *Ab* · *Bb*
   **4.**  *Ad* ∨ *Bd*
   **6.**  *Ef* ∨ (*Gf* · *Kf*)
   **8.**  *Ph* ≡ ~*Qh*
   **10.**  ~*Ek* ⊃ ~(*Bk* ∨ *Uk*)
**B.**  Application of Universal Generalization.
   **2.**  None
   **4.**  (*x*) [*Sx* ⊃ (*Tx* ∨ *Rx*)]
   **6.**  (*x*) (*Ax* ⊃ *Bx*)
   **8.**  None
   **10.**  (*x*) [*Mx* ∨ (*Tx* ≡ *Qx*)]

# EXERCISES 10.7

**A.**  Application of Existential Instantiation. (The selection of individual constants is in all cases arbitrary.)
   **2.**  *Sb* · *Pb*
   **4.**  *Ld* ≡ *Md*

6.   $Af \cdot \sim Bf$
8.   $Kh \cdot (Lh \equiv \sim Mh)$
10.   $\sim Pk \cdot \sim (Qk \lor Rk)$

B.    Application of Existential Generalization.
2.   $[(\exists x) \, Sx] \cdot [(\exists x) \, Sx]$ (The statement is redundant but permissible.)
4.   $(\exists x) \, [Sx \supset (Tx \lor Rx)]$
6.   $(\exists x) \, (Ax \supset Bx)$
8.   None
10.   $(\exists x) \, [Mx \lor (Tx \equiv Qx)]$

# EXERCISES 10.8

A.    Formal proofs using Universal Instantiation and Universal Generalization. (Alternative proofs are possible in all cases.)

(2)   1. $(x) \, (Px \supset \sim Mx)$
      2. $(x) \, (Sx \supset Mx) \; / \therefore (x) \, (Sx \supset \sim Px)$
      3. $Py \supset \sim My$                        1 UI
      4. $Sy \supset My$                          2 UI
      5. $\sim My \supset \sim Sy$                4 Trans.
      6. $Py \supset \sim Sy$                  3, 5 HS
      7. $\sim\sim Sy \supset \sim Py$            6 Trans.
      8. $Sy \supset \sim Py$                  7 DN
      9. $(x) \, (Sx \supset \sim Px)$         8 UG

(4)   1. $(x) \, (Px \supset Mx)$
      2. $(x) \, (Mx \supset \sim Sx) \; / \therefore (x) \, (Sx \supset \sim Px)$
      3. $Py \supset My$                          1 UI
      4. $My \supset \sim Sy$                  2 UI
      5. $Py \supset \sim Sy$                  3, 4 HS
      6. $\sim\sim Sy \supset \sim Py$            5 Trans.
      7. $Sy \supset \sim Py$                  6 DN
      8. $(x) \, (Sx \supset \sim Px)$         7 UG

B.    Formal proofs using Existential Instantiation, Universal Instantiation, and Existential Generalization. (The selection of individual constants is in all cases arbitrary. Alternative proofs are possible in all cases.)

(2)   1. $(x) \, (Px \supset Mx)$
      2. $(\exists x) \, (Sx \cdot \sim Mx) \; / \therefore (\exists x) \, (Sx \cdot \sim Px)$
      3. $Sb \cdot \sim Mb$                    2 EI
      4. $Pb \supset Mb$                     1 UI
      5. $\sim Mb \supset \sim Pb$             4 Trans.
      6. $\sim Mb$                           3 Simp.
      7. $\sim Pb$                           5, 6 MP
      8. $Sb$                               3 Simp.
      9. $Sb \cdot \sim Pb$                    8, 7 Conj.
     10. $(\exists x) \, (Sx \cdot \sim Px)$       9 EG

(4)   1. $(x) \, (Px \supset \sim Mx)$
      2. $(\exists x) \, (Mx \cdot Sx) \; / \therefore (\exists x) \, (Sx \cdot \sim Px)$
      3. $Md \cdot Sd$                       2 EI
      4. $Pd \supset \sim Md$                1 UI

|   |   |   |
|---|---|---|
| 5. | $\sim\sim Md \supset \sim Pd$ | 4 Trans. |
| 6. | $Md \supset \sim Pd$ | 5 DN |
| 7. | $Md$ | 3 Simp. |
| 8. | $\sim Pd$ | 6, 7 MP |
| 9. | $Sd$ | 3 Simp. |
| 10. | $Sd \cdot \sim Pd$ | 9, 8 Conj. |
| 11. | $(\exists x) (Sx \cdot \sim Px)$ | 10 EG |

**(6)**
|   |   |   |
|---|---|---|
| 1. | $(x) (Mx \supset Px)$ | |
| 2. | $(\exists x) (Mx \cdot Sx) \ / \ \therefore (\exists x) (Sx \cdot Px)$ | |
| 3. | $Mf \cdot Sf$ | 2 EI |
| 4. | $Mf \supset Pf$ | 1 UI |
| 5. | $Mf$ | 3 Simp. |
| 6. | $Pf$ | 4, 5 MP |
| 7. | $Sf$ | 3 Simp. |
| 8. | $Sf \cdot Pf$ | 7, 6 Conj. |
| 9. | $(\exists x) (Sx \cdot Px)$ | 8 EG |

**(8)**
|   |   |   |
|---|---|---|
| 1. | $(\exists x) (Px \cdot Mx)$ | |
| 2. | $(x) (Mx \supset Sx) \ / \ \therefore (\exists x) (Sx \cdot Px)$ | |
| 3. | $Ph \cdot Mh$ | 1 EI |
| 4. | $Mh \supset Sh$ | 2 UI |
| 5. | $Mh$ | 3 Simp. |
| 6. | $Sh$ | 4, 5 MP |
| 7. | $Ph$ | 3 Simp. |
| 8. | $Sh \cdot Ph$ | 6, 7 Conj. |
| 9. | $(\exists x) (Sx \cdot Px)$ | 8 EG |

# EXERCISES 10.9

**A.** Formal proofs of validity. (The selection of individual constants is arbitrary except in cases in which the conclusion is a quantified universal statement. Alternative proofs are possible in all cases.)

**(2)**
|   |   |   |
|---|---|---|
| 1. | $(x) [Px \supset (Qx \cdot Rx)]$ | |
| 2. | $(\exists x) (Tx \cdot \sim(Qx \vee Rx)] \ / \ \therefore (\exists x) (Tx \cdot \sim Px)$ | |
| 3. | $Tb \cdot \sim(Qb \vee Rb)$ | 2 EI |
| 4. | $Pb \supset (Qb \cdot Rb)$ | 1 UI |
| 5. | $\sim(Qb \vee Rb)$ | 3 Simp. |
| 6. | $\sim Qb \cdot \sim Rb$ | 5 De M. |
| 7. | $\sim Qb$ | 6 Simp. |
| 8. | $\sim Qb \vee \sim Rb$ | 7 Add. |
| 9. | $\sim(Qb \cdot Rb)$ | 8 De M. |
| 10. | $\sim Pb$ | 4, 9 MT |
| 11. | $Tb$ | 3 Simp. |
| 12. | $Tb \cdot \sim Pb$ | 11, 10 Conj. |
| 13. | $(\exists x) (Tx \cdot \sim Px)$ | 12 EG |

**(4)**
|   |   |   |
|---|---|---|
| 1. | $(x) [Jx \supset (Ax \equiv Rx)]$ | |
| 2. | $(\exists x) (Jx \cdot \sim Ax) \ / \ \therefore (\exists x) (Jx \cdot \sim Rx)$ | |
| 3. | $Jd \cdot \sim Ad$ | 2 EI |

4. $Jd \supset (Ad \equiv Rd)$      1 UI
5. $Jd$          3 Simp.
6. $Ad \equiv Rd$       4, 5 MP
7. $(Ad \supset Rd) \cdot (Rd \supset Ad)$   6 Equiv.
8. $Rd \supset Ad$       7 Simp.
9. $\sim Ad$        3 Simp.
10. $\sim Rd$        8, 9 MT
11. $Jd \cdot \sim Rd$       5, 10 Conj.
12. $(\exists x)(Jx \cdot \sim Rx)$     11 EG

**(6)** 1. $(x)[Ax \supset (Bx \lor Cx)]$
2. $(x)(Cx \supset Dx)$
3. $(x) \sim Dx$ / $\therefore$ $(x)(Ax \supset Bx)$
4. $Ay \supset (By \lor Cy)$     1 UI
5. $Cy \supset Dy$       2 UI
6. $\sim Dy$        3 UI
7. $\sim Cy$        5, 6 MT
8. $\sim Ay \lor (By \lor Cy)$    4 Impl.
9. $(\sim Ay \lor By) \lor Cy$    8 Assoc.
10. $\sim Ay \lor By$      9, 7 DS
11. $Ay \supset By$       10 Impl.
12. $(x)(Ax \supset Bx)$     11 UG

**(8)** 1. $(x)(Jx \supset Kx)$
2. $(x)(Rx \supset \sim Kx)$
3. $(\exists x)(Tx \cdot Rx)$ / $\therefore$ $(\exists x)(Tx \cdot \sim Jx)$
4. $Tg \cdot Rg$       3 EI
5. $Jg \supset Kg$       1 UI
6. $Rg \supset \sim Kg$      2 UI
7. $Rg$         4 Simp.
8. $\sim Kg$        6, 7 MP
9. $\sim Jg$        5, 8 MT
10. $Tg$         4 Simp.
11. $Tg \cdot \sim Jg$       10, 9 Conj.
12. $(\exists x)(Tx \cdot \sim Jx)$     11 EG

**(10)** 1. $(x)[Ax \supset (Bx \lor Cx)]$
2. $(x)(Bx \equiv Cx)$
3. $(\exists x)(Dx \cdot \sim Bx)$ / $\therefore$ $(\exists x)(Dx \cdot \sim Ax)$
4. $Dm \cdot \sim Bm$      3 EI
5. $Am \supset (Bm \lor Cm)$    1 UI
6. $Bm \equiv Cm$       2 UI
7. $(Bm \supset Cm) \cdot (Cm \supset Bm)$   6 Equiv.
8. $Cm \supset Bm$       7 Simp.
9. $\sim Bm$        4 Simp.
10. $\sim Cm$        8, 9 MT
11. $\sim Bm \cdot \sim Cm$     9, 10 Conj.
12. $\sim (Bm \lor Cm)$     11 De M.
13. $\sim Am$        5, 12 MT
14. $Dm$         4 Simp.
15. $Dm \cdot \sim Am$      14, 13 Conj.
16. $(\exists x)(Dx \cdot \sim Ax)$    15 EG

**B.**   Formal proofs of restated arguments. (The selection of individual constants is arbitrary except when the conclusion is a quantified universal statement. Alternative proofs are possible in all cases.)

**(2)**  1. $(x) (Bx \supset Tx)$
    2. $(x) (Tx \supset {\sim}Rx)$ / $\therefore$ $(x) (Bx \supset {\sim}Rx)$
    3. $By \supset Ty$                        1 UI
    4. $Ty \supset {\sim}Ry$                2 UI
    5. $By \supset {\sim}Ry$                3, 4 HS
    6. $(x) (Bx \supset {\sim}Rx)$        5 UG

**(4)**  1. $(x) (Mx \supset {\sim}Px)$
    2. $(x) (Sx \supset Mx)$ / $\therefore$ $(x) (Sx \supset {\sim}Px)$
    3. $My \supset {\sim}Py$             1 UI
    4. $Sy \supset My$                2 UI
    5. $Sy \supset {\sim}Py$              4, 3 HS
    6. $(x) (Sx \supset {\sim}Px)$        5 UG

**(6)**  1. $(x) (Px \supset {\sim}Ox)$
    2. $(x) (Sx \supset Ox)$ / $\therefore$ $(x) (Px \supset {\sim}Sx)$
    3. $Py \supset {\sim}Oy$             1 UI
    4. $Sy \supset Oy$                2 UI
    5. ${\sim}Oy \supset {\sim}Sy$          4 Trans.
    6. $Py \supset {\sim}Sy$              3, 5 HS
    7. $(x) (Px \supset {\sim}Sx)$        6 UG

**(8)**  1. $(x) [Cx \supset (Vx \cdot Tx)]$
    2. $(x) (Gx \supset {\sim}Vx)$ / $\therefore$ $(x) (Gx \supset {\sim}Cx)$
    3. $Cy \supset (Vy \cdot Ty)$            1 UI
    4. $Gy \supset {\sim}Vy$              2 UI
    5. ${\sim}Gy \vee {\sim} Vy$           4 Impl.
    6. $({\sim}Gy \vee {\sim} Vy) \vee {\sim}Ty$    5 Add.
    7. ${\sim}Gy \vee ({\sim}Vy \vee {\sim} Ty)$   6 Assoc.
    8. $(Gy \supset ({\sim} Vy \vee {\sim} Ty)$    7 Impl.
    9. $Gy \supset {\sim} (Vy \cdot Ty)$       8 De M.
  10. ${\sim}(Vy \cdot Ty) \supset {\sim} Cy$    3 Trans.
  11. $Gy \supset {\sim}Cy$            9, 10 HS
  12. $(x) (Gx \supset {\sim}Cx)$       11 UG

**(10)** 1. $(x) (Ox \supset {\sim}Yx) \cdot (Rx \supset {\sim}Px)$
    2. $(x) [Cx \supset (Ox \cdot Px)]$ / $\therefore$ $(x) [Cx \supset ({\sim}Yx \cdot {\sim}Rx)]$
    3. $(Oy \supset {\sim}Yy) \cdot (Ry \supset {\sim}Py)$      1 UI
    4. $Cy \supset (Oy \cdot Py)$                 2 UI
    5. ${\sim}Cy \vee (Oy \cdot Py)$              4 Impl.
    6. $({\sim}Cy \vee Oy) \cdot ({\sim}Cy \vee Py)$    5 Dist.
    7. ${\sim}Cy \vee Oy$                    6 Impl.
    8. $Cy \supset Oy$                       7 Impl.
    9. $Oy \supset {\sim} Yy$                  3 Simp.
  10. $Cy \supset {\sim}Yy$                 8, 9 HS
  11. ${\sim}Cy \vee {\sim}Yy$              10 Impl.
  12. ${\sim}Cy \vee Py$                 6 Simp.
  13. $Cy \supset Py$                    12 Impl.
  14. $Ry \supset {\sim}Py$                 3 Simp.

15. $\sim\sim Py \supset \sim Ry$                              14 Trans.
16. $Py \supset \sim Ry$                                 15 DN
17. $Cy \supset \sim Ry$                                 13, 16 HS
18. $\sim Cy \lor \sim Ry$                               17 Impl.
19. $(\sim Cy \lor \sim Yy) \cdot (\sim Cy \lor \sim Ry)$   11, 18 Conj.
20. $\sim Cy \lor (\sim Yy \cdot \sim Ry)$               19 Dist.
21. $Cy \supset (\sim Yy \cdot \sim Ry)$                 20 Impl.
22. $(x) [Cx \supset (\sim Yx \cdot \sim Rx)]$           21 UG

# EXERCISES 10.10

**A.**   Truth-functional restatements of quantified statements. (The selection of individual constants is arbitrary.)

**2.** $[Ka \supset (Ma \lor Na)] \cdot [Kb \supset (Mb \lor Nb)] \cdot [Kc \supset (Mc \lor Nc)] \cdot [Kd \supset (Md \lor Nd)] \cdot [Ke \supset (Me \lor Ne)] \cdot [Kf \supset (Mf \lor Nf)] \cdot [Kg \supset (Mg \lor Ng)] \cdot [Kh \supset (Mh \lor Nh)]$

**4.** $(Da \lor Aa) \cdot (Db \lor Ab) \cdot (Dc \lor Ac) \cdot (Dd \lor Ad)$

**6.** $Aa \lor Ba$

**8.** $[Aa \cdot (Ca \lor Da)] \lor [Ab \cdot (Cb \lor Db)] \lor [Ac \cdot (Cc \lor Dc)] \lor [Ad \cdot (Cd \lor Dd)] \lor [Ae \cdot (Ce \lor De)] \lor [Af \cdot (Cf \lor Df)] \lor [Ag \cdot (Cg \lor Dg)] \lor [Ah \cdot (Ch \lor Dh)]$

**10.** $[Ka \cdot (La \equiv Ma)] \lor [Kb \cdot (Lb \equiv Mb)] \lor [Kc \cdot (Lc \equiv Mc)] \lor [Kd \cdot (Ld \equiv Md)] \lor [Ke \cdot (Le \equiv Me)] \lor [Kf \cdot (Lf \equiv Mf)] \lor [Kg \cdot (Lg \equiv Mg)] \lor [Kh \cdot (Lh \equiv Mh)]$

**B.**   Reductio Ad Absurdum test for validity.

**2. Premise 1:**   $(Aa \lor Ca) \cdot (Ab \lor Cb) \cdot (Ac \lor Cc) \cdot (Ad \lor Cd)$
                        F T  ?  T T T  F T T T  F T T T  F

**Premise 2:**   $\sim Aa \lor \sim Ab \lor \sim Ac \lor \sim Ad$
                  T      T F      F F      F F

**Conclusion:**   $Ca \lor Cb \lor Cc \lor Cd$
                   ?    F    F    F    F    F    F

The argument is valid.

**4. Premise 1:**   $(La \supset Qa) \cdot (Lb \supset Qb) \cdot (Lc \supset Qc) \cdot (Ld \supset Qd)$
                       ?  T    F T F  T    F T F  T    F T F  T    F
                  $\cdot (Le \supset Qe) \cdot (Lf \supset Qf) \cdot (Lg \supset Qg) \cdot (Lh \supset Qh)$
                    T F T    F T    F T    F T    F T    F T    F T    F

**Premise 2:**   $[Qa \supset (Pa \lor Ma)] \cdot [Qb \supset (Pb \lor Mb)] \cdot [Qc \supset (Pc \lor Mc)]$
                  F T     F F    F T    F T     F F    F T    F T     F F    F
                  $\cdot [Qd \supset (Pd \lor Md)] \cdot [Qe \supset (Pe \lor Me)] \cdot [Qf \supset (Pf \lor Mf)]$
                    T    F T    F F    F T    F T    F F    F T    F T    F F    F
                  $\cdot [Qg \supset (Pg \supset Mg)] \cdot [Qh \supset (Ph \lor Mh)]$
                    T    F T    F F    F T    F T    F F    F

**Conclusion:**  [La ⊃ (~Pa ⊃ Ma)] · [Lb ⊃ (~Pb ⊃ Mb)] · [Lc ⊃ (~Pc ⊃ Mc)]
         ? F T   F   F F    F T T    F   F T    F T T    F   F

· [Ld ⊃ (~Pd ⊃ Md)] · [Le ⊃ (~Pe ⊃ Me)] · [Lf ⊃ (~Pf ⊃ Mf)]
T   F T T     F   F T    F T T     F   F T    F T T     F   F

· [Lg ⊃ (~Pg ⊃ Mg)] · [Lh ⊃ (~Ph ⊃ Mh)]
T   F T T     F   F T    F T T    F   F

The argument is valid.

**6. Premise 1:**  [Ca ⊃ (Da · Za)] · [Cb ⊃ (Db · Zb)] · [Cc ⊃ (Dc · Zc)]
         ? T   F F   T T    T T   T T    T T   T T

· [Cd ⊃ (Dd · Zd)] · [Ce ⊃ (De · Ze)] · [Cf ⊃ (Df · Zf)]
T   T T   T T    T T   T T    T T   T T

· [Cg ⊃ (Dg · Zg)] · [Ch ⊃ (Dh · Zh)]
T   T T   T T    T T   T T

**Premise 2:**  (Na · ~Da) ∨ (Nb · ~Db) ∨ (Nc · ~Dc) ∨ (Nd · ~Dd)
        T T T     T    T F F     F    T F F     F    T F F

∨ (Ne · ~De) ∨ (Nf · ~Df) ∨ (Ng · ~Dg) ∨ (Nh · ~Dh)
F   T F F     F   T F F     F   T F F     F   T F F

**Conclusion:**  (Na · ~Ca) ∨ (Nb · ~Cb) ∨ (Nc · ~Cc) ∨ (Nd · ~Cd)
        T F?    F   T F F     F   T F F     F   T F F

∨ (Ne · ~ Ce) ∨ (Nf · ~Cf) ∨ (Ng · ~Cg) ∨ (Nh · ~Ch)
F   T F F     F   T F F     F   T F F     F   T F F

The argument is valid.

**8. Premise 1:**  (Da ⊃ Za) · (Db ⊃ Zb) · (Dc ⊃ Zc) · (Dd ⊃ Zd)
         T T   T T    T T   T T    T T   T T    T T   T

· (De ⊃ Ze) · (Df ⊃ Zf) · (Dg ⊃ Zg) · (Dh ⊃ Zh)
T   T T   T T    T T   T T    T T   T T    T T   T

**Premise 2:**  [Za ⊃ ~ (Qa · Ta)] · [Zb ⊃ ~ (Qb · Tb)] · [Zc ⊃ ~ (Qc · Tc)]
        T T T    TF   F T   T T T    TF   F T   T T T    TF   **F**

· [Zd ⊃ ~ (Qd · Td)] · [Ze ⊃ ~ (Qe · Te)] · [Zf ⊃ ~ (Qf · Tf)]
T   T T T    TF   F T   T T T    TF   F T   T T T    TF   **F**

· [Zg ⊃ ~ (Qg · Tg)] · [Zh ⊃ ~ (Qh · Th)]
T   T T T    TF   F T   T T T    TF   F

**Conclusion:**  [Qa ⊃ (Ta · Da)] · [Qb ⊃ (Tb · Db)] · [Qc ⊃ (Tc · Dc)]
        T F    F F   T F   T F    F F   T F   T F    F F   T

· [Qd ⊃ (Td · Dd)] · [Qe ⊃ (Te · De)] · [Qf ⊃ (Tf · Df)]
F   T F    F F   T F   T F    F F   T F   T F    F F   T

· [Qg ⊃ (Tg · Dg)] · [Qh ⊃ (Th · Dh)]
F   T F    F F   T F   T F    F F   T

The argument is invalid.

**10. Premise 1:**  (Ka · Sa) ∨ (Kb · Sb) ∨ (Kc · Sc) ∨ (Kd · Sd)
        ? T   T T    FF   T F    FF   T F    FF   T

∨ (Ke · Se) ∨ (Kf · Sf) ∨ (Kg · Sg) ∨ (Kh · Sh)
F   FF F F    FF T F    FF T F    FF T

**Premise 2:**  [Sa ⊃ (Ta · Ra)] · [Sb ⊃ (Tb · Rb)] · [Sc ⊃ (Tc · Rc)]
        T T    TT   T T    T T    TT   T T    T T    TT   T

$$\cdot \; [Sd \supset (Td \cdot Rd)] \cdot \; [Se \supset (Te \cdot Re)] \cdot \; [Sf \supset (Tf \cdot Rf)]$$
T   TT      TT   T T      T T      TT   T T      T T      TT   T

$$\cdot \; [Sg \supset (Tg \cdot Rg)] \cdot \; [Sh \supset (Th \cdot Rh)]$$
T   TT      TT   T T      T T      TT   T

**Conclusion:**   $[Ka \cdot (Ta \supset Ra)] \lor [Kb \cdot (Tb \supset Rb)] \lor [Kc \cdot (Tc \supset Rc)]$
?F      T T      T   F      FF      T T      T   F      FF      T T      T

$\lor \; [Kd \cdot (Td \supset Rd)] \lor [Ke \cdot (Te \supset Re)] \lor [Kf \cdot (Tf \supset Rf)]$
F      FF      T T      T   F      FF      T T      T   F      FF      T T      T

$\lor \; [Kg \cdot (Tg \supset Rg)] \lor [Kh \cdot (Th \supset Rh)]$
F      FF      T T      T   F      FF      T T      T

The argument is valid.

# EXERCISES 11.1–11.2

**A.**   (C = conclusion; T = type.)
  **2.**   **C:** Cigarette smoking causes lung cancer.
     **T:** Causal theory.
  **4.**   **C:** Adult male chickens have combs, adult female chickens do not.
     **T:** Empirical generalization.
  **6.**   **C:** It will rain tomorrow.
     **T:** Specific alleged matter of fact.
  **8.**   **C:** We have been robbed.
     **T:** Specific alleged matter of fact.
  **10.**   **C:** The blood circulates through the human body, flowing away from the heart via the arteries and returning to it via the veins.
     **T:** Theoretical hypothesis.
**B.**   Open-ended.
**C.**   Open-ended.

# EXERCISES 12.1–12.2

**A.**   See definitions in Section 12.1.
**B.**   **2.**   The probability that either $A$ is true or $B$ is not true is $\frac{2}{3}$.
  **4.**   The probability that either $A$ is true or $B$ and $C$ are true is $\frac{2}{7}$.
  **6.**   The probability that either $A$ or not-$A$ is true is 1.
  **8.**   The probability that $A$ is true in conjunction with $B$ or not-$C$ is $\frac{5}{11}$.
  **10.**   The probability that $A$, not-$B$, and $C$ are all true is $\frac{5}{12}$.
**C.**   Open-ended.

# EXERCISES 12.3–12.4

**A.**   **2.**   Throwing a pair of dice once is equivalent to throwing a single die twice. Thus the probability of throwing a pair of 3s on a single throw of two dice is the same as the probability of throwing two

3s in successive throws of a single die. The probability of throwing a 3 on a single throw of a die is $\frac{1}{6}$. Therefore:

$$P(3_a \cdot 3_b) = P(3_a) \times P(3_b)$$
$$P(3_a \cdot 3_b) = \frac{1}{6} \times \frac{1}{6} = \frac{1}{36}$$

4. **b.** The probability of drawing a spade on each draw is $\frac{13}{52} = \frac{1}{4}$. Therefore:

$$P(S_1 \cdot S_2) = P(S_1) \times P(S_2)$$
$$P(S_1 \cdot S_2) = \frac{1}{4} \times \frac{1}{4} = \frac{1}{16}$$

**d.** The probability of drawing a red card on each draw is $\frac{1}{2}$. Therefore:

$$P(R_1 \cdot R_2) = P(R_1) \times P(R_2)$$
$$P(R_1 \cdot R_2) = \frac{1}{2} \times \frac{1}{2} = \frac{1}{4}$$

**f.** The probability of drawing an even-numbered card on each draw is $\frac{20}{52} = \frac{5}{13}$. Therefore:

$$P(E_1 \cdot E_2) = P(E_1) \times P(E_2)$$
$$P(E_1 \cdot E_2) = \frac{5}{13} \times \frac{5}{13} = \frac{25}{169}$$

**h.** The probability of drawing the ace of spades on the first draw is $\frac{1}{52}$, and the probability of drawing a face card on the second draw is $\frac{12}{52} = \frac{3}{13}$. Therefore:

$$P(A \cdot F) = P(A) \times P(F)$$
$$P(A \cdot F) = \frac{1}{52} \times \frac{3}{13} = \frac{3}{676}$$

**j.** The probability of drawing the ace of hearts on the first draw is $\frac{1}{52}$, and the probability of drawing the king of diamonds on the second draw is also $\frac{1}{52}$. Therefore:

$$P(A \cdot K) = P(A) \times P(K)$$
$$P(A \cdot K) = \frac{1}{52} \times \frac{1}{52} = \frac{1}{2704}$$

**B.** 1. **b.** $P(R_1) = \frac{1}{26}$, and $P(R_2 \text{ given } R_1) = \frac{25}{52}$. Therefore:

$$P(R_1 \cdot R_2) = P(R_1) \times P(R_2 \text{ given } R_1)$$
$$P(R_1 \cdot R_2) = \frac{1}{26} \times \frac{25}{52} = \frac{25}{1352}$$

**d.** $P(E_1) = \frac{5}{13}$, and $P(E_2 \text{ given } E_1) = \frac{19}{51}$. Therefore:

$$P(E_1 \cdot E_2) = P(E_1) \times P(E_2 \text{ given } E_1)$$
$$P(E_1 \cdot E_2) = \frac{5}{13} \times \frac{19}{51} = \frac{95}{663}$$

2. $P(H_1) = .32$, and $P(H_2 \text{ given } H_1) = .34$. Therefore:

$$P(H_1 \cdot H_2) = P(H_1) \times P(H_2 \text{ given } H_1)$$
$$P(H_1 \cdot H_2) = .32 \times .34 = .1088$$

3. **b.** $P(R_1) = \frac{1}{2}$, and $P(R_2 \text{ given } R_1) = \frac{49}{99}$. Therefore:

$$P(R_1 \cdot R_2) = P(R_1) \times P(R_2 \text{ given } R_1)$$
$$P(R_1 \cdot R_2) = \frac{1}{2} \times \frac{49}{99} = \frac{49}{198}$$

**d.** $P(G) = \frac{1}{2}$, and $P(R$ given $G) = \frac{50}{99}$. Therefore:

$P(G \cdot R) = P(G) \times P(R$ given $G)$
$P(G \cdot R) = \frac{1}{2} \times \frac{50}{99} = \frac{50}{198} = \frac{25}{99}$

## EXERCISES 12.5–12.7

**A.**  Exclusive Disjunction Rule.
   **1.** **b.** $P(E) = \frac{1}{2}$ and $P(3) = \frac{1}{6}$. Therefore:

   $P\sim(E \equiv 3) = \frac{1}{2} + \frac{1}{6} = \frac{2}{3}$

   **d.** $P(O) = \frac{1}{2}$ and $P(E$ other than 6$) = \frac{1}{3}$. Therefore:

   $P\sim(O \equiv E$ other than 6$) = \frac{1}{2} + \frac{1}{3} = \frac{5}{6}$

   **2.** **b.** $P(RF) = \frac{3}{26}$ and $P(BF) = \frac{3}{26}$. Therefore:

   $P\sim(RF \equiv BF) = \frac{3}{26} + \frac{3}{26} = \frac{3}{13}$

   **d.** $P(OR) = \frac{5}{26}$ and $P(B) = \frac{1}{2}$. Therefore:

   $P\sim(OR \equiv B) = \frac{5}{26} + \frac{1}{2} = \frac{9}{13}$

   **3.** **b.** $P(Int) = .05$ and $P(S) = .03$. Therefore:
   $P\sim(Int \equiv S) = .05 + .03 = .08$

   **d.** $P(C) = .40$ and $P(Int) = .05$. Therefore:

   $P\sim(C \equiv Int) = .40 + .05 = .45$

**B.**  General Disjunction Rule.
   **2.** $P(M \vee T) = P(M) + P(T) - P(M \cdot T)$
   $P(M \vee T) = .60 + .80 - (.60 \times .80)$
   $P(M \vee T) = 1.40 - .48 = .92$
   **4.** $P(M \vee V) = P(M) + P(V) - P(M \cdot V)$
   $P(M \vee V) = 0 + \frac{2}{100} - (0 \times \frac{2}{100})$
   $P(M \vee V) = \frac{2}{100} - 0 = \frac{2}{100} = \frac{1}{50}$
   **5.** **b.** $P(D \vee >6) = P(D) + P(>6) - P(D \cdot >6)$
   $P(D \vee >6) = \frac{6}{36} + \frac{21}{36} - \frac{3}{36} = \frac{24}{36} = \frac{2}{3}$
   **d.** $P(7 \vee O>7) = P(7) + P(O>7) - P(7 \cdot O>7)$
   $P(7 \vee O>7) = \frac{6}{36} + \frac{6}{36} - 0 = \frac{12}{36} = \frac{1}{3}$

**C.**  **2.** $P(\sim R) = .55$
   **4.** $P(\sim R) = .09$
   **6.** $P(\sim R) = \frac{1}{5}$
   **8.** $P(\sim R) = \frac{8}{17}$
   **10.** $P(\sim R) = \frac{206}{313}$

## EXERCISE 13.1

(Correct answers are in some cases a matter of judgment.)
   **2.**  To prevent it from occurring.

4. To satisfy curiosity.
6. To prevent it from occurring.
8. To satisfy curiosity; to acquire power to make it happen—or perhaps to prevent its occurrence.
10. To establish responsibility.
12. To prevent it from occurring.
14. To satisfy curiosity; to make it occur in the sense of determining the conditions under which there is a likelihood of finding more petroleum.
16. To prevent it from occurring.
18. To satisfy curiosity.
20. To satisfy curiosity; to prevent it from occurring; to establish responsibility.

## EXERCISE 13.2

2. Long list of grievances: probably proximate and remote, tractability unknown, sufficient condition for the occurrence of a revolution.
4. Jeering of the crowd: proximate, tractable, sufficient condition to make him angry.
6. Rash speech: remote, tractable, sufficient condition for him to lose the election.
8. Switchman neglected to throw the switch: probably proximate, tractable, sufficient condition for the derailment.
10. Design defect: remote, tractable, sufficient condition for brake failure to occur.
12. Corporate avarice: remote, tractable, sufficient for design defect to go unreported.
14. Eating certain foods: proximate, tractable, sufficient.
16. Overwork: proximate, tractable, sufficient.
18. Poor study habits and lack of effort: proximate, tractable, sufficient.
20. An increase of nitrogen in the soil: proximate, tractable, sufficient.

## EXERCISES 13.3–13.4

A. 2 and 3.
C. 3, 6, 10.

## EXERCISES 13.5

A. 1.
C. 3, 5, 6, 8.

## EXERCISE 13.6

2. *C, E.*

## EXERCISE 13.7

2.   An investigator would study the school with the high absentee rate and some schools with normal absentee rates in an attempt to determine what is uniquely different about the former. If the research were successful, one or more characteristics would be found in the "normal" schools that is/are absent in the school with the abnormally high absentee rate.

4.   Automotive engineers know, in general, the characteristics of automobiles that achieve "ordinary" mileage. The 80-mpg automobile would be studied to determine how it differs from "ordinary" automobiles.

## EXERCISE 13.8

2.   The absence of $B$ was a sufficient condition for the occurrence of event $\sim Z$ in case 0, and the occurrence of events of type $B$ is a sufficient condition for the occurrence of events of type $Z$.

## EXERCISE 14.1

Observation statements: 3, 4, 7, 9, 10, 11, 15, 16, 17.

## EXERCISES 14.2

B.   See pages 312–313.

## EXERCISES 14.3

A.   A universal empirical generalization affirms that some characteristic is present in all members of a certain class—for example, "All birds are feathered." A statistical generalization affirms a statistical regularity about a class. A universal empirical generalization, therefore, is a statement about every member of the class, whereas a statistical generalization is a statement about the class (not about its individual members).

## EXERCISES 14.4

B.   To say that empirical laws are testable by means of a direct appeal to empirical facts means that such laws are empirical generalizations, and as such their truth or falsity is determined by the relevant empirical facts.

## EXERCISES 14.5

**B.**  1. Theoretical hypotheses posit unobserved entities (atoms, gravitational force, etc.), empirical laws do not.
  2. Theoretical hypotheses cannot be verified directly, empirical laws can.
  3. Theoretical hypotheses are broader in scope than empirical laws.

**D.**  Open-ended.

## EXERCISES 14.6

**A.**  A revolutionary hypothesis is a theoretical hypothesis that, if true, requires a substantial revision of prevailing theories and beliefs. It differs from other theoretical hypotheses only in the extent of its impact on currently prevailing theories and beliefs.

## EXERCISES 14.7

**B.**  The informed consensus would be as follows:
  2. Scientific (but false).
  4. Pseudoscientific.
  6. Scientific.
  8. Scientific.
  10. Pseudoscientific.

# index

**399**

# about the author

William H. Halverson is Adjunct Professor of Philosophy and Associate Dean of University College at Ohio State University. He received a B.A. from Augsburg College in 1951, an M.A. from Princeton University in 1959, and a Ph.D. from Princeton in 1961. His primary areas of interest are logic, ethics, aesthetics, and the philosophy of religion. He is the author of numerous articles and books, including *A Concise Introduction to Philosophy*, 4th ed. (Random House, 1981), and *Concise Readings in Philosophy* (Random House, 1981).

# formal proof system

## ELEMENTARY VALID ARGUMENT FORMS

**MODUS PONENS (MP)**
1. $p \supset q$
2. $p / \therefore q$

**MODUS TOLLENS (MT)**
1. $p \supset q$
2. $\sim q / \therefore \sim p$

**HYPOTHETICAL SYLLOGISM (HS)**
1. $p \supset q$
2. $q \supset r / \therefore p \supset r$

**ADDITION (ADD.)**
1. $p / \therefore p \vee q$

**ABSORPTION (ABS.)**
1. $p \supset q / \therefore p \supset (p \cdot q)$

**CONSTRUCTIVE DILEMMA (CD)**
1. $(p \supset q) \cdot (r \supset s)$
2. $p \vee r / \therefore q \vee s$

**SIMPLIFICATION (SIMP.)**
1. $p \cdot q / \therefore p$     OR:     1. $p \cdot q / \therefore q$

**CONJUNCTION (CONJ.)**
1. $p$
2. $q / \therefore p \cdot q$

**DISJUNCTIVE SYLLOGISM (DS)**
1. $p \vee q$     OR:     1. $p \vee q$
2. $\sim p / \therefore q$              2. $\sim q / \therefore p$

## LOGICALLY EQUIVALENT STATEMENTS

1. Association (Assoc.):     $p \vee (q \vee r)$ is equivalent to $(p \vee q) \vee r$
$p \cdot (q \cdot r)$ is equivalent to $(p \cdot q) \cdot r$

2. Commutation (Com.):     $(p \vee q)$ is equivalent to $(q \vee p)$
$(p \cdot q)$ is equivalent to $(q \cdot p)$

3. Distribution (Dist.):     $p \cdot (q \vee r)$ is equivalent to $(p \cdot q) \vee (p \cdot r)$
$p \vee (q \cdot r)$ is equivalent to $(p \vee q) \cdot (p \vee r)$

4. Double Negation (DN):     $p$ is equivalent to $\sim\sim p$

5. Tautology (Taut.):     $(p \vee p)$ is equivalent to $p$
$(p \cdot p)$ is equivalent to $p$

6. DeMorgan's Theorems (DeM.):     $\sim(p \cdot q)$ is equivalent to $(\sim p \vee \sim q)$
$\sim(p \vee q)$ is equivalent to $(\sim p \cdot \sim q)$

7. Exportation (Exp.)     $(p \cdot q) \supset r$ is equivalent to $p \supset (q \supset r)$

8. Transposition (Trans.):     $(p \supset q)$ is equivalent to $(\sim q \supset \sim p)$

9. Material Implication (Impl.):     $(p \supset q)$ is equivalent to $(\sim p \vee q)$
$(p \supset q)$ is equivalent to $\sim(p \cdot \sim q)$

10. Material Equivalence (Equiv.):     $(p \equiv q)$ is equivalent to $(p \supset q) \cdot (q \supset p)$
$(p \equiv q)$ is equivalent to $(p \cdot q) \vee (\sim p \cdot \sim q)$